HANDBOOK OF HUMAN PERFORMANCE

VOLUME 3

STATE AND TRAIT

HANDBOOK
OF
HUMAN PERFORMANCE

VOLUME 3

STATE AND TRAIT

Edited by

A.P. Smith & D.M. Jones

ACADEMIC PRESS

Harcourt Brace Jovanovich, Publishers

LONDON SAN DIEGO NEW YORK BOSTON SYDNEY TOKYO TORONTO

ACADEMIC PRESS LIMITED
24–28 Oval Road
London NW1 7DX

United States Edition published by
ACADEMIC PRESS INC.
San Diego, CA 92101

This book is printed on acid-free paper

A catalogue record for this book is available from the British Library
ISBN 0-12-650353-2

Typeset by P&R Typesetters Ltd, Salisbury, Wilts
and printed and bound in Great Britain by
Hartnolls Ltd., Bodmin, Cornwall

Contents

Contributors

M. Anderson, Department of Psychology, The University of Western Australia, Nedlands, Western Australia 6009, Australia

S. Brown, Department of Psychology, University of Queensland, St Lucia, Queensland, Australia 4072

S.S. Campbell, Institute of Chronobiology, New York Hospital/Cornell Medical Center, 21 Bloomingdale Road, White Plains, New York, USA

R.E. Cooper, MRC/ESRC Social and Applied Psychology Unit, Department of Psychology, University of Sheffield, Sheffield, S10 2TN, UK

A. Craig, MRC/ESRC Social and Applied Psychology Unit, Department of Psychology, University of Sheffield, Sheffield, S10 2TN, UK

D.R. Davies, Human Factors Research Unit, Aston Business School, Aston University, Birmingham, UK

L. Dorn, Human Factors Research Unit, Aston Business School, Aston University, Birmingham, UK

K. Hänecke, Universität Oldenburg, Fachbereich 5, Birkenweg 3, D-2900 Oldenburg, Germany

G. Matthews, Department of Psychology, University of Dundee, Dundee, DD1 4HN, UK

J.H. Mueller, Educational Psychology Department, University of Calgary, Calgary, Alberta T2N, 1N4, Canada

F. Nachreiner, Universität Oldenburg, Fachbereich 5, Birkenweg 3, D-2900 Oldenburg, Germany

A.P. Smith, Health Psychology Research Unit, School of Psychology, University of Wales College of Cardiff, PO Box 901, Cardiff, CF1 3YG, UK

A. Taylor, Department of Psychology, University of Leicester, Leicester, UK

A. Tilley, Department of Psychology, University of Queensland, St Lucia, Queensland, Australia 4072

J. Ussher, Department of Psychology, University of Sussex, Brighton, BN1 9QN, UK

General Preface

In this three volume series, the effects of different states and environments on performance are examined. That contemporary research in this area could not be encompassed in one volume marks not just the diversity of effects which now come under this rubric but also its maturity as a subject area. Twenty years ago, this would have been a slim volume indeed!

What are the factors which caused the growth of interest which led to the book? No single factor can be identified, rather the interplay of several factors seems to be responsible. Initially, interest centred on the use of task-performance as measures of central nervous system efficiency and as indices which by-passed the difficulty of obtaining objective measures of the person's state. Models of human performance became more refined in the decades after the Second World War, because the judicious selection of tasks meant that a more analytic approach could be used. This approach yielded more than a simple index of performance to represent overall efficiency. Rather, using a battery of tasks or by careful analysis of the microstructure of individual tasks (often focusing on the interplay of several measures), qualitative judgements could be made about the action of the agent. The term 'efficiency' in this context is somewhat misleading because it seems to imply that the main interest is in loss of efficiency and in obtaining some single quantitative index of the person's state. Although this might be part of the motivation, particularly for the early studies, latterly much more interest has centred upon discerning different classes of response. This helps to further our understanding of the physiological basis for each of the effects and the likely interplay of factors.

The increasing portability and cheapness of microprocessors has also played a role in the increasing scope of work. By using microprocessors, field observations may now be made with the accuracy that was hitherto only possible in laboratories. We can now judge the effect of a particular factor at the place of work and moreover for extended periods of time. In each of the contributions, authors have provided an up-to-date account of the empirical work in the area. Where possible, findings are presented from both laboratory and field settings and in each case discussion of methodological issues will also be found. Some work is still in the very early stages and hence highly developed and integrated theories are not always the rule. The volumes provide, in their breadth and depth, a cross-section of interesting work in the area of human performance.

The three volumes reflect the division of work in the area into three distinct but often interacting domains. Volume 1 has its roots in occupational health and work psychology. It contains some of the longest established areas of interest: noise, heat, distraction and vibration. New industrial processes and machines have introduced new concerns such as the increasing use of solvents in the chemical industry, the concern about hyperbaric environments in the search for oil and the behavioural effects of electrical fields and ionization in the distribution of electricity. The contents of Volume 1 also reflect the fact that much more work is now undertaken in offices than in factories (at least in the Western world). Visual display units, once a rarity, now seem ubiquitous. Although the settings in which they are used are by and large more hospitable in some respects than the traditional shop-floor, the pace, content and organization of work will still have consequences on efficiency.

Volume 2 contains research which is very much less traditional and which has been marked by enormous growth in the last decade. Here the emphasis is on the relationship between health and behaviour. Three complementary approaches can be discerned. First, there is growing evidence and concern about the effect of behaviours such as smoking and alcohol consumption on performance and well-being. Second, the behavioural consequences of illness (acute and chronic, mental and physical) in terms of the effects on performance are examined. Third, and perhaps the longest recognized is the interest in psychological side-effects of treatment both on mental and physical health.

Volume 3 continues to regard the state of the person, but its scope is in terms of chronic, long term, slowly-changing effects of state. This volume also takes up the theme of chronic and acute change in state by setting aside a section to the study of individual differences in state and trait. The periodicity of the day–night cycle has implications for efficiency because alertness varies with the time of day, the nature and, more particularly, the length of work. Even when undisturbed, these factors produce a change in efficiency. When disturbed, by shiftwork or emergencies, the consequences are normally much more dramatic. There is obvious practical interest in knowing what effects new patterns of work will have on the person both in the short term for efficiency and in the long term, for health.

Preface to Volume 3

There has been considerable research on individual differences in behaviour, and interest has focused on demographic factors, such as age and gender, stable personality traits and differences which reflect the current state of the person. The present volume reviews what is known about individual differences in human performance, and considers both effects related to stable characteristics and those which are a product of either endogenous changes in state or induced by task performance itself.

The first chapter is concerned with one of the most frequently discussed topics in psychology, namely intelligence. This is followed by two chapters on important demographic factors—age and gender.

The second section of the volume covers the relationship between personality and performance. Chapter 4 considers a most widely studied personality trait, extraversion, and Chapter 5 provides a link between the trait and state parts of the volume by reviewing the different aspects of anxiety.

The third section of the volume examines the effect of mood (Chapter 6) and endogenous changes in state on performance. Chapters 7, 8, and 9 are concerned with sleep, circadian rhythms, and time of day effects in performance and the studies reviewed here are both of theoretical and applied importance. Furthermore, they demonstrate that diurnal variation in performance reflects both circadian rhythms and the effects of exogenous events which are often associated with particular times of day.

The final section of the book describes research on changes in performance efficiency as a function of time on task (Chapter 10—Vigilance), and as a result of prior performance of other tasks (Chapter 11—Fatigue).

Overall, the chapters in this volume provide wide-ranging coverage of the effects of traits and different states on performance. All chapters not only provide detailed descriptions of the different areas of research but give critical evaluations of the methodology, theory and practical importance of the work.

The volume has achieved the dual aims of covering a wide range of topics and yet linking these in a consistent manner to human performance. We would like to thank the authors for their contributions and to also thank everyone who has helped us in the various stages of producing this volume.

Andrew Smith and Dylan Jones

List of Contents for Volumes 1, 2 & 3

VOLUME 1
THE PHYSICAL ENVIRONMENT

VOLUME 2
HEALTH AND PERFORMANCE

VOLUME 3
STATE AND TRAIT

1

Intelligence

M. ANDERSON

Is there such a thing as intelligence? Such a question may appear somewhat gratuitous to the layperson who has little doubt that people can be discriminated on the basis of how 'bright' or 'dim' they are (Fitzgerald and Mellor, 1988). Yet there are psychologists who believe that intelligence is the fictional invention of intelligence testers (Howe and Smith, 1988; Howe, 1990; Ceci, 1990). This view is not simply the more usual objection to equating intelligence with a single global measure such as IQ; the grounds for objection being that intelligence tests measure too narrow a range of the abilities that contribute to intelligence (see, for example, Gardner, 1983). Rather, the belief is that the notion of intelligence is vacuous as an explanatory construct since it is simply a *description* of performance. To describe those who perform well on intelligence tests as 'intelligent' adds nothing by way of explanatory power and simply seduces us into believing that intelligence is a real psychological attribute. Put simply, the argument runs like this:

1. Intelligence tests simply sample what we know.
2. It is true that some people know more than others but...
3. to explain *why* some people know more than others by saying that they are more intelligent is vacuous (being a tautology).
4. We only think that there is such a thing as intelligence because we have been told that this is so by those who claim to be able to measure it with intelligence tests.

Although this view is clearly eccentric and has been cogently rebutted by others (Sternberg, 1988; Nettelbeck, 1990) it provides a sharp focus for the central question addressed in this chapter. Is it the case that the indisputable ability of intelligence tests to 'predict' many aspects of human performance

HANDBOOK OF HUMAN PERFORMANCE
VOLUME 3 ISBN 0-12-650353-2

in education and the workplace is because: (1) the tests simply sample the range of knowledge and experience relevant to the performance they predict, or (2) the tests measure (albeit indirectly) underlying information processing capacities? Proposition 1 corresponds to what Jensen (1984) has called the *specificity doctrine*, henceforth referred to as the *specificity hypothesis*. The specificity hypothesis proposes that intelligence is nothing more than a rag-bag of knowledge acquired through experience and ingenuously sampled by intelligence tests. My position is that the specificity hypothesis is false and that proposition 2 is true: that is, intelligence tests measure, in part, stable individual differences in information processing capacities.

Research on the relationship between psychometric measures of intelligence and information processing is vast (see, for example, Sternberg, 1982). Consequently, the presentation of relevant data and issues in this chapter must be selective. I concentrate here on the central issue: whether intelligence should be regarded as synonymous with knowledge or whether it reflects properties of information processing that constrain knowledge *acquisition*. This takes us, by way of introduction, through brief discussions of the psychometrics of intelligence and the domain specificity of knowledge, to a consideration of the relationship between information processing capacities and intelligence. In particular, the relationship between putatively *knowledge-free* information processing measures, such as inspection time, and individual differences in psychometric intelligence is focused upon.

PSYCHOMETRICS OF INTELLIGENCE

Psychometric theories of intelligence are notoriously contradictory. They range from the earliest suggestion of Spearman (1904) that intelligence tests primarily measure a unitary factor, *g*, through Thurstone's (1938) proposal that there are eight primary mental abilities (verbal, spatial, number and so forth), to Guilford's (1966) contention that there are at least 120 independent abilities. The fact that such contradictory theories have co-existed for much of the century is not so surprising: theoretical conflict can be a healthy sign in a developing science. It is not, then, the conflicting theories *per se* that have damned psychometrics in the eyes of many non-psychometrists so much as the fact that the conflict shows no sign of resolution. As a result, psychometric theories are often regarded as sterile. This state of affairs is especially surprising when we consider that this sterility exists despite the fact that intelligence tests provide an unequivocal database with a reliability and applicability that is unsurpassed in the rest of psychological science. Modern intelligence tests go through rigorous procedures of item selection; they are subjected to tests of reliability and validity, and they are published with precise norming and standardization data. As a result, we know precisely what pattern of results to expect when the test is administered to different populations and we can make well-defined comparisons between individuals on the basis of these results. Why is it, then, that this branch of psychological science, with such high quality data, has not solved the scientific problem of the nature of intelligence? To understand why this is so, and why, therefore, psychometric theories are considered sterile, we need only look at the most robust data of all: the fact that cognitive abilities covary.

General intelligence

If a heterogeneous set of cognitive tests is given to a random sample of the population, performance on these tests will correlate. For example, individuals who are better than average on tests of vocabulary will be better than average on tests of mechanical reasoning. They will also be better at solving analogies, better at making inferences, better at arithmetical calculations, know more general information, be faster at substituting digits for other symbols, and so forth. The fact that the correlation matrix of ability tests yields correlations that are all significantly positive has been termed *positive manifold*. When the variance in the matrix is analysed into underlying factors (see below) a general factor on which all the tests have moderate to high loadings will be found. This general factor is found even in cases where the test constructors set out with the explicit intention to measure independent abilities. For example, the British Ability Scales (Elliott, 1983) set out to measure twenty-three conceptually distinct cognitive abilities and yet the general factor accounts for more variance than any other single factor in the battery (Elliott, 1986). This covariation of abilities has been designated *general intelligence* since the time of Spearman (1904): but it is just this designation that has been the object of an unresolved dispute. While everyone agrees that the data (covariation of abilities) are what they are, the same data are open to radically different interpretations. Why is this so?

The difference between psychometric theories rests on differences in methods of *factor analysis*, which is the major analytic tool used by psychometricians. Simply put, the variance in a matrix of correlations can be distributed among underlying, hypothetical factors, or latent traits, in a variety of ways. For example, the main criterion for a factor solution might be that the factors should be orthogonal to each other. Such a criterion will result in a solution that produces a large general factor, or Spearman's *g*, where all the tests have moderately high loadings on the factor. On the other hand, we might search for factors that maximize the number of high and low loadings for each of the tests in the battery. This will produce a solution more like Thurstone's primary mental abilities (PMA), but the factors themselves will be moderately correlated and not orthogonal. The point is that these radically different psychometric structures are mathematically equivalent, in the sense that they both account for the same amount of variance. So, mathematically, there is no good reason to choose one solution rather than another. Thus, we are left with the peculiar (some may say damning) situation of the same data matrix, containing the undeniable covariation of abilities, being analysed in different ways to support diametrically opposed theories.

Psychometricians have tried to find objective methods to find the 'best' factor structure. The details of these methods are unimportant. It is enough to know that at the end of the day the choice of factor solution appears arbitrary but is, in fact, driven by the psychometrists 'theory' of the structure of intelligence. In other words, the structure is not inherent in the data. This has reinforced the view of those who believe that the whole notion of intelligence is an artifact of the psychometric method. Such a fundamental theoretical dispute as the existence or non-existence of general intelligence, or *g*, turns out, they claim, to be nothing more than a dispute over mere mathematical abstractions arbitrarily chosen from among an infinite supply (Gould, 1981). Yet, things are not as ambiguous as some would have us believe. In particular, there are at least two good psychometric reasons favouring the view that there is a general property to intelligence, akin to Spearman's conception of *g*:

1. More modern analytic techniques such as LISREL (Joreskog and Sorbom, 1981) have shown that while there is good support for more specific factors (roughly equivalent to the PMA of Thurstone), *hierarchical* models with a unitary *g* factor at the apex of the hierarchy fit the data better than any model without such a *g* factor (Gustafson, 1984). In short, solutions that exclude a general factor appear to be non-optimal solutions as judged by the new yardstick of LISREL.
2. While we can design tests that load almost exclusively on a general factor, no-one has been able to construct a test battery intended to measure a collection of independent abilities where no general factor can be extracted. For example, the logical step for Thurstone after 'discovering' the PMA was to design tests that would measure only a single ability. Unfortunately this project failed. Nearly all the tests specifically designed to test each independent PMA had higher *g*-loadings than they did on the particular PMA factor they were designed to measure (Eysenck, 1939).

These two observations on the status of psychometric *g* merely scratch the surface of what has been a protracted debate. The interested reader is referred to Jensen (1984, 1987) for the pro-*g* case, and to Schonemann (1985, 1987) and Gould (1981) for a critique. However, I should make it clear that, in my opinion, the central criticism of psychometric theories is valid: the issue of data interpretation is unresolvable within a purely psychometric framework. What we need is some kind of external validation of the contested psychometric constructs. I hope to provide this validation for general intelligence below. First, though, the other side of the central issue of this chapter – the domain specificity of knowledge – must be addressed.

THE DOMAIN SPECIFICITY OF KNOWLEDGE

The specificity hypothesis claims that intelligence is simply a rag-bag of specific skills and knowledge. In the context of the predictive validity of intelligence tests (the indisputable ability of intelligence test performance to predict real-life performance measures in education and at the workplace) the specificity hypothesis amounts to the claim that the basis of their predictive validity is overlapping knowledge content between the predictor (tests) and criteria (educational or occupational performance).* Similarly, the covariation of abilities is to be explained on the basis of overlapping content between different tests. Yet, the specificity hypothesis, in its opposition to the construct of general intelligence, takes as axiomatic the notion of domain specificity in knowledge (see, for example, Ceci and Liker, 1986). In addition, I argue, if we take the domain specificity of knowledge at all seriously we will find that the specificity hypothesis is both logically flawed and empirically false. There are two main empirical falsifications: (1) the inability to find general transfer of training, and (2) the superiority of general ability tests over specific tests for predicting real-world performance. The logical flaw is that the notion of domain specificity makes the idea that intelligence tests 'sample' knowledge incoherent. Let us take each point in turn.

Knowledge and transfer

To test the specificity hypothesis we might look to evidence on the transfer of knowledge and cognitive skills. What we find is that knowledge is indeed highly domain (situation) specific and heavily influenced by experience. For example, undergraduates in physics, who have received considerable instruction but are not yet 'experts', can still fail simple mechanics problems because of an inability to apply what they 'know' (i.e. what they have been instructed in) to a novel but related problem (Larkin, 1983). If knowledge is so domain-specific, then perhaps intelligence is nothing other than a rag-bag of skills picked up over the years and which are sampled on intelligence tests, as is claimed by the specificity hypothesis. However, it seems that knowledge is so domain-specific that unless an intelligence test overlapped considerably

* As this chapter makes clear, intelligence test scores predict two kinds of performance. Real-world performance refers primarily to occupational or educational success and should be distinguished from laboratory performance measures to be discussed later in the chapter.

with the knowledge content of the criterion performance, then they would have little, if any, predictive validity. We shall see in a moment that it is not only wrong to suppose that the best predictors of performance are those tests whose content mirrors closely criterion performance, but that it is also not the case that test content must even come *fairly close* to the criterion content.

Before I justify this let us look at a more moderate version of the specificity hypothesis: intelligence tests predict criterion performance because individuals with more knowledge (those that score higher on intelligence tests) can use existing knowledge as the basis of *learning* new skills. That is, particular items of knowledge are not directly transferred from one situation to another but, rather, constitute the basis for learning new tasks. Data from the transfer of cognitive skills should be relevant to this issue.

Transfer of training occurs when having learned one task aids (positive transfer) or hinders (negative transfer) performance on another task. If general transfer from one domain of knowledge to another was possible (learning any task would have positive effects on learning any other) then a moderate specificity hypothesis would be more plausible: the more we know the more positive transfer there will be to novel tasks. Unfortunately, evidence for general transfer is weak.

Theories of transfer were first proposed in a behaviourist framework. For example, Thorndike's identical elements theory (e.g. Thorndike and Woodworth, 1901) proposed that the degree of transfer from one task to another depended on the number of 'elements' the tasks had in common, an element being defined as some kind of stimulus–response connection. The central problem for a behaviourist conception of transfer of identical elements is that no two situations are exactly alike (they are not even nearly alike in the case of the abilities in a typical intelligence test battery that are known to covary: for example, What are the common identical elements in knowing who wrote *Faust* and performance on a digit span test?). The advent of cognitive psychology gave impetus to those who believed that general transfer was possible, because it held out some hope that the basis of transfer might not be identical elements but some abstract attribute of knowledge. Thus, the emphasis was in generating structural descriptions of knowledge more abstract than the 'elemental' (e.g. Simon, 1975). Yet, what these more abstract descriptions could be has eluded some of the best thinkers in the field. It is not that there are no deep abstract specifications of problems: indeed, the move from novice to expert may be characterized as the acquisition of such abstractions (e.g. Chi *et al.*, 1982), it is just that the abstract specification varies from one problem domain to another. Structural descriptions of expertise in chess, for example, are very different from structural descriptions of expertise in medical diagnosis.

The lack of theories of how general transfer of knowledge might work has led to a move back towards specific transfer. One of the most influential of modern cognitive theories of learning and transfer, the ACT framework of J.R. Anderson (1983), is very *un*-abstract in flavour. The carrying out of a cognitive skill requires the operation of domain-specific *productions*. Productions consist of condition–action pairs with the basic form 'If X then Y', i.e. if condition X is met then action Y will result. Production systems are very similar in flavour to theories such as Thorndike's identical elements, with the crucial difference being that an 'element' is a cognitive representation rather than a stimulus–response connection. However, for the ACT framework, transfer between tasks is determined by the number of productions shared by two tasks, just as for Thorndike it was determined by the number of common identical elements.

In arguing that transfer of cognitive skills is based on the number of specific productions two tasks hold in common, Singley and J.R. Anderson (1989) make the following point about theories of transfer based on general knowledge:

> There is another way in which general transfer might occur ... based on two premises: (1) the mind is a general-purpose computing system, and (2) it is something whose computation can improve. The appropriate analogy is muscle. Strengthening muscle in one task improves its performance in another task. It is now abundantly clear that the mind is not a muscle in this sense. Thus, the conjunction of premises (1) and (2) cannot be true. Moreover, premise (2) is known to be true because the mind can improve its performance on specific tasks in very much the same way that muscle gains strength. Thus, premise (1) must be the problem. Hence, we can conclude that the units of knowledge in the mind are functionally separate *with respect to their potential for improvement*. (pp. 28–9, my italics)

To understand the significance of this quote, another central tenet of the ACT framework should be borne in mind. J.R. Anderson (1987) has argued for two levels of description in cognition, the algorithmic and the implementational. Algorithms are the abstract procedures that form the steps that the mind goes through when thinking. Implementation refers to properties of those steps, such as their speed. The quote from Singley and Anderson argues that, because there is no evidence for general transfer of training, it is unlikely that transfer operates by improving (or strengthening, in the muscle analogy) a general-purpose computational system. It is, then, inappropriate to think of the mind as a general-purpose computational system, at an *algorithmic level of description*. But here is the rub. Although there is no evidence for general transfer, there is plenty for the covariation of abilities, or general intelligence. It is implausible that such generality as is captured, for example, by the correlations between vocabulary scores, digit span tests and block design, could be explained in terms of common productions. It follows, then, from Anderson's analysis that such generality can only be captured at the implementational level. Thus, from within a bastion of modern cognitive science, we have a convincing argument that the covariation of abilities cannot be based on shared properties of knowledge content.

So the representation of knowledge is highly specific and possesses no general properties that could form the basis of learning new knowledge.

Therefore, even the more moderate specificity hypothesis (to remind the reader: the covariation of abilities simply reflects the fact that having more knowledge makes it easier to acquire new knowledge) is unlikely to be true. This means that the only specificity hypothesis that can work is the strong one: the ability of intelligence tests to predict real-world performance can only be due to shared knowledge content between predictor and criterion.

The predictive validity of intelligence tests

Is it the case that the predictive validity of intelligence tests is related to the degree of similarity between the test and the criterion?

In the case of the prediction of educational success there is no doubt that many intelligence tests use material that children may learn at school. Tests of arithmetic abilities, general information, vocabulary and so forth, may correlate with academic achievement because academic achievement measures the same things. However, it is equally clear that many intelligence tests test abilities that are not explicitly taught nor do they form the content of scholastic tests. Who has ever been taught 'how to do' a block design test? Who has ever been taught how to do Raven's progressive matrices? Indeed, it is only recently that there have been systematic attempts to discover just what it is we do when we solve such problems (Just and Carpenter, 1985; Carpenter *et al.*, 1990). Of great significance in this context is the predictive validity of intelligence tests during cognitive development. Measures of IQ show substantial stability from five to seventeen (Hindley and Owen, 1978). If the predictive validity of the tests depended on shared content how could it be that estimates of intelligence taken at the age of five predict performance based on very different kinds of knowledge measured again at seventeen? For example, vocabulary scores at five years predict mathematics scores at sixteen (Yule *et al.*, 1982). Indeed, more recently measures of information processing in the first few months of infancy have been shown to be predictive of later IQ differences (Rose *et al.*, 1986). The fact that intelligence test performance predicts real-world performance over such a developmental time span (and, indeed, the fact that there is substantial stability in IQ despite major changes in the content of the tests) belies the belief that intelligence tests have predictive validity because of overlapping content between predictor and criterion.

In the case of the prediction of occupational success we find a similar picture. In a review of hundreds of studies Hunter (1986) shows that general intelligence predicts performance on all jobs, even so-called manual jobs. Even more damning for the specificity hypothesis is that general ability estimates, derived from a simple averaging of performance on many tests, are as good predictors of job performance as complex regression techniques where different tests are given different weights tailored for particular jobs. For example, for a mechanics job it might be thought that giving increased weighting to tests of mechanical reasoning might increase the predictive validity of the test battery compared with just taking an average of scores on diverse tests such as mechanical reasoning, vocabulary, digit span, verbal comprehension and so forth. However, 'tweaking' the weightings in this way makes little or no difference to the predictive validity of the test battery.

We have seen that the specificity hypothesis is almost certainly wrong because: (1) training studies have shown that there is no evidence for general transfer between tasks, and (2) the predictive validity of intelligence tests is not related to overlapping knowledge content. In any case, if we take the domain specificity of knowledge seriously (and the anti-general intelligence school most certainly does) then the specificity hypothesis is surely incoherent. How could a 'sample' of an essentially arbitrary collection of skills allow us to predict an individual's performance on any other task? If the specificity hypothesis were true then individual differences in any truly arbitrary sample could not predict individual differences in a second sample. To argue, on the one hand, that what we know is domain-specific, and, on the other, that intelligence tests can predict performance because they 'sample' what any individual knows is hand-waving of hurricane proportions. If the domain specificity of knowledge is accepted and if intelligence is nothing other than knowledge, then intelligence tests should have little or no predictive validity. The specificity hypothesis, then, depending as it does on the domain-specificity of knowledge for its empirical justification, is theoretically incoherent.

The inability of the specificity hypothesis to explain either the covariation of abilities or the predictive validity of intelligence tests rules out a trivial dismissal of intelligence as a non-causal construct. Intelligence is a stable attribute of an individual that intelligence tests indirectly assess. Of course, it does not follow, necessarily, that this stable attribute is cognitive, it could be (given the discussion to this point) a non-cognitive attribute. For example, individuals may differ systematically in levels of motivation which causes some to be both successful in their occupation and good at intelligence tests. The history of such non-cognitive explanations of general intelligence shows that they have been discounted shortly after each new possibility is suggested. It is beyond the scope of this chapter to review this literature. We turn now to the positive case, that is, the arguments in favour of an information processing basis for general intelligence. In particular, I want to argue that variations in intelligence are, in part, determined by differences in the *speed* of information processing.

INFORMATION PROCESSING AND INTELLIGENCE

Cognitive correlates and components

Since the late 1970s, when cognitive psychologists finally became interested in individual differences in intelligence, the source of those differences has been sought in two main locations within the information processing system; either in *knowledge-rich* or in *knowledge-free* processes.

The cognitive correlates approach, pioneered by Hunt and his colleagues (Hunt, 1978, 1980; Hunt *et al.*, 1975), took what were fast becoming standard measures of cognitive processes and correlated individual differences in those processes with differences in psychometric measures of abilities. The work originally focused on verbal abilities principally because the most robust information processing measures had been derived from theories of verbal learning and memory. So, for example, the experimental paradigm first developed by Posner and Mitchell (1967) is thought to provide an index of the time taken to retrieve information from semantic memory. Subjects make judgements about whether pairs of letters (e.g. AA or Aa) are the same or different. They make this judgement in two different conditions, a name identity condition (Aa = same) or a physical identity condition (Aa = different). The typical result is that longer reaction times are found for the name identity condition. This is attributed to the extra time required to retrieve the name code from long-term memory. The approach taken by cognitive correlates research was to correlate individual differences in the speed of this hypothetical process with verbal ability as measured by standard psychometric tests. Other paradigms were used similarly, for example, short-term memory scanning (Sternberg, 1966) and sentence verification (Clark and Chase, 1972), in an attempt to find which processes best predicted psychometric verbal ability. Subsequently, spatial abilities were also investigated, principally by correlating psychometric measures with information processing measures of mental imagery, for example, the mental rotation of images (Shepard and Metzler, 1971).

Hunt himself considered that, as an attempt to isolate the major influences on individual differences in intelligence, the cognitive correlates approach failed (see Hunt, 1980). He noted that the correlations between the speed or efficiency of individual mechanisms and measured ability rarely exceeded 0.3, or about 10 per cent of the variance. Hunt argued that the major individual differences were to be found, not in the operation of processing components (knowledge-free mechanisms), but in how those components are selected and organized to solve a particular problem. Intelligence, proposed Hunt, is not a function of low-level properties of the processing system, but a property of processing *strategies* and *metacognitive* functions.

Robert Sternberg, the most influential and prolific of current researchers in intelligence, took a different tack from Hunt but came to much the same conclusion. Sternberg explicitly represents the cognitive processes involved in intelligent problem-solving as a hierarchy of three kinds of information processing component: performance components, knowledge acquisition components and metacomponents.

At the bottom of the hierarchy are *performance* components. These are the information processing mechanisms invoked by a particular sequence of information processing operations (for example, encoding, mapping, inference). The theory derives these performance components by testing alternative process models against experimental data gathered using Sternberg's technique of componential analysis (Sternberg, 1977, 1983), which is a variety of Donder's subtractive reaction time method. Basically, reaction time in one task condition is subtracted from reaction time in another condition that is thought to require an additional processing component for its successful solution. By comparing many conditions that differ only by a single processing component, alternative information processing models (and, consequently, the validity of their constituent components) are tested by their ability to model the RT data. Sternberg, like Hunt before him, came to the conclusion that, although performance components contribute to individual differences in intelligence, overall the contribution is weak, with correlations rarely exceeding 0.3.

At the top of the Sternberg's processing hierarchy are *metacomponents*. These are executive processes responsible for planning task solutions and monitoring feedback from performance and knowledge acquisition components. Sternberg claims that it is in these metacomponent processes that the major individual differences related to intelligence are to be found. That is, intelligence is the province of the processes involved, principally, in organizing problem solving *strategies* rather than the information processing components which implement the problem solving routines.

The cognitive correlates and cognitive components research represents the earliest incursions of cognitive psychologists into the study of individual differences in intelligence. This research has clearly favoured the 'high-level', knowledge-rich conception of intelligence and disfavoured the 'low-level', knowledge-free one. Inevitably, this research programme is not without its own problems. A major one, which applies more to the cognitive components than the cognitive correlates research, is the often dubious theoretical status of the particular information processing components and how they have been operationalized in different tasks. For example, it is not clear that a performance component labelled 'encoding' in one task bears any relationship to a performance component given the same label in any other, given that they often have quite different operating characteristics in each task (Neisser, 1983). Indeed, the metacomponents seem to embody the area of residual ignorance (to borrow Alan Baddeley's phrase) in the componential framework. So, for example, one of Sternberg's metacomponents is responsible for 'recognition of just what the nature of the problem is'. This reads more like a restatement of how intelligence is manifested rather than an explanation of it. A second problem concerns the kinds of subject used in the cognitive correlates and components research programmes. In the main, they have been American undergraduates. Using undergraduate subjects reduces the natural variance of intelligence and necessarily restricts the size of the relationship that can be expected with simple measures of the speed of elementary processes. It is of some interest, then, that more recently there have been discoveries of putatively simple knowledge-free measures that do seem to account for a substantial proportion of the variance in intelligence.

Reaction time and inspection time

In the 1970s Jensen began a research programme investigating the possibility that psychometric *g* may have its basis in speed of information processing. To measure speed of processing Jensen used a reaction time procedure, illustrated in Figure 1.1. Subjects hold down a home key until one of the surrounding lights is illuminated. They must then move their finger from 'home' to press a button immediately below the light. In such a procedure there are two principal dependent measures. Reaction time (RT) is the length of time between the onset of the stimulus light and the time at which the subjects lifts his or her finger off the home button. Movement time is the time from the offset of the home button to the press of the button below the stimulus light. The major independent variable is the number of lights.

According to the information theory of Shannon and Weaver (1949) the information in a task rises as a $\log_z$ of the number of alternatives, which is, in the case of Jensen's procedure, the number of lights. That is, increasing the number of lights increases the information load of the task (doubling the number of lights increases the information load by one 'bit'). Hick (1952) and Hyman (1953) had shown that the increase in RT is a linear function of the number of bits of information in the task, a result that became known as the Hick/Hyman Law. Eysenck (1967) cited research by Roth (1964) who

Figure 1.1 Jensen's reaction time task.

found that the slope of the function relating bits of information to RT was correlated with IQ. In other words, higher IQ subjects process a single bit of information faster than low IQ subjects, and the more bits there are the greater the difference in RT between high and low IQ subjects.

Jensen has fleshed out the empirical basis of the reaction time work in a number of studies. He claims that:

1. The *slope* of the function relating RT to bits is correlated with IQ (Jensen and Munro, 1979; Jenkinson, 1983).
2. The *correlation* between IQ and RT increases with task complexity, that is, number of bits (Lally and Nettelbeck, 1977; Smith and Stanley, 1983).
3. Intra-individual variability (measured by the standard deviation of the subject's RTs over trials, for any given number of bits) is the single best predictor of IQ of any of the RT parameters (Jensen, 1980, 1982).
4. RT parameters discriminate between IQ criterion groups, e.g. groups with retarded and normal IQ (Nettelbeck and Kirby, 1983; Jensen, 1982; Vernon, 1981).

All of these effects have been interpreted by Jensen (1982) in terms of a model of intelligence based on the rate of oscillation of excitatory and inhibitory phases of neuronal firing. He claims that these studies show that the basis of individual differences in intelligence is to be found not in differences in knowledge, or knowledge use, but in the speed of processing a single bit of information.

Jensen's conclusion, that differences in intelligence do not depend on complex cognitive processes, clearly contradicts the views of Sternberg and Hunt outlined above and represents a serious challenge to a cognitive view of intelligence. It is no surprise, therefore, to discover that Jensen's interpretations of the data are not uncontested.

Jensen's theory is based on strong assumptions about his RT procedure. The major assumption is that performance in the RT procedure only indexes processing speed and will not be influenced by differences in knowledge or knowledge use. This conclusion has been vigorously challenged (Longstreth, 1984, 1986; Rabbitt, 1985). The challenges centre around the contrary assertion that performing well in a reaction time task is actually a complicated business. Rather than RT reflecting the speed of operation of something as straightforward as the processing of a variable number of bits of information, it reflects the operation of a complex processing system which, itself, contains many different components, including attention, motivation, visual search and visual encoding. In addition, the instructions in an RT task to be 'accurate but respond as fast as possible' requires that subjects monitor their speed–accuracy trade-off functions in order to optimize performance. Such monitoring is complex, and is subject to large effects of age, IQ and practice (Rabbitt, 1979; Rabbitt and Goward, 1986). Differences in RT, then, may reflect differences in one or more of these diverse processes, or even more congenially for the cognitivist, in the organization and control of these processes.

Indeed, there are some indications that Jensen was too simplistic in his analysis of the cognitive requirements of his RT procedure. For example, even he acknowledges that the linear relationship between RT and complexity (number of bits) breaks down at an information load of about four or five bits (Jensen, 1982). He attributes this to the invocation by the subject of different mental processes to cope with the increased information load. However, cognitive psychologists have claimed that processing strategies are invoked at all levels of complexity in RT tasks and it is the variance in their use, with higher IQ subjects having more efficient (i.e. 'clever') strategies, that creates the correlation between RT and IQ. Thus, the major assumption of Jensen has been called into question. The correlation between RT and IQ may be created by the intelligent use of cognitive processing in both RT and IQ tasks and not on their shared reliance on processing speed.

The claim that Jensen's RT task is rather complex should be treated with a fair measure of scepticism given that the basis of the original opposition from cognitive psychology to the idea of an RT/IQ correlation, was that an RT task is too simple to be related to intelligence. As Jensen (1985, p. 254) has put it: 'Those investigators who have pursued only the experimental psychology of RT... may have forgotten that a few years ago it was conventional wisdom in psychology that RT had no relationship to intelligence.' Yet, there can be no doubt that the RT task is much more complex than Jensen originally supposed. This leaves room for differences in performance strategies to cause the IQ/RT correlation. However, another kind of information processing task, that purportedly measures speed of processing but does not have the procedural problems of the RT task, has been shown to have substantial correlations with measured intelligence.

In an *inspection time* task a subject is required to make a perceptual discrimination at different exposure durations of a stimulus (see Figure 1.2). For example, in a visual inspection time task, a stimulus, usually two lines of markedly different length which are joined at the top with a short horizontal bar, is presented for a varying duration before the inset of a masking stimulus. The subject is required to make a discriminative judgement (is the longer line on the left or the right?) and his or her accuracy is recorded at different stimulus–mask onset asyncronies. At longer exposures (greater than 500 ms) performance is virtually error-free. It is important to note that the decision to be made in an inspection time task is extremely simple: given a long enough stimulus exposure (and by long enough I mean only a second or so), virtually anyone, irrespective of intellectual ability, can accurately perform the task. As the exposure duration of the stimulus decreases, errors increase until the stimulus exposure is so short that discriminative judgements approach chance levels. The relationship of accuracy to exposure duration follows a standard psychophysical function – the cumulative normal ogive (Vickers and Smith, 1986) and for each subject a measure of inspection time can be calculated

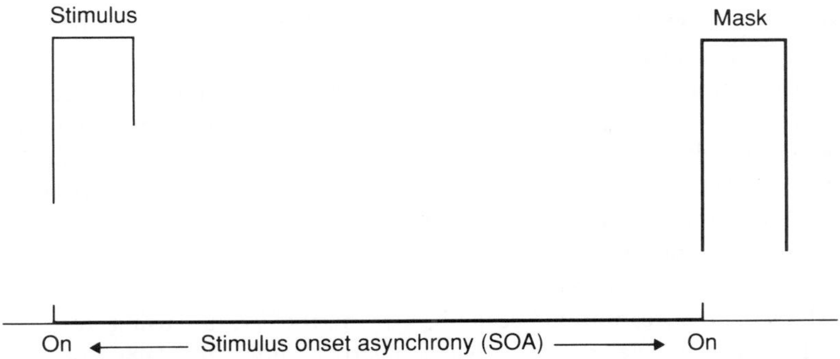

Figure 1.2 Inspection time. A stimulus is presented for a variable interval (SOA) before the onset of a masking stimulus which prevents further processing of the stimulus.

from this function. Thus, inspection time (IT) reflects individual differences in the exposure duration required to maintain a given level of accuracy. Since decreasing the exposure duration of stimuli increases the difficulty of the task without changing task complexity, IT is thought to estimate an individual's speed of information processing. In considered reviews of many studies, both Nettelbeck (1987) and Kranzler and Jensen (1989) came to the conclusion that inspection time and IQ correlate, negatively, at about 0.5. In other words, the speed of processing a 'simple' unit of information predicts about 25 per cent of the variance in knowledge-rich performance measured by a typical intelligence test. That such a simple measure, with well described *psychophysical* properties (Vickers and Smith, 1986), can predict individual differences in a range of knowledge domains, for example vocabulary scores, has led some to conclude that speed of processing is the basis of general intelligence (Anderson, 1989; 1992; Brand and Deary, 1982; Nettelbeck, 1987). Certainly, IT tasks obviate some of the criticisms levelled at the RT procedures and seem, for this reason alone, to be a better measure of speed of processing.

The major procedural advantage of the IT task over an RT task is that there is no requirement for speed of response, and therefore little possibility of the processing strategies (particularly speed–accuracy trade-offs) that have blighted the RT/IQ research. In an IT task some subjects will be highly accurate at exposures of 100 ms and will only start making errors at 80 ms. For others the figures might be 130 ms and 120 ms, or 70 ms and 55 ms. The crucial dimension of difficulty is simply the exposure duration of the stimulus. There is no need to trade off speed and accuracy, since subjects can take as long as they like to report their decision. The speed variable, this time, is not within the control of the subject but is an attribute of the stimulus.

There are, however, two principal criticisms of the IT work. The first is that the studies have used too few subjects and too many of those have been mentally retarded. The second is that despite having a simpler procedure there is still room for variations in processing strategies.

The early IT studies used small samples, with non-normal distributions of IQ, and usually included mentally retarded subjects: factors which are likely to over-estimate the size of the true population correlation with intelligence (see Mackintosh, 1986). While it is true that some studies which excluded subjects of subnormal intelligence have found low and/or insignificant correlations (Hulme and Turnbull, 1983; Irwin, 1984), there have been many studies since then which have used representative samples of subjects and have found a significant correlation between IT and intelligence. For example, Nettelbeck (1985) reported correlations of −0.38, −0.55 and −0.46 with verbal, performance and full-scale IQs from the WAIS, using forty adult subjects in the normal range of IQ. Similarly, Anderson (1986) reported a correlation of −0.41 with WAIS full scale IQ for forty-three schoolchildren attending a normal school, and Anderson (1988) found a correlation of −0.39 with Raven's matrices for one hundred and thirteen normal schoolchildren. Further, Longstreth, the doyen of the RT/IQ critics and a self-proclaimed sceptic of the IT research, reported a correlation of −0.44 between inspection time and IQ with a sample size of eighty-one and admitted: 'We are "Doubting Thomases" no more' (Longstreth *et al.*, 1986).

As for the influence of processing strategies, it is true that they have been found. In particular, some subjects report adopting, spontaneously, an apparent motion strategy (looking for the way the stimulus appears to 'move' into the mask) which substantially lowers their estimated IT. However, there is no relationship between intelligence and strategy use and, further, there is no correlation between IT and IQ within the strategy-using group. Indeed, removing those subjects who use strategies increases the size of the correlation for the remaining subjects (Egan, 1986; Mackenzie and Bingam, 1985; Mackenzie *et al.*, 1991). In short, strategy use detracts from, rather than causes, the IT/IQ correlation.

In conclusion, despite some initial concerns about the number and nature of subjects in the early studies and the possibilities of strategic influences on performance, there can now be little doubt that IT is related to intelligence in the normal population. The question now is, what are we to make of this?

SPEED OF PROCESSING, THOUGHT AND HUMAN PERFORMANCE

We have established a case for the view that individual differences in measured intelligence may indirectly reflect differences in the speed of information processing. We can now re-examine the relationship between intelligence and performance in this light.

Fluid and crystallized *g*

The major implication from the speed of processing studies is that intelligence tests predict human performance because of a shared reliance on speed of processing. It should be made clear that the correlation between measures of speed of processing and intelligence test performance is not based on a 'surface' correlation between speed of processing and speed of completing a test (in fact, the correlation of speeded and unspeeded versions of tests is fairly high). Measures of speed of processing predict performance on a variety of intelligence tests, including recognized 'power' tests of abilities, such as Raven's progressive matrices and tests of information and knowledge, such as vocabulary tests. But how can processing speed convert itself into breadth of knowledge and problem solving power?

Cattell (1963) has proposed that general intelligence can be subdivided into two related parts. Broadly speaking, *fluid g* is measured by tasks which require thought and reasoning, and can be conceived of as the biological basis of intelligence. In so far as we can associate fluid *g* with information processing notions such as speed of processing or cognitive capacity, many researchers would claim that fluid *g* increases with development (Case, 1985; Halford, 1987; Kail, 1986) and declines in old age (Salthouse, 1985). *Crystallized g*, on the other hand, is considered to be the conversion of fluid ability into stored knowledge. Although crystallized intelligence is related to levels of fluid *g*, it should show some independence too because factors such as motivation and experience also influence the contents of crystallized intelligence. It is interesting, therefore, that crystallized knowledge bases, such as the ability to solve crossword puzzle problems (Rabbitt, personal communication), can be maintained well into old age when fluid *g* has substantially declined. The distinction between fluid and crystallized intelligence has been clouded of late by Horn (1986), a collaborator of Cattell's, with the revelation that there are, in fact, a plethora of *g* abilities (belying, one might think, the label) and the claim that, in fact, even fluid and crystallized *g* are independent of each other. Nevertheless, Cattell's original insight provides a clue to how we might resolve the relationship among intelligence, knowledge and human performance.

The theory of the minimal cognitive architecture

I have recently proposed a theory of intelligence which has as its central core the relationship between intelligence and knowledge (Anderson, 1989; 1992). In brief, the theory proposes that knowledge is acquired through the implementation of knowledge acquisition routines, or algorithms, generated by a pair of specific processors (see Figure 1.3). These processors acquire knowledge using different kinds of routine (perhaps best thought of as verbal/propositional, on the one hand, and spatial/analogue on the other). These processors are akin to computer languages that solve problems (acquire knowledge) using different codes. In principle, each can solve any problem that can be solved by the other (being Turing machines) but, in practice, each will be better suited to different knowledge domains. The implementation

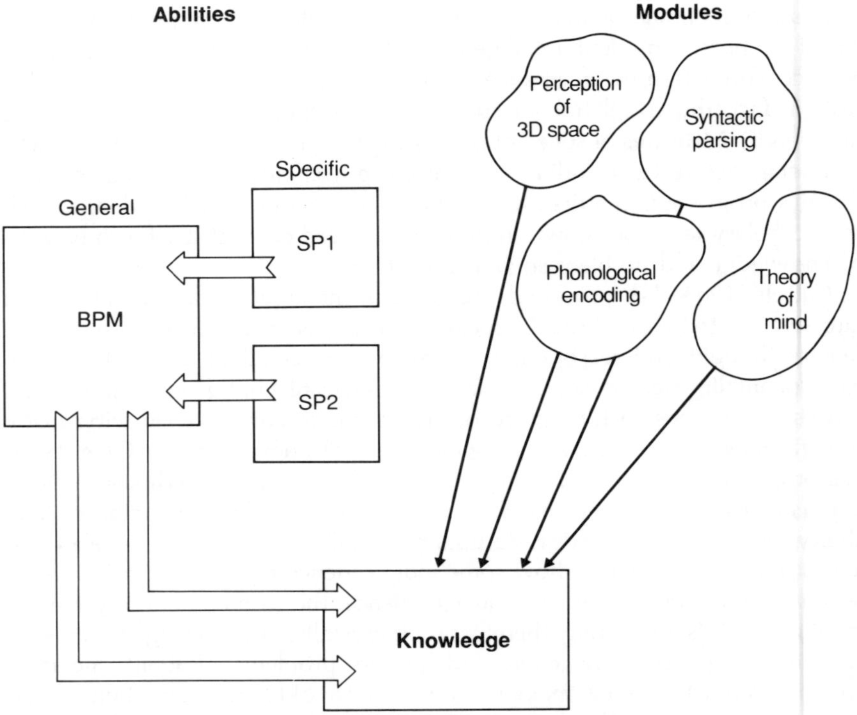

Figure 1.3

of an algorithm generated by a specific processor is what constitutes *thinking*. Variations in the latent power of the specific processors are the basis of differences in specific abilities (or the ability to think in different 'modes'). However, the complexity of specific processor algorithms that can be implemented is constrained by the speed of a *basic processing mechanism* (see Figure 1.3). Individuals with higher processing speeds will be able to implement more complex knowledge acquisition routines generated by the specific processors. In this way, variations in speed of processing will be the basis of individual differences in general intelligence. There is quite a separate dimension to intelligence in the developmental theory. Cognitive development is underlain by processing modules that are unconstrained by the speed of the basic processing mechanism. While the developmental dimension need not concern us here, it may be worth noting that I have adopted the hypothesis that speed of processing is unchanging during development (making individual differences and major aspects of developmental change truly orthogonal) but that I hold no view on the possibility that the speed of the basic processing mechanism may decline in old age.

I cannot, of course, present here the array of evidence that I have mustered in support of the theory of the *minimal cognitive architecture* represented in Figure 1.3 (Anderson, 1992). However, to conclude this chapter I would like to present three bald statements about the relationship between intelligence and human performance that are derived from the theory. In this way I hope to give some idea about how this relationship might best be conceived and perhaps provoke some new research questions.

1. Since differences in general intelligence are caused, in the main, by differences in the speed of the basic processing mechanism, processing tasks that ensure that individuals use the *same* processing algorithm (generated by a specific processor) should show the highest correlation between speed measures and IQ. Isolating identical algorithms and measuring their run-time should give the best estimate of individual differences in speed of processing, just as benchmark tests are used to compare different computers. Excising identical algorithms is likely to be more feasible in simple tasks where there is little or no room for alternative processing strategies. Such tasks (varieties of inspection time spring to mind) should, in the long run, show the clearest relationships with intelligence. This view runs counter to that currently in vogue in information processing circles. So, while it is correct to claim that more complex information processing tasks show the highest correlations with IQ and that this may be due to the fact that complex tasks consume more processing capacity (Larson and Saccuzzo, 1989), this is, on the one hand, an unsurprising proposition (intelligent people are better at more complex tasks) and, on the other, one which is potentially ambiguous. Variations in speed of processing in complex tasks are as likely to be due to variations in problem-solving algorithms used as they are to be due to variations in speed or capacity *per se.*
2. The theory does propose, however, that the speed of the basic processing mechanism only constrains thought and is not a general constraint on all kinds of information processing. Most obviously, modular processes that are either hardwired or have been 'over-learned' through practice and have become automatic (Shiffrin and Schneider, 1977) will be unrelated to measures of speed of processing and, consequently, intelligence. This hypothesis has been proposed before but for quite independent reasons (e.g. Hasher and Zacks, 1984). More novel, perhaps, is the more specific prediction that it is only *symbolic* processes that are constrained by the speed of the basic processing mechanism and that, therefore, those processing functions that are accommodated comfortably by connectionist systems are unlikely to be related to either processing speed or intelligence. Indeed, if a symbolic judgement in any discrimination task, whose speed is usually related to differences in intelligence (such as the judgement made in an inspection time task), can be made non-symbolically

(becoming, strictly, not a 'judgement' but a kind of implicit detection), then the relationship between speed of processing in the task and intelligence should disappear.

3. Since the speed of the basic processing mechanism constrains the complexity of thought (i.e. the complexity of the algorithms or routines generated by the specific processors) variation in specific abilities will be least at low processing speeds and greatest at high processing speeds. In short, specific abilities should be more differentiated at higher levels of IQ. Further, speed of processing measures should correlate more with variations in intelligence in below-average IQ groups than in above-average IQ groups. Partial empirical support for this *differentiation hypothesis* already exists: the *g*-factor is larger for lower IQ groups than those of average IQ (Spitz, 1988; Detterman and Daniel, 1989); the relationship between verbal and performance IQ changes with level of intelligence (Lawson and Inglis, 1985); simple information processing tasks are more highly intercorrelated for lower IQ groups than for higher IQ groups, and the tasks also correlate more highly with IQ within the lower group (Detterman and Daniel, 1989). Another major prediction of the differentiation hypothesis is that the influence of differential experience (environment) will be greatest at higher levels of intelligence, which is at least consistent with the finding of a higher heritability of IQ in lower IQ groups (Spitz, 1988).

The basic picture painted by this theory of intelligence shows that individual differences in intelligence are underlain, in the main, by differences in the speed of information processing. Individuals with high processing speed will not only be able to process information faster (accumulating, on average, more knowledge) but will also be able to entertain more complex thoughts. This will make such an individual better at coping both with novel tasks and tasks with high information loads. In turn, more complex thoughts will lead to the acquisition of more complex knowledge systems. The contents of an individual's knowledge base, then, although influenced by his or her experience, will depend primarily on his or her speed of processing.

The theory argues that, while it is likely that enough practice and experience can, in the long run, be more important for performance in a specific domain, the ability of intelligence tests to predict human performance across many different domains lies in the fact that these tests indirectly measure an individual's speed of information processing.

REFERENCES

Anderson, J.R. (1983) *The Architecture of Cognition*. Cambridge, Mass.: Harvard University Press.
Anderson, J.R. (1987) Methodologies for studying human knowledge. *Behavioral and Brain Sciences* **10**: 467–505.

Anderson, M. (1986) Inspection time and IQ in young children. *Personality and Individual Differences* **7**: 677–86.
Anderson, M. (1988) Inspection time, information processing and the development of intelligence. *British Journal of Developmental Psychology* **6**: 43–57.
Anderson, M. (1989) New ideas in intelligence. *The Psychologist: Bulletin of the British Psychological Society* **3**: 92–4.
Anderson, M. (1992) *Intelligence and Development: A cognitive theory*. Oxford: Blackwell.
Brand, C. and Deary, I.J. (1982) Intelligence and inspection time. In *A Model for Intelligence*, edited by H.J. Eysenck. New York: Springer.
Carpenter, P.A., Just, M.A. and Shell, P. (1990) What one intelligence test measures: a theoretical account of the processing in the Raven Progressive Matrices test. *Psychological Review* **97**: 404–31.
Case, R. (1985) *Intellectual Development: Birth to Adulthood*. New York and London: Academic Press.
Cattell, R.B. (1963) Theory of fluid and crystallised intelligence: a critical experiment. *Journal of Educational Psychology* **54**: 1–22.
Ceci, S.J. and Liker, J.K. (1986) A day at the races: a study of IQ, expertise, and cognitive complexity. *Journal of Experimental Psychology: General* **115**: 255–66.
Ceci, S.J. (1990) *On Intelligence... More or Less. A Bioecological Treatise on Intellectual Development*. Englewood Cliffs, NJ: Prentice Hall, Inc.
Chi, M.T.H., Glaser, R. and Rees, E. (1982) Experts in problem solving. In *Advances in the Psychology of Human Intelligence*, Vol. 1, edited by R. Sternberg. Hillsdale, NJ: Erlbaum, pp. 7–75.
Clark, H.H. and Chase, W.G. (1972) On the process of comparing sentences against pictures. *Cognitive Psychology* **3**: 472–517.
Detterman, D.K. and Daniel, M.H. (1989) Correlations of mental tests with each other and with cognitive variables are highest for low IQ groups. *Intelligence* **13**: 349–59.
Egan, V. (1986) Intelligence and inspection time: do high-IQ subjects use cognitive strategies? *Personality and Individual Differences* **7**: 695–700.
Elliott, C.D. (1983) *British Ability Scales: Technical Handbook*. Windsor: NFER–Nelson.
Elliott, C.D. (1986) The factorial structure and specificity of the British Ability Scales. *British Journal of Psychology* **77**: 175–85.
Eysenck, H.J. (1939) Review of Primary Mental Abilities by L.L. Thurstone. *British Journal of Educational Psychology* **9**: 270–5.
Eysenck, H.J. (1967) Intelligence assessment: a theoretical and experimental approach. *British Journal of Educational Psychology* **37**: 81–98.
Fitzgerald, J.M. and Mellor, S. (1988) How do people think about intelligence? *Multivariate Behavioral Research* **23**: 143–57.
Gardner, H. (1983) *Frames of Mind: The Theory of Multiple Intelligences*. London: Heinemann.
Gould, S.J. (1981) *The Mismeasure of Man*. Pelican.
Guilford, J.P. (1966) Intelligence: 1965 model. *American Psychologist* **21**: 20–6.
Gustafson, J.E. (1984) A unifying model for the structure of mental abilities. *Intelligence* **8**: 179–203.
Halford, G.S. (1987) *A Structure Mapping Analysis of Conceptual Complexity: Implications for Cognitive Development*. Technical Report 87/1, Centre for Human Information Processing and Problem-solving (CHIPPS).
Hasher, L.H. and Zacks, R.T. (1984) Automatic processing of fundamental information: the case of frequency of occurrence. *American Psychologist* **39**: 1372–88.
Hick, W.G. (1952) On the rate of gain of information. *Quarterly Journal of Experimental Psychology* **4**: 11–26.
Hindley, C.B. and Owen, C.F. (1978) The extent of individual changes in IQ for ages between 6 months and 17 years, in a British longitudinal sample. *Journal of Child Psychology and Psychiatry* **19**: 329–50.

Horn, J. (1986) Intellectual ability concepts. In *Advances in the Psychology of Human Intelligence,* edited by R.J. Sternberg. Hillsdale, NJ: Erlbaum.

Howe, M.J.A. (1990) *The Origins of Exceptional Abilities.* Oxford: Blackwell.

Howe, M.J.A. and Smith, J. (1988) Calendrical calculating in 'idiots savants': how do they do it? *British Journal of Psychology* **79**: 371–86.

Hulme, C. and Turnbull, J. (1983) Intelligence and inspection time in normal and mentally retarded subjects. *British Journal of Psychology* **74**: 365–70.

Hunt, E. (1978) Mechanics of verbal ability. *Psychological Review* **85**: 109–30.

Hunt, E. (1980) Intelligence as an information processing concept. *British Journal of Psychology* **71**: 449–74.

Hunt, E., Lenneborg, C. and Lewis, J. (1975) What does it mean to be high verbal? *Cognitive Psychology* **7**: 194–227.

Hunter, J.E. (1986) Cognitive ability, cognitive aptitudes, job knowledge and job performance. *Journal of Vocational Behaviour* **29**: 340–62.

Hyman, R. (1953) Stimulus information as a determinant of reaction time. *Journal of Experimental Psychology* **45**: 188–96.

Irwin, R.J. (1984) Inspection time and its relation to intelligence. *Intelligence* **8**: 47–65.

Jenkinson, J.C. (1983) Is speed of information processing related to fluid or to crystallized intelligence? *Intelligence* **7**: 91–106.

Jensen, A.R. (1980) Chronometric analysis of mental ability. *Journal of Social and Biological Structures* **3**: 181–224.

Jensen, A.R. (1982) Reaction time and psychometric *g*. In *A Model for Intelligence,* edited by H.J. Eysenck. Berlin: Springer.

Jensen, A.R. (1984) Test validity: *g* versus the specificity doctrine. *Journal of Social and Biological Structures* **7**: 93–118.

Jensen, A.R. (1985) The nature of the black–white difference on various psychometric tests: Spearman's hypothesis. *Behavioral and Brain Sciences* **8**: 193–263.

Jensen, A.R. (1987) The *g* beyond factor analysis. In *The Influence of Cognitive Psychology on Testing,* edited by R.R. Ronning, J.A. Glover, J.C. Conoley and J.C. Witt. Hillsdale, NJ: Erlbaum.

Jensen, A.R. and Munro, E. (1979) Reaction time, movement time and intelligence. *Intelligence* **3**: 121–6.

Joreskog, K.G. and Sorbom, D. (1981) *LISREL V: Analysis of Linear Structural Relationships by Maximum Likelihood and Least Squares Methods.* Research report, Department of Statistics, University of Uppsala.

Just, M.A. and Carpenter, P.A. (1985) Cognitive coordinate systems: accounts of mental rotation and individual differences in spatial ability. *Psychological Review* **92**: 137–72.

Kail, R. (1986) Sources of age differences in speed of processing. *Child Development* **57**: 969–87.

Kranzler, J.H. and Jensen, A.R. (1989) Inspection time and intelligence: a meta-analysis. *Intelligence* **13**: 329–48.

Lally, M. and Nettelbeck, T. (1977) Intelligence, reaction time and inspection time. *American Journal of Mental Deficiency* **82**: 273–81.

Lally, M. and Nettelbeck, T. (1980) Intelligence, inspection time, and response strategy. *American Journal of Mental Deficiency* **84**: 553–60.

Larkin, J.H. (1983) The role of problem representation in physics. In *Mental Models,* edited by D. Gentner and A.L. Stevens. Hillsdale, NJ: Erlbaum.

Larson, G.E. and Saccuzzo, D.P. (1989) Cognitive correlates of general intelligence: toward a process theory of *g*. *Intelligence* **13**: 5–31.

Lawson, J.S. and Inglis, J. (1985) Learning disabilities and intelligence test results: a model based on a principal components analysis of the WISC-R. *British Journal of Psychology* **76**: 35–48.

Longstreth, L.E. (1984) Jensen's reaction time investigations of intelligence: a critique. *Intelligence* **8**: 139–60.

Longstreth, L.E. (1986) The real and the unreal: a reply to Jensen and Vernon. *Intelligence* **10**: 181–91.

Longstreth, L.E., Walsh, D.A., Alcorn, M.B., Szeszulski, P.A. and Manis, F.R. (1986) Backward masking, IQ, SAT and reaction time: interrelationships and theory. *Personality and Individual Differences* **7**: 643–51.

Mackenzie, B. and Bingham, E. (1985) IQ, inspection time and response strategies in a university population. *Australian Journal of Psychology* **37**: 257–68.

Mackenzie, B., Molloy, E., Martin, F., Lovegrove, W. and McNicol, D. (1991) Inspection time and the content of simple tasks: a framework for research on speed of information processing. *Australian Journal of Psychology* **43**: 37–43.

Mackintosh, N.J. (1986) The biology of intelligence? *British Journal of Psychology* **77**: 1–18.

Neisser, U. (1983) Components of intelligence or steps in routine procedures? *Cognition* **15**: 189–97.

Nettelbeck, T. (1985) Inspection time and IQ. Paper presented at the second meeting of the International Society for the Study of Individual Differences, Santa Feliu de Guixols, Catalonia, Spain.

Nettelbeck, T. (1987) Inspection time and intelligence. In *Speed of Information Processing and Intelligence*, edited by P.A. Vernon. New York: Ablex.

Nettelbeck, T. (1990). Intelligence does exist. *The Psychologist: Bulletin of the British Psychological Society* **3**: 494–7.

Nettelbeck, T. and Kirby, N.H. (1983) Measures of timed performance and intelligence. *Intelligence* **7**: 39–52.

Posner, M.I. and Mitchell, R.F. (1967) Chronometric analysis of classification. *Psychological Review* **74**: 392–409.

Rabbitt, P.M.A. (1979) How old and young subjects monitor and control responses for accuracy and speed. *British Journal of Psychology* **70**: 305–11.

Rabbitt, P.M.A. (1985) Oh *g* Dr. Jensen! or, *g*-ing up cognitive psychology? Open peer commentary. *Behavioral and Brain Sciences* **8**: 238–9.

Rabbitt, P.M.A. and Goward, L. (1986) Effects of age and raw IQ test scores on mean correct and mean error reaction times in serial choice tasks: a reply to Smith and Brewer. *British Journal of Psychology* **77**: 69–73.

Rose, D.H., Slater, A.S. and Perry, H. (1986) Prediction of childhood intelligence from habituation in early infancy. *Intelligence* **10**: 251–63.

Salthouse, T.A. (1985) *A Theory of Cognitive Ageing*. Amsterdam: North-Holland.

Schonemann, P.H. (1985) On artificial intelligence. Open peer commentary. *Behavioral and Brain Sciences* **8**: 241–2.

Schonemann, P.H. (1987) Jensen's *g*: outmoded theories and unconquered frontiers. In *Arthur Jensen: Concensus and Controversy*, edited by S. Mogdil and C. Modgil. Brighton: Falmer Press.

Shannon, C.E. and Weaver, W. (1949) *The Mathematical Theory of Communication*. Urbana: University of Illinois Press.

Shiffrin, R.M. and Schneider, W. (1977) Controlled and automatic human information processing. II: Perceptual learning, automatic attending and a general theory. *Psychological Review* **84**: 127–90.

Shepard, R.N. and Metzler, J. (1971) Mental rotation of three-dimensional objects. *Science, New York* **171**: 701–3.

Simon, H.A. (1975) The functional equivalence of problem solving skills. *Cognitive Psychology* **7**: 268–88.

Singley, M.K. and Anderson, J.R. (1989) *The Transfer of Cognitive Skill*. Cambridge, Mass.: Harvard University Press.

Smith, G.A. and Stanley, G. (1983) Clocking *g*: relating intelligence and measures of timed performance. *Intelligence* **7**: 353–68.

Spearman, C. (1904) 'General intelligence', objectively determined and measured. *American Journal of Psychology* **15**: 201–93.

Spitz, H.H. (1982) Intellectual extremes, mental age, and the nature of human intelligence. *Merrill–Palmer Quarterly* **28**: 167–92.

Spitz, H.H. (1988) Wechsler subtest patterns of mentally retarded groups: relationship to *g* and estimates of heritability. *Intelligence* **12**: 279–97.

Sternberg, R.J. (1977) *Intelligence, Information Processing and Analogical Reasoning: The Componential Analysis of Human Abilities.* Hillsdale, NJ: Erlbaum.

Sternberg, R.J. (ed.) (1982) *Handbook of Human Intelligence.* Cambridge University Press.

Sternberg, R.J. (1983) Components of human intelligence. *Cognition* **15**: 1–48.

Sternberg, R.J. (1988) Explaining away intelligence: a reply to Howe. *British Journal of Psychology* **79**: 527–33.

Sternberg, S. (1966) High speed scanning in human memory. *Science, New York* **153**: 652–4.

Thorndike, E.L. and Woodworth, R.S. (1901) The influence of improvement in one mental function upon the efficiency of other functions. *Psychological Review* **8**: 247–61.

Thurstone, L.L. (1938) *Primary Mental Abilities.* University of Chicago Press.

Vernon, P.A. (1981) Reaction time and intelligence in the mentally retarded. *Intelligence* **5**: 345–55.

Vernon, P.A. (1983) Speed of information processing and intelligence. *Intelligence* **7**: 53–70.

Vickers, D. and Smith, P.L. (1986) The rationale for the inspection time index. *Personality and Individual Differences* **7**: 609–23.

Yule, W., Gold, R.D. and Busch, C. (1982) Long-term predictive validity of the WPPSI: an 11-year follow-up study. *Personality and Individual Differences* **3**: 65–71.

2

Aging and Human Performance

D.R. DAVIES, A. TAYLOR & L. DORN

INTRODUCTION

Human performance is dependent upon a chain of mechanisms, beginning with the sensory systems which receive stimulation from the external and internal environments and ending with the neuro-muscular systems which effect responses to stimulation (Welford, 1985). Intervening between sensory and motor systems are a number of central mechanisms responsible for selective attention, for the recognition and identification of sensory stimuli, for the integration of incoming information with information already stored in memory, for the selection and initiation of appropriate actions, for the timing and co-ordination of muscular responses, and for the formulation and implementation of system goals. The aging process can impair the operational efficiency of sensory, motor and central mechanisms quite markedly, although since both individuals and mechanisms age at different rates, some people show few effects of normal (non-pathological) aging until relatively late in life. Moreover, neuro-biological mechanisms may vary considerably in their susceptibility to age-related deterioration.

Research designs

In investigating the relation between aging and human performance most studies have employed cross-sectional designs, comparing groups of younger and older adults working at the same task in the same situation at roughly the same time. Usually the average level of performance of the younger group is found to be significantly superior to that of the older group, though

HANDBOOK OF HUMAN PERFORMANCE
VOLUME 3 ISBN 0-12-650353-2

it has frequently been observed that within age-group differences exceed between age-group differences, and the extent of within age-group differences becomes greater as age increases. The level of performance achieved by some older individuals may therefore equal, or even exceed, the average performance level of younger individuals, and the performance of some younger individuals may be inferior to that of the average older individual. But cross-sectional designs are unable to separate age effects from cohort or generational effects, broadly defined as the collection of life experiences and socio-cultural influences that people of different ages bring to the task situation as a result of having been born at a particular historical time. Successive cohorts or generations are likely to possess higher levels of education, usually defined by the number of years of formal schooling (though this definition is not entirely problem-free; see Krauss, 1980), to have been exposed to more cognitively stimulating environments, and to have had access to more effective health care. To the extent that educational level, cognitive stimulation and health status are positively related to task performance, earlier cohorts will be disadvantaged relative to later ones and any age differences in task performance will not be solely due to the effects of aging. For instance, educational level is positively related to performance on intelligence (IQ) tests (e.g. Baltes, 1987), and health status and physical fitness are positively related to performance on psycho-motor tasks (e.g. Spirduso, 1980). Controlling cohort differences statistically, or through matching procedures (e.g. Green, 1969), usually reduces and sometimes eliminates age differences in performance.

A less frequently used alternative to the cross-sectional design, since it is both time-consuming and expensive, is the longitudinal design, in which the performance of the same individuals in the same task situation is sampled at different ages. Longitudinal designs control cohort effects, but confound effects due to aging with those due to time of measurement. Since only one birth cohort is tested, age effects observed in a longitudinal design are cohort specific. Time-of-measurement effects reflect the impact on behaviour of specific events, such as wars or economic depressions, which affect all individuals regardless of cohort membership. The longitudinal design faces the difficulties of selective 'drop-out' or attrition, the necessity of retaining the original methods of performance assessment, even though they may have become outdated and supplanted by more sensitive measures, and the generally beneficial effects of practice, despite the fact that encounters with the testing situation may be relatively infrequent, and quite widely spaced over time. Although longitudinal studies tend to give a more favourable picture of the intellectual ability of older individuals than do cross-sectional studies (see Salthouse, 1988) they have rarely been used in research on human performance, and the two designs have been even more rarely compared with respect to outcome. But in a recent study of age and vigilance, in which both longitudinal and cross-sectional comparisons were conducted, both comparisons indicated that age did not affect overall detection rate, or the vigilance decrement, though some differences were observed for detection latencies and a physiological measure of arousal, skin potential (Giambra and Quilter, 1988).

A third design, the time-lag design, controls age effects, but confounds time-of-measurement and cohort effects. In this design groups from several different cohorts are investigated, but the testing sessions are so spaced that each group is assessed at the same chronological age, say sixty. The 1900 cohort would thus be tested in 1960, the 1910 cohort in 1970, the 1920 cohort in 1980, and the 1930 cohort in 1990. In the time-lag design the problems of selective attrition and of practice effects do not arise, since each cohort is tested only once. By combining the three designs, it is possible to separate, at least in principle, effects due to age, cohort and time of measurement (see Schaie, 1977). This separation can be accomplished by the utilization of three bi-factor designs, the cohort-sequential, time-sequential and cross-sequential designs, in which age and cohort membership, age and time of measurement, and cohort membership and time of measurement are the respective independent variables. Despite their advantages, sequential designs may nevertheless encounter the problems associated with selective attrition, practice effects, and the retention of what may be less sophisticated methods of behavioural assessment. Moreover, since age, cohort membership and time of measurement are not truly independent of one another, once the levels of two of the variables are set, the level of the third is automatically determined. Each sequential design can thus manipulate two independent variables, but must leave the third uncontrolled, as a potential source of confounding. Baltes (1968) has argued that time-of-measurement effects are less important than are age and cohort effects, and has proposed a bi-factorial approach in which cross-sectional and longitudinal sequences are employed to estimate age effects.

A number of research designs are thus available for investigating both age differences and age changes in human performance. As already indicated, most studies of age and human performance have employed cross-sectional designs and have therefore focused on age differences, which may be confounded by cohort effects. In the absence of sequential studies, the extent to which cohort differences confound age differences in the kind of tasks typically used in studies of human performance is uncertain, but it has been suggested that cohort effects are likely to be minimal, if indeed they operate at all. Kausler (1982, pp. 169–73) pointed out that data for some such tasks, obtained under similar conditions, are available for young adults from different cohorts, in certain cases extending back to the last century. On the basis of an analysis of between-cohort comparisons, Kausler concluded that for several tasks, including paired-associate learning, serial learning, digit span and span of apprehension, the evidence for cohort effects on performance was negligible. Moreover, when cohort effects are obtained, as in a sequential study of the susceptibility of different age groups to two well-known visual illusions, they can be difficult to interpret (Kausler, 1982). But even if cohort differences do confound age differences in some kinds of human performance, establishing under what circumstances age differences in performance occur, and determining which factors enhance, reduce or perhaps even eliminate them, can help to facilitate the development and implementation of intervention techniques which may enable older individuals to function more effectively, more safely and more independently in a number of everyday situations. These include task/job/environment redesign, training and educational procedures, or changes in product packaging and labelling (see Smith, 1990, for further discussion).

AGE DIFFERENCES IN TASK PERFORMANCE

In this section we consider age differences in task performance in laboratory situations. Laboratory tasks often do not have an obvious correspondence with tasks encountered outside the laboratory and are likely to be relatively unfamiliar to older individuals. Moreover, laboratory studies of task performance, which usually emphasize both the speed and accuracy of performance, are frequently designed to push individuals close to their performance limits. Laboratory studies thus tend to assess maximal performance in novel and frequently highly abstract task situations, and are liable to exacerbate age-related performance differences, whether or not cohort effects are operating. Most work situations, in contrast, do not push people very close to their sensory, intellectual, or physical performance limits, and objective measures of work performance, such as output or production records, are more likely to be assessing typical, rather than maximal performance. Such measures may well be less sensitive to age effects than are laboratory measures. Two main topics are considered in this section: firstly, age-related performance slowing, frequently regarded as a fundamental contributor to age-related performance differences, and secondly, age differences in cognitive performance.

Age-related performance slowing

The slowing of behaviour with increasing age is generally regarded as the most widely documented finding in geropsychology (Salthouse, 1985; Welford, 1977). While behavioural slowing can be observed in simple tasks, it increases with task complexity, defined in terms of the computational processing time required to perform a particular task (Cerella *et al.*, 1980), both in psycho-motor tasks and, especially, in cognitive tasks. Absolute age differences in the speed of performance tend to be larger in complex tasks than in simpler ones, because complex tasks require more information-processing/cognitive operations, thereby producing greater cumulative slowing.

PSYCHO-MOTOR TASKS

Tasks typically employed to assess age differences in psycho-motor speed include simple movements (for example, tapping), paced tasks, and, most frequently, simple and choice reaction time (RT) tasks. There is considerable variation in the results obtained from studies of age differences in simple movement times, due in part to the nature of the task, but age differences are apparent to a greater or lesser degree in virtually all such studies, regardless of whether maximum or 'comfortable' response speeds are being assessed (see Welford, 1977). In tasks involving more complex responses, which require more time to select, programme and execute, the response latencies of older adults increase to a greater extent relative to those of younger adults (Spirduso and MacRae, 1990). In paced tasks, in which signals requiring action are presented at a fixed rate which is not under the respondent's control, performance deteriorates from the fifties onwards, especially if signals are presented at high rates (Davies, 1968; Welford, 1977).

Literature surveys suggest that response latencies in simple RT tasks increase by 20 per cent to 26 per cent from the twenties to the sixties, although in absolute terms these differences are slight, usually being less than one-twentieth of a second (Welford, 1977). In choice RT tasks, age-related psycho-motor slowing is generally more pronounced than in simple RT tasks (see Salthouse, 1985; Welford, 1977). Dirken and Wartna (1972), for example, who tested a sample of 320 Dutch industrial workers aged thirty to sixty-nine years, observed a correlation of +0.26 between age and simple RT. The correlation increased slightly for a two-choice task (+0.29), but when the number of choices was increased to four, the correlation rose to +0.48, remaining at or around this level as the number of choices was increased from five to eight. Task complexity can also be increased by manipulating stimulus–response (S–R) compatibility. S–R incompatibility increases RTs, but disproportionally so for older adults (Spirduso and MacRae, 1990).

Age-related psycho-motor slowing is not confined to tasks presented to a particular sensory modality, or to tasks requiring a particular motor response. Similar age-related decrements in response speed are observed in visual and auditory simple RT tasks (e.g. Koga and Morant, 1923) and in tasks comparing release responses made with the finger, jaw or foot (Birren and Botwinick, 1955). Moreover, attempts to localize age-related performance slowing in a particular processing stage, such as encoding, comparison or response selection and execution, suggest that all processing stages are characterized by slowing, and hence that age-related differences in the speed of performance cannot be attributed solely to any one stage (e.g. Salthouse and Somberg, 1982a). It is generally held, however, that the effects of aging are greater for information processing / cognitive components of performance than for perceptual–motor components, and age differences in response speed are believed to be mediated primarily by central rather than by peripheral factors (Salthouse, 1985). Although both sensory and motor processes are adversely affected by aging, input–output deficits have been generally regarded as accounting for relatively little of the overall slowing of performance with age (Welford, 1977). Stimuli are usually presented well above threshold and can be easily seen or heard; age differences in the latencies of retinal or pupillary responses are minimal; motor reactions are usually relatively simple and highly practised, and motor times (the delay between electro-myographic and mechanical responses) show very small changes with age. Moreover, age differences in peripheral nerve conduction velocities and in synaptic and neuro-muscular delay, have been estimated to contribute only about four per cent and two per cent respectively to the slowing of speeded voluntary reactions with age (see Surwillo, 1968).

However, the findings of a recent study conducted by Strayer *et al.* (1987) suggest that in some task situations at least, input–output processes may account for a substantial proportion of the age difference in response speed. Strayer *et al.* recorded event-related brain potentials (ERPs) from individuals ranging in age from twenty to sixty-five during the performance of a memory search task. They examined specifically the latency of the P_{300} component of the ERP, which has been shown to be sensitive to changes in information / cognitive processing, while being unaffected by response-related processes (see Duncan-Johnson, 1981). Strayer *et al.* found that P_{300} latencies increased with age by only 50 ms, while memory search RTs increased by 150 ms. Further analysis indicated that age differences in the speed of memory search were attributable to a roughly equal combination of age differences in the speed of perceptual encoding, in the speed of response execution, and in the position adopted along the speed–accuracy trade-off function. This result suggests that age differences in memory search response speed are due mainly to age differences in the speed of input–output processes rather than to age differences in central processing times.

COGNITIVE TASKS

Age-related performance slowing has also been observed in the performance of a wide variety of cognitive tasks, for instance, memory scanning, visual search, digit symbol substitution and mental rotation. Absolute age differences in cognitive slowing appear to be more substantial than in psycho-motor slowing, because a greater number of mental operations, each of which is performed more slowly in older individuals, intervene between stimulus presentation and response execution. Age differences in the speed of cognitive performance also markedly increase as the task becomes more complex (Cerella *et al.*, 1980). For example, in mental rotation tasks individuals are presented with pairs of stimuli and have to decide whether the elements of each pair are identical. As the rotational difference becomes greater, the number of cognitive operations required, and the time taken to reach a decision about whether or not the two are identical, increase. If each cognitive operation becomes slower with age, response time differences between younger and older adults should increase as the rotational difference increases. This prediction has been confirmed in several studies (e.g. Cerella *et al.*, 1981), which suggest that cognitive slowing in mental rotation tasks begins to become apparent in the sixties, although there may be no age difference in accuracy levels (Sharps and Gollin, 1987).

EXPLANATION OF AGE-RELATED PERFORMANCE SLOWING

These findings indicate that age-related performance slowing is widespread, if not ubiquitous, and Birren (1974) has suggested that behavioural slowing reflects a fundamental neural slowing, primarily in central brain mechanisms, which reduces the speed with which mental operations can be carried out. Analyses of RT data obtained from a wide variety of psycho-motor and cognitive tasks indicate that the RTs of younger and older individuals are linearly related, with the RTs of older individuals being increased by a constant proportion, varying from around 1.4 to 2.0, depending upon task complexity (e.g. Cerella *et al.*, 1980; Salthouse, 1985). Moreover, the proportion of the variance accounted for by the equation describing the linear relation between the RTs of older and younger individuals typically exceeds 0.9, despite the diversity of the tasks from which the RT data are drawn. Age-related differences in RTs would thus appear to result from a general slowing of performance, regardless of the nature of the task being performed. Correlations between measures of the speed of performance across different tasks also increase with age, and factor analyses indicate that the performance of older adults is characterized by a general speed factor, whereas that of younger adults is not (Birren *et al.*, 1962).

The most convincing exception to the general finding that response speed is slower in older than in younger adults comes from studies of healthy, active and physically fit older individuals, aged between fifty and seventy, who tend to be unrepresentative of their age cohort. Such individuals not only respond much more quickly in simple and choice RT tasks than do their sedentary and less healthy peers, but have also been shown to perform at levels comparable to those achieved by physically inactive college students in their twenties, and in some cases to exceed them (Spirduso and Clifford, 1978). However, younger active students still performed at higher levels than did older active individuals in both simple and choice RT tasks, though the age difference was relatively small. Both within- and between-subjects variabilities in RTs, which usually increase markedly with age, have been found to be essentially the same across age groups for physically active individuals. Exercise intervention programmes have also been shown to improve psycho-motor performance in older people, and since they are likely to be functioning at lower levels of health and fitness, their psycho-motor performance may show larger gains from such intervention programmes relative to those of younger people who are more likely to be functioning at higher levels (Spirduso and MacRae, 1990). Factors relating to activity, health and fitness may also be implicated in the greater RT slowing with age shown by men compared with women (Bleecker *et al.*, 1987), although men tend to respond more quickly than do women at most ages (e.g. Bellis, 1933).

Practice is another variable which might be expected to minimize or eliminate age differences in the speed of performance. However, while benefiting the performance of both older and younger individuals, practice does not seem to reduce the response speed of older individuals disproportionally (Salthouse, 1990). It is worth noting, however, that in one small-scale study, in which massive amounts of practice (20,000 trials) on a simple RT task were given to three women aged 17, 18 and 57, the initial age difference in RT was eventually abolished (Murrell, 1970). Age differences in RT have also been reported to be minimized, or even abolished, in task situations requiring vocal, rather than, manual responses (e.g. Nebes, 1978), although the evidence is somewhat inconsistent and the effect may be confined to tasks in which fast reactions (less than 400 ms) are called for (Spirduso and MacRae, 1990). It may be concluded that physically active life-styles and the maintenance of fitness during young and middle adulthood considerably attenuate, although do not completely eliminate, the effects of normal aging on the speed of psycho-motor reactions. Practice benefits young and old alike, although initial age differences in response speed do not appear to be abolished, at least with amounts of practice up to about fifty hours, which represents the upper limit so far examined in laboratory studies of psycho-motor and cognitive performance. More evidence would seem to be required as to whether age differences in response speed are reliably eliminated in tasks where the response requirement is vocal rather than manual.

A wide variety of explanations of age-related performance slowing have been proposed (see Salthouse, 1985) and these may be broadly divided into explanations emphasizing age-related strategic changes and those emphasizing age-related changes in neuro-biological mechanisms. Strategic explanations of age-related performance slowing suggest that older and younger individuals adopt different strategies when performing psycho-motor and cognitive tasks. Older individuals employ more cautious response strategies, favouring accuracy over speed, while younger individuals adopt more risky strategies, favouring speed over accuracy; older individuals thus adopt more conservative response criteria. As noted earlier, the adoption of a more conservative response criterion may account for some proportion of age-related performance slowing (Strayer *et al.*, 1987), but the finding that age differences in response speed persist when individuals of different ages are compared at exactly the same level of accuracy (Salthouse and Somberg, 1982b) suggests that differences among age groups in speed–accuracy trade-offs cannot provide a complete explanation of age-related performance slowing. Indeed, in the Strayer *et al.* study, the proportion of overall response slowing in memory search times which could be accounted for in this way was estimated to be about one-third.

Rabbitt (1981) suggested that response criteria can be adjusted in order to maintain an optimal balance between the speed and accuracy of performance. He showed that RTs become progressively faster until an error is made, whereupon they become slower before speeding up once more until the next error, and so on. Errors thus provide information about whether the respondent is performing at the right speed, and enable the response criterion to be adjusted. Older individuals appear to be less sensitive to error feedback information, so inappropriate adjustments are made to their response criteria. Consequently older people may make more errors, and their RTs are both longer and show greater variability. In these individuals, therefore, the system responsible for monitoring response speed, and for responding to error feedback, may be deficient, perhaps because of age-related deficits in attentional capacity.

One of the principal neuro-biological explanations of age-related performance slowing suggests that aging affects the timing of neuro-biological processes in the central nervous system (e.g. Birren, 1974). Surwillo (1968), for example, put forward an explanation of behavioural slowing in terms of the well-documented slowing of the EEG alpha rhythm with age (see, for example, Obrist, 1965; Woodruff-Pak, 1985). The alpha rhythm was hypothesized to function as an internal clock or 'master timing mechanism' for co-ordinating neural activities and organizing behaviour, and this internal clock was held to operate at a slower rate in older individuals. The alpha rhythm was also thought to have an arousing effect upon the cortex, so that alpha slowing would be liable to produce a state of under-arousal in the elderly. While Surwillo reported evidence broadly consistent with the internal clock hypothesis, subsequent tests have produced mixed results (see Salthouse *et al.*, 1979). Hicks and Birren (1970) reviewed evidence suggesting that the brain mechanism principally responsible for both psycho-motor slowing and the increased variability of RT with age was 'a system consisting of extrapyramidal centres of the basal ganglia, midbrain and thalamic reticular formation, and their rostral and caudal connections' (p. 389), although they pointed out that most of the evidence they reviewed was indirect. Welford (1985) discussed research indicating that external stimuli have to be discriminated against a background of random activity or 'noise' which arises partly from stimulus factors and partly from neural activity within sensory pathways and the brain itself ('neural noise'). It has been suggested that neural noise, or 'perceptual noise', increases with age (e.g. Gregory, 1959) since the number of functioning brain cells diminishes over the years: after the age of seventy, for example, around one per cent of cortical neurons are lost each year (Henderson *et al.*,

1980). The detection of external stimuli depends upon the signal-to-noise ratio. If neural noise does increase with age, then this ratio would be lowered, although older individuals might be able to compensate for this in various ways (see Welford, 1985). A lower signal-to-noise ratio would result in stimuli appearing 'weaker', and it would thus take longer for the stimuli to be detected and for a motor response to be elicited.

Any definitive explanation of age-related performance slowing will have to take into account both the effects of aging on neuro-biological mechanisms, and their psychological consequences. It appears more likely that age-related changes in central rather than peripheral mechanisms are responsible for behavioural slowing, but whether the principal results of such changes are to alter signal-to-noise ratios, to lower internal clock rates (and hence the operating speed of which the processing system as a whole is capable), to bring about a fundamental shift in strategies, or to weaken specific processing systems such as an error feedback system, remains unclear.

Cognitive performance

More research appears to have been conducted on the effects of age on cognitive functioning than on any other topic in geropsychology (Baltes, 1987). The discussion that follows is highly selective, and focuses on two main topics: intelligence, and learning and memory.

INTELLIGENCE

The relation between age and intellectual ability has usually been investigated by means of standard intelligence tests, many of which were originally developed for use with children and young adults. Early cross-sectional studies of age and intelligence indicated that there was a steady and seemingly irreversible decline in most, if not all, intellectual abilities from the late teens or early twenties onwards (see Jones, 1959). Later research, beginning in the 1950s, has considerably modified this picture although the nature and extent of any intellectual decline with age remain a matter for debate. Apparent declines in performance with age are partly artefactual, resulting from the use of cross-sectional designs in which age differences are confounded with cohort differences, especially educational level. Educational level is positively related to performance on standard tests of intelligence, and later cohorts are assumed to have spent more time in formal education than earlier ones. Indeed, the past fifty or so years have seen 'massive gains' in intelligence test scores in Western industrialized countries which render cross-sectional comparisons problematic (Flynn, 1984, 1987). However, since there is evidence that (presumably as a result of socio-historical changes) cohort differences are less substantial for later cohorts (see Schaie, 1990), it is likely that the use of cross-sectional designs will in future provide a less vitiated description of age differences in intelligence test scores.

In contrast to cross-sectional studies, longitudinal and cohort-sequential investigations of age and intelligence have usually reported that intelligence test scores either remain relatively stable or improve with increasing age, at least up to age sixty, although some individuals show no intellectual decline until their early eighties. Comparisons of cohort and age effects within cohort-sequential designs suggest that cohort differences are more important than age differences up to about age sixty, after which age differences tend to be more influential, although they are not always substantial. The attenuation or elimination of age-related declines in intellectual performance observed in longitudinal and cohort-sequential studies is obscured by the strong probability of selective attrition whereby it is predominantly the initially more able and motivated who tend to be available for retesting over the period under investigation (e.g. Siegler and Botwinick, 1979). Moreover, many longitudinal studies are not strictly comparable with cross-sectional studies with respect to the types of intellectual ability assessed or to the age ranges examined. In both cases longitudinal studies tend to be far more restricted (Salthouse, 1982, 1988). For example, for practical reasons, the age ranges investigated in longitudinal studies are typically less than half those investigated in cross-sectional studies. On the other hand, in both cross-sectional and longitudinal designs, comparisons among age groups may be affected by age differences in motivation, test anxiety, test fatigue, and other ability-extraneous factors (Furry and Baltes, 1973), by age-related differences in health status, which will tend to exacerbate any intellectual decline even if such differences are restricted to mild sensory deficits (Hertzog *et al.*, 1978; Granick *et al.*, 1976), and by a lack of 'age fairness' in test items (Schaie, 1988).

Where decline is reliably observed as a function of adult age, it is rarely global. Rather, it typically follows the 'classic aging pattern'. Scores on performance subtests, such as the digit symbol substitution test in the Wechsler adult intelligence scale (WAIS), show more marked declines, and from an earlier age, than do scores on verbal subtests, such as the WAIS information or vocabulary tests. Verbal scores either remain relatively unimpaired or show improvement until late adulthood or well into old age. A partial explanation of the discrepancy is in the particular susceptibility of performance subtests to behavioural slowing, since they are typically speeded while verbal subtests are not. Behavioural slowing cannot completely account for the classic aging pattern, however, since procedural modifications which remove time criteria from performance tests do not eliminate and may even enhance age differences (e.g. Storandt, 1976, 1977).

A further possible explanation of the classic aging pattern utilizes the distinction between fluid and crystallized intelligence (e.g. Horn and Donaldson, 1976), although according to Horn (1982) the correspondence between fluid and crystallized intelligence and performance and verbal abilities is far from exact. Fluid intelligence (G_f) is held to be unaffected by experience (being determined largely by hereditary factors), to depend upon the integrity and efficiency of physiological and neurological functioning, and therefore to be subject to decline from early adulthood onwards. Crystallized intelligence (G_c), in contrast, is a function of accumulated experience, knowledge and training, is largely independent of G_f after early or middle adulthood, and can be expected to increase through adulthood into old age. However, since the development of G_c depends upon the exercise of G_f, the rate of growth of G_c diminishes with age (see Figure 2.1). Generally speaking, the pattern of susceptibility, or resistance, of intelligence subtests to the effects of aging is in line with these hypotheses in that scores on subtests which appear primarily to be measuring G_c hold up better with age than do scores on subtests which appear primarily to be measuring G_f (e.g. Hayslip and Sterns, 1979). As an explanation of age effects, however, the G_f/G_c distinction presents some difficulties. Firstly, the independence of G_c from G_f is a matter of debate (see e.g. Kausler, 1982, pp. 584–7). Secondly, the distinction between fluid and crystallized intelligence established by factor-analytic techniques from the intercorrelational patterns of test batteries applied to young adults has not been equally apparent when older adults furnish the correlational data (Baltes *et al.*, 1980). This has led to the suggestion that

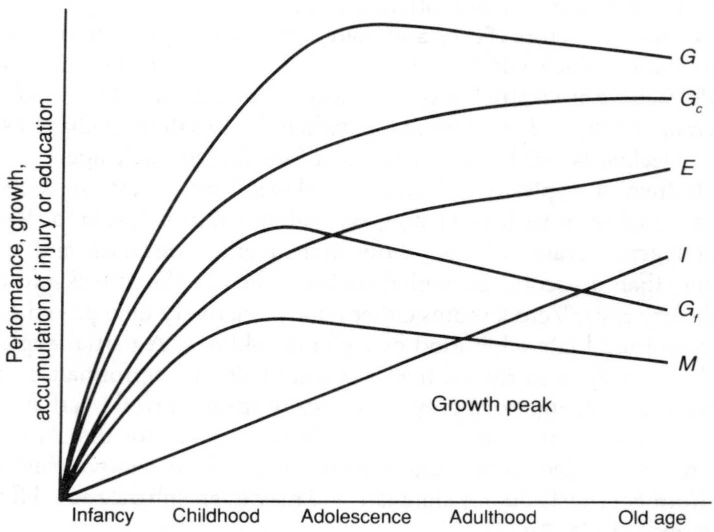

Figure 2.1 Development of fluid intelligence (G_f) and crystallized intelligence (G_c) in relation to maturational growth and decline of neural structures (M), accumulation of injury to neural structures (I), accumulation of educational exposures (E), and overall ability (G). (From Horn, 1970.)

while fluid and crystallized intelligence may become differentiated and functionally distinct in late childhood, they may converge and become re-integrated in late adulthood, and thus could not be used to explain the classic aging pattern. Further, there is evidence that the performance of older adults at certain age-sensitive and ostensibly 'fluid intelligence' tasks may be improved by 'cognitive' training, even after a decline in performance of some years' duration (e.g. Schaie and Willis, 1986). This casts doubt on the view that fluid intelligence is independent of experience and directly dependent upon levels of physiological and neurological functioning, as does the finding that the massive gains in intelligence test scores in Western countries over the past few decades are almost entirely due to improvements in performance on subtests measuring fluid rather than crystallized intelligence (Flynn, 1987).

As already indicated, the investigation of age-related changes in intellectual ability has been dominated by the use of standard intelligence tests, such as the WAIS and the primary mental abilities (PMA) test. While the tasks included in such test batteries may be defended as being representative of the 'everyday' adaptive tasks and exercises of young people in (or only recently out of) the formal education system, their validity as predictors of everyday adaptive capacity in older adults is much more questionable, and there is a strong presumption that formal and artificial measures are likely to under-estimate the abilities of older people in real-life settings. Nevertheless, age-related declines have also been observed in psychometric tests designed to assess competence in real-life situations, such as the Educational Testing Service basic skills test (see Salthouse, 1990). On the other hand, while studies of formal problem-solving tasks in the laboratory typically show poorer performance in older than in younger adults, the age difference is considerably less marked, and later in onset, when practical problems are employed (e.g. Denney and Palmer, 1981), or when skilled tasks, such as symbolic logic, chess or bridge, are carried out by experts (e.g. Charness, 1985). To the extent that some age-related decline is still observed in situations in which the effects of practice, motivation and perceived 'relevance' do not discriminate against older people, the decline appears to be principally attributable to response-slowing, to the inefficient use of strategies or to a reduction in the capacity of working memory. Evidence for response-slowing was described in the previous section, while strategy use and working memory are discussed below.

LEARNING AND MEMORY

Older adults often perform less well than younger ones with respect to both the acquisition and retrieval of information. As with intelligence, the comparative difficulties of older adults are selective rather than across-the-board and much research effort has been devoted to distinguishing among those tasks which are, and those which are not, sensitive to age differences.

Generally speaking, age-related deficits are more consistently found in learning than in memory tasks. Age differences have been reliably reported, for example, in conditioning, in maze learning, in paired-associate and in serial learning tasks. The clearest evidence for such deficits is in adults aged sixty and over, with much less clear evidence for earlier declines. The age difference does not appear to be attributable to cohort effects since it is observed in longitudinal studies as well as in cross-sectional ones in which older and younger groups are matched for educational level and for vocabulary scores (see e.g. Kausler, 1982). Studies of primary memory, by contrast, have typically reported no substantial age decrement, although there are some findings of extremely modest but consistent reductions in memory (digit or word) span (e.g. Hayslip and Kennelly, 1982), and in the extent of the recency effect in free recall. Both memory span and the recency effect are, of course, acknowledged to depend upon secondary, as well as primary memory. Decrements in immediate memory tasks become substantial only when some additional load is imposed in the form of divided attention or active manipulation of the material, in other words, when working memory is involved (see e.g. Craik, 1977).

Age differences in secondary memory are more varied. Decrements are frequently reported in longitudinal as well as cross-sectional studies, and while in some cases the decrement may be attributable to difficulties at acquisition, and hence to learning rather than memory in the strict sense, there is also abundant evidence for retrieval difficulties. Indeed, a number of studies have found that age differences in memory tasks are attenuated, or even abolished, when recognition is tested rather than recall, and also that older participants benefit more than younger ones from cueing and other contextual aids to retrieval (see e.g. Craik, 1977; Kausler, 1982). However, the occurrence and extent of age decrements depend not only upon the test procedures adopted but also upon the nature of the task. For example, it has often been claimed that while episodic memory tasks may reliably exhibit age decrements, semantic memory tasks do not. Certainly, semantic memory appears to be more resistant to age effects, and some studies have reported age increments rather than decrements in tasks such as vocabulary recall or memory for factual information (e.g. Mitchell, 1989). However, other evidence suggests that older participants may nevertheless experience difficulties in retrieving material from semantic memory in some circumstances, particularly when fluency or speed of response is demanded (e.g. Eysenck, 1975), or when word retrieval is required, for example in response to a dictionary definition (Bowles and Poon, 1985). The latter finding is in agreement with the common complaint of older people that they have difficulty in accessing desired words in speaking and writing (Burke and Light, 1981).

While age-related decrements are commonplace in explicit memory tasks they are less likely to be found when the memory component of the task is implicit, for example, when participants are asked to spell words which are in fact homophones, or to complete word fragments, having been primed in the direction of specific spellings or completions by a prior orientating task. There is some suggestion of poorer implicit memory in the case of older adults asked to complete word fragments (Chiarello and Hoyer, 1988), but the effect appears to be slight and perhaps unreliable since it has failed to attain significance in other studies (Light and Singh, 1987). Lastly, the evidence so far available indicates that age differences do not occur reliably in prospective memory, or memory for activities to be performed in the future, such as remembering to make a telephone call at a specified time, to pass on a message, or to take medication (e.g. Einstein and McDaniel, 1990), although an age decrement was found by Dobbs and Rule (1987) in one task when a lenient, but not when a strict, scoring criterion was used. The absence of an age difference for prospective memory is curious given that contexts and cues to retrieval are particularly helpful to older individuals, since prospective memory can be regarded as the most self-initiated task of all (Craik, 1986). It might be argued that prospective memory is preserved in elderly people by their use of external cues such as written reminders, but Einstein and McDaniel (1990) found that their age-equal finding was unaffected by the provision or prohibition of external aids.

To a degree, age-related decrements in learning and memory may be artefactually produced by ability-extraneous factors such as test anxiety, test fatigue and age-fairness, already referred to in the context of intelligence. Learning and memory tasks may also be susceptible to the effects of response slowing, and there is considerable evidence that performance, particularly of older participants, may be depressed by cautiousness or response reluctance. Older adults typically make more errors of omission rather than commission in learning tasks (e.g. Eisdorfer, 1968), and when responding is encouraged, notably by monetary incentives, errors of omission are largely replaced not by errors of commission but by correct responses (e.g. Leech and Witte, 1971); comparable findings have been observed with respect to intelligence test performance (Birkhill and Schaie, 1976). Apart from such essentially response-related factors, deficits in learning and memory can be ascribed in part to generalized response slowing, and more specifically to age differences in the use of strategies, and to age-related declines in working memory and other processing resources.

It is frequently reported that older adults are less likely than younger ones spontaneously to adopt effective strategies. For example, they are less likely to use mediators in paired-associate tasks, especially imaginal mediators which promote more effective learning, particularly in older adults (Canestrari, 1968). Similarly, in free recall tasks, older adults rehearse items less frequently than do younger adults, notably items early in the list to be recalled (Sanders *et al.*, 1980), and are less likely to categorize and cluster items in recall. All of these techniques are beneficial to performance. To some extent failure to use effective strategies reflects not lessened capacity but a production deficiency, since when they are instructed to use effective strategies, older adults appear able to adopt them, with a corresponding improvement in performance. Moreover, in many cognitive tasks, training and practice can induce changes in the strategies adopted by middle-aged or older adults, and thereby enhance their performance (see, for example, Hultsch and Dixon, 1990). On the other hand, age differences are rarely eliminated by such procedures, and there is evidence that older adults may have more difficulty in employing strategies once they have been adopted (e.g. Eysenck, 1974).

One possible reason for the failure to adopt effective strategies might be a failure of meta-memory, and specifically of memory monitoring. According to this view, older individuals may under-estimate the need for active learning or retrieval attempts in a particular task. While most studies of meta-memory in older and younger people have failed to find age differences, there are some findings indicating that older adults, by various criteria, tend to over-estimate their likely performance in laboratory memory tasks (e.g. Lovelace and Marsh, 1985). The direction of the inaccuracy is interesting, since complaints of failing memory are frequent among elderly people, and are often unrelated in degree to their own memory performance or to spouses' and others' ratings of their abilities. Memory complaints, however, seem to be very largely a function of depression (see Sunderland *et al.*, 1986).

It is also possible that older learners do not adopt active learning strategies because they require effort and hence impose greater demands upon attentional capacity. Schneider and Shiffrin (1977) distinguished between 'effortful' or 'controlled' processing, on the basis of their studies of the effects of extensive practice on the performance of consistently mapped (CM) and variably mapped (VM) memory search/visual search tasks (Shiffrin and Schneider, 1977). Effortful or controlled processing is characterized as 'slow, sequential, and attention demanding', while automatic processing is 'rapid, parallel, and makes few demands on attention' (Fisk and Scerbo, 1987, pp. 654–5). Since attentional capacity is thought to decline with age (Craik and Simon, 1980), it would be expected that age differences should be much smaller in automatic processing tasks, such as CM search tasks, than in processing tasks requiring effort, such as VM search tasks. This expectation has been confirmed in several studies (e.g. Madden and Nebes, 1980; Plude and Hoyer, 1986). The evidence most directly relevant to the hypothesis that attentional capacity declines with age comes from dual-task studies employing the secondary task method (see Ogden *et al.*, 1979). In a dual-task situation, performance on the secondary task can be regarded as reflecting the attentional capacity remaining after the capacity required for the primary task has been allocated. If older adults possess less attentional capacity than do younger adults, then their secondary task performance should show greater impairment relative to that of younger adults than when the same task is performed alone. This result has been obtained in several studies using relatively complex primary tasks (e.g. McDowd and Craik, 1988; Salthouse *et al.*, 1984), though when simple tasks have been employed the evidence is less conclusive (see McDowd and Birren,

1990). It thus appears, both from 'effortful'/automatic processing studies and from dual-task studies, that there is some decline in attentional capacity with age.

Attentional capacity is frequently regarded as a processing resource, as are processing speed and working memory (e.g. Salthouse, 1988), all of which are held to be essential for the efficient performance of a wide variety of tasks. Working memory refers to 'the temporary storage of information that is being processed in any of a range of cognitive tasks' (Baddeley, 1986, p. 34), and, like attentional capacity, is believed to be impaired by aging (Craik and Rabinowitz, 1984). Working memory is held to be a limited capacity system operating across a wide range of tasks, which may involve different processing codes and input modalities. It is thus a system in which information is actively manipulated rather than being passively stored, and is similar to the active short-term memory system hypothesized by Welford (1958) to be especially vulnerable to the effects of aging. An early example of the effects of age on active short-term memory is a study conducted by Kirchner (1958). In this study, older (64–78 years) and younger (18–25 years) individuals performed a task utilizing a row of twelve lights under each of which a response key was situated. When a light came on, it had to be put out by depressing the appropriate key. In this version of the task, the percentage of correct responses for younger individuals was 100 per cent, and for older individuals 99 per cent. The task was then made more difficult by the requirement to respond not to the light which had just come on, but to the previous one, which had already been extinguished. The percentage of correct responses hardly changed for younger individuals, falling to 99 per cent, but for older individuals it fell to 90 per cent. The task was then made even more difficult by the requirement to work 'two back' in the series. The percentage of correct responses fell to 93 per cent for younger individuals, but dropped dramatically to 33 per cent for older individuals. Kirchner's task necessitated the simultaneous storage of recently presented information and the processing of current information: a critical aspect of working memory (Baddeley, 1986), and one which clearly poses difficulties for older individuals. Dobbs and Rule (1989) compared the performance of individuals aged between thirty and ninety-nine years on three memory tasks: two of them 'passive' and the third a working memory task. The passive tasks were digit span (forwards and backwards), and the Peterson–Peterson (1959) short-term memory tasks, in which digit triplets have to be retained for varying short durations while a distractor task is performed. The working memory task was based on Kirchner's task, and required individuals to listen to a series of digits, presented in random order, and then to recall either the digit just heard (the zero lag condition), the digit prior to the one just heard (the 'one back' or lag one condition), or the digit two before the one just heard (the 'two back' or lag two condition). Dobbs and Rule's results for the two passive tasks are presented in Table 2.1, from which it can be seen that age differences in the

Table 2.1 Performance of different age groups on two 'passive' short-term memory tasks. (From Dobbs and Rule, 1989, p. 501.)

Measure	*Age range*				
	30–39	40–49	50–59	60–69	70+
Mean recall digit span					
Forwards	7.02	6.48	6.93	6.29	6.60
Backwards	5.57	5.30	5.67	5.28	5.02
Percentage correct Peterson–Peterson task					
Retention interval					
3s	87.8	84.2	85.2	85.8	80.5
6s	71.2	69.0	70.0	71.5	67.0
12s	63.3	64.3	66.0	65.2	56.8

performance of both tasks were slight; indeed, educational level, but not age, was found to be a significant predictor of performance in these tasks. Their results for the working memory task are shown in Figure 2.2, which indicates that performance markedly declined in the two oldest groups tested; in this task, age was a reliable predictor of performance.

Processing resources such as processing speed, attentional capacity and working memory all decline with age, and they all affect performance in a wide range of tasks. Resource explanations of age-related declines in cognitive performance have therefore become popular in recent years (see Salthouse, 1988), although resources are often vaguely defined and their mode of

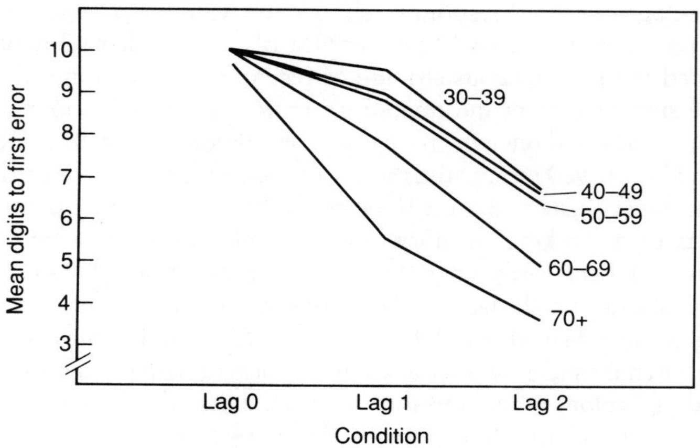

Figure 2.2 The performance of different age groups under different lag conditions in a working memory task. (From Dobbs and Rule, 1989, p. 501.)

operation is seldom specified in any detail. Resources have been conceptualized as one or more reservoirs of 'fuel' supporting information processing operations (e.g. Hirst and Kalmar, 1987), a view which emphasizes the energizing aspect of resources, although alternative conceptualizations emphasize spatial and temporal aspects (see Salthouse, 1988). Age-related resource deficits have been invoked to explain age decrements in cued recall (Rabinowitz *et al.*, 1982), and, as Salthouse (1988) observes, in discourse recall (Hartley, 1986), prose comprehension (Stine *et al.*, 1986), and even the absence of an age difference in memory for pictorial information (Park *et al.*, 1986).

Salthouse *et al.* (1989a) tested predictions derived from a resource interpretation of the effects of task complexity upon the magnitude of age differences in cognitive performance, mentioned earlier. Since processing resources are limited, and task performance depends upon a variety of processing operations each of which consumes resources, more complex cognitive tasks, presumably involving a greater number of processing operations, will consume more resources than will simple cognitive tasks. As older individuals are assumed to possess lower quantities of resources such as attentional capacity and working memory, increasing task complexity will impair their performance to a greater extent than it will impair the performance of younger individuals. If a particular processing resource, such as working memory, is involved in several different cognitive tasks, then the effects of increasing task complexity in those tasks should have similar effects on the underlying resource; that is, the effects of task complexity across different tasks should be positively and significantly correlated. Moreover, statistically controlling an index of the hypothesized underlying resource should eliminate, or at least attenuate, any age differences observed. Using an index of working memory, and varying task complexity in verbal and spatial tasks, Salthouse *et al.* (1989a) found that performance declined with age as task complexity increased, that the magnitude of the complexity-related performance declines in the verbal and spatial tasks were significantly positively correlated (+0.63), and that statistically controlling the working memory index attenuated, but did not eliminate, age differences in verbal and spatial performance. Salthouse *et al.* concluded that their results, and others reported by Salthouse (1988), while consistent with resource explanations of age differences in cognitive performance, nevertheless suggested that age-related resource reductions account for less than 50 per cent (and perhaps only around 15–20 per cent) of age-related performance decrements. They argued that, 'greater understanding is needed of the nature of working memory, and how it can best be measured' (p. 516), an argument which could be extended to other kinds of processing resource. The major difficulties with resource approaches to age differences in performance are in securing quantitative measures of resources which are independent of performance, and in demonstrating that there is a causal relationship between resource deficits and performance differences.

AGE DIFFERENCES IN EVERYDAY PERFORMANCE

In this section the effects of aging on task performance outside the laboratory are considered. The focus is on two main areas: the effects of age on driving—an 'everyday' activity for increasing numbers of older adults—and the effects of age on work performance.

Driving

Recent statistics indicate that in the United States and the United Kingdom around one in eight of all drivers is aged 65 and over, and the number is growing rapidly (*Lex Report on Motoring*, 1991). However, accident statistics show that in the United States, mileage-adjusted accident rates for the over-65 driver are higher than for all other age groups (National Research Council, 1988), although high levels of accident involvement are also found in young male drivers aged 25 and under. The same finding is apparent in the United Kingdom, with the exception of drivers under the age of 25. Compared with younger drivers, older drivers tend to be involved in different types of accident, and to be cited for different types of traffic violation. For example, older drivers are more frequently involved in accidents which are due to failures to heed signs, to give way or to negotiate junctions (Huston and Janke, 1986). Similarly, with respect to traffic violations, Brainin (1980) observed that older drivers were over-represented in citations related to unsafe left turns (right turns in the United Kingdom), inattention, and failure to yield right of way.

Although many road accidents have multiple causes, including mechanical failure, bad weather and so on, several investigators have concluded that 'driver error' is either a definite or probable cause in around ninety per cent of such accidents (see Shinar, 1978). Approaches to road accident causation have tended, therefore, to focus upon human factors, particularly perceptual–cognitive factors which may predict accident rates. Given that ninety per cent of the information processed during driving is visual (Hills, 1980), the visual system plays a crucial role in driving. But the visual system is particularly vulnerable to the effects of aging, and survey data indicate that, compared with young adults, older people are much more likely to report themselves as experiencing difficulties with visual functioning in everyday life (Kosnick *et al.*, 1990). These include the speed of processing of visually presented information, visual sensitivity under extreme levels of illumination, recognition of moving objects, visual acuity over short distances, peripheral vision, and locating target objects in an array. Most of these difficulties result from age-related changes in the structure of the eye, which produce, for example, a loss of accommodative power in the lens, especially at short viewing distances, a decline in the ability of the lens to transmit light, and a decrease in the size of the aperture of the pupil, so that less light reaches the retina (see Fozard, 1990; Kline and Scheiber, 1985).

Kosnick *et al.* (1990) observed that older drivers who had recently given up driving reported more visual problems than older drivers who continued to drive. In questioning drivers about visual problems experienced while driving, difficulties with speed judgements, with cars 'appearing' in the visual periphery, in reading road signs, in seeing the instrument panel, and in perceiving the position of other cars through windscreen glare, have been commonly reported by older drivers. Many older drivers attempt to counteract such difficulties by driving fewer miles (*Lex Report*, 1991), avoiding high-risk situations, such as rush-hour traffic (Yee, 1983), and reducing or eliminating night driving (Hakkinen, 1984). Nevertheless, while many older drivers may reduce their frequency of travel, they appear to be resistant to changing their preferred mode of transport, so that self-regulation may not be an effective means of reducing the older driver's exposure to road accident risk (Jetté and Branch, 1992).

Several investigators have attempted to relate measures of perceptual–cognitive functioning in the elderly to measures of driving performance, such as police accident and traffic violation statistics, self-reported accident rates, observational on-the-road tests, and, with some potential loss of fidelity, performance in driver simulators. (For a discussion of the relative merits of these different measures see Ball and Owsley (1991).) As an example of such an attempt, since the results of both cross-sectional (e.g. Weale, 1978) and longitudinal (e.g. Gittings and Fozard, 1986) studies indicate that visual acuity deteriorates with age, with the greatest loss taking place between the ages of sixty and ninety (e.g. Verriest, 1971), it might be expected that visual acuity would be related to driving performance. However, although significant correlations have been obtained between accident rates and both static and dynamic visual acuity in the elderly (e.g. Shinar, 1977), these correlations are relatively modest, and account for only small amounts of the total variance.

In-depth studies of accident causation have highlighted attentional and perceptual errors as important direct causes of road accidents (Shinar, 1978). In one of the most extensive studies of this kind, the Indiana University tri-level study (Treat *et al.*, 1977), which investigated over thirteen thousand accidents, the four main causes were, in order of importance:

1. Improper look-out.
2. Excessive speed.
3. Inattention.
4. Improper evasive action.

Each of these was a probable cause in over ten per cent of accidents, with improper look-out being a probable cause in over twenty per cent. Improper look-out was most frequently cited as the cause of accidents at intersections when drivers either failed to look before pulling out, or looked but failed to see an oncoming vehicle. Improper look-out has been considered to be principally a failure of selective attention (Shinar, 1978). In the Indiana study, inattention was most frequently cited as the cause of a road accident in 'rear-end' collisions, where, as a result of being preoccupied with 'task-irrelevant thoughts', the driver failed to notice that the preceding vehicle had either slowed or stopped. Inattention during driving has been linked to failures of sustained attention (Shinar, 1978).

Of the four causes of accidents suggested by Treat *et al.*, only excessive speed is unlikely to be a major contributor to accident rates in the elderly, who report themselves as driving more slowly (Case *et al.*, 1970; Rackoff, 1974), and who have been found to drive at low speeds, compared with young and middle-aged drivers, in a computer-based driving simulator (Dorn, 1991). Since, though, accident probability appears to be lowest for vehicles travelling at or around the mean, and increases as drivers move away from the mean (Brehmer, 1990), it is possible that the relatively slow speeds at which older drivers tend to travel may pose problems for other road users, and thereby contribute to accident causation. However, excessive speed is a major contributor to the accident involvement rates of young male drivers (aged 25 and under), who generally exhibit poorer risk perception than do older drivers and tend to be more confident about their driving skills, especially in relation to their peers (Dorn *et al.*, 1992).

Both auditory and visual measures of selective attention have been shown to correlate significantly with road accident involvement in male drivers (Avolio *et al.*, 1985; Kahneman *et al.*, 1973), although such correlations are relatively modest (around 0.30) and non-significant correlations have also been reported. Measures of selective attention have usually been derived from laboratory tasks such as dichotic listening, and subsequently related to accident involvement rates. Virtually no study has investigated selective attention in the driving task itself, although Ponds *et al.* (1988) reported divided attention deficits in a group of older drivers during the performance of a simulated driving task. The ability to switch attention is also an important aspect of driving and correlations between measures of attention-switching and accident rates are somewhat higher than for measures of selective attention (Kahneman *et al.*, 1973). Moreover, older drivers report finding this aspect of driving increasingly difficult compared with other age groups (Parasuraman, 1989; Ranney and Pulling, 1989).

One of the principal ways of measuring visual selective attention is to use a visual search paradigm, and visual search performance is known to decline with age (see Ball *et al.*, 1990). In order to examine the role of visual attention in driving, Ball, Owsley and their colleagues (Ball and Owsley, 1991; Owsley *et al.*, 1991) have employed the useful field of view (UFOV) task, which assesses the extent of the visual field required for the performance of a particular task (see Sanders, 1970). The UFOV is measured binocularly, and involves the detection, localization and/or identification of supra-threshold targets in complex displays. Several studies have reported that the UFOV is reduced with age for detection, localization and identification (Ball *et al.*, 1988, 1990; Scialfa *et al.*, 1987; Sekuler and Ball, 1986). Using several measures of sensory, perceptual and cognitive functioning, Owsley *et al.* (1991) found that the best predictor of accident frequency in a group of fifty-three older drivers aged 57–83 years was the size of the UFOV, coupled with a measure of mental status and cognitive functioning, the Mattis organic mental status syndrome examination (Mattis, 1976). Together these measures accounted for twenty per cent of the overall accident frequency among the older drivers examined, and for twenty-nine per cent of the variance for intersection accidents. Low scorers on the UFOV task had three to four times as many accidents overall as high scorers, and fifteen times as many intersection accidents. As noted earlier, age differences in attentional performance become much more substantial when processing places greater demands on attentional capacity, as in heavy traffic, or when difficult roundabouts or intersections have to be negotiated. Such conditions may over-reach the capacity of the older driver (Hancock *et al.*, 1989) and increase the risk of accidents.

A further aspect of inattention in driving situations is a failure of sustained attention. While in laboratory studies of vigilance and sustained attention older individuals show generally minimal declines, and in some studies no decline at all, relative to younger individuals (Davies and Griew, 1965; Davies and Parasuraman, 1982; Giambra and Quilter, 1988), several studies of male drivers have reported finding significant decrements in sustained attention during prolonged driving (see Davies and Parasuraman, 1982). However, most of the reported decrements have been for measures such as lane drift frequency, which could be influenced by fatigue effects on perceptual–motor performance, rather than representing a genuine impairment of sustained attention. But in a study of age and driving, Korteling (1990) observed significant age differences in a vehicle-following task, with older drivers (61–73 years) being less accurate than younger drivers (21–43 years) at reproducing the speed of the car in front, which may reflect an age-related decline in sustained attention. Lastly, there are virtually no direct studies of age differences in evasive action while driving, but indirect evidence on brake RTs suggests that there are no differences between older and younger drivers (Olsen and Sivak, 1986). Moreover, Korteling (1990) also observed no age differences in brake RTs in a simulated driving task, even when task load was increased. At present, then, although individual differences among older drivers are considerable (Ball and Owsley, 1991), the principal direct causes of accident rates in older drivers would appear to be improper look-out and inattention, and these appear to be attributable in turn to perceptual and cognitive deficits.

Work performance

Research on aging and work involves both practical and methodological problems, which may explain why studies of age and work performance are relatively rare compared, for instance, with studies of age and cognitive performance. One reason for conducting research on age and work performance is to investigate ways of counteracting any age-related declines in performance through training, job redesign and environmental modification; another reason is to assess prevailing stereotypes of older workers, which tend to be predominantly negative (Davies *et al.*, 1991; Stagner, 1985). There is ample evidence that older workers (defined here, following the US Age Discrimination in Employment Act 1967, as workers aged 40 and over) are widely believed by both employers and younger employees to be less productive, more resistant to change, and less well suited to particular kinds of job such as those involving rapid decision-making or the use of complex skills, especially information technology skills. Since it is also widely believed that older workers are poorer learners, older workers are less likely to gain access to training schemes. Other consequences of the prevailing stereotype of older workers include a greater risk of long-term unemployment, due in part to age-related hiring limits, poorer promotion prospects and lower earnings. Following the upsurge of private and public early retirement programmes introduced in several industrialized countries during the 1970s and 1980s (see Mirkin, 1987), fewer older workers, especially men, remain in the labour force, though this is an acceleration of a long-term trend which goes back to the end of the last century (Easterlin *et al.*, 1984).

Studies of age and work performance indicate that age-related performance differences occur less frequently than might be expected from laboratory studies, and when they do occur, such differences are often relatively slight (Davies *et al.*, 1991; Davies and Sparrow, 1985). Table 2.2 provides the results for productivity measures (output or production records) from two meta-analyses of the relation between age and work performance (McEvoy and Cascio, 1989; Waldman and Avolio, 1986). As can be seen from the table, Waldman and Avolio obtained a modest, positive correlation (+0.27) between age and productivity, indicating that productivity improved slightly

Table 2.2 Mean correlations (r) between age and productivity reported in two meta-analyses

Study	*Productivity measures*	
	N	r
Waldman and Avolio, 1986	2745	0.27
McEvoy and Cascio, 1989	13184	0.07

Adapted from Davies *et al.*, 1991, p. 168.

with age. The positive correlation was of similar magnitude for both professional ($r = +0.27$, $N = 1764$) and non-professional ($r = +0.26$, $N = 981$) workers. McEvoy and Cascio obtained an even more modest, positive correlation ($+0.07$), suggesting that age and work performance are essentially unrelated.

OUTPUT AND PRODUCTION RECORD DATA

The use of data derived from output or production records is almost certainly the most satisfactory way of assessing the relationship between age and work performance, provided that certain practical and methodological difficulties can be minimized. For example, one practical difficulty is that of obtaining production record data over a sufficient period of time to be certain of their reliability, because companies may keep the data only for short periods. A second difficulty is that of obtaining sufficient numbers of workers in the older age groups, particularly in the 60+ group. A further problem is, that even within the same job, older and younger workers may be differentially allocated to tasks which are more or less complex, strenuous or demanding. Moreover, when assessing age differences in the performance of a particular job, a number of selection factors may be operating which either inflate or reduce the apparent efficiency of older workers. On the one hand, less productive workers are likely to be transferred to other work, sacked or persuaded to take early retirement (Welford, 1958). The more productive older workers remaining in the job will be unrepresentative of their age cohort, and any comparison of the productivity of different age groups will tend to favour older workers. Conversely, older workers with relatively good production records may be promoted to supervisory positions, leaving less productive older workers behind, so that any age group comparison will tend to favour younger workers. Furthermore, the most efficient younger workers may leave for jobs elsewhere, especially in industries where there is a high demand for labour. In general, therefore, age comparisons of work performance are most likely to be useful when turnover and internal transfer rates are low, and when checks are made on task allocation within particular jobs (Davies and Sparrow, 1985).

The relationship between age and work performance in studies using output or production records is somewhat variable. Some studies have reported that productivity improves with age, others have found declines in output, while yet others have obtained no relation between age and work performance (Davies *et al.*, 1991; Davies and Sparrow, 1985). For skilled and semi-skilled manual and technical jobs, an inverted U relationship between age and work performance is relatively common, with performance peaking in the late thirties or early forties. Usually, the performance decline in older workers is fairly gradual, so that the productivity of workers in their fifties exceeds that of workers in their teens or twenties (Davies and Sparrow, 1985). An example of such a relationship, from a study by Sparrow and Davies (1988) of the performance of skilled, technical workers is shown in Figure 2.3. In this study, the performance of 1308 service engineers employed by a multinational office equipment company was investigated. Turnover and internal transfer rates were low, and educational levels were similar across age cohorts. In addition to age, Sparrow and Davies also examined the effects of tenure, recency of training, and job complexity, indexed by the size of the machine to be serviced, and the range of functions of which it was capable. Checks were made to ensure that older and younger engineers were not differentially allocated to machines of different complexity. Two output measures were collected: (1) quality of performance, assessed as the rate of machine performance between services compared with the national average for machines of its type, and (2) speed of performance, assessed by the time taken to service a machine. Surprisingly, although job complexity significantly affected both performance measures, in neither case did it interact significantly with age. As can be seen from Figure 2.3, age and the quality of performance were curvilinearly related, with performance peaking in the mid-thirties and early forties. Speed of performance was affected more strongly by training and tenure than by age, although the youngest group was significantly faster than the other age groups. But for both performance measures, each main effect or interaction involving age accounted for less than one per cent of the variance.

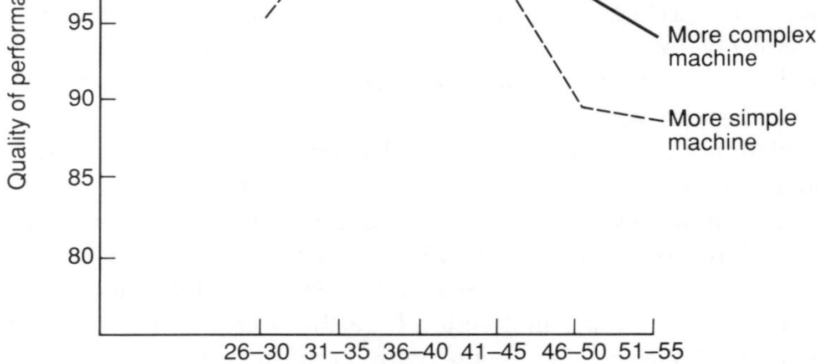

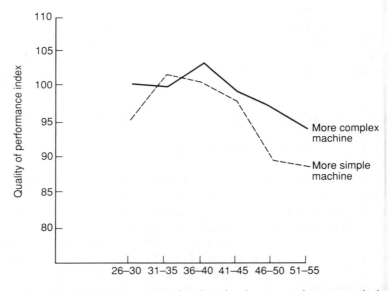

Figure 2.3 The relation between age and quality of performance at the most simple (level 1) and most complex (level 4) complexity levels. (From Sparrow and Davies, 1988, p. 311.)

The curvilinear relationship between age and work performance is not confined to skilled and semi-skilled manual and technical jobs. For example, a study of salespeople working in two large department stores showed that performance tended to improve with both age and experience, peaking in the early fifties (Kelleher and Quirk, 1973). Studies of publication output in research scientists have also consistently obtained a curvilinear relationship between age and productivity, although the age at which performance peaks varies with the research domain (Simonton, 1988). In contrast, a number of other studies have failed to find such a relationship. For instance, Salvendy (1972) obtained no effects of age on performance for workers in manufacturing jobs. Similarly, Gordon and Fitzgibbon (1982) observed no relationship between either age or seniority and performance in a sample of sewing machine operators, following a change of job in a garment manufacturing plant. Eisenberg (1980), however, found a negative relationship between age and the piece-rate earnings of sewing machine operators. He attributed this finding to the speeded nature of the work. In the same manufacturing plant, age was positively related to productivity for examiners and material handlers, whose jobs were more dependent on skill.

PERFORMANCE RATINGS

An alternative method of assessing work performance is by means of performance ratings, usually made by supervisors or managers. Ratings are less satisfactory than objective measures of work performance, since there tends to be unreliability across raters and over time, and ratings can be susceptible to bias on the part of the rater (Cattell and Kline, 1977). Table 2.3 shows the results for supervisor's ratings from the meta-analyses conducted by McEvoy and Cascio (1989) and Waldman and Avolio (1986), referred to earlier. As can be seen from Table 2.3, McEvoy and Cascio obtained a similar result for supervisory ratings to that obtained for productivity measures, a correlation approaching zero between age and performance. But Waldman and Avolio obtained a modest negative correlation (−0.14), indicating that performance ratings fell slightly with age, the opposite result to that obtained for productivity measures. Peer rating data, also shown for Waldman and Avolio's study in Table 2.3, are difficult to compare across the two meta-analyses because McEvoy and Cascio included only three studies involving peer ratings and so were unable to analyse these studies as a separate category. Despite the possibility of rater bias, however, several studies have obtained no significant differences in the job performance ratings given to older and younger clerical and industrial workers (e.g. Arvey and Muscio, 1973). Age differences in job performance ratings are more likely to be reported in studies of technical and managerial jobs. Dalton and Thompson (1971) and Price *et al.* (1975), for example, obtained managerial ratings of the work performance of a large sample of engineers employed by six large

Table 2.3 Mean correlations (r) between age and rating measures of performance reported in two meta-analyses

Study	*Rating measures*					
	Supervisor		*Peer*		*Non-supervisor*[a]	
	N	*r*	*N*	*r*	*N*	*r*
Waldman and Avolio, 1986	3660	−0.14	3622	0.10	—	—
McEvoy and Cascio, 1989	18781	0.03	—	—	3227	−0.09

[a] Ratings by peers, subordinates, self and outsiders. Adapted from Davies *et al.*, 1991, p. 168.

technological companies. Rated performance rose with age initially, peaked in the mid-thirties, and declined thereafter, reaching a level of 75 per cent of peak performance in the 55–65 age group. Price *et al.* emphasized the high degree of overlap between performance levels in different age groups. Ratings appeared to be biased by the difficulty of the job being performed and by the differential assignment of younger engineers to more difficult jobs. Age tended to become a progressively stronger predictor of performance over the period of the study (1960–1968). Dalton and Thompson (1971) attributed this effect to an acceleration during the 1960s of the obsolescence of technological expertise.

EFFECTS OF EXPERIENCE

It is widely believed that experience with a task or set of tasks in some way protects performance from the effects of aging. It migh therefore be expected that experience, usually measured by tenure, or length of service, which tends to be highly positively correlated with age, would counteract the effects of age on work performance. Some studies of industrial and clerical jobs have shown that when length of service is controlled for, age effects on performance disappear; conversely when age is controlled for, the effects of experience remain (e.g. Giniger *et al.*, 1983). Experience can, therefore, be a stronger predictor of job performance than is age. Studies of drill-press operators (Murrell *et al.*, 1962), and of simultaneous language translators (Murrell and Humphries, 1978), have reported no performance differences between old and young experienced workers, while finding that inexperienced older adults performed at lower levels than did inexperienced younger adults.

Not all studies find that experience reduces the effects of age on performance. For example, Salthouse *et al.* (1989b) measured spatial visualization abilities in a group of practising architects, much of whose work consisted of the production of two-dimensional drawings of three-dimensional objects, thereby exercising fairly continuously their visuo-spatial abilities. Salthouse *et al.* compared the performance of architects with that of unselected adults whose relevant experience was much lower; they obtained significant age-related declines in spatial visualization in both groups (if anything, the decline was greater for architects than for non-architects).

As Salthouse (1990) points out, the role of experience may also be remedial, that is, added experience may reverse age-related ability declines. Practice and training might therefore reduce or eliminate age differences. As noted earlier, the effects of practice on laboratory tasks benefit old and young alike but do not seem to benefit older individuals to a greater extent than younger ones. Additionally, age differences apparent before practice sessions begin are still present when they are completed, even when practice is fairly extensive. The effects of practice on job performance may be rather different, however; for example, in a study of skilled typists, Salthouse (1984) noted that the inter-key RTs of older, experienced typists were virtually identical to those of young typists, whereas they were 80–150 ms slower in laboratory choice PT tasks. Salthouse also observed that in seventeen minutes of typing at sixty words per minute, an experienced typist would produce as many key-presses as in 5000 choice RT trials in the laboratory. Further, Sparrow and Davies (1988) did not find any interaction between age and job complexity with respect to work performance, although such an interaction almost invariably appears in studies of laboratory task performance. Although a great deal is known about the training procedures most appropriate for, and most acceptable to, older workers (e.g. Belbin, 1965), the effects of training on age differences in job performance have seldom been examined, although in the study by Sparrow and Davies (1988) there was some indication that training, especially if it was recent, did reverse age-related declines.

The role of experience may also be important for the manner in which component processes contribute to the performance of skilled tasks. Various studies of skilled performance, reviewed by Salthouse (1989), suggest that while there may be age-related declines in component processes, there may be no such decline in the overall level of skilled performance. The role of component processes in a molar skill may thus change with age and experience. Several mechanisms were proposed by Salthouse to explain how effective skilled performance may be maintained, while component processes deteriorate. These include compensation, whereby declines in some component processes are offset by improvements in others; accommodation, whereby individuals adapt to their perceived age-related deficiencies, and employ different strategies in order to prevent these deficiencies being put at risk; and compilation, whereby once the molar skill has been acquired, or compiled, it becomes relatively independent of its component processes.

Lastly, if the performance of a particular job exacerbates perceived age-related deficiencies, then the job may simply be avoided, or eliminated, and, where possible, a worker may assign himself or herself to a different job entirely. In a series of studies of the age structure of jobs, conducted during the 1950s, it was shown that older workers tended to be found less frequently in jobs making heavy demands on abilities known to decline with age than would be expected on the basis of population or company employment statistics, and that older workers tended to move to jobs in which these demands were minimized (e.g. Belbin, 1953; Murrell and Griew, 1958). Moreover, Griew (1959) demonstrated that older workers working in 'young' jobs experienced higher accident rates than would be expected. Later research on the age structures of occupations, using United Kingdom census data (Smith, 1975), has strongly suggested that the age structures of occupations reflect the degree of difficulty that job demands make on particular age groups. The sensory, perceptual and cognitive demands of some jobs can pose problems for older workers, though these may be to some extent alleviated through job redesign (e.g. Griew, 1964). Nevertheless, for at least some older workers who continue to perform such jobs, age differences in job performance are likely to be found. One of the advantages conferred by experience, which may in part explain the greater job satisfaction of older workers (see Davies *et al.*, 1991; Davies and Sparrow, 1985), may be the greater opportunity to match jobs and their component tasks to the individual's perceived abilities.

REFERENCES

Arvey, R.D. and Muscio, S.J. (1973) Test discrimination, job performance, and age. *Industrial Gerontology* **16**: 22–9.

Avolio, B.J., Kroeck, K.G. and Panek, P.E. (1985) Individual differences in information processing ability as a predictor of motor vehicle accidents. *Human Factors* **27**: 577–87.

Baddeley A.D. (1986) *Working Memory*. Oxford: Clarendon Press.

Ball, K. and Owsley, C. (1991) Identifying correlates of accident involvement for the older driver. *Human Factors* **33**: 583–5.

Ball, K., Beard, B., Roenker, D.L., Miller, R. and Griggs, D. (1988) Age and visual search: expanding the useful field of view. *Journal of the Optical Society of America* **5**: 2110–19.

Ball, K., Roenker, D.L. and Bruni, J.R. (1990) Developmental changes in attention and visual search throughout adulthood. In *The Development of Attention: Research and Theory*, edited by J.T. Enns. Amsterdam: Elsevier.

Baltes, P.B. (1968) Cross-sectional and longitudinal sequences in the study of age and generation effects. *Human Development* **11**: 145–71.

Baltes, P.B. (1987) Theoretical propositions of life-span developmental psychology: on the dynamics between growth and decline. *Developmental Psychology* **23**: 611–26.

Baltes, P.B., Cornelius, S.W., Spiro, A. Nesselroade, J.R. and Willis, S.L. (1980) Integration vs. differentiation of fluid/crystallized intelligence in old age. *Developmental Psychology* **16**: 625–35.

Belbin, R.M. (1953) Difficulties of older people in industry. *Occupational Psychology* **27**: 177–90.

Belbin, R.M. (1965) *Training Methods for Older Workers*. Paris: OECD.

Bellis, C.J. (1933) Reaction time and chronological age. *Proceedings of the Society for Experimental Biology and Medicine* **30**: 801–3.

Birkhill, W.R. and Schaie, K.W. (1976) The effect of differential reinforcement of cautiousness in intellectual performance among the elderly. *Journal of Gerontology* **30**: 578–83.

Birren, J.E. (1974) Translations in gerontology–from lab to life: psychophysiology and the speed of response. *American Psychologist* **29**: 808–15.

Birren, J.E. and Botwinick, J. (1955) Age differences in finger, jaw, and foot reaction time to auditory stimuli. *Journal of Gerontology* **10**: 429–32.

Birren, J.E., Riegel, K.F. and Morrison, D.F. (1962) Age differences in response speed as a function of controlled variations of stimulus conditions: evidence of a general speed factor. *Gerontologia* **6**: 1–18.

Bleecker, M.L., Bolla-Wilson, K., Agnew, J. and Meyers, D.A. (1987) Simple visual reaction time: sex and age differences. *Developmental Neuropsychology* **3**: 93–99.

Bowles, N.L. and Poon, L.W. (1985) Aging and retrieval of words in semantic memory. *Journal of Gerontology* **40**: 71–7.

Brainin, P.A. (1980) *Safety and Mobility Issues in Licensing and Education of Older Drivers*. Final Report DOT HS-805 492 NHTSA. US Department of Transportation, Washington DC.

Brehmer, B. (1990) Variable errors set a limit to adaptation. *Ergonomics* **33**: (10/11), 1231–9.

Burke, D.M. and Light, L.L. (1981) Memory and aging: the role of retrieval processes. *Psychological Bulletin* **90**: 513–46.

Canestrari, R.E. (1968) Age changes in acquisition. In *Human Aging and Behavior: Recent Advances in Research and Theory*, edited by G.A. Talland. New York and London: Academic Press.

Case, H.W., Hulbert, S. and Beers, J. (1970) *Driving Ability as Affected by Age*. Final Report No. 70-18. University of California at Los Angeles, Institute of Transportation and Traffic Engineering.

Cattell, R.B. and Kline, P. (1977) *The Scientific Analysis of Personality and Motivation*. New York and London: Academic Press.

Cerella, J., Poon, L.W. and Williams, D.M. (1980) Age and the complexity hypothesis. In *Aging in the 1980s: Psychological Issues*, edited by L.W. Poon and K.W. Schaie. Washington, DC: American Psychological Association.

Cerella, J., Poon, L.W. and Fozard, J.L. (1981) Mental rotation and age reconsidered. *Journal of Gerontology* **36**: 604–24.

Charness, N. (1985) Aging and problem-solving performance. In *Aging and Human Performance*, edited by N. Charness. Chichester: Wiley.

Chiarello, C. and Hoyer, W.J. (1988) Adult age differences in implicit and explicit memory: time course and encoding effects. *Psychology and Aging* **3**: 358–66.

Craik, F.I.M. (1977) Age differences in human memory. In *Handbook of the Psychology of Aging*, edited by J.E. Birren and K.W. Schaie. New York: Van Nostrand Reinhold.

Craik, F.I.M. (1986) A functional account of age differences in memory. In *Human Memory and Cognitive Capabilities: Mechanisms and Performances*, edited by F. Klix and H. Hagendorf. Amsterdam: Elsevier.

Craik, F.I.M. and Rabinowitz, J.C. (1984) Age differences in the acquisition and use of verbal information: a tutorial review. In *Attention and Performance*, Vol. X, edited by H. Buoma and D.G. Bouwhuis. Hillsdale, NJ: Erlbaum.

Craik, F.I.M. and Simon, E. (1980) Age differences in memory: the roles of attention and depth of processing. In *New Directions in Memory and Aging*, edited by L.W. Poon, J.L. Fozard, L.S. Cermak, D. Arenberg and L.W. Thompson. Hillsdale, NJ: Erlbaum.

Dalton, G.W. and Thompson, P.H. (1971) Accelerating obsolescence of older engineers. *Harvard Business Review* **49**: 57–68.

Davies, D.R. (1968) Age differences in paced inspection tasks. In *Human Aging and Behavior: Recent Advances in Research and Theory*, edited by G.A. Talland. New York and London: Academic Press.

Davies, D.R. and Griew, S. (1965) Age and vigilance. In *Behavior, Aging, and the Nervous System*, edited by A.T. Welford and J.E. Birren. Springfield, Ill.: Charles C. Thomas.

Davies, D.R. and Parasuraman, R. (1982) *The Psychology of Vigilance*. New York and London: Academic Press.

Davies, D.R. and Sparrow, P.R. (1985) Age and work behaviour. In *Aging and Human Performance*, edited by N. Charness. Chichester: Wiley.

Davies, D.R., Matthews, G. and Wong, C.S.K. (1991) Ageing and work. In *International Review of Industrial and Organizational Psychology 1991*, Vol. 6, edited by C.L. Cooper and I.T. Robinson. Chichester: Wiley.

Denney, N.W. and Palmer, A.M. (1981) Adult age differences in traditional and practical problem-solving measures. *Journal of Geronotology* **36**: 323–8.

Dirken, J.M. and Wartna, G.F. (1972) Ageing and mental functions. In *Functional Age of Industrial Workers*, edited by J.M. Dirken. Groningen: Wolters-Noordhof.

Dobbs, A.R. and Rule, B.G. (1987) Prospective memory and self-reports of memory abilities in older adults. *Canadian Journal of Psychology* **41**: 209–2.

Dobbs, A.R. and Rule, B.G. (1989) Adult age differences in working memory. *Psychology and Aging* **4**: 500–3.

Dorn, L. (1991) Unpublished data.

Dorn, L., Davies, D.R., Matthews, G., Glendon, A.I. and Taylor, R.G. (1992) Risk perception and driving competence as a function of age and sex. Submitted for publication.

Duncan-Johnson, C.D. (1981) P300 latency: a new metric of information processing. *Psychophysiology* **18**: 207–15.

Easterlin, R.A., Crimmins, E.M. and Ohanian, L. (1984) Changes in labor force participation of persons 55 and over since World War II: their nature and causes. In *Aging and Technological Advances*, edited by P.K. Robinson, J. Livingston and J.E. Birren. New York: Plenum Press.

Einstein, G.O. and McDaniel, M.A. (1990) Normal aging and prospective memory. *Journal of Experimental Psychology (Learning, Memory, and Cognition)* **16**: 717–26.

Eisdorfer, C. (1968) Arousal and performance: experiments in verbal learning and a tentative theory. In *Human Aging and Behavior: Recent Advances in Research and Theory*, edited by G.A. Talland. New York and London: Academic Press.

Eisenberg, J. (1980) Relationship between age and effects upon work. Doctoral dissertation, City University of New York.

Eysenck, M.W. (1974) Age differences in incidental learning. *Developmental Psychology* **10**: 936–41.

Eysenck, M.W. (1975) Retrieval from semantic memory as a function of age. *Journal of Gerontology* **30**: 174–80.

Fisk, A.D. and Scerbo, M.W. (1987) Automatic and control processing approach to interpreting vigilance performance: a review and reevaluation. *Human Factors* **29**: 653–60.

Flynn, J.R. (1984) The mean IQ of Americans: massive gains 1932 to 1978. *Psychological Bulletin* **95**: 29–51.

Flynn, J.R. (1987) Massive IQ gains in 14 nations: what IQ tests really measure. *Psychological Bulletin* **101**: 171–91.

Fozard, J.L. (1990) Vision and hearing in aging. In *Handbook of the Psychology of Aging*, 3rd edn, edited by J.E. Birren and K.W. Schaie. New York and London: Academic Press.

Furry, C.A. and Baltes, P.B. (1973). The effect of age differences in ability-extraneous performance variables on the assessment of intelligence in children, adults, and the elderly. *Journal of Gerontology* **28**: 73–80.

Giambra, L.M. and Quilter, R.E. (1988) Sustained attention in adulthood: a unique, large-sample, longitudinal and multicohort analysis using the Mackworth Clock-test. *Psychology and Aging* **3**: 75–83.

Giniger, B., Dispenzieri, A. and Eisenberg, J. (1983) Age, experience and performance on speed and skill jobs in an applied setting. *Journal of Applied Psychology* **68**: 469–75.

Gittings, N.S. and Fozard, J.L. (1986) Age related changes in visual acuity. *Experimental Gerontology* **21**: 423–33.

Gordon, M.E. and Fitzgibbon, W.J. (1982) Empirical test of the validity of seniority as a factor in staffing decisions. *Journal of Applied Psychology* **67**: 811–9.

Granick, S., Klehan, M.H. and Weiss, A.D. (1976) Relationships between hearing loss and cognition in normally hearing aged persons. *Journal of Gerontology* **31**: 434–40.

Green, R.F. (1969) Age-intelligence relationship between ages sixteen and sixty-four: a rising trend. *Developmental Psychology* **1**: 618–27.

Gregory, R.L. (1959) Increase in 'neurological noise' as a factor in ageing. *Proceedings of the 4th Congress of the International Association of Gerontology, Vol. 1, Merano.*

Griew, S. (1959) A study of accidents in relation to occupation and age. *Ergonomics* **2**: 17–23.

Griew, S. (1964) *Job Re-design for Older Workers.* Paris: OECD.

Hakkinen, L. (1984) Vision in the elderly and its use in the social environment. *Scandinavian Journal of Social Medicine* **35**: 5–60.

Hancock, P.A., Wulf, G., Thom, D.R. and Fassnacht, P. (1989) Contrasting driver behavior during turns and straight driving. *Proceedings of the 33rd Annual Meeting of the Human Factors Society.* Santa Monica, Ca.: Human Factors Society, pp. 918–22.

Hartley, J.T. (1986) Reader and text variables as determinants of discourse memory in adulthood. *Psychology and Aging* **1**: 150–8.

Hayslip, B. and Kennelly, K. (1982) Short-term memory and crystallized–fluid intelligence in adulthood. *Research on Aging* **4**: 314–32.

Hayslip, B. and Sterns, H.L. (1979) Age differences in relationships between crystallized and fluid intelligence and problem solving. *Journal of Gerontology* **34**: 404–14.

Henderson, G., Tomlinson, B.E. and Gibson, P.H. (1980) Cell counts in human cerebral cortex in normal adults throughout life using an image analyzing computer. *Journal of the Neurological Sciences* **46**: 113–36.

Hertzog, C., Schaie, K.W. and Gribbin, N. (1978) Cardiovascular disease and changes in intellectual function from middle to old age. *Journal of Gerontology* **33**: 872–83.

Hicks, L.H. and Birren, J.E. (1970) Aging, brain damage, and psychomotor slowing. *Psychological Bulletin* **74**: 377–96.

Hills, B.L. (1980) Vision, visibility, and perception in driving. *Perception* **9**: 183–216.

Hirst, W. and Kalmar, D. (1987) Characterizing attentional resources. *Journal of Experimental Psychology (General)* **116**: 68–81.

Horn, J. (1970) Organization of data on life-span development of human abilities. In *Life-span Developmental Psychology: Research and Theory,* edited by L. Goulet and P.B. Baltes. New York and London: Academic Press, p. 465.

Horn, J.L. (1982) The aging of human abilities. In *Handbook of Developmental Psychology,* edited by B. Wolman. Englewood Cliffs, NJ: Prentice Hall, Inc.

Horn, J.L. and Donaldson, G. (1976) On the myth of intellectual decline in adulthood. *American Psychologist* **31**: 701–19.

Hultsch, D.F. and Dixon, R.A. (1990) Learning and memory in aging. In *Handbook of the Psychology of Aging,* 3rd edn, edited by J.E. Birren and K.W.Schaie. New York and London: Academic Press.

Huston, R. and Janke, M. (1986) *Senior Driver Facts.* Technical Report CAL-DNMV-RSS-86-82, Department of Motor Vehicles, Sacramento, Ca.

Jetté, A.M. and Branch, L.G. (1992) A ten-year follow-up of driving patterns among the community-dwelling elderly. *Human Factors* **34**: 147–53.

Jones, H.E. (1959) Intelligence and problem solving. In *Handbook of Aging and the Individual,* edited by J.E. Birren. University of Chicago Press.

Kahneman, D., Ben-Ishai, R. and Lotan, M. (1973) Relation of a test of attention to road accidents. *Journal of Applied Psychology* **58**: 113–5.

Kausler, D.H. (1982) *Experimental Psychology and Human Aging.* New York: Wiley.

Kelleher, C.H. and Quirk, D.A. (1973) Age, functional capacity and work: an annotated bibliography. *Industrial Gerontology* **19**: 80–98.

Kirchner, W.K. (1958) Age differences in short-term retention of rapidly changing information. *Journal of Experimental Psychology* **55**: 352–8.

Kline, D.W. and Scheiber, F. (1985) Vision and aging. In *Handbook of the Psychology of Aging,* edited by J.E. Birren and K.W. Schaie. New York: Van Nostrand Reinhold.

Koga, Y. and Morant, G.M. (1923) On the degree of association between reaction times in the case of different senses. *Biometrika* **15**: 346–72.

Korteling, J.E. (1990) Perception–response speed and driving capabilities of brain-damaged and older drivers. *Human Factors* **32**: 95–108.

Kosnick, W.D., Sekuler, P. and Kline, D.W. (1990) Self-reported visual problems of older drivers. *Human Factors* **32**: 95–108.

Krauss, I.K. (1980) Between- and within-group comparisons in aging resarch. In *Aging in the 1980s: Psychological Issues,* edited by L.W. Poon and K.W. Schaie. Washington, DC: American Psychological Association.

Leech, S. and Witte, K.L. (1971) Paired-associate learning in elderly adults as related to pacing and incentive conditions. *Developmental Psychology* **5**: 180.

Lex Report on Motoring (1991) London: Lex Services.

Light, L.L. and Singh, A. (1987) Implicit and explicit memory in younger and older adults. *Journal of Experimental Psychology (Learning, Memory, and Cognition)* **13**: 531–41.

Lovelace, E.A. and Marsh, G.R. (1985) Prediction and evaluation of memory performance by young and old adults. *Journal of Gerontology* **40**: 192–7.

Madden, D.J. and Nebes, R.D. (1980) Aging and the development of automaticity in visual search. *Developmental Psychology* **16**: 377–84.

Mattis, S. (1976) Mental status examination for organic mental syndrome in the elderly patient. In *Geriatric Psychiatry,* 2nd edn, edited by L. Bella and T.B. Karasu. New York: Oxford University Press.

McDowd, J.M. and Birren, J.E. (1990) Aging and attentional processes. In *Handbook of the Psychology of Aging,* 3rd edn, edited by J.E. Birren and K.W. Schaie. New York and London: Academic Press.

McDowd, J.M. and Craik, F.I.M. (1988) Effects of aging and task difficulty on divided attention performance. *Journal of Experimental Psychology (Human Perception and Performance)* **14**: 267–80.

McEvoy, G.M. and Cascio, W.F. (1989) Cumulative evidence of the relationship between employee age and job performance. *Journal of Applied Psychology* **74**: 11–17.

Mirkin, B.A. (1987) Early retirement as a labor force policy: An international overview. *Monthly Labor Review,* March, 19–33.

Mitchell, D.B. (1989) How many memory systems? Evidence from aging. *Journal of Experimental Psychology (Learning, Memory, and Cognition)* **15**: 31–49.

Murrell, K.F.H. (1970) The effect of extensive practice on age differences in reaction time. *Journal of Gerontology* **25**: 268–74.

Murrell, K.F.H. and Griew, S. (1958) Age structure in the engineering industry: a study of regional effects. *Occupational Psychology* **32**: 1–13.

Murrell, K.F.H. and Humphries, S. (1978) Age, experience, and short-term memory. In *Practical Aspects of Memory,* edited by M.M. Gruneberg, P.E. Morris and R.N. Sykes. New York and London: Academic Press.

Murrell, K.F.H., Powesland, P.F. and Forsaith, B. (1962) A study of pillar-drilling in relation to age. *Occupational Psychology* **36**: 45–52.

National Research Council (1988) *Transportation in an Aging Society: Improving Mobility and Safety for Older Persons,* Vol. 1. Washington, DC: US National Research Council.

Nebes, R.D. (1978) Vocal versus manual response as a determinant of age differences in simple reaction time. *Journal of Gerontology* **33**: 884–9.

Obrist, W.D. (1965) Electroencephalographic approach to age changes in response speed. In *Behavior, Aging and the Nervous System,* edited by A.T. Welford and J.E. Birren. Springfield, Illinois: Charles C. Thomas.

Ogden, G.D., Levine, J.M. and Eisner, E.J. (1979) Measurement of workload by secondary tasks. *Human Factors* **21**: 529–48.

Olsen, O.P. and Sivak, M. (1986) Perception–response time to unexpected roadway hazards. *Human Factors* **28**: 91–96.

Owsley, C., Ball, K., Sloane, M.E., Roenker, D.L. and Bruni, J.R. (1991) Visual/perceptual/cognitive correlates of vehicle accidents in older drivers. *Psychology and Aging* **6**: 403–15

Parasuraman, R. (1989) *Selective Attention and Motor Vehicle Accidents in Young and Older Drivers.* Report No. 89-2, Catholic University of America, Cognitive Science Laboratory, Washington, DC.

Park, D.C., Puglisi, J.T. and Smith, A.D. (1986) Memory for pictures: Does an age-related decline exist? *Psychology and Aging* **1**: 11–7.

Peterson, L.R. and Peterson, M.J. (1959) Short-term retention of individual verbal items. *Journal of Experimental Psychology* **58**: 193–8.

Plude, D.J. and Hoyer, W.J. (1986) Aging and the selectivity of visual information processing. *Psychology and Aging* **1**: 1–9.

Ponds, R.M., Brouwer, W.H. and Van Wolffelaar, P.C. (1988) Age differences in divided attention in a simulated driving task. *Journal of Gerontology* **43**: 151–6.

Price, J.L., Thompson, P.H. and Dalton, G.W. (1975) A longitudinal study of technological obsolescence. *Research Management*, November 22–3.

Rabbitt, P.M.A. (1981) Cognitive psychology needs models for changes in performance with old age. In *Attention and Performance*, Vol. X, edited by J. Long and A.D. Baddeley. Hillsdale, NJ: Erlbaum.

Rabinowitz, J.C., Craik, F.I.M. and Ackerman, B.P. (1982) A processing resource account of age differences in recall. *Canadian Journal of Psychology* **36**: 325–44.

Rackoff, N. (1974) An investigation of age-related changes in drivers' visual search patterns and driving performance and the relation of tests of basic functional capacities. Doctoral dissertation, Ohio State University.

Ranney, T.A. and Pulling, N.H. (1989) Relation of individual differences in information-processing ability to driving performance. *Proceedings of the 33rd Annual Meeting of the Human Factors Society*. Santa Monica, Ca.: Human Factors Society.

Salthouse, T.A. (1982) *Adult Cognition: An Experimental Psychology of Human Aging*. New York: Springer.

Salthouse, T.A. (1984) Effects of age and skill in typing. *Journal of Experimental Psychology (General)* **113**: 345–71.

Salthouse, T.A. (1985) Speed of behavior and its implications for cognition. In *Handbook of the Psychology of Aging*, 2nd edn, edited by J.E. Birren and K.W. Schaie. New York: Van Nostrand Reinhold.

Salthouse, T.A. (1988) Resource-reduction interpretations of cognitive aging. *Developmental Review* **8**: 238–72.

Salthouse, T.A. (1989) Aging and skilled performance. In *The Acquisition and Performance of Cognitive Skills*, edited by A. Colley and J. Beech. Chichester: Wiley.

Salthouse, T.A. (1990) Influence of experience on age differences in cognitive functioning. *Human Factors* **32**: 551–69.

Salthouse, T.A. and Somberg, B.L. (1982a) Isolating the age deficit in speeded performance. *Journal of Gerontology* **37**: 59–63.

Salthouse, T.A. and Somberg, B.L. (1982b) Time-accuracy relationships in young and old adults. *Journal of Gerontology* **37**: 349–53.

Salthouse, T.A., Wright, R. and Ellis, C.L. (1979) Adult age and the rate of an internal clock. *Journal of Gerontology* **34**: 53–7.

Salthouse, T.A., Mitchell, D.R.D., Skovronek, E. and Babcock, R.L. (1989a) Effects of adult age and working memory on reasoning and spatial abilities. *Journal of Experimental Psychology (Learning, Memory, and Cognition)* **15**: 507–16.

Salthouse, T.A., Babcock, R.L., Skovronek, E., Mitchell, D.R.D. and Palmon, R. (1989b) Age and experience effects in spatial visualization. *Developmental Psychology* **26**: 128–36.

Salthouse, T.A., Rogan, J.D. and Prill, K.A. (1984) Division of attention: age differences on a visually presented memory task. *Memory and Cognition* **12**: 613–20.

Sanders, A.F. (1970) Some aspects of the selective process in the functional field of view. *Ergonomics* **13**: 101–17.

Sanders, R.E., Murphy, M.D., Schmitt, F.A. and Walsh, K.K. (1980) Age differences in free recall rehearsal strategies. *Journal of Gerontology* **35**: 550–8.

Salvendy, G. (1972) Effects of age on some test scores of production criteria. *Studia Psychologica* **14**: 186–89.

Schaie, K.W. (1977) Quasi-experimental designs in the psychology of aging. In *Handbook of the Psychology of Aging*, edited by J.E. Birren and K.W. Schaie. New York: Van Nostrand Reinhold.

Schaie, K.W. (1988) Ageism in psychological research. *American Psychologist* **43**: 179–88.

Schaie, K.W. (1990) Intellectual development in adulthood. In *Handbook of the Psychology of Aging*, 3rd edn, edited by J.E. Birren and K.W. Schaie. New York and London: Academic Press.

Schaie, K.W. and Willis, S.L. (1986) Can decline in intellectual functioning in the elderly be reversed? *Developmental Psychology* **22**: 223–32.

Schneider, W. and Shiffrin, R.M. (1977) Controlled and automatic human information processing: I. Detection, search, and attention. *Psychological Review* **84**: 1–66.

Scialfa, C.T., Kline, D.W. and Lyman, B.J. (1987) Age differences in target identification as a function of retinal location and noise level: An examination of the useful field of view. *Psychology and Aging* **2**: 14–19.

Sekuler, R. and Ball, K. (1986) Visual localization: age and practice. *Journal of the Optical Society of America* **3**: 864–7.

Sharps, M.J. and Gollin, E.S. (1987) Speed and accuracy of mental image rotation in young and elderly adults. *Journal of Gerontology* **42**: 342–4.

Shiffrin, R.M. and Schneider, W. (1977) Controlled and automatic human information processing. II: Perceptual learning, automatic attending, and a general theory. *Psychological Review* **84**: 127–90.

Shinar, D. (1977) Driver visual limitations: diagnosis and treatment. Technical Report No. NTIS PB-278-84, US Department of Transportation, Washington, DC.

Shinar, D. (1978) *Psychology on the Road: The Human Factor in Traffic Safety*. New York: Wiley.

Siegler, I.C. and Botwinick, J. (1979) A long-term longitudinal study of intellectual ability of older adults: the matter of selective subject attrition. *Journal of Gerontology* **34**: 242–5.

Simonton, D.K. (1988) Age and outstanding achievement: What do we know after a century of research? *Psychological Bulletin* **104**: 251–67.

Smith, J.M. (1975) Occupations classified by their age structure. *Industrial Gerontology* **2**: 209–15.

Smith, D.B.D. (1990) Human factors and aging: an overview of research needs and application opportunities. *Human Factors* **32**: 509–26.

Sparrow, P.R. and Davies, D.R. (1988) Effects of age, tenure, training, and job complexity on technical performance. *Psychology and Aging* **3**, 307–14.

Spirduso, W.W. (1980) Physical fitness, aging, and psychomotor speed: A review. *Journal of Gerontology* **35**: 850–65.

Spirduso, W.W. and Clifford, P. (1978) Neuromuscular speed and consistency of performance as a function of age, physical activity level, and type of physical activity. *Journal of Gerontology* **33**: 26–30.

Spirduso, W.W. and MacRae, P.G. (1990) Motor performance and aging. In *Handbook of the Psychology of Aging*, 3rd edn, edited by J.E. Birren and K.W. Schaie. New York and London: Academic Press.

Stagner, R. (1985) Aging in industry. In *Handbook of the Psychology of Aging*, 2nd edn, edited by J.E. Birren and K.W. Schaie. New York: Van Nostrand Reinhold.

Stine, E.L., Wingfield, A. and Poon, L.W. (1986) How much and how fast: rapid processing of spoken language in later adulthood. *Psychology and Aging* **1**: 303–11.

Storandt, M. (1976) Speed and coding effects in relation to age and ability level. *Developmental Psychology* **12**: 177–8.

Storandt, M. (1977) Age, ability level, and scoring the WAIS. *Journal of Gerontology* **32**: 175–8.
Strayer, D.L., Wickens, C.D. and Braune, R. (1987) Adult age differences in the speed and capacity of information processing: 2. An electrophysiological approach. *Psychology and Aging* **2**: 99–110.
Sunderland, A., Watts, K., Baddeley, A.D. and Harris, J.E. (1986) Subjective memory assessment and test performance in elderly adults. *Journal of Gerontology* **41**: 376–84.
Surwillo, W.W. (1968) Timing of behavior in senescence and the role of the central nervous system. In *Human Aging and Behavior: Recent Advances in Research and Theory*, edited by G.A. Talland. New York and London: Academic Press.
Treat, J.R., Tumbas, N.S., McDonald, S.T., Shinar, D., Hume, R.D., Mayer, R.E., Stansiffer, R.L. and Castellan, N.J. (1977) *Tri-level Study of the Causes of Traffic Accidents*. Report No. DOT-HS-034-3-535-77. (TAC), Indiana University.
Verriest, G. (1971) L'influence de l'age sur les fonctions visuelles de l'homme. *Bulletin de L'Académie Royale de Médecine Belgique* **11**: 527–78.
Waldman, D.A. and Avolio, B.J. (1986) A meta-analysis of age differences in job performance. *Journal of Applied Psychology* **71**: 33–8.
Weale, R.A. (1978) The eye and aging. In *Interdisciplinary Topics in Aging*, Vol. 13, edited by O. Hockivin. New York: Karger.
Welford, A.T. (1958) *Ageing and Human Skill*. London: Oxford University Press.
Welford, A.T. (1977) Motor performance. In *Handbook of the Psychology of Aging*, edited by J.E. Birren and K.W. Schaie. New York: Van Nostrand Reinhold.
Welford, A.T. (1985) Changes of performance with age: an overview. In *Aging and Human Performance*, edited by N. Charness. Chichester: Wiley.
Woodruff-Pak, D.S. (1985) Arousal, sleep, and aging. In *Handbook of the Psychology of Aging*, 2nd edn, edited by J.E. Birren and K.W. Schaie. New York: Van Nostrand Reinhold.
Yee, D. (1983) A survey of the traffic safety needs and problems of drivers aged 55 and over. In *Driver 55 plus: Needs and problems of older drivers. Survey Results and Recommendations*. Falls Church, Va.: AAA Foundation for Traffic Safety.

3

Sex Differences in Performance: Fact, Fiction or Fantasy?

J.M. USSHER

INTRODUCTION: CONTROVERSY AND CONTRADICTION

The case thus far:

Science

The man of science is deficient on the purely emotional element [and that] in many regards the character of the scientific men is strongly anti-feminine; their mind is directed to facts and abstract theories, and not to persons or human interests... they have little sympathy with female ways of thought. (Galton, 1874, quoted in Easlea, 1986, p. 137)

Gender ideology [was] a crucial mediator between the birth of modern science and the economic and political transformation surrounding that birth... neither the equations between mind, reason and masculinity, not the dichotomies between mind and nature, reason and feeling, masculine and feminine, are historically invariant. (Keller, 1985, p. 44)

Mathematical reason

The sex related differences in spatial abilities are thought to be part of the sex-related differences in mathematical reasoning and /or mathematical skills and achievement; for example see Harris (1978) and Sherman (1978)... Yes, of course, there are sex-related group differences, primarily favouring males in selected spatial skills and mathematical skills. (Anderson, 1986, pp. 46, 51)

Constantly and continually, girls have to be proved to fail or to be inferior at mathematics, despite the extreme ambiguity of the evidence. In spite of many obvious successes (Walden and Walkerdine, 1983) girls' performance is constantly demonstrated to be different from, other than that of boys. (Walkerdine, 1990, p. 62)

HANDBOOK OF HUMAN PERFORMANCE
VOLUME 3 ISBN 0-12-650353-2

Menstruation

> The periodic disturbances, to which girls and women are constitutionally subject, condemn many of them to a recurring, if temporary, diminution of mental efficiency. Moreover, it is during the more important years of school life that these disturbances are most intense and pervasive, and whenever one of them coincides with some emergency, for example, an examination, girls are heavily handicapped as compared to boys... (Board of Education, 1923, quoted in Richardson, 1991a)

> The discourse of menstrual cycle vulnerability, reified in the premenstrual syndrome, is not based on fact. There is no evidence for menstrual cycle effects on mood or performance, of increases in accident or violence – despite the prevalent stereotype. The fact that we still believe that women are weakened by menstruation is testimony to the tenacity of the misogynistic beliefs associated with the female body, rather than because of reliable or valid evidence of the effects of this supposed syndrome. (Ussher, 1992b, p. 25)

These illustrative quotes demonstrate the diversity of opinion on the subject of sex differences in performance. There seems to be little room for agreement between the opposing camps. On the one hand, experts declare unequivocally that sex differences do exist, and that it is women who are clearly inferior to men in many spheres of performance, with the only disagreement being over the *causes* of this disparity – uncertainty as to whether it is a biological or social phenomenon. On the other hand, there is an equally vociferous argument that sex differences do not exist, that the very interest in sex differences is based on misogynistic assumptions, and that the perpetuation of the discourse of female fallibility and lability serves to maintain woman's position as the Other,* as outside the world of men; outside the world of power and privilege.

Empirical research in a number of different areas of human performance is wielded by the proponents of both viewpoints in support of their arguments, but the conclusions reached are far from simple or incontrovertible. Whether sensory functioning, cognition, learning and memory, social cognition, stress reactivity, menstrual cycle variability or occupational performance is the object of analysis, there are differences of interpretation and contradictions in this field. This controversy is the subject of this chapter. The established 'truths' within the sex differences research are examined, but just one area of study, that of menstrual cycle performance change, is focused upon in order to illustrate the problems inherent within the literature. Others have carried out similar analyses looking specifically at the field of mathematics (Walkerdine, 1990) or scientific reasoning (Fee, 1988; Keller, 1985; Blier, 1988; Harding, 1986b) – these are equally valid as focuses for discussion. Whatever area of

---

* The concept of the Other originates from both Simone De Beauvoir and more latterly Lacanian theory, where the woman is seen as always secondary in relation to the man within the symbolic order: he is and I and she is the not-I, the second sex.

performance is the focus of analysis, simple interpretations of sex differences research, based on little or no theoretical underpinnings, have for too long been allowed to go unchallenged.

Discourse and truth

Many researchers in this field base their arguments about sex differences in performance on unquestioning acceptance of the existing empirical research material (as evidenced by Anderson on mathematics, quoted above) and conduct narrative reviews consisting solely of descriptions of the research literature. My approach, however, does not take any of our present system of knowledge about sex differences in performance as pre-given truths. Instead I deconstruct the discursive practices which make up our present system of knowledge and examine the history of the production of this knowledge in order to challenge the assumptions and accepted truths which underlie our present prejudices and practices.†

In this context, I use the term discourse in the Foucauldian sense of a regulated system of statements, which has a particular history (which Foucault termed a genealogy), and a set of rules which distinguishes it from other discourses whilst establishing both links and difference.‡ The discourse is what organizes our knowledge about a subject (in this case about sex differences in performance) and about the relation of both the individual and society to that subject. The 'truth' we adhere to will depend on whichever discourse is currently dominant – whichever discourse is adhered to by those in power. Thus our knowledge and belief in the 'facts' about women's and men's performance, the way in which we use the knowledge we have at our disposal, is governed by these evolving discourses. Within psychology, the dominant discourse positions woman as unequal to man in many spheres of performance, reinforcing the notion that women's inability in arenas such as science or mathematics is real.

To understand our present system of knowledge we need to look to its genealogy, as the roots of our beliefs and practices are firmly located in the past. It is only the language and the context which has changed, the method of proving truths; the underlying discourse is the same.

---

† Much of this work is based on a post-structuralist analysis of language, in which 'those practices which constitute our everyday lives are produced and reproduced as an integral part of the production of signs and signifying systems' (Henriques *et al.*, 1984: 99).

‡ See Henriques *et al.*, 1984 for a more complete explanation of this use of 'discourse' and deconstruction. I am following these authors in 'extending signification to produce the notion of the discursive' (1984, p. 99).

THE HISTORICAL LEGACY

Science positions the female

> The chief distinction in the intellectual powers of the two sexes is shown by man attaining to a higher eminence, in whatever he takes up, than women can attain – whether requiring deep thought, reason, or imagination, or merely the use of senses and hands. (Darwin, 1871)

The discourse of woman as vulnerable, labile and unequal to man in the world of education, politics, art or work has been prevalent in society for many centuries. However, it was in the nineteenth century that experts in the area of medicine, education and science became more prolific in the pronouncements about the weakness in the female sex, and women's consequent unsuitability for intellectual exertion.

The establishment of the scientific discourse in the nineteenth century reified both the powerful position of men and the fallibility of women, for woman and science were seen as bipolar opposites (Jordanova, 1989; Keller, 1985). In the nineteenth century, women's supposed weaknesses meant that they were positioned as unsuitable for and incapable of any form of intellectual exercise or employment, at risk of endangering themselves and their future offspring should they attempt to try: a belief maintained by both scientific theory and the vociferous experts who pronounced upon it.

For example, a woman doctor or psychiatrist was unthinkable, for it was thought, as argued by a Dr Augustus Gardener in 1872, that, 'medicine [is] disgusting to women, accustomed to softness and the downy side of life' (Barker-Benfield, 1976, p. 87). Swinburne, in 1902, claimed that, 'when it comes to science we find women are simply nowhere. The feminine mind is quite unscientific'. Her position was clearly not in the public sphere, as Prime Minister of Britain Asquith commented: 'the grant of the parliamentary franchise to women in this country would be a political mistake of a very disastrous kind' (Morgan, 1989, p. 64), a belief echoed by Enoch Powell MP over half a century later when he declared: 'A woman in the House of Commons is a contradiction in terms' (Morgan, 1989, p. 66). And the arts were not immune: the composer Sir Thomas Beecham commented, 'there are no women composers, never have been, and never will be' (Morgan, 1989, p. 163); Charlotte Brontë was informed that, 'literature cannot be the business of a woman's life, and it ought not to be' (Morgan, 1989, p. 160); John Ruskin confidently commented that 'no woman can paint' (Morgan, 1989, p. 165).

Reproduction as liability

The discourse within which women's biology, and particularly her sexuality and reproductive capabilities, marked her as different (and deficient), was promulgated in the nineteenth century. It was assumed that women has a finite amount of energy which could be used either for study or for reproduction, and if women were to work then a 'decreased fulfilment of the maternal functions' would inevitably result (Spencer, 1873, p. 31). The absence of 'reproductive power' in many middle class women as evidenced by the low fertility of educated women, was 'attributed to the overtaxing of their brains – an overtaxing which was said to produce a serious reaction on the physique' (Sayers, 1982, p. 8). The counter-argument was that reproduction was a liability in itself. Thus in 1916 women were advised that:

> All heavy exercise should be omitted during the menstrual week... a girl should not only retire earlier at this time, but ought to stay out of school from one to three days as the case may be, resting the mind and taking extra hours of rest and sleep. (Scott Hall, 1916)

Brain inferiority

If fecundity and raging hormones were not at the seat of women's apparent weakness, the theory of brain inferiority could be brought forward. For women were deemed to have 'less cerebral activity to exercise' due to the supposed differences in brain organization (Topinard, 1894, p. 121).

Man's physical strength was also seen as an asset and advantage, resulting in his 'natural' superiority. As Thomas in 1897 (p. 761) claimed:

> In view of his superior power of making movements and applying physical force, the male must inevitably assume control... there has never been a moment in the history of society when the law of might, tempered by sexual affinity, did not prevail.

At the same time, those aspects of performance or skills at which women might be thought to excel were denigrated or dismissed. For as Darwin argued,

> It is generally admitted that with women the powers of intuition, of rapid perception, and perhaps of imitation, are more strongly marked than in man; but some, at least, of these faculties are characteristic of the lower races, and therefore of a past and lower state of civilisation. (Darwin, 1871, p. 563)

So the conclusions were clear. Women were positioned as *naturally* unequal to men because of their biology, whether it be the fault of reproduction, physical weakness or differences in the structure of the brain.

Sex or gender?

Researchers proclaim confidently upon the reality of sex differences in performance, reinforcing the popular belief that girls are 'heavily handicapped as compared with boys' (Dalton, 1969b) in both examinations and overall educational abilities, and thus justifying disparities in achievement. The fact that it is *sex* that they focus on implies interest in the biological distinction between men and women, based on hormonal, anatomical or chromosomal differences. A focus on *gender* implies the social construction of any differences, as gender is seen as a social category learnt through differential socialization processes. The implications of there being sex differences are more serious for women, as these can be posited as immutable differences, linked to biology, positioning women as irrevocably outside and Other; a position which is continued in the twentieth century psychology which perpetuates the same discourse perpetuated by the nineteenth century experts.

THE TWENTIETH CENTURY: MATHS, SCIENCE, RATIONALITY – NOT WOMEN'S WORK

Sex differences in achievement

While the nineteenth century experts looked only to their own clinical judgements or to subjective (and arguably prejudicial) interpretations made of women's apparent lack of achievement, the second half of the twentieth century has seen an explosion of empirical research which sets out to examine the existence (or attempts to prove the non-existence) of sex differences in performance.

One of the major motivations for this research has been to provide an explanation for the apparent lack of achievement exhibited by women, and by their predominance in low paid, low status work. Women are almost completely absent from many spheres of employment, particularly science, engineering, mathematics – notably those which are often of a higher status (and certainly more highly paid) within Western industrialized society. Yet this is a division which is evidenced early in life, and throughout education, as is clearly demonstrated by recent statistics on examinations (see Table 3.1). Boys are represented in higher numbers in mathematics and science, girls in the arts subjects. This disparity continues into higher education, as is evidenced by the statistics on sex differences in degree subjects (see Table 3.2).

After schooling, women continue to be under-represented in many of the professions. For despite apparent comparability of ability and education, women do not succeed in the world of work to the same extent as men. Women make up only five per cent of management positions (Alban-Metcalf and West, 1991), and men still dominate in all professions, even those which are positioned as 'female' such as nursing or teaching (Hansard, 1990). As the Hansard commission report concluded: 'To achieve promotion to senior jobs, women too often have to be better than men' (Hansard, 1990, p. 3). Even when women do work along side men, they earn less (Table 3.3).

Table 3.1 School divisions by subject

1987–88	*Girls*		*Boys*	
	Attempts	*Passes*	*Attempts*	*Passes*
CSE/O level				
English language	297.3		291.0	
Mathematics	270.7		279.8	
Biology	168.5		94.8	
French	142.8		95.8	
Music, Drama, Arts	122.8		102.7	
History	115.4		112.9	
Chemistry	86.1		110.6	
Physics	67.3		167.5	
Computer science	31.2		59.1	
GCE A level				
English	29.6	25.0	13.5	11.3
Mathematics	19.0	14.3	37.6	29.2
Physics	8.0	6.2	27.2	21.5

All figures are in thousands.

Table 3.2 Undergraduate degrees

	Females	*Males*
Language and related	18.3	7.6
Social sciences	15.2	17.1
Multi-disciplinary studies	13.5	15.0
Medicine and dentistry	13.5	15.0
Biological sciences	8.8	7.3
Humanities	6.8	7.6
Physical sciences	6.8	7.6
Studies allied to medicine	4.2	2.0
Mathematical sciences	3.3	10.5
Business and financial studies	3.7	5.5
Engineering and technology	3.0	24.5
Veterinary science, argiculture, etc.	2.1	2.4
Creative arts	2.1	1.4
Education	1.5	0.5
Architecture and related	0.9	2.3
Librarianship and information science	0.1	0.1
All subjects	98.6	130.0

All figures are in thousands.

The statistics in the three tables provide a powerful picture of women's seeming inability to achieve at the same level as men, maintaining the notion of woman's inferiority in the 'masculine' spheres of science, mathematics and engineering, and of women's unsuitability for responsibility or power in business or the professions: notions at the basis of the nineteenth century pronouncements on woman and at the foundation of the twentieth century sex differences research which took up the challenge of the case with positivism.

Table 3.3

	Occupational group	Females			Males		
		N	%	£	N	%	£
I	Professional and related supporting management and administration	383	4	270.4	1110	8	365.4
II	Professional and related in education, welfare and health	1490	14	206.9	733	5	290.8
III	Literary, artistic and sports	135	1	228.7	204	1	310.0
IV	Professional and related in science, engineering, technology and similar fields	111	1	197.7	936	7	291.8
V	Managerial (excluding general management)	691	6	198.9	1920	13	289.7
VI	Clerical and related	3250	30	150.5	1011	7	194.1
VII	Selling	1044	10	128.5	746	5	221.5
VIII	Security and protective servicing	45	0	232.1	357	3	255.4
IX	Catering, cleaning, hairdressing and other personal service	2311	22	116.7	577	4	158.7
X	Farming, fishing and related	97	1	–	365	3	151.2
XI	Materials processing (excl. metals)	477	5	125.6	1158	8	201.2
	Making and repairing (exclu. metals and electrics)			120.3			207.2
XII	Processing, making, repairing and related (metal and electrical)	112	1	140.2	2260	16	223.4
XIII	Painting, repetitive assembling, products inspection, packaging and related	390	4	130.4	558	4	194.0
XV	Construction and mining	4	0	–	870	6	200.7
XVI	Transport operating, materials moving and storing and related	86	0	132.8	1341	9	196.4
XVII	Miscellaneous	5	0	–	39	–	181.5

N is in thousands; £, average gross weekly earnings; %, percentage of female population in employment. Source: EOC Statistics Unit, 1990.

SEX DIFFERENCES RESEARCH

The uncontested truth?

> Sex differences can clearly be demonstrated in only four areas: (1) Girls have greater verbal ability than boys; (2) boys excel in visual–spatial ability; (3) boys excel in mathematical ability; (4) boys are more aggressive. (Unger, 1979, p. 86)

The previously generalized statements on women's lack of ability have been transformed through empirical analysis of specific aspects of performance (for reviews see Maccoby and Jacklin, 1974; Fairweather, 1976; Wittig and Peterson, 1979; Sherman, 1978; Harris, 1978; MacLeod, 1979; McGee, 1979; Cooper and Reagan, 1982; Baker, 1986; Richardson, 1991b). While a cornucopia of abilities and skills have been examined for possible sex differences, the main findings are generally summarized succinctly as by Unger above. These conclusions have become the truths of the discourse on sex differences, but it is not as clear and unproblematic as the researchers might have us believe. A brief overview of some of the specific areas of research indicates the contradictions in the literature and highlights the problems inherent in interpreting the results.

Cognition, learning and memory

As it is thought that 'sex differences in cognitive skill are reflected in the choice of career and professional achievement' (Newcombe and Ratcliff, 1978, p. 195), and more specifically that ability in mathematics is the 'critical factor' in women's lower achievement (Sells, 1973), the realm of cognition has provided much fruit for the researcher attempting to understand inequalities between men and women.

MATHEMATICAL ABILITY

In a now classic review of sex differences Maccoby and Jacklin (1974, p. 352) claimed that 'boys excel in mathematical ability'; a finding which a recent review concludes is still 'robust' (Halpern, 1986, p. 56). Yet global assertion of male superiority when examined more carefully is shown to be tenable only when applied to post-adolescent children, as sex differences do not emerge before age 13–16 and they are not found across the board (Halpern, 1986; Fennema, 1974; Stage *et al.*, 1985; Hyde *et al.*, 1990). For while the research suggests that boys out-perform girls on tasks requiring mathematical reasoning and on tests of algebra and mathematical knowledge, girls are said to 'occasionally out-perform boys on tests of computational skills' (Stage *et al.*, 1985, p. 240). In addition, recent reviews argue that 'a general statement about gender differences is misleading because it masks the complexity of the pattern' (Hyde *et al.*, 1990, p. 151). In a meta-analysis of one hundred studies, these authors conclude that 'females are superior in computation, [and] there are no gender differences in understanding of mathematical concepts' (Hyde *et al.*, 1990, p. 151). They also report that effect sizes are very small, in the order of 0.15, which is in line with other research (i.e. Stage *et al.*, 1985).

One interesting finding is that any difference between boys and girls on any aspect of mathematical ability has declined over the past twenty years (Feingold, 1988), and that the differential is evident only at higher levels of mathematical ability (Becker and Hedges, 1984; Benbow and Stanley, 1980;

Feingold, 1988). So the very existence of sex differences in mathematical ability can certainly be questioned.

SPATIAL ABILITIES

One of the explanations for any sex differences in mathematical ability, and thus women's under-representation in engineering and science (Colthart *et al.*, 1975), is supposed sex differences in visual spatial skills. One of the main means of measuring visual spatial skills has been the 'rod and frame test' (RFT) which provides the measure of analytical ability, termed field independence, indicating the extent to which the person's perceptions are independent of environmental cues.§ Field independence is deemed to be related to analytical ability, supposedly equipping men for success in the professions (see Maccoby and Jacklin, 1974; Fairweather, 1976; McGee, 1979; Nyborg, 1983).

Based on research using the RFT it has been argued that men are more efficient and rapid than women at carrying out mental rotation tasks (Shepard and Metzler, 1971; Vandenberg and Kuse, 1978; Kail *et al.*, 1979; Sanders *et al.*, 1982) and that males participate more readily in activities which are related to spatial ability (Newcome *et al.*, 1983). Equally, men are said to be faster and more accurate in comparing computer-generated images of three-dimensional objects (Blough and Salvin, 1987). So, the claim that boys' performance is superior to that of girls in the area of geometry (Marshall, 1984; Fennema and Carpenter, 1981), and that boys are said to be more competent in the field of rational thinking and logical reason (Benbow and Stanley, 1983), is being explained simply by recourse to the sex differences in spatial ability and logical thought.

However, these conclusions are not as clear-cut as many would make out. It has been suggested (i.e. Sherman, 1978; Linn and Peterson, 1985; Richardson, 1991b) that any gender differences in spatial ability are small, and that they may be an artefact of the experimental setting. Indeed, when spatial ability tasks are designed to be more appropriate for females, women are more successful (Birkett, 1976).

LEARNING AND MEMORY

The results of the research on learning and memory are equivocal. For example, experimenters have claimed that women are slower at scanning tasks than men (Chaing and Atkinson, 1976; Longstreth and Madigan, 1982), suggesting

§ The RFT involves a luminous rod contained in a square luminous frame, which is shown to the subject in a darkened room. The rod and frame are presented out of alignment in a tilted position and the subject is instructed to tell the experimenter to rotate the rod until it is vertical. The accuracy of the positioning of the rod in the face of discrepant information from the frame is the object of investigation.

poorer recall from short-term memory, but that women are superior to men in the recognition and recall of pictures and names of objects (Ernest, 1983; Harshman *et al.*, 1983; Marks, 1973; Richardson, 1991b), and in the recall of verbal descriptions of particular situations (McGuiness and Maclaughlin, 1982; see Richardson, 1991a, for a review of this literature). In their 1974 review, Maccoby and Jacklin argued that girls' verbal ability matures earlier than that of boys, and that girls are more competent at tasks requiring memory of verbal materials.

Yet again these are not incontrovertible sex differences for, as Richardson (1991b, p. 293) concludes in a review of the literature on mental imagery: 'There is no reliable difference between males and females in terms of the effects of stimulus imageability... [or] imagery instructions in tests of learning and memory'. A conclusion echoed by Feingold (1988, p. 101) who reviewed gender differences in cognition between 1947 and 1983 and claimed that:

> the analysis of... normative data question the validity of the findings that girls out-perform boys in the verbal domain... [and] the analyses of the norms from the maths tests... suggested that girls narrowed the gender difference in quantitative abilities over the years.

SENSORY FUNCTIONING

In a review of sensory functioning, Baker (1986, p. 26) claims that, 'sex differences are well-established in pure-tone thresholds, visual acuity, and pressure threshold. Females show lower thresholds for pure-tone threshold above 1000 Hz and for pressure all over the body and, on average, have poorer static and dynamic visual acuity'. Drawing analogous conclusions, Maccoby and Jacklin (1974) argued that girls have greater tactile sensitivity than boys. One of the explanations for these apparent sex differences is menstrual cycle variations, as it has been noted that 'changes in threshold occur within the menstrual cycle, during pregnancy, or when oral contraceptives are taken' (Baker, 1986, p. 26). This apparent variability in sensory modalities has been claimed to be one of the most consistent aspects of functioning which varied with the menstrual cycle (see Parlee, 1983; Dye, 1991 for reviews of this literature).

It is interesting that these apparent differences in sensory functioning do not necessarily favour males. In the areas of auditory functioning, differences in pure-tone threshold favour women (Roche *et al.*, 1978), and it has been reported that men show a greater hearing loss with age than do women (Berger *et al.*, 1977), particularly at levels above 1000 Hz (Corso, 1959). However, the research examining sex differences in vision tends to suggest that men have better visual acuity than women (Farrimond, 1967), and that female vision declines at an earlier age, after the age of 35, rather than 45 for men (Roberts, 1968; Baker, 1986).

Conclusion

The results of research on performance are equivocal. Many researchers would argue that there are no sex differences in the majority of aspects of performance (Fairweather, 1976; Feingold, 1988), reinforcing conclusions from analyses of sex differences in areas such as social cognition (Durkin, 1986), reactions to environmental stress (Green and Bell, 1986) and work in an applied setting (Redgrove, 1986). Others clearly support the notion of the existence of sex differences, but not necessarily across the board. This level of disagreement is also reflected in the various theories offered to explain the supposed differences.

Theories of sex differences in performance

Much of the sex differences research is not theory-driven (see Ussher, 1991b), and thus explanations for any significant results are invariably posited retrospectively rather than being based on experimental work being carried out in relation to particular theoretical predictions. These explanations for difference fall clearly along the well trodden nature–nurture path, with many sitting firmly in the middle, arguing that both biology and environment have an influence. This is a division not unique to the question of sex differences in performance: it mirrors the debate surrounding the existence and etiology of sex differences in depression (see Ussher, 1991a), or sex differences in aggression (Hyde, 1984).

BIOLOGICAL FACTORS

> The genetic basis [of sex differences] is intense enough to cause a substantial division of labour even in the most free and most egalitarian of... societies (Wilson, 1975, p. 50, quoted in Sayers, 1982, p. 29)

The most pervasive explanation is that sex differences in performance and achievement are the result of biological differences between men and women (reviewed by Halpern, 1986). In particular, sex differences in spatial ability have been attributed to hormonal or genetic factors (Dawson, 1972; Elliot and Fralley, 1976; McGee, 1979), or to a possible X chromosome linked recessive trait for spatial skills (Stafford, 1961), to the greater lateralization of males (Buffery and Grey, 1972); or the hormonal profiles of women (Caplan *et al.*, 1985; McKeever and Deyo, 1990; Harris, 1981). In this vein, Harris confidently concludes:

> Fetal testicular hormones act on an initially sexually undifferentiated nervous system to bring about sensitization to visual input... earlier right-cerebral hemisphere development and ultimately greater lateral separation of function with consequent enhancement of right-hemisphere functional efficiency. (1981, p. 111, quoted by Anderson, 1986, p. 45)

RAGING HORMONES

The hormonal arguments are supported by the finding that any sex differences in performance which are reported are generally not manifested until after puberty, coinciding with the start of the reproductive hormones circulating in the woman's body. That any other factor coincident with the hormonal changes taking place at puberty could provide explanation for performances differences is generally overlooked. So the confident conclusion of Noble (1978) that, 'males are better on speeded tasks... males excel in athletic skills requiring strength and stamina... Olympic records in swimming and track and field tests are lower for females, and... men do better on the Seguin form board and the Porteus Maze' (quoted in Anderson, 1986, p. 48) has been interpreted by researchers (i.e. Broverman *et al.*, 1981) as factors resulting from sex differences in levels of circulating oestrogen and androgen. The research literature on sex differences in sensory functioning (see Dye, 1991; Baker, 1986; Parlee, 1983) has also been related to physical or biological differences between men and women, particularly at the time of menstruation. Menstruation is again posited as the underlying cause of women's supposed lability.

PHYSICAL WORK CAPACITY

As the physical differences between men and women were used as a justification for women's absence in the workforce in the nineteenth century, so the physical differences in size and strength are today deemed to be at the root of woman's inability to perform:

> Men are taller, have greater sitting height, longer arms, and longer legs. These factors can affect responses especially when they are combined with greater strength... Men also have a more efficient oxygen transport system. The cardiac output is smaller for women so that the heart must pump more oxygenated blood for a woman than for a man to perform the same amount of work. (Wardle *et al.*, 1986, p. 116)

Researchers proclaim with confidence that 'women have significantly smaller capacities to perform physical work and to perform specific work activities than do men' (Wardle *et al.*, 1986, p. 118). Yet does this apparent physical disadvantage have the negative implications which might first appear? In a review of anthropometric factors in performance, Perival and Quinkert (1986, p. 138) concluded that, 'significant differences exist between man and women with regard to size, strength and flexibility'. Yet, rather than assuming that these put women at a 'natural' disadvantage they go on to say that, 'these differences have a major impact on the proper design of equipment, tasks, jobs, environments, and systems for a user population composed of men and women', as they demonstrate 'the negative consequences of designing equipment to be used by women on the basis of male anthropometric data'. So while women may be smaller than men, or have less physical strength, this is only a disadvantage in a world designed (literally) for men.

BIOLOGICAL MYTHS

Although the biological explanations which perpetuate the reductionist belief that women are inherently unstable cannot be entirely substantiated by empirical research, they are as valid and reliable as the edicts of the reactionary experts of the nineteenth century. They continue the discourse of female fallibility which divides and denigrates. The lack of size of the female brain has been translated into arguments about lateralization. The wandering womb of the ancient Greeks has been replaced by genetic and hormonal explanation to be assessed by hormonal assay and developments in DNA research: by empirical research investigating menstrual cycle phenomena. Yet as Richardson argues (1991b, p. 285),

> The theory of differential brain lateralization proposed by Buffery and Gray (1972) was intended to explain the supposed greater incidence of bilateral representation of spatial abilities in women and men, but a number of commentators have insisted that the relevant empirical data are simply not reliable and in many cases simply show no gender difference at all. (Annett, 1980; Caplan *et al.*, 1985; Fairweather, 1976; Kinsbourne, 1980; McGlone, 1980; Sherman, 1978; Wolff, 1980)

Equally, the research which has been carried out to examine the supposed X-linkage for spatial abilities, which would predict high within-family correlations, has failed to reproduce significant results (Vandenberg and Kuse, 1978; Bouchard and McGee, 1977). Menstruation has not been found to have any consistent effect on women's performance, as outlined below. These genetic and hormonal arguments are naive in their insistence on the influence of biological over all other factors, as if environmental or social factors have no sway. Even the strict reductionists would be hard-pressed to produce a convincing case in this sphere. They are looking to an *apparent* (for there is still no conclusive case) correlation between performance and sex, and assuming that one or other of the physical differences between the sexes must underlie the effect. There is no primary theoretical justification in the main, but to the reductionist steeped in the discourse of woman as biologically inferior it rings true, and consequently holds sway.

SOCIO-CULTURAL FACTORS

> Sex differences in performance are the outcome of collective, social–cognitive interactions dependent in part upon individually held expectations and beliefs and in part upon the constraints within which social perception is fashioned. (Durkin, 1986, p. 142)

Socialization. The socio-cultural explanation posits that any differences in performance are due to the different socialization of boys and girls (Unger, 1979), or to factors such as birth order, age, family size and culture (Fairweather, 1976). For example, the evidence that men respond more negatively to crowding and invasion of physical space (Stokols *et al.*, 1973;

Epstein and Karlin, 1975; Levitt and Leventhal, 1978), and are therefore at a disadvantage in performance situations which involve such conditions, has been attributed to socio-cultural factors, as different meanings are attributed to close physical contact by men and women (Green and Bell, 1986).

At the level of scholastic performance, it is argued that boys are encouraged to compete and achieve, girls to affiliate and acquiesce, and that girls are socialized into choosing particular career paths which avoid science and maths, instead moving towards 'women's' professions of nursing, teaching, and arts and social-based degree courses. As Keller argues:

> The metaphor of a marriage between Mind and Nature necessarily does not look the same to [a male scientist] as it does to women... In a science constructed around the naming of object (nature) as female and the parallel naming of subject (mind) as male, any scientist who happens to be a woman is confronted with an *a priori* contradiction in terms. (Keller, 1985, p. 174)

Science as male. It is argued that the gendering of science is internalized by schoolchildren (Dwyer, 1973; Weinreich-Haste, 1979), affecting their attitude to work and choice of examination subject early on in their careers. Thus, as it was believed that it was dangerous for the nineteenth century women to engage in such masculine pursuits as reasoning, so girls today are dissuaded from engaging in mathematics, science and engineering. Girls may not be encouraged in such subjects at school, and therefore achieve less, or believe they can achieve less (Walden and Walkerdine, 1983). The fact that girls are more likely to succeed at mathematics and science in single sex schools (Deem, 1984) suggests not an absence of ability but a different set of expectations.

Recently, researchers have presented models to explain these socially constructed sex differences, including the expectation × value model (Eccles, 1987) which explains gender differences in mathematical selection, and the autonomous learning model (Fennema and Peterson, 1985) which argues that women are dissuaded from engaging in autonomous learning in maths, and therefore fall behind.

In the classroom, girls are encouraged to be nice, kind and helpful (Walkerdine, 1990, p. 76) rather than to be academic, achieving or successful. A 'good' girl is a quiet girl who follows the rules: not the natural training for a mathematician or scientist who must think in an innovative way. And if she dare challenge in the classroom she is viewed very differently from the boy who does so, often painted as lazy or wilful by the teachers, and lacking in femininity by her peers, as in this example:

> Emma displayed those characteristics considered positive when displayed in boys. According to the [male] teacher she is 'interested in ideas and abstract problems', 'a great problem-solver, natural talent'. She is 'constantly trying out ideas'; this makes her 'lazy, selfish...' Of the girls in the class many picked Emma as the very person they were glad they were not. They were afraid of being like her and noted a lack of femininity, saying of her, 'She's skinny'. (Walkerdine, 1990, p. 78).

It seems that from a very early age the girl must choose either to be feminine or to achieve; that the majority still choose the former is not surprising given the negative experiences of many women who do step outside their allotted path. Many women may be reluctant to succeed in such fields for fear of contravening the confines of their expected sex role; a contravention which can lead to diagnosis of psycho-pathology (see Ussher, 1991a). Equally, there are few female role models, few female mentors, and no 'old girls network' in the majority of professions, particularly in the fields of mathematics, engineering and science (Ussher, 1992b).

Interactionism

Moving away from the dichotomy of biological versus social, interactionist explanations have been put forward, such as that of Sherman (1977), who argued that gendered education and women's reliance on their dominant hemisphere for verbal and spatial functioning combine to impede women's performance. This is a position also adopted by Harris (1978) who, while focusing on hemispheric differences between men and women as the root of performance differences, acknowledged that verbal skills are encouraged and facilitated in female children by their mothers, leading to reliance on the dominant hemisphere for processing of linguistic and spatial information.

Artefactual results

> An experiment employing male and female subjects is likely to be a different experiment for the males and for the females. Because experimenters behave differently to male and female subjects even while administering the same formally programmed procedures, male and female subjects may, psychologically, simply not be in the same experiment at all. (Rosenthal, 1976, p. 56, quoted in Richardson, 1991b, p. 256)

A further persuasive argument is that any sex differences which *are* reported are merely artefacts of the experimental situation, or a result of experimenter expectations or influence. It has been clearly demonstrated (i.e. Rosenthal, 1976; Richardson, 1982; Gralton *et al.*, 1979) that experimenters behave differently towards male and female subjects and that this can have a significant effect on outcome. Women often feel anxious when being tested by a male experimenter (Jacklin, 1981; Sherman, 1978), particularly if the situation contains cues which would provoke anxiety in any other context. For example, Sherman (1978) has presented a convincing case to the effect that any sex differences found on the rod and frame test are due to experimental conditions. Any woman placed in an experimental setting which involves giving instructions to a man in the dark (the RFT setting) may be seriously disadvantaged, particularly, as Sherman has argued, as anecdotal evidence suggests that sexual harassment is not uncommon in such circumstances.

It has also been argued that certain experimental situations have different meanings for males and females. For example, Unger (1979) points to the research which showed that females react with greater anxiety in insulting situations (Frodi *et al.,* 1977). Equally, many of the tasks chosen by experimenters in sex differences research are more familiar to boys, such as the use of computer graphics, or three-dimensional games, as boys spend more of their leisure time engaged in such activities and have more access to problem solving experiences outside the classroom (Kimball, 1989). Thus *gender* differences, in terms of socialization or reaction to artefacts of the experimental situation may underlie the apparent *sex* differences on which the researchers proclaim.

The case so far

Is there a clear genealogy of the present discourse of sex differences in performance? Have the claims of the nineteenth century experts been borne out by empirical research carried out by their positivistically minded descendants? One might say yes, and conclude this overview with a few suggestions for future research, or move on to examine in greater depth the details of individual studies claiming to support a particular theory of sex differences, as others have done. But this would serve only to perpetuate the positioning of woman as Other, and the reification of those attributes of behaviour which are conceived of as male within our current discursive regimes: reason over emotion, rationality over subjectivity.

VALUING MALE/DEVALUING FEMALE

What is striking in all of this research is that those aspects of performance or ability at which men are supposedly advantaged are positioned as more important than those at which females are supposedly advantaged. For example, take the claim that:

> When significant differences did appear they were more apt to be in the boys' favour when higher level cognitive tasks were being measured and in the girls' favour when lower level cognitive tasks were being measured. (Fennema, 1974, p. 137)

This claim clearly positions the girls' ability as lower-level. It is seen again in a British government report published in 1982 on the teaching of mathematics in schools, in which Shuard described girls as hard-working and diligent in the classroom, and competent at those aspects of mathematics which are 'taken to require low-level rule following' as well as better than boys at tests that were 'easy' (Walkerdine, 1990, p. 64). As Walkerdine comments:

> The view of mathematics learning dominant in primary schools [is] that proper success is produced on the basis of real understanding... success at reasoning. Mathematics is seen as the *development* of the reasoned and logical mind... Those explanations that allow girls success at all say that is it based on rule following and rote-learning, not on proper understanding... something that amounts to nothing. (1990, pp. 65–6)

Thus those aspects of performance at which females might be shown to excel are dismissed and downgraded as irrelevant and unimportant. The language used is no coincidence.

Yet there is a danger in this debate, for it is easy to become embroiled in questions of methodological sophistication and intent upon upstaging or disproving one's colleagues and professional adversaries (see Gardner, 1985, p. 135), rather than looking more widely to the significance of the research. Rather than posing the question 'Is there a sex difference?' in any aspect of performance, and looking for either biological or social explanations, perhaps we should be asking why this particular question is of interest.

In examining this issue we need to take a step back. Rather than accept the research studies which claim to demonstrate sex differences in performance, or the contradictory studies which claim no such effect, we should ask what is the function of such research. Whose interests does it serve, and is it in any way useful or meaningful? Is it in any way part of the wider discursive practices which position woman within patriarchal society, and can the claims of the positivistic scientists as to their objectivity and neutrality be justified? For does not the focus on sex differences serve mainly the interests of those who would perpetuate the discourse of woman as labile and irrational? Is simplistic research, with questionable reliability and validity, invariably based on naive empiricism not merely an effective justification for maintaining women's exclusion for positions of authority or power?

Would such research conclusions be accepted so readily in other spheres, for example if we were positing racial differences in performance? Even to discuss racial differences in performance or intelligence, even to carry out research on such issues, provokes heated controversy today.¶ Why is the same outcry not forthcoming when we examine sex differences? The assumptions of the researchers and the theoretical justification for their research are often as spurious. The interpretations of their findings are as fallible. And the function of the research is to mark woman as Other as firmly as the race research marks the Black person as Other. It is not coincidental that sex has interested psychologists and physiologists as a variable in their exacting studies. It is because sex is one of the major ways in which power is

¶ See successive 1990 issues of *The Psychologist* for the heated debate on the publication of Rushton's research on race and performance.

differentiated and divided in our society. To produce empirical evidence apparently supporting the notion of divisions of ability or performance on the basis of sex merely perpetuates the divide.

The iniquitous implications of this are illustrated most clearly in the research literature associated with the menstrual cycle, which has passed into popular discourse as 'fact', yet is as insubstantial and unfounded as many of the other fictions about women. As the literature on menstrual cycle performance variability epitomizes the methodological and theoretical difficulties inherent in all sex differences research, it deserves detailed examination here, and can serve as a case in point.

MENSTRUATION: THE WANDERING WOMB RESURRECTED IN SCIENTIFIC DISCOURSE

Menstruation and behaviour

> The headline on the *New York Times* reads 'Female Sex Hormone Tied to Ability to Perform Tasks' (Blakeslee, 1988)... My local paper announced 'Sex Hormones, Women's Thinking Linked in Study' (Maugh, 1988). The sex hormones in question were those that fluctuate with the mentrual cycle, and the conclusion was based on a study of women's performance across the menstrual cycle. (Sommer, 1991)

The nineteenth century belief in woman's fallibility and weakness centred around the body and reproduction (see Ussher, 1989), as argued above. The wandering womb, menstruation and pregnancy were deemed to mark women as weak and labile, and in need of care not strenuous work (unless they were of the lower classes, when reproduction seemingly had no effect). This discourse continued into the twentieth century, as in both popular and scientific discourse menstruation is believed to affect detrimentally work and examination ability (Dalton, 1969a), mood (Moos, 1969), athletic ability (Ederli, 1968), potential for accidents (Lees, 1965; Dalton, 1960), admissions to psychiatric hospital (Luggin *et al.*, 1984), ability to look after one's child (Tuch, 1975; Shreeve, 1984), and result in increases in violent behaviour (Morton *et al.*, 1953) and suicide (Mandell and Mandell, 1967).

Yet there is much controversy over the validity of the claims for *any* reliable menstrual cycle effects in women's behaviour (see Laws, 1990; Ussher, 1989, 1992b; Richardson, 1991c), as many of the claims of a menstrual cycle effect are based on single unreplicated studies (i.e. Dalton, 1969b) which have been severely criticized (Parlee, 1973; Sommer, 1991; Ussher, 1991b), and evidence for an *absence* of a menstrual cycle influence on behaviours such as accidents or violence is strong (Nicolson, 1992; Ussher, 1989). However, it is the question of menstrual cycle effects on performance which has been at the centre of the vast body of empirical research – and where the conclusions are the most unequivocal, and of most interest here.

Menstruation and performance

The interest in menstrual cycle effects on performance is not new. Yet from one of the first empirical studies carried out in 1914 (Hollingsworth, 1914) to recent reviews of the literature (Sommer, 1983, 1991) the findings are clear: there is no consistent effect of menstruation on women's performance. Yet, despite this, researchers continue to point to menstrual cycle variations as explanations for generalized sex differences in performance (i.e. Hines, 1982; Waber, 1979).

One of the problems in this area is that cyclical change is found only on single tests or subtests (Slade and Jenner, 1980; Asso, 1986; Sommer, 1983, 1991; Richardson, 1991c; Ussher and Wilding, 1991). Thus there are reports of premenstrual performance decrement on subtests such as perceptual motor tasks (Hampson and Kimura, 1988, Hudgens *et al.*, 1988; Jensen, 1982; Klaiber *et al.*, 1974; Zimmerman and Parlee, 1973), or reaction time (Engel and Hildebrandt, 1974; Garrett and Elder, 1984; Landauer, 1974; Hunter *et al.*, 1979) or on particular aspects of performance tasks. For example, Becker *et al.* (1982) reported improved performance in addition on arithmetic tests in the follicular phase of the cycle, but only when the task demanded immediate memory. Cycle variation in numerical addition, but not subtraction, were reported by Graham (1980), with performance reportedly improving premenstrually. Improved cognitive processing on a task requiring work matching was reported by Ussher and Wilding (1991), and Hampson (1986) reported improvements in speech articulation in the second half of the cycle.

To balance this there are a number of studies which report no cyclical change in a range of performance tasks (Golub, 1976; Baisden and Gibson, 1975; Hunter *et al.*, 1979; Loukes and Thompson, 1968; Kopell *et al.*, 1969; Pierson and Lockhart, 1963; Ussher and Wilding, 1991).

Yet even though there is little evidence for any performance variation across the cycle, it is still possible for the author of a 'self-help' book on women to declare:

> It is an indisputable, if regrettable, fact that if you suffer from the premenstrual syndrome, you are likely to work less efficiently for a few days each month, and that your poorer powers of concentration and reduced memory ability will inevitably affect your overall efficiency. (Shreeve, 1984, p. 78)

As 95 per cent of women are deemed to suffer from PMS (Ussher, 1989), is this not merely part of the same discourse as that which warned nineteenth century women to 'rest the mind and take extra hours of rest and sleep' during the menstrual phase of the cycle? The function of the discourse is the same, women are encouraged not to work for they are incapable of such exertions because of their biology.

Menstrual cycle performance research is only one example of an area of empirical research wherein the discourse of the debilitated woman, at the mercy of her biology, has not been borne out by the positivists' enquiries. Sommer (1991) concludes that what needs to be explained is not why or how menstruation affects performance, but rather why is there a continuation of the belief in the debilitating effects of menstruation. The answer is simple. The discourse of female weakness serves to maintain the position of women outside the realms of power, to maintain woman's position as Other. It serves to persuade women that their performance is not up to the stresses and strains of the marketplace: that their place is in the home. The psychological research on sex differences, on menstrual cycle performance variations, may *seem* to be objective rational and clear, but it is not. Conclusions are based on spurious and often methodologically weak studies, supporting dominant discourses of sexual inequality, rather than being based on objective value free science, as their proponents would insist.

Deconstructing the discourse of female performance debilitation

Many of the problems inherent within the field of menstrual cycle research are also those which beset the field of sex differences research in general. We turn now to look at some of these methodological inadequacies.

SPURIOUS METHODOLOGY

The research which is published, and reported time and time again, is often based on dubious methodology, such as the reporting of Whitehead in 1934 that women pilots were more likely to crash premenstrually, based merely on a police report which found that six women had crashes when they were *said* to be menstruating (Parlee, 1973). Dalton's oft-quoted finding that schoolgirls are likely to fail examinations during particular phases of the menstrual cycle has also been criticized for its methodology and the absence of statistical analysis of the results (Parlee, 1989; Sommer, 1983).

One of the major problems is that the research which examines the question of sex differences has been what Unger termed 'scattered and disorganised... as "Sex" effects may be related tangentially to every conceivable psychological phenomenon, but they are found tacked onto investigations of other "major" variables' (1979, p. 82). This is epitomized by the 'accidental tourist' (Ussher, 1991a) in menstrual cycle research who adds in menstruation as a variable in experiments almost as an afterthought. The converse to adding 'sex' as a variable is to ignore it altogether and to concentrate on male subjects, as many psychologists have chosen to do. Thus considerations of sex and gender may be omitted from the design of the original experiment, overlooked in the data analysis, or eliminated from the final article (Richardson, 1991b, p. 5), producing a body of findings which is based on male subjects.

PUBLICATION BIAS

There is a clear publication bias in the research, as it is nigh on impossible to publish research results which show *no* significant difference as only five per cent of published papers are of statistically non-significant results (Smart, 1963). The research which shows *no* sex difference suffers from the 'file drawer problem' (Rosenthal, 1979), and thus in the eyes of the academic research community does not exist. Yet the spurious results, which may often be chance, and which cannot be replicated, remain part of the research literature (Eichler, 1988) and thus form the 'truths' about sex differences in performance. There is no research literature on gender *similarities*, but rather a patchy and atheoretical literature on sex differences. As Unger points out:

> Examination of sex differences obscures the examination of sex similarities. In fact the sexes are similar in far more ways than they are different, but this is not considered startling psychological news. (Unger, 1979, p. 83)

If psychology considers only statistically significant results as 'findings' worthy of publication, it will continue to develop in the narrow and limited framework in which it is currently confined. In the area of menstrual cycle research, or sex differences research in general, *no* difference is certainly an important 'finding'.

SCIENTIFIC BIASES

Of equal importance is the fact that research findings which support the dominant discourse, the current *zeitgeist* in any field, are more likely to be accepted for publication in scientific journals (Mahoney, 1979; Kitzinger, 1990). Therefore, research showing no sex differences in performance, if it is not rejected on the grounds of statistically non-significant (but not insignificant) results, may be rejected because it contradicts current theories and established scientific discourses.

Equally, the values of the researchers may have a significant effect on both their research design, their methodology and the interpretations they make from their data. To take the case of the menstrual cycle researcher (see Ussher,

1991b), the liberal feminist striving to demonstrate an absence of sex differences may view the research literature as only evidencing spurious findings of menstrual cycle performance variability, which may be chance, and which serve to perpetuate women's oppression. The biological reductionist may seize on the few significant findings and offer them as evidence for a hormonal substrate underying women's behaviour. Both are looking at the same literature, their conclusions are very different.

The gender of the researcher may in many cases influence their position in this debate. Women are still over-represented at the lower ends of the scientific professions, including psychology (Nicolson, 1992), and under-represented at the top (Keller, 1985). Women are in the minority as journal editors and thus as academic gatekeepers (Over, 1981). Is it a coincidence that research demonstrating the frailty of the findings of sex difference research, or questioning the assumptions made by these researchers is rarely part of the psychological agenda, but that the studies which claim to demonstrate sex differences are regularly published and thus part of the official discourse?

RELEVANCE OF RESEARCH

Much of the work on sex differences in performance has little relevance outside of the naive empiricists' papers through which it is promulgated. To take the example of menstrual cycle research again, even if menstrual cycle effects can be demonstrated in performance measures such as reaction time, or visual acuity (ie, Dye, 1991; Parlee, 1983), the relevance of this to women's behaviour, work or general well-being is questionable. Menstrual cycle effects on *any* aspect of behaviour are so slight as to be undetectable in the majority of cases, and as there are so many individual differences between women (and men) that to talk of generalized menstrual cycle effects on performance becomes a nonsense. The same argument applies to sex differences research in general: men and women are not homogeneous groups, easily categorized as different, and sex (or gender) is not a category which cuts across all others in importance in the sphere of performance. For as Unger argues:

> Even on a given trait males and females form two overlapping distributions, with a minority of people of either sex at the extremes. It might be more valuable for the understanding of psychological processes to examine the individuals who are high or low on a particular trait within a sex rather than looking at trait differences between groups. (1979, p. 83)

It is interesting that the mass of research showing *no* sex difference in performance tends to be dismissed by many of those reviewing the literature (see the chapters in Baker, 1986). Are these authors aware of their selective interpretation of the research literature, and the fact that they are echoing the comments of their nineteenth century predecessors when they assert that women are not as able, or are labile?

CONCLUSION

The fiction of sex differences

Despite persistent and pejorative stereotypes, there appears to be no consistent difference between men and women in the main spheres of performance. Researchers have examined sensory functioning, aspects of cognitive ability, including learning and memory, spatial ability, and mathematical achievement, and failed to provide conclusive evidence for the existence of sex differences. Any differences which do exist are small and not a uniform effect, with greater differences within groups of women and men than between them. Sex differences in areas such as mathematical or scientific achievement may be explained by artefacts of experimental situations, questionable methodology, or the effects of the pervasive positioning of woman outside these spheres of opportunity. There is only spurious evidence for a basic biological substrate underlying performance: theories of hemispherical differences or of the effect of menstruation on performance have little basis in reality, serving only to perpetuate the belief in women's biological inferiority. The differences in physical size and strength between men and women may have advantaged the cave man, but they will only be a disadvantage for women in a world physically designed for men – a situation which ergonomists have long been able to overcome.

ACHIEVEMENT

Sex differences in certain aspects of achievement undoubtedly do exist – the EOC statistics clearly demonstrate this. There are clear sex differences in the position of men and women in terms of access to wealth, power and privilege. This may suggest that women fail; that they do not have the same ability; that their unequal position is natural and right. Or it may suggest that it is the misogynistic discourse which continues to position women outside of the world of power and prestige, and that the rhetoric associated with the field of sex differences in performance serves only to maintain that position, presenting fictions and fantasies as facts.

HISTORICAL PRECEDENTS

The discourse of women's inferiority in the field of performance has a genealogy that can been traced back for centuries, for although I have chosen to start with the nineteenth century experts, women have been marked as Other through the supposed existence of sex difference in performance and ability since the time of the ancient Greeks when Plato declared that the womb travelled about the body and produced women's monthly madness

(Veith, 1964). To focus on sex differences in performance today is to perpetuate this same discourse, even if we reify our pronouncements through the guise of rational science and pseudo-objectivity.

THE POWER OF DISCURSIVE PRACTICES

The discourse of sex differences in performance can be related to other powerful discursive practices, such as that of woman as mad (see Ussher, 1991a), woman as sexually dangerous (Foucault, 1979), or lesbians as 'sick' (Kitzinger, 1987). These discourses impart knowledge and thus power to those who promulgate them, maintaining the position of those outside of the sphere of knowledge as powerless. We should not be focusing on which sex differences in performance exist, but look at the question of why is this question deemed important. Do any demonstrated differences explain women's lack of achievement, or do they merely move attention away from the reality of the problem which is an inequality in opportunity, a continuous denigration of the female, and the impossibility of women entering bastions of male power and prestige.

It is no coincidence that women are positioned as Other: this serves the interests of the One, men. If women believe that they cannot perform at the same level as men, a belief perpetuated by current sex difference research, they will not challenge their position and will remain on the outside. It is time for an end to naive empiricism. It is a time for an end to atheoretical, simplistic assumptions which do not serve either women or men, but only the researchers whose publications record increases as a consequence. There is no truth in the majority of the 'facts' of sex differences research: it is fiction, fantasy, fable. Only when we acknowledge this can we move forwards.

THE FUTURE

In 1991, following other developed countries, the first British person was sent into space. Out of possible thousands this person was a woman. She may have been an exception, in the way that the former British Prime Minister, Margaret Thatcher was often positioned as an exception. Or she may present clear irrefutable evidence of the fact that at the most demanding level of performance, after arduous and painful trials and training, gender or sex are irrelevant.

Whether we view these two women as evidence of woman's ability to achieve as much (or more) than man, or as an unholy exception to the rule, depends on the discourse to which we adhere. As with all questions of sex and performance, there can be no rational, objective and unbiased reading of the evidence: the stakes to be played for are too high, the implications of the different conclusions too far-reaching. Those who pronounce calmly and confidently on the reality of sex differences in performance, whether they be nineteenth century experts or twentieth century empiricists, do so with the acknowledgement that theirs is only one voice maintaining the discursive practices which control women and empower men. It is in this light that we should evaluate their words and their work.

Discourses of the past may have prejudicially positioned women as unequal and unable – creating a set of negative expectations which many women could do little but follow. Things are changing. There is clear evidence that those few (often negligible) sex differences in performance which were previously evident are disappearing (Feingold, 1988). Educators are being encouraged to recognize that boys and girls have different experiences which affect their learning, and that skills such as problem solving should be taught in schools so as not to disadvantage girls in important areas of schooling such as mathematics (Hyde *et al.*, 1990). Women are starting to enter professions and academic disciplines previously closed to them, and by the year 2000 will make up fifty per cent of the workforce in Britain at least (Firth-Cozens and West, 1991). By example women are challenging the negative assumptions. Disproving the notion that sex (womanhood) is a handicap. Those who are interested in the psychology of sex differences in performance should do the same.

REFERENCES

Alban-Metcalf, B. and West, M. (1991) Women managers. In *Women at Work: Psychological and Organizational Perspectives*, edited by J. Firth-Cozens and M. West. Milton Keynes: Open University Press.

Anderson, N.S. (1986) Cognition, learning and memory. In *Sex Differences in Human Performance*, edited by M.A. Baker. Chichester: Wiley, pp. 37–54.

Annett, M. (1980) Sex differences in laterality: meaningfulness versus reliability. *Behavioral and Brain Sciences* **3**: 227–8.

Asso, D. (1986) Psychology degree examinations and the premenstrual phase of the menstrual cycle. *Women and Health* **10**: 91–104.

Baisden, C. and Gibson, W. (1975) Effects of the menstrual cycle on the performance of complex perceptual psychomotor tasks. Paper presented at the 19th Annual Meeting of the Human Factors Society, Dallas, Texas.

Baker, H. (1986) *Sex Differences in Human Performance*. Wiley: London.

Barker-Benfield, G.J. (1976) *The Horrors of the Half Known Life: Male Attitudes towards Women and Sexuality in Nineteenth Century America*. New York: Harper and Row.

Becker, B.J. and Hedges, L.V. (1984) Meta-analysis of cognitive gender differences: a comment on an analysis by Rosenthal and Rubin. *Journal of Educational Psychology* **76**: 583–7.

Becker, D., Creutzfelt, O.D., Schwibbe, M. and Wuttke, W. (1982) Changes in physiological, EEG and psychological parameters in women during the spontaneous menstrual cycle and following oral contraceptives. *Psychoneuroendocrinology* **7**: 75–90.

Benbow, C.P. and Stanley, J.C. (1980) Sex differences in mathematical ability: fact or artifact? *Science, New York* **210**: 1262–4.

Benbow, C.P. and Stanley, J.C. (1983) Sex differences in mathematical reasoning ability: more facts. *Science, New York* **222**: 1029–31.

Berger, E.H., Royster, L.H. and Thomas, W.G. (1977) Hearing levels of non-industrial noise exposed subjects. *Journal of Occupational Medicine* **19**: 664–70.

Birkett, P. (1976) Sex differences and reasoning versus imagery strategies in the solution of visual and auditorily presented family relationship problems. *Bulletin of the Psychonomic Society* **8**: 139–42.

Blakeslee, S. (1988) Female sex hormone is tied to ability to perform tasks. *New York Times* 18 November, p. 16.

Blier, R. (1988) *Feminist Approaches to Science*. New York: Pergamon.

Blough, P.M. and Slavin, L.K. (1987) Reaction time assessments of gender differences in visual–spatial performance. *Perception and Psychophysics* **41**: 276–81.

Bouchard, T.J., Jr. and McGee, M.G. (1977) Sex differences in human spatial ability: not an X linked recessive gene effect. *Social Biology* **24**: 332–5.

Broverman, D.M., Vogel, W., Klaiber, E.L., Majcher, D., Shea, D. and Paul, V. (1981) Changes in cognitive task performance across the menstrual cycle. *Journal of Comparative and Physiological Psychology* **95**: 646–54.

Buffery, A.W.H. and Grey, J.A. (1972) Sex differences in the development of spatial and linguistic skills. In *Gender Differences: Their Ontogency and Significance*, edited by C. Ounsted and D.C. Taylor. Edinburgh: Churchill Livingstone, pp. 173–175.

Caplan, P.J., McPherson, G.M. and Tobin, P. (1985) Do sex related differences in spatial abilities exist? A multi-level critique with new data. *American Psychologist* **40**: 786–99.

Chiang, A. and Atkinson, R.C. (1976) Individual differences and interrelations among a select set of cognitive skills. *Memory and Learning* **4**: 661–72.

Colthart, M., Hull, E. and Slater, D. (1975) Sex differences in imagery and reading. *Nature, London* **253**: 438–40.

Cooper, L.A. and Regan, D.T. (1982) Attention, perception and intelligence. In *Handbook of Human Intelligence*, edited by R.J. Sternberg. New York: Cambridge University Press, pp. 123–69.

Corso, J.F. (1959) Age and sex differences in pure-tone thresholds: survey of hearing levels from 18–65 years. *Archives of Otolaryngology* **77**: 53–73.

Dalton, K. (1960) Menstruation and accidents. *British Medical Journal* **2**: 1425–6.

Dalton, K. (1969a) *The Menstrual Cycle*. Harmondsworth: Penguin.

Dalton, K. (1969b) Menstruation and examinations. *Lancet* **ii**: 1386–8.

Darwin, C. (1871) *The Descent of Man* (Reprint). Princeton University Press.

Dawson, J.L.M. (1972) Effects of sex hormones on cognitive style in rats and men. *Behavior Genetics* **2**: 21–42.

Deem, R. (1984) *Conflict and Change in Education: A Sociological Introduction.* Milton Keynes: Open University Press.

Durkin, K. (1986) Social cognition and social context in the construction of sex differences. In *Sex Differences in Human Performance*, edited by M.A. Baker. London: Wiley, pp. 142–70.

Dwyer, C.A. (1973) Children's sex role standards and sex role identification and their relationship to achievement. Doctoral dissertation, University of California, Berkeley.

Dye, L. (1991) Psychophysical measures of visual information processing. In *Cognition and the Menstrual Cycle*, edited by J.T.E. Richardson. New York: Erlbaum.

Easlea, B. (1986) The masculine image of science: how much does gender really matter? In *Perspectives on Gender and Science*, edited by J. Harding. Brighton: Falmer Press.

Eccles, J.S. (1987) Gender roles and women'a achievement-related decisions. *Psychology of Women Quarterly* **11**: 135–72.

Ederli, G. (1968) Gynaecological study of female athletes. *Journal of Sports and Medical Fitness* **2**: 174–9.

Eichler, M. (1988) *Non-sexist Research Methods*. Boston, Ma: Allen and Unwin.

Elliot, J. and Fralley, J.S. (1976) Sex differences in spatial abilities. *Young Children* **31**: 487–98.
Engel, P. and Hildebrandt, G. (1974) Rhythmic variations in reaction time, heart rate and blood pressure at different durations of the menstrual cycle. In *Biorhythms and Human Reproduction*, edited by M. Ferin, F. Halberg, R.M. Richart and R.L. Vande Wiele. New York: Wiley.
Epstein, Y.M. and Karlin, R.A. (1975) Effects of acute experimental crowding. *Journal of Applied Psychology* **5**: 34–53.
Ernest, C.H. (1983) Imagery and verbal ability and recognition memory for pictures and words in males and females. *Educational Psychology* **3**: 227–44.
Fairweather, H. (1976) Sex differences in cognition. *Cognition* **4**: 231–80.
Farrimond, T. (1967) Visual and auditory performance variation with age: some implications. *Australian Journal of Psychology* **19**: 193–201.
Fee, E. (1988) Critique of modern science: the relationship of feminism to other radical epistemologies. In *Feminist Approaches to Science*, edited by R. Blier. New York: Pergamon. pp. 42–56.
Feingold, A. (1988) Cognitive gender differences are disappearing. *American Psychologist* **43**: 95–103.
Fennema, E. (1974) Mathematics learning and the sexes. *Journal for Research in Mathematics Education* **5**: 126–9.
Fennema, E. and Carpenter, T.P. (1981) Sex related differences in mathematics: Results from the National Assessment. *Mathematics Teacher* **74**: 554–9.
Fennema, E. and Peterson, P. (1985) Autonomous learning behaviour a possible explanation of gender related differences in mathematics. In *Gender Influences in Class Room Interaction*, edited by L.S. Wilkinson and C.B. Marrett. New York: Academic Press, pp. 17–36.
Firth-Cozens, J. and West, M., eds (1991) *Women at Work: Psychological and Organizational Perspectives*. Milton Keynes: Open University Press.
Foucault, M. (1979) *A History of Sexuality: I.* London: Penguin.
Frodi, A., Macaulay, J. and Thome, P.R. (1977) Are women always less aggressive than men? *Psychological Bulletin* **84**: 634–60.
Gardener, A. (1872) in Barker-Benfield (1976) *op. cit.*
Gardner, H. (1985) *The New Mind's Science: A History of the Cognitive Revolution.* New York: Basic Books.
Garrett, K. and Elder, S. (1984) The menstrual cycle from a bio-behavioural approach: a comparison of oral contraceptive and non-oral contraceptive users. *International Journal of Psychophysiology* **1**: 209–14.
Golub, S. (1976) The effect of premenstrual anxiety and depression on cognitive function. *Journal of Personality and Social Psychology* **34**: 99–104.
Graham, E.A. (1980) Cognition as related to menstrual cycle phase and estrogen level. In *The Menstrual Cycle*, Vol. 1, edited by A.J. Dan, E.A. Graham and C.P. Beecher. New York: Springer.
Gralton, M.A., Hayes, Y.A. and Richardson, J.T.E. (1979) Introversion–extroversion and mental imagery. *Journal of Mental Imagery* **3**: 1–10.
Green, T. and Bell, P.A. (1986) Environmental stress. In *Sex Differences in Human Performance*, edited by M.A. Baker. London: Wiley, pp. 81–106.
Halpern, D.F. (1986) *Sex Differences in Cognitive Abilities.* Hillsdale, NJ.: Erlbaum.
Hampson, E. (1986) Variations in perceptual and motor performance related to the menstrual cycle. Paper presented at the meeting of the Canadian Psychological Association.
Hampson, E. and Kimura, D. (1988) Reciprocal effects of hormonal fluctuations on human motor and perceptual–spatial skills. *Behavioral Neuroscience* **102**: 456–9.
Hansard (1990) Hansard commission report. HMSO.
Harding, J. (1986a) *Perspectives on Gender and Science.* Brighton: Falmer Press.
Harding, S. (1986b) *The Science Question in Feminism.* Ithaca: Cornell University Press.
Harris, LJ. (1978) Sex differences in spatial ability: possible environmental, genetic and

neurobiological factors. In *Asymmetrical Function of the Brain*, edited by M. Kinsbourne. Cambridge University Press, pp. 405–552.

Harris, L.J. (1981) Sex related variations in spatial skills. In *Spatial Representation and Behaviour across the Lifespan: Theory and Application*, edited by L.S. Liben, A.H. Patterson and N. Newcombe. New York and London: Academic Press, pp. 83–125.

Harshman, R.A., Hampson, E. and Berenbaum. S.A. (1983) Individual differences in cognitive abilities and brain organization. Part 1: Sex and handedness differences in ability. *Canadian Journal of Psychology* **37**: 144–92.

Henriques, J., Holloway, W., Urwin, C., Venn, C. and Walkerdine, V. (1984) Changing the subject: psychology, social regulation and subjectivity. London and New York: Methuen.

Hines, M. (1982) Prenatal gonadal hormones and sex differences in human behaviour. *Psychological Bulletin* **92**: 56–80.

Hirsch, M.J. (1963) The refraction of children. In *Vision in Children: An Optometric Symposium*, edited by J. Hirsch and E.R. Wicks. Philadelphia: Chiltern Books.

Hollingsworth, L.S. (1914) *Functional Periodicity: An Experimental Study of the Mental and Motor Abilities of Women during Menstruation.* Columbia University Contributers to Education, Teachers College Series, No. 69.

Hudgens, G., Fatkin, L., Billingsley, P. and Mazurczak, J. (1988) Effects of sex, menstrual phase, oral contraceptives, practice, and handgun weight. *Human Factors* **30**: 51–60.

Hunter, S., Schraer, R., Landers, D.M., Buskirk, E. and Harris, D.V. (1979) The effects of total oestrogen concentration and menstrual cycle phase on reaction time performance. *Ergonomics* **22**: 263–8.

Hyde, J.S. (1984) How large are gender differences in aggression? A developmental meta-analysis. *Developmental Psychology* **20**: 722–36.

Hyde, J.S., Fennema, E. and Lamon, S.J. (1990) Gender differences in mathematical performance: a meta-analysis. *Psychological Bulletin* **107**: 139–55.

Jacklin, CN. (1981) Methodological issues in the study of sex related differences. *Developmental Review* **1**: 266–273.

Jensen, B. (1982) Menstrual cycle effects on task performance examined in the context of stress research. *Acta Psychologia* **50**: 159–78.

Jordanova, L.J. (1989) *Sexual Visions: Images of Gender in Science and Medicine between the Eighteenth and Twentieth century*. Brighton: Harvester Wheatsheaf.

Kail, R., Carter, P. and Pelligrino, J. (1979) The locus of sex differences in spatial ability. *Perception and Psychophysics* **26**: 182–6.

Keller, E.F. (1985) *Reflections on Gender and Science*. London: Vale University Press.

Kimball, M.M. (1989) A new perspective on women's maths achievement. *Psychological Bulletin* **105**: 198–214.

Kinsbourne, M. (1980) If sex differences in brain lateralization exist, they have yet to be discovered. *Behavioral and Brain Sciences* **3**: 241–42.

Kitzinger, C. (1987) *The Social Constructions of Lesbianism.* London: Sage.

Kitzinger, C. (1990) The rhetoric of pseudo-science. In *Deconstructing Social Psychology*, edited by I. Parker and J. Shotter. London: Routledge, pp. 61–75.

Klaiber, E., Broverman, D., Vogel, W. and Kobayashi, Y. (1974) Rhythms in plasma MAO activity, EEG, and behaviour during the menstrual cycle. In *Bioryhthms and Human Reproduction*, edited by M. Ferin, F. Halberg, R. Richart, and R. Vande Wiele. New York: Wiley.

Kopell, B., Lunde, D., Clayton, R., Moos, R. and Hamburg, D. (1969) Variations in some measures of arousal during the menstrual cycle. *Journal of Nervous and Mental Disorders* **148**: 180–7.

Landauer, A.A. (1974). Choice decision time and the menstrual cycle. *Practitioner* **213**: 703–6

Laws, S. (1990) *Issues of Blood.* London: Macmillan.

Lees, P. (1965) *The Vulnerability to Trauma of Women in Relation to Periodic Stress.* The Medical Commission on Accident Prevention, second annual report (abstract).

Levitt, L. and Leventhal, G. (1978) The effects of density and environmental noise on perception of time, the situation, onself, and others. *Perceptial and Motor Skills* **47**: 999–1009.
Linn, M.C. and Petersen, A.C. (1985) Emergence and characterisation of sex differences in spatial ability: a meta-analysis. *Child Development* **56**: 1479–98.
Longstreth, L.E and Madigan, S. (1982) Sex differences in the correlation of memory span with scan and other episodic memory tasks. *Intelligence* **6**: 37–56.
Loukes, J. and Thompson, H. (1968) Effect of menstruation on reaction time. *Research Quarterly* **39**: 407–8.
Luggin, R., Bensted, L., Petersson, B. and Jacobsen, A. (1984) Acute psychiatric admission related to the menstrual cycle. *Acta Psychiatrica Scandanavica* **69**: 461–5.
Maccoby, E.E. and Jacklin, C.N. (1974) *The Psychology of Sex Differences*. Stanford, Ca.: Stanford University Press.
MacLeod, C.M. (1979) Individual differences in learning and memory: a unitary information processing approach. *Journal of Research in Personality* **13**: 530–45.
Mahoney, M.J. (1979) Psychology of the scientist: an evaluative review. *Social Studies of Science* **9**: 349–75.
Mandell, J. and Mandell, M.P. (1967) Suicide and the menstrual cycle. *Journal of the American Medical Association* **200**: 792–3.
Marks, D.F. (1973) Visual imagery differences in recall of pictures. *British Journal of Psychology* **64**: 17–24.
Marshall, S.P. (1984) Sex differences in children's mathematics achievements: solving computations and story problems. *Journal of Educational Psychology* **76**: 194–204.
Maugh, T.H. II (1988) Sex hormones, women's thinking linked in study. *Sacremento Bee*, 17 November, p. 12.
McGee, MG. (1979) Human spatial abilities: psychometric studies and environmental, genetic, hormonal, and neurological influences. *Psychological Bulletin* **86**: 889–918.
McGlone, J. (1980) Sex differences in human brain asymmetry: a critical survey. *Behavioral and Brain Sciences* **3**: 215–63.
McGuiness, D. and Maclaughlin, L. (1982) An investigation of sex differences in visual recognition and recall. *Journal of Mental Imagery* **6**: 203–12.
McKeever, W.F. and Deyo, RA. (1990) Testosterone, dihydrotestosterone, and spatial task performance in males. *Bulletin of the Psychonomic Society* **28**: 305–8.
Moos, R.H. (1969) Typology of menstrual cycle symptoms. *American Journal of Obstetrics and Gynaecology* **103**: 390–402.
Morgan, F. (1989) *A Misogynist's Source Book*. London: Jonathan Cape.
Morton, J., Additon, H., Addison, R., Hunt, L. and Sullivan, J.J. (1953) A clinical study of premenstrual tension. *American Journal of Obstetrics and Gynaecology* **65**: 1182–91.
Newcombe, F. and Ratcliffe, G. (1978) The female brain: a neuropsychological viewpoint. In *Defining Females*, edited by S. Ardener. London: Croom Helm.
Newcombe, N., Bandura, M.M. and Taylor, D.G. (1983) Sex differences in spatial ability and spatial activities. *Sex Roles* **9**: 377–86.
Nicolson, P. (1992) Gender issues the organisation of clinical psychology. In *Gender Issues in Clinical Psychology*, edited by J.M. Ussher and P. Nicolson. London: Routledge.
Noble, C.E. (1978) Age, race and sex in learning and performance of psychomotor skills. In *Human Variation: The Biopsychology of Age, Race and Sex*, edited by R.T. Osborne, C.E. Noble and N. Weyle. New York and London: Academic Press, pp. 287–378.
Nyborg, H. (1983) Spatial abilities in men and women: review and new theory. *Advances in Behavioural Research and Therapy* **5**: 89–140.
Over, R. (1981) Representation of women on the editorial boards of psychology journals. *American Psychologist* **36**: 885–91.
Parlee, M.B. (1973) The premenstrual syndrome. *Psychological Bulletin* **80**: 454–65.
Parlee, M. (1983) Menstrual rhythms in sensory processes: a review of fluctuations in vision, olfaction, audition, taste and touch. *Psychological Bulletin* **93**: 539–48.

Parlee, M. (1989) The science and politics of PMS research. Paper presented at the Association for Women in Psychology Annual Research Conference, Newport, Rhode Island, 10–12 March.

Perival, L. and Quinkert, K. (1986) Anthropomorphic factors. In *Sex Differences in Human Performance*, edited by M.A. Baker. London: Wiley, pp. 121–39.

Pierson, W.R. and Lockhart, A. (1963) Effect of menstruation on simple reaction time and movement time. *British Medical Journal* **1**: 796–7.

Redgrove, J. (1986) Applied settings. In *Sex Differences in Human Performance*, edited by M.A. Baker. London: Wiley, pp. 171–86.

Richardson, J.T.E. (1982) Introversion–extroversion and experimenter effects on memory tasks. *Personality and Individual Differences* **3**: 327–8.

Richardson, J.T.E. (1991a) Paramenstrual symptomatology. In *Cognition and the Menstrual Cycle*, edited by J.T.E. Richardson. London: Erlbaum.

Richardson, J.T.E. (1991b) Gender differences in imagery, cognition, and memory. In *Mental Images in Human Cognition*, edited by R. Logie and M. Denis. Amsterdam: Elsevier.

Richardson, J.T.E. (1991c) Learning, memory and the menstrual cycle. In *Cognition and the Menstrual Cycle*, edited by J.T.E. Richardson. London: Erlbaum.

Roberts, J. (1968) *Monocular–Binocular Visual Acuity of Adults: United States 1960–1962.* Public Health Service Publication, Vital and Health Statistics, Series 11, No. 3, US Government Printing Office, Washington, DC.

Roche, A.F., Siervogel, R.M. and Hines, J.H. (1978) Longitudinal study of hearing in children: baseline data concerning auditory thresholds, noise exposure, and biological factors. *Journal of Acoustical Society of America* **64**: 1593–601.

Rosenthal, R. (1976) *Experimenter Effects in Behavioural Research.* New York: Irvington.

Rosenthal, R. (1979) The 'file drawer problem' and tolerance for null results. *Psychological Bulletin* **86**: 638–40.

Sanders, B., Soares, M.P. and D'Aquila, J.M. (1982) The sex difference on one test of SV: a nontrivial difference. *Child Development* **53**: 1106–10.

Sayers, J. (1982) *Biological Politics: Feminist and Anti-Feminist Perspectives.* London: Tavistock.

Scott Hall, W. (1916) *Sexual Knowledge.* Philadelphia: Winston.

Sells, L.W. (1973) High school mathematics as the critical filter in the job market. In *Developing Opportunities for Minorities in Graduate Education*, edited by R.T. Thomas. Berkeley: University of California Press, pp. 37–9.

Shepard, R.N and Metzler, J. (1971) Mental rotation of three-dimensional objects. *Science, New York* **171**: 701–3.

Sherman, J. (1977) Effects of biological factors on sex-related differences in mathematics achievement. In *Women and Mathematics: Research Perspectives for Change*, edited by L.H. Fox, E. Fennema and J. Sherman. Washington: National Institute for Education.

Sherman, J.A. (1978) *Sex-related Cognitive Differences: An Essay on Theory and Evidence.* Springfield, Il.: Thomas.

Shreeve, C. (1984) *The Premenstrual Syndrome.* Wellingborough: Thorsons.

Slade, P. and Jenner, F.A. (1980) Performance tests in different phases of the menstrual cycle. *Journal of Psychosomatic Research* **24**: 5–8.

Smart, R. (1963) The importance of negative results in psychological research. *The Canadian Psychologist* **5**: 225–32.

Sommer, B. (1983) How does menstruation affect cognitive competence and physiological response? *Women and Health* **8**: 53–90.

Sommer, B. (1991) Cognitive performance and the menstrual cycle. In *Cognition and the Menstrual Cycle*, edited by J.T.E. Richardson. London: Erlbaum.

Spencer, H. (1983) Psychology of the senses. *Popular Science Monthly* **4**: 30–8.

Stafford, R.E. (1961) Sex differences in spatial visualization as evidence of sex-linked inheritance. *Perceptual and Motor Skills* **13**: 428.

Stage, E.K., Kreinberg, N., Eccles, J.R. and Becker, J.R. (1985) Increasing the participation and achievement of girls and women in mathematics, science, and engineering. In *Handbook for achieving Sex Equity through Education*, edited by S.S. Klein. Baltimore: Johns Hopkins University Press, pp. 237–69.

Stokols, D., Rall, M. and Schopler, J. (1973) *Environment and Behavior* **5**: 87–115.

Thomas, W.I. (1897) On a difference in the metabolism of the sexes. *American Journal of Sociology* **3**: 31–63.

Topinard, P. (1894) *Anthropology* (translated by R.T.H. Bartley). London: Chapman and Hall.

Tuch, R. (1975) The relationship between a mother's menstrual status and her response to illness in her child. *Psychosomatic Medicine* **37**: 388–94.

Unger, R.K. (1979) *Female and Male: Psychological Perspectives*. New York: Harper and Row.

Ussher, J.M. (1989) *The Psychology of the Female Body*. London: Routledge..

Ussher, J.M. (1991a) *Women's Madness: Misogyny or Mental Illness?* Hemel Hempstead: Harvester Wheatsheaf.

Ussher, J. M. (1991b) The demise of dissent and the rise of cognition in menstrual cycle research. In *Cognition and the Menstrual Cycle*, edited by J.T.E. Richardson. London: Erlbaum.

Ussher, J.M. (1992a) Science sexing psychology. In *Gender Issues in Clinical Psychology*, edited by J. Ussher and P. Nicolson. London: Routledge.

Ussher, J.M. (1992b) Reproductive rhetoric and the blaming of the body. In *The Psychology of Women's Health and Health Care*, edited by P. Nicolson and J.M. Ussher. London: Macmillan.

Ussher, J.M. and Wilding, J. (1991) Performance and state changes during the menstrual cycle, conceptualised within broad band testing framework. *Social Science and Medicine* **32**: 535–43.

Vandenberg, S.G. and Kuse, A.R. (1978) Mental rotations: a group test of three-dimensional spatial visualization. *Perceptual and Motor Skills* **47**: 599–604.

Veith, I. (1964) *Hysteria: The History of a Disease*. University of Chicago Press.

Waber, D.P. (1979) Cognitive abilities and sex related variations on the maturation of cerebral cortical functions. In *Sex Related Issues in Cognitive Functioning: Developmental Issues*, edited by M.A. Wittig and A.C. Petersen. New York and London: Academic Press.

Walden, R. and Walkerdine, V. (1983) *Girls and Mathematics: From Primary to Secondary Schooling*. London: Heinemann.

Walkerdine, V. (1990) *Schoolgirl Fictions*. London: Virago.

Wardle, M.G., Gloss, M.R. and Gloss III, D.S. (1986) Response differences. In *Sex Differences in Human Performance*, edited by M.A. Baker. London: Wiley.

Weinreich-Haste, H. (1979) What sex is science? In *Sex Role Stereotyping*, edited by O. Hartnett, G. Boden and M. Fuller. London: Tavistock.

Whitehead, R. (1934) Women pilots. *Journal of Aviation Medicine* **5**: 47–9.

Wilson, E. (1975) Human decency is animal. *New York Times Magazine*, 12 October.

Wittig, M.A. and Peterson, A.C. (eds) (1979) *Sex Related Issues in Cognitive Functioning: Developmental Issues*. New York and London: Academic Press.

Wolff, P.H. (1980) A difference that may make no difference. *Behavioural and Brain Sciences* **3**: 250–1.

Zimmerman, E. and Parlee, M. (1973) Behavioural changes associated with the menstrual cycle: an experimental investigation. *Journal of Applied Social Psychology* **3**: 335–44.

4

Extraversion

G. MATTHEWS

One of the most salient aspects of individual differences in personality is the person's level of extraversion or introversion, associated with qualities such as sociability, impulsiveness, assertiveness and vivacity. The existence of a trait of extraversion is strongly supported psychometrically by many independent factor analyses of various kinds of personality data (Eysenck and Eysenck, 1985; Matthews, 1989a). There is a growing consensus that extraversion is one of the replicable 'big five' personality factors (Brand, 1984; McCrae and Costa, 1987). Extraversion scales typically show moderate or high stability over many years (Costa *et al.*, 1983).

Extraversion has been shown to correlate with a number of aspects of performance. Superficially, it is surprising that extraversion scales, which typically rely heavily on self-reports of social attitudes and behaviours, should predict performance of simple laboratory tasks such as short-term memory (STM) and vigilance. One possibility is that it is not so much extraversion which predicts task performance but impulsivity, a narrower trait correlated with extraversion (Revelle *et al.*, 1980). Alternatively, individual differences in social behaviour are just one manifestation of a more general quality of the person. The first aim for the cognitive psychologist is to describe this quality in contemporary, information processing terminology. A second aim is to determine the causal influences on individual differences in performance associated with extraversion.

Empirical work on extraversion and performance falls into three areas. Firstly, simple performance correlates of extraversion may be determined across a range of tasks. Work of this kind corresponds to what Hockey and Hamilton (1983) term broad-band stress research, which aims to construct a detailed picture of the cognitive state or patterning of performance associated

HANDBOOK OF HUMAN PERFORMANCE
VOLUME 3 ISBN 0-12-650353-2

with extraversion. The prediction and explanation of this cognitive patterning is an important test for any theory of extraversion. A second area of research is driven by the hypothesis that individual differences in extraversion are associated with individual differences in arousal (Eysenck and Eysenck, 1985). Since arousal–performance relationships are often considered to be non-linear, it is expected that extraversion and stressors such as caffeine or noise should have interactive effects on performance. There is a sizeable body of research on extraversion × stressor interactions: in general, extraverts tend to perform better under stress than introverts (Eysenck and Eysenck, 1985). A third research area is driven by the proposal that extraversion is correlated with sensitivity to signals of reward and punishment (Gray, 1981). A number of empirical studies show that extraversion effects on performance are indeed affected by appropriate stimuli.

The theoretical challenge of research on extraversion and performance is the range of psychological functions sensitive to the personality dimension, including perception, attention, memory, higher cognitive functions and motor processes (Eysenck and Eysenck, 1985). A satisfactory theory must explain why extraversion affects this diversity of tasks. In some respects, contemporary cognitive psychology, with its emphasis on specific, discrete processes is not ideally suited to the description of individual differences in quite global properties of the mind affecting tasks with little in common superficially. Perhaps for this reason, theories of extraversion and performance are predominantly psycho-biological: individual differences in performance are said to reflect individual differences in brain functioning. In particular, extraversion has often been linked to arousal or arousability (Eysenck, 1967). The advantage of this approach is that it allows for integration of both behavioural and psycho-physiological data on extraversion. There is extensive evidence relating extraversion to indices of autonomic and central nervous system activity or excitability (Stelmack, 1981). Even some very simple aspects of neural activity, such as speed of axonal or synaptic transmission in the peripheral nervous system may be linked to extraversion, as evidenced by correlations between extraversion and auditory brainstem evoked potentials (Stelmack, 1990). Application of psycho-biological theories to performance data is problematic, though. Such theories frequently tend to jump from the neural to the behavioural level of description, without specifying extraversion effects at the intermediate cognitive level. Brain processes are linked to performance by naive concepts such as the overall efficiency or excitation of the brain. Psycho-biological theories also raise difficult causal questions. It is unsafe to assume that neural processes which are empirically correlated with extraversion play any direct role in effects of extraversion on performance, particularly as psycho-physiological and performance data tend to be collected under rather different laboratory conditions. It is conceivable, for example, that if extraversion has a genetic component, the genes concerned independently affect neural and cognitive functioning. Thus, in assessing psycho-biological theories, we must consider both their success in predicting the performance correlates of extraversion, and the individual differences in information processing responsible for those correlates.

Structure of the chapter

This chapter has two aims: to review the effects of extraversion on the processing of information, and to assess the success of psycho-biological and cognitive theories in explaining these effects. There are several detailed reviews of performance correlates of extraversion which cover research up to the early 1980s, such as those of Eysenck and Eysenck (1985), Eysenck (1976, 1981) and Davies and Parasuraman (1982). The approach of the present chapter is to use these reviews to summarize much of the earlier empirical work, updated with more detailed accounts of more recent studies. The next section of this chapter outlines the main psycho-biological (Eysenck, 1967) and cognitive (Humphreys and Revelle, 1984) theories of the performance correlates of extraversion. Next, each of the three areas of empirical research described previously is reviewed, with the aim of describing the cognitive patterning of the empirical effects of extraversion, and of evaluating the success of the main theories in accounting for these effects. Lastly, some general conclusions are outlined.

THEORIES OF EXTRAVERSION

Arousal theory

The most detailed and influential approach to extraversion is Eysenck's (1967; Eysenck and Eysenck, 1985) arousal theory of extraversion. According to Eysenck, extraversion is determined most strongly by genetic factors, with within-family environmental factors also playing an important role. These genetic and environmental influences control extraversion via a neural circuit, a feedback loop connecting the cortex to the ascending reticular activating system (ARAS). This 'reticulo-cortical loop' is said to regulate the level of arousal of the cortex, and hence the general efficiency of information processing. This circuit is claimed to be less arousable in extraverts, so that, by and large, extraverts will be lower in tonic cortical arousal than introverts. The Eysenck theory then proposes two links between individual differences in cortical arousal and performance. Firstly, arousal and performance are *directly* linked by the Yerkes–Dodson law, the hypothesis that the regression of performance on arousal is described by an inverted U (see Mueller, this volume). In addition, the optimal level of arousal for performance decreases as task difficulty increases. Thus, extraversion will combine with other endogenous and environmental influences to affect the person's state of cortical arousal, which in turn will affect performance. Two main predictions follow from the Yerkes–Dodson law. Firstly, extraverts should tend to perform better than introverts in highly arousing conditions because they are less prone to over-arousal, and they should perform worse than introverts in de-arousing conditions because they are more susceptible to under-arousal relative to optimal arousal level for performance. Secondly, extraversion should interact with task difficulty, such that extraverts perform relatively better on more difficult tasks, and relatively worse on easier tasks, compared to introverts. Both hypotheses receive a degree of empirical support (Eysenck and Eysenck, 1985).

The second, *indirect* link between arousal and performance is derived from a further hypothesis: that there is an inverted U relationship between arousal and subjective hedonic tone (Eysenck, 1967). (There is no particular relationship between optimal levels of arousal for performance and for hedonic tone.) If arousal deviates from the optimal for pleasant hedonic tone, the person is motivated to avoid or seek arousal to return it to the most pleasant, moderate level. This need to maintain a moderate level of arousal may affect the person's behaviour during task performance If the task provides low levels of stimulation and tends to reduce arousal, people may arouse themselves by increasing their response rate. Since extraverts tend to be tonically low in arousal, they will respond more frequently and vigorously than introverts. Task strategy will be affected by such active attempts to regulate arousal. The simplest prediction is that extraverts should be more ready to respond, as expressed by performance measures of response criterion (β), and speed–accuracy trade-off. Again, there is at least some evidence for the hypothesis (Eysenck and Eysenck, 1985).

Shortcomings of arousal theory

The success of the Eysenck theory in explaining each of the areas of empirical research is considered subsequently. The theory does have some general shortcomings for the cognitive psychologist, though. Firstly, the reliability of the negative correlation between extraversion and cortical arousal is questionable. Although many studies do show the predicted negative correlation, the extraversion–arousal correlation seems to vary with level of ambient stimulation (Stelmack, 1981; Gale, 1981). The negative correlation is most reliable under moderately low levels of stimulation but tends to disappear or even reverse under higher levels of stimulation. Since performance-testing environments are often stimulating, they are rather unsuitable for obtaining the negative extraversion–arousal correlation. Fowles *et al.* (1977)

provide a direct demonstration of this problem: following performance of a difficult, and probably stressful, task, extraverts tended to be higher in skin conductance than introverts. H.J. Eysenck (1981) claims that under stressful conditions a protective inhibitory process ('transmarginal inhibition') tends to *reduce* arousal in introverts as stimulation increases. This proposal is more helpful to the psycho-physiologist than to the performance researcher, who must face the possibility of the extraversion–arousal correlation varying within different task conditions.

A second problem is the theory's vagueness about cognitive processes. It is assumed that the reticulo-cortical loop controls the general efficiency of cortical functioning, but the nature of individual differences in general efficiency are not specified in cognitive terms. Hence the theory is unable to predict whether extraversion should have differing effects on two tasks of equal difficulty but differing information processing requirements. The use of the Yerkes–Dodson law to describe relationships between individual differences in arousal and performance has also been criticized, as discussed by Mueller (this volume).

Cognitive theories

Humphreys and Revelle (1984) attempted to integrate a modification of the Eysenck (1967) theory with contemporary cognitive psychology. Like Eysenck, these authors see individual differences in arousal as being central to extraversion effects on performance. However, they suggest that it is impulsivity rather than extraversion which affects performance, and that the impulsivity–arousal relationship varies with time of day. Impulsivity is said to be linked to a phase difference in circadian arousal rhythm, such that high impulsives (equivalent to extraverts) are lower in arousal in the morning, but higher in arousal in the evening, relative to low impulsives. Personality effects on performance are associated with individual differences in capacity or resources, reservoirs of 'energy' or 'fuel' for particular types of processing. The performance of certain tasks only is limited by resource availability: performance is otherwise limited by the quality of signal or memory data. Humphreys and Revelle (1984) propose that increasing arousal increases the availability of attentional or sustained information processing (SIT) resources, but decreases availability of short-term memory (STM) resources. For complex tasks, requiring both types of resource, the arousal–performance relationship is an inverted U. Hence, the theory predicts that in the morning, high impulsives, and to some extent extraverts, should perform worse on predominantly attentional tasks, such as vigilance and serial reaction time, but better on STM tasks, relative to low impulsives. Impulsivity will interact with arousal level in its effects on complex tasks. All personality–performance relationships will tend to reverse in the evening. The Humphreys and Revelle

(1984) model is thus a distinct improvement on psycho-biological theories in its use of cognitive theory, which allows it to be tested by reasonably straightforward task parameter manipulations. However, it is vulnerable to disconfirmation by physiological data inconsistent with the posited time of day dependent relationship between impulsivity and arousal. The evidence for this relationship is weak (Matthews, 1988; Vidacek *et al.*, 1988).

Other theories of extraversion and performance are of more limited scope, seeking to account for only a subset of the performance correlates of extraversion or impulsivity, such as speed–accuracy trade-off (Dickman and Meyer, 1988), conditioning (Gray, 1981) and arousal-dependent correlates (Matthews and Harley, 1989). Such theories are described more fully in the context of the type of data they attempt to explain.

SIMPLE EFFECTS OF EXTRAVERSION ON PERFORMANCE

Many studies have simply tested correlations between extraversion and performance without testing for interactions between extraversion and arousal level. Many of these, particularly older studies, have aimed to test predictions from the Eysenck (1967) theory with tasks of limited interest to the cognitive psychologist, such as conditioning. Eysenck and Eysenck (1985) provide a comprehensive review of such research. This section focuses primarily on more recent studies of extraversion and information processing concerned with attention, memory and task strategy. Predictions can be derived from the Eysenck (1967) and Humphreys and Revelle (1984) theories as follows. The main prediction from Eysenck (1967) is that extraversion should interact with task difficulty. If extraverts are under-aroused, and lower levels of arousal are optimal for more difficult tasks, then extraverts should tend to perform better on more difficult tasks, and worse on easier ones relative to introverts. The Eysenck (1967) theory also predicts that extraverts should show behaviour associated with seeking of stimulation to raise arousal, such as responding more rapidly. Humphreys and Revelle (1984) predict that in the morning high impulsives (and so, to some extent, extraverts) should perform more poorly on attention-demanding tasks (since arousal is positively correlated with SIT resource availability), but better on STM tasks (arousal is negatively correlated with STM resources). These effects should become stronger as the resource demands of the task increase.

Attention

A variety of types of task have been used to assess the relationship between extraversion and attention, including measures of vigilance and sustained attention, and selective and divided attention. Two issues are put aside for discussion later in the chapter: the incidence of correlations between extraversion and response criterion, and the variation of correlations between extraversion and attention with arousal level. Tasks requiring continuous performance, such as continuous serial reaction, letter cancellation and card sorting, typically show arousal-dependent relationships between extraversion and performance, rather than main effects of extraversion (Corcoran, 1972; Matthews *et al.*, 1989).

VIGILANCE

The most popular paradigm for testing attentional correlates of extraversion has been the vigilance task in which performance of a simple target detection task must be sustained over time. Typically, extraverts detect a lower proportion of signals than introverts in both visual and auditory modalities (Davies and Parasuraman, 1982). However, a number of well designed studies fail to show any extraversion effects at all (e.g. Gale *et al.*, 1972). A few studies also show greater temporal decrement in detection rate in extraverts, but this effect appears to be unreliable (Davies and Parasuraman, 1982). Many studies have methodological weaknesses, such as use of non-standard measures of extraversion, and tasks on which performance is close to ceiling levels. Few studies have manipulated task parameters to test whether extraversion effects vary with the information processing demands of the task. Signal detection theory suggests that detection rates in vigilance depend on two underlying qualities of the observer: perceptual sensitivity (indexed by d'), and response criterion, or readiness to respond (indexed by β). Unfortunately, the majority of studies of extraversion fail to measure these two separate performance indices, making the detection rate data rather ambiguous. Extraverts' poorer detection rates appear to be most reliable when subjects must detect a physically encoded visual stimulus such as a line or pattern of lines rather than symbolic stimuli such as digits (e.g. Gange *et al.*, 1979; Singh, 1989). Studies using simple visual stimuli conducted by Harkins and Geen (1975) and Geen *et al.* (1985) have shown lower perceptual sensitivity (d') in extravert subjects, at least in quiet, de-arousing conditions.

THE ROLE OF AROUSAL

A few vigilance studies have also simultaneously measured autonomic arousal. For a strong test of the Eysenck (1967) theory, we need studies which both find a negative association between personality and vigilance, and report the full set of relationships among personality, vigilance and arousal. The theory then predicts that arousal should be negatively related to extraversion and positively related to vigilance. There are three such studies which report significant associations between extraversion and vigilance. Carr (1969) found that extraverts were lower than introverts in both autonomic arousal and perceptual sensitivity. However, the arousal index, tonic skin conductance, was not itself correlated with detection rate or perceptual sensitivity. Hastrup (1979) found that both extraversion and electro-dermal lability predicted performance, in some task conditions, but there was no relationship between extraversion and electro-dermal lability. Giambra *et al.* (1988) obtained a negative correlation between sociability and vigilance, but two electro-dermal measures of arousal were not significantly correlated with either performance or sociability. That is, neither an arousal–performance correlation (Carr, 1969; Giambra *et al.*, 1988) nor a personality–arousal correlation (Hastrup, 1979; Giambra *et al.*, 1988) is a necessary condition for a personality–vigilance correlation. These studies provide no compelling evidence for the proposition that extraversion–vigilance correlations are mediated by individual differences in arousal.

PREDICTIONS FROM THE HUMPHREYS AND REVELLE (1984) MODEL

Humphreys and Revelle (1984) predict that extraverts should show poorer vigilance in the morning, but only a small number of studies have manipulated time of day. Colquhoun (1960) found that extraversion was negatively related to detections on a visual vigilance task in the morning, but positively related in the afternoon, as expected. However, Blake (1971), Gale *et al.* (1972), and Vidacek *et al.* (1988) failed to replicate this finding. Humphreys and Revelle (1984) also predict that impulsivity should be a stronger correlate of vigilance than sociability. Giambra *et al.* (1988) provide directly contradictory evidence. Sociability was significantly negatively correlated with detections on the Mackworth clock test, but extraversion and impulsivity were unrelated to detections. Two studies showing extraversion–vigilance relationships (Bakan, 1959; Colquhoun, 1960) used part II of the Heron scale, which is made up of sociability items. Studies of vigilance thus offer little positive support for the Humphreys and Revelle (1984) theory.

RESOURCE-LIMITED SUSTAINED ATTENTION

Recent vigilance research suggests that performance of demanding, high event-rate visual sustained attention tasks appears to depend on attentional resource availability (Parasuraman *et al.*, 1987). If stimuli are degraded with visual noise, a rapid perceptual sensitivity decrement is found, over five to ten minutes. Matthews *et al.* (1990a,b) ran five studies of these tasks, manipulating several task parameters including type of stimulus (symbolic or physical). In all studies, time of day was manipulated, and arousal was monitored with a validated self-report measure. In general, extraversion was an inconsistent predictor of sustained attention. In two out of the four studies using symbolic material, including the largest single study ($N = 100$), extraverts showed a *smaller* perceptual sensitivity decrement than introverts on more demanding task versions. Extraverts were lower in overall perceptual sensitivity on one out of four physical, line length discrimination tasks. A further study ($N = 108$) of dual-task performance of sustained attention tasks, found higher perceptual sensitivity in extraverts only in dual-task conditions, a finding suggestive of greater resource availability in extraverts (Matthews *et al.*, 1990c). A corresponding result was significant for impulsivity but not for sociability. Matthews *et al.* (in press) showed a comparable facilitative effect of extraversion on skilled sustained performance ($N = 53$): extraverted post office trainees were faster and more accurate than introverts at semi-automated mail sorting.

These studies provide some evidence for the extraversion × difficulty interaction predicted by Eysenck (1967). Analysis of self-report arousal data showed that none of these extraversion effects was mediated by individual differences in arousal though. If anything, there was a tendency towards small positive correlations between extraversion and arousal, irrespective of time of day. Apart from the greater predictive power of impulsivity found by Matthews *et al.* (1990c), no evidence favouring the Humphreys and Revelle (1984) theory was found. In particular, there was no evidence for the extraversion/impulsivity × time of day interaction predicted by Humphreys and Revelle.

Selective and divided attention

SELECTIVE ATTENTION

A number of studies have investigated attentional selectivity in extraverts and introverts. If extraverts are less aroused, they should use a wider range of cues (see Easterbrook, 1959), and so be more easily distracted by extraneous information. M.W. Eysenck (1981) discusses three studies of verbal learning, in which, contrary to expectation, extraverts were less distracted than introverts by irrelevant information presented at encoding. The dependent measures in these experiments were related to learning, and so are a rather indirect index of the subjects' allocation of attention during performance. The breadth of attention can also be assessed by the Stroop test. If introverts are more aroused, they should be less distracted by the colour of the ink when reporting the written colour name. In fact, either extraverts are less affected by the ink colour (Davies, 1967), or there is no effect of extraversion at all (Murphy and McKelvie, 1984). Eysenck (1982) suggests that introverts are more distractable in these studies because they allocate a greater proportion of their attentional resources to primary task performance. Introverts, then, have fewer 'spare' attentional resources available for resisting environmental distraction. Dunne and Hartley (1985) used a dichotic listening task, where subjects were instructed to attend to words presented at one ear, and ignore the other. Extraversion affected subsequent recognition memory in that extraverts showed superior recognition for attended words but poorer recognition of unattended words, suggesting that extraverts had better voluntary control over the focus of their attention. Again, the extraversion × difficulty interaction was not in the predicted direction. Extraverts' better recognition of attended material is incompatible with Eysenck's (1982) hypothesis that introverts allocate more attention to the primary task. Dunne and Hartley also manipulated administration of a drug, the cholinergic antagonist scopolamine, which reduced arousal, but no interactive effects of extraversion and scopolamine were found.

Two studies have used incidental recall as a measure of allocation of attention. Imam (1974) instructed subjects to learn nonsense syllables enclosed in geometric shapes, and found no effect of extraversion on incidental recall of the pairing of syllables and shapes. Bermudez *et al.* (1988) followed a letter cancellation task with a test of incidental recall of the text used for the cancellation task. Textual recall was analysed in terms of propositions of different level of detail, varying from major themes to specific episodes. Although there was no effect of extraversion on cancellation, extraverts showed better incidental recall of higher level propositions, main themes and plot of the story. Here, contrary to expectation, extraverts were superior in recall to introverts only for easily recalled material. In contrast to studies of distraction, this result also suggests that extraverts have a wider focus of attention than introverts.

DIVIDED ATTENTION

Eysenck and Eysenck (1979) investigated dual-task performance using a version of the Sternberg paradigm requiring either physical or semantic category matching. Extraverts tended to be faster at scanning memory for a serial match, but there was no personality effect on physical matching speed. Furthermore, introverts were more adversely affected when both types of match were to be sought simultaneously. Eysenck and Eysenck interpret these results in terms of poorer parallel processing by introverts, although there appears to be no evidence to suggest that dual-task performance induced a switch from serial to parallel processing. Another interpretation is that extraverts responded faster in more difficult conditions, since task difficulty was greater in both semantic matching and dual-task conditions, relative to physical matching and single-task conditions respectively. A white noise manipulation had no effect at all, suggesting that the extraversion effects were not mediated by arousal. Schwartz (1979) obtained a comparable single-task effect in a two-word matching task. Extraverts and introverts were equally fast at detecting a physical match, but introverts were slower at responding to phonemic and semantic matches, which took longer to perform.

Attention: conclusions

The most consistent findings from studies of attention are introverts' superior vigilance, and extraverts' superiority on more demanding attentional tasks such as dual-task performance, resistance to distraction, and incidental recall of text. The latter finding is predicted by Eysenck (1967), although there are some exceptions to the rule. Direct measurement of autonomic or self-report arousal in studies of vigilance and sustained attention does not support the contention that extraversion effects are mediated by individual differences in arousal. Likewise, those studies of divided and selective attention which have manipulated arousal fail to obtain interactive effects of extraversion and arousal consistent with arousal theory. Support for the Humphreys and Revelle (1984) theory is limited to isolated studies, although it has yet to be adequately tested, particularly in studies of selective and divided attention.

Memory

ROLE OF TASK PARAMETERS

Much of the literature on extraversion and memory has been reviewed in detail by M.W. Eysenck (1976, 1981). Eysenck (1976) identifies three task parameters which appear to modify the relationship between extraversion and memory: retention interval, response competition, and response dominance. Extraverts tend to show better recall over retention intervals of up to five minutes or so, whereas, rather less reliably, introverts show superior long-term recall. The studies concerned most commonly used paired associate learning tasks. To account for this effect in terms of arousal theory, Walker's (1958) action decrement theory is invoked, which claims that high arousal facilitates consolidation of information in long-term memory (LTM) but impairs STM. Hence, on memory tasks, extraverts appear to behave as though they were low in arousal, as the Eysenck (1967) theory predicts. In support of arousal theory, Amelang *et al.* (1977) found that introverts' poor short-term memory was associated with reduced EEG alpha activity and slower reaction times early in the retention interval, effects attributed to greater consolidation by introverts. Difficulties for the arousal theory interpretation include uncertainties over the mechanism for the arousal × retention interval interaction, and empirical and theoretical problems of the action decrement theory (Eysenck, 1982; Humphreys *et al.*, 1983). Recent studies provide somewhat inconsistent evidence. Recall of television news stories appears to show the typical extraversion × retention interval interaction (Gunter and Furnham, 1986; Gunter *et al.*, 1984), although extraverts showed superior short-term recall only when news was presented audio-visually, rather than in the auditory or visual modality alone (Gunter and Furnham, 1986). The audio-visual condition was easier than the other two, so the extraversion × difficulty interaction was in the opposite direction to expectation. However, two further studies failed to show the predicted effects of extraversion on short-term recall of noun lists (Dunne and Hartley, 1985) and ordered digit sequences (Matthews *et al.*, 1989).

Studies of response competition and response dominance provide quite a good fit to the extraversion × task difficulty interaction predicted from the Eysenck (1967) theory. Several studies of paired associate learning show that extraverts tend to show better recall mainly when there is response competition between two or more associates of the stimulus words (Eysenck, 1976). There is little evidence to indicate whether this is a direct effect of response complexity or an indirect effect of task difficulty. M.W. Eysenck (1981) has suggested that one influence on extraverts' short-term recall may be more efficient retrieval. Studies reviewed by M.W. Eysenck (1981) suggest that extraverts tend to show faster retrieval from both semantic and episodic storage, particularly when (in semantic memory) items are of low dominance. These retrieval effects are quite strongly modified by arousal level though.

STUDIES OF AROUSAL AND TIME OF DAY

There have been few direct tests of whether extraversion effects on memory are mediated by individual differences in arousal. In Eysenck's (1981) studies of retrieval, a positive association between extraversion and retrieval was obtained in some task conditions, but in these studies the trend was actually towards a *positive* correlation between extraversion and self-report arousal (Eysenck, 1977, p. 201). Mangan and Hookway (1988) assessed free recall of neutral and aversive film segments, along with several psycho-physiological responses. Extraverts showed superior recall of both kinds of information, but psycho-physiological responses to the films varied with both extraversion and type of film. These data suggest a dissociation between the psycho-physiological and mnemonic correlates of extraversion. In particular, extraverts showed better recall of neutral information even though they were no less aroused than introverts during both exposure to the film and recall.

Few studies of personality and memory have tested the Humphreys and Revelle (1984) theory, although a successful outcome is reported by Puchalski (1988). In this experiment, impulsivity was positively correlated with immediate recall of text in the morning, but not in the early afternoon. The opposite pattern of results was obtained for delayed recall. Matthews *et al.* (1989) failed to find an equivalent effect for immediate recall of digit sequences. Gunter *et al.* (1984) found a rather peculiar pattern of interaction between time of day and extraversion in delayed recall of television news. Introverts showed better free and cued recall in the morning and late afternoon, but extraverts recalled somewhat more material in the early afternoon. A general problem for the Humphreys and Revelle (1984) model is uncertainty over the role of resources in immediate retention tasks (e.g. Klapp and Netick, 1988).

INFORMATION PROCESSING IN MEMORY

There have also been several attempts to investigate whether extraversion is correlated with theoretically relevant processing components of memory. Two studies (Schwartz, 1975; Craig *et al.*, 1979) have contrasted learning of semantically and phonemically related paired associates to test the role of processing codes in extraversion effects on memory. Results were inconclusive and mutually inconsistent. Extraversion effects varied with neuroticism, and, in the Craig *et al.* study, with caffeine dosage also, but there was no straightforward interaction between extraversion and processing code or task difficulty. Craig *et al.* demonstrate that their results are inconsistent with a unitary arousal model. They also failed to find any clear-cut differences between effects of extraversion, impulsivity and sociability. Other studies have investigated degree of semantic clustering of responses in recall, often taken as an index of the active processing and organization of material, again with conflicting results. The correlation between extraversion and amount of clustering has been found to be positive (Eysenck, 1974), negative (Stein and Harrison, 1967), and dependent on neuroticism (Schwartz, 1975).

Matthews (1987a) reported a study of relationships between extraversion, free recall of a sixteen-item word list, and a working memory task, which tested recall of words embedded in sentences. In both tasks, concurrent memory load and articulatory suppression were manipulated, to test the role of three specific stores posited by Hitch (1980): the central executive (affected by memory load), the articulatory loop (affected by articulatory suppression), and the verbal input register. In free recall, extraversion affected the recency but not the pre-recency items, irrespective of memory load and articulatory suppression manipulations, as shown in Figure 4.1. This pattern of results suggests that extraverts are able to hold more items in the verbal input register than introverts, which explains extraverts' superior STM, but not its dependence on task difficulty. A comparable effect was found with self-report arousal, in that low arousal subjects had a smaller recency effect, but the extraversion and arousal effects were independent and additive. There were no simple effects of extraversion on working memory: other experiments show no correlation between extraversion and performance on a high memory load visual search task (Matthews *et al.*, 1989), and on controlled memory search (Matthews *et al.*, 1990a).

Memory: conclusions

Extraverts appear to show better short-term retention than introverts, and recall better under conditions of response competition and response dominance.

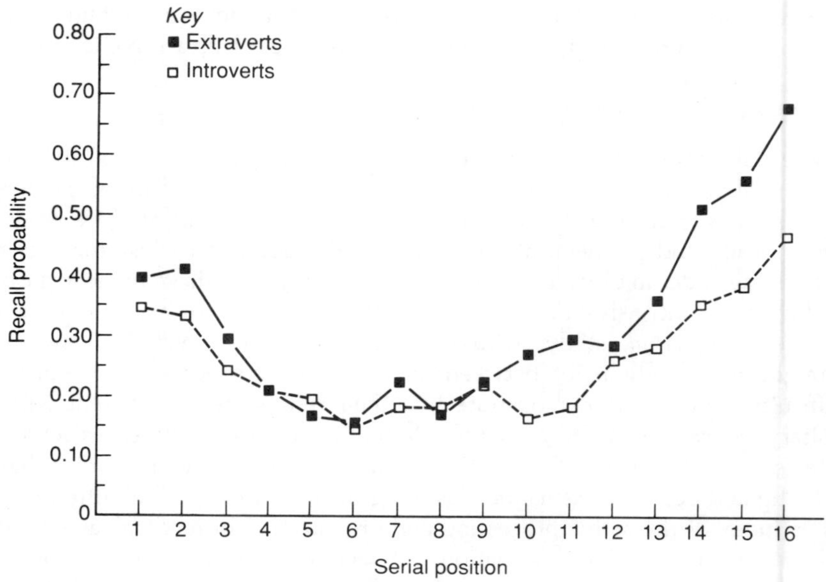

Figure 4.1 Free recall as a function of extraversion and serial position. (From Matthews, 1987a.)

Superficially, these findings are consistent with arousal theory, but there is little direct evidence that extraversion effects on memory are mediated by individual differences in arousal. Cognitively orientated studies have been somewhat disappointing, so far.

Extraversion, speed of response and task strategy

SPEED–ACCURACY TRADE-OFF AND RESPONSE CRITERION

Effects of extraversion on measures of simple response speed appear to be weak (e.g. Amelang and Ullwer, in press), although Robinson and Zahn (1988) have reported that extraversion is negatively correlated with simple RT provided that there is a preparatory interval of at least four seconds. On more complex, self-paced tasks there are some reports of extraverts responding more quickly but less accurately than introverts, at least in the early stages of performance (Eysenck and Eysenck, 1985). There is a weak tendency for extraverts to make more false positive errors, and to set a lower response criterion, on traditional vigilance tasks (Davies and Parasuraman, 1982). Similar findings for response criterion have been reported for recognition memory (Gillespie and Eysenck, 1980; Danzinger and Larsen, 1989). These results are consistent with the hypothesis that extraverts respond more frequently and rapidly to raise their arousal level towards the optimal for subjective contentment (Eysenck, 1967). Several studies fail to find the predicted relationships though (e.g. Matthews *et al.*, 1990), possibly because effects of extraversion on motor reactivity vary with neuroticism and motivation (Wallace and Newman, 1990).

Brebner and Cooper (1985) provide an alternative account of effects of extraversion on response speed. They suggest that extraversion affects the balance of excitation and inhibition associated with stimulus analysis and response excitation, such that extraverts are 'geared to respond' and introverts 'geared to inspect'. Extraverts' tendency to generate excitation from response organization explains these subjects' general behavioural impulsivity. The theory predicts phenomena such as extraverts' propensity to respond on 'catch trials' where response should be withheld (Brebner and Flavel, 1978), and depression of response rate ('learned helplessness') in introverts following exposure to uncontrollable performance decrement (Tiggeman *et al.*, 1982). However, the analysis of task performance in terms of excitation and inhibition is of uncertain validity, and it is unclear how the theory would account for extraversion effects on more 'cognitive' tasks such as memory tasks.

IMPULSIVITY

There is a somewhat separate literature on impulsivity and speed–accuracy trade-offs, which finds, in general, that high scorers on questionnaire measures of impulsivity do indeed tend to respond faster and less accurately (e.g. Edman *et al.*, 1983), although Barrett (1987) suggests that high impulsives tend to respond more slowly than low impulsives when extensive stimulus processing is necessary. A series of studies by Dickman (1985; Dickman and Meyer, 1988) have attempted to investigate the exact mechanism for the effect of impulsivity on speed–accuracy trade-off. Dickman (1985) investigated a card sorting task where stimuli were large letters composed of smaller ones. Impulsivity had no effects on selective attention or response interference in this paradigm, but high impulsives were disadvantaged when local and global information had to be integrated. Dickman suggests that high impulsives tend to adopt a strategy of attending to one type of information only: an hypothesis which seems to relate impulsivity to a bias in stimulus processing rather than in responding. Dickman and Meyer (1988) applied additive-factors methods to a visual comparison task, and again found that impulsivity affects speed–accuracy trade-off relatively early in processing. Processing of response execution was identical in high and low impulsive groups, but high impulsives were faster and more inaccurate at the feature comparison stage. These studies provide considerable insight into impulsivity, but it is unclear whether Dickman's findings are mediated by arousal or whether relationships between extraversion and responsivity are controlled by similar mechanisms. A similar result was obtained by Weinman *et al.* (1985) who showed that on a maze solution task extraverts spent less time than introverts on the initial search phase but not on later phases.

Explaining the cognitive patterning of extraversion

This selective review of the data suggests that there are at least four aspects of performance which show fairly reliable simple effects of extraversion.

1. Extraverts show poorer detection of visual stimuli in traditional vigilance paradigms. There is a possible link here with studies showing poorer visual perception in extraverts. Eysenck and Eysenck (1985) review studies suggesting that extraverts show poorer perception of flicker, greater sensitivity to masking by meta-contrast, and higher sensory thresholds (for hearing as well as vision).
2. Extraverts show better short-term recall, and possibly poorer long-term recall, although there is uncertainty over which memory tasks other than paired associate learning are sensitive to the effect.
3. There are several paradigms in which extraverts tend to out-perform introverts when task difficulty is increased, including short-term retention (M.W. Eysenck, 1981), and high event-rate sustained attention tasks (e.g. Matthews *et al.*, 1990a). Not all difficulty manipulations result in this effect: introverts appear to be better at solving difficult problems (Kumar and Kapila, 1987).
4. Extraverts sometimes require less sensory evidence for response, at least on de-arousing tasks.

How well can existing theories of extraversion account for this cognitive patterning? The tendency for extraverts to perform better on relatively difficult memory and attention tasks is consistent with Eysenck's (1967) arousal theory. However, there are too many exceptions to the general rule (e.g. Bermudez *et al.*, 1988; Gunter and Furnham, 1986; Dunne and Hartley, 1985; Matthews *et al.*, 1990b) to posit confidently that difficulty is the only, or even the main, factor controlling the nature of extraversion effects. Furthermore, studies which have measured arousal as well as performance have frequently failed to find the relationships among arousal, extraversion and performance predicted by Eysenck (1967), even within studies showing the predicted extraversion × difficulty interaction (e.g. Matthews *et al.*, 1990a, c). It is possible that factors such as transmarginal inhibition (H.J. Eysenck, 1981), variation between task versions in the extraversion–arousal correlation, and use of less than optimal indices of cortical arousal are obscuring interrelationships among extraversion, arousal and performance. More sophisticated, multivariate studies may yet vindicate the Eysenck (1967) theory, but the evidence to date does not convincingly explain the patterning of performance claimed to be associated with extraversion.

It is difficult to assess the predictive success of the Humphreys and Revelle (1984) theory because of the paucity of studies which have manipulated, or even controlled for time of day. Of these studies, for every result which supports Humphreys and Revelle (1984), there seems to be a counter-example. It is possible that those studies which obtained the predicted personality × time of day interaction (e.g. Colquhoun, 1960; Puchalski, 1988) used appropriately resource-limited tasks, and unsuccessful studies did not. However, the only set of studies which both manipulated time of day (Matthews *et al.*, 1990a, b), and used an explicit resource theory framework, did not obtain the predicted interaction with time of day. It is also difficult to conclude that impulsivity is a more reliable predictor of performance than sociability.

Eysenck (1982) makes an interesting *post hoc* suggestion that introverts typically have fewer processing resources available than extraverts, which accounts for extraverts' tendency to out-perform introverts on demanding tasks, particularly in dual-task paradigms. The resource hypothesis accounts straightforwardly for extraverts' resistance to distraction (M.W. Eysenck, 1981) and superior dual-task performance (Eysenck and Eysenck, 1979; Matthews *et al.*, 1990c). It also partially explains why effects of extraversion on attentional selectivity vary with task demands (M.W. Eysenck, 1981; Dunne and Hartley, 1985; Bermudez *et al.*, 1988), since the impact on performance of individual differences in resource availability will be modified by resource allocation policy and strategy. The resource hypothesis also does not require extraversion to facilitate every difficult task; only those where difficulty results from high resource demands. The hypothesis can account for only a part of the cognitive patterning of extraversion. It cannot explain why extraverts tend to be poor at traditional vigilance tasks or why they sometimes set a lower response criterion. It is also unclear whether extraverts' superior STM can be attributed simply to greater resource availability, because of the complexity of short-term recall. It may be important that the majority of tasks showing superior performance in extraverts employed verbal stimuli, and inferior levels of performance by extraverts are most marked on sensory tasks (although there are a number of exceptions to these generalizations, such as introverts' superior verbal conditioning; Eysenck and Eysenck, 1985). Very speculatively, a multiple resource interpretation of the data may eventually be possible, perhaps with extraversion affecting the balance of resources available for verbal and sensory processing (see Wickens, 1984). Greater availability of resources for verbal processing might account for extraverts' greater social interest and skills.

In summary, existing research indicates a number of paradigms where extraversion has reasonably replicable effects, and others where it does not. We can describe the cognitive patterning associated with these effects as for any other 'stressor' (Hockey and Hamilton, 1983). None of the theories of extraversion described accounts for all the data, and it may be that extraversion is associated with a constellation of functionally independent individual differences in cognitive functioning.

EXTRAVERSION AND COGNITIVE RESPONSE TO STRESS

On many tasks, extraversion interacts with the subject's level of stress or arousal. Typically, introverts perform more efficiently than extraverts at low levels of stress, but extraverts are superior under high stress. A striking feature of such findings is their generalization across tasks and stressors. Interactions of this kind have been reported for sensory thresholds (Shigehisa and Symons, 1973), vigilance (see Davies and Parasuraman, 1982), continuous serial reaction, card sorting and letter cancellation (Corcoran, 1972), intelligence and creativity test performance (Gupta, 1988; Matthews, 1986; Revelle *et al.*, 1976) and memory tasks (see Eysenck, 1981). Sources of stress in these studies included noise, caffeine, anxiety and incentive. The interaction may also generalize to applied settings such as vehicle operation (Fagerstrom and Lisper, 1977): extraverts' driving is improved by playing the car radio. Introverts also perform relatively better under de-arousing manipulations such as sleep deprivation (Corcoran, 1972) and alcohol ingestion (Jones, 1974). These data have been interpreted as providing particularly strong support for the arousal theory of extraversion (Eysenck and Eysenck, 1985). Increased stress or arousal improves extraverts' performance because they are under-aroused under normal testing conditions, but impairs introverts' because they are normally near the optimal level of arousal (Figure 4.2).

The first difficulty for the Eysenck (1967) theory derives from time of day effects first demonstrated by Blake (1971), using a letter cancellation task. Blake showed that incentive (provided through knowledge of results) and noise tended to improve the performance of extraverts in the morning, as expected. However, in the evening these supposedly arousing stressors impaired the performance of extraverts but did not much affect introverts: a finding inconsistent with extraverts being lower in arousal than introverts.

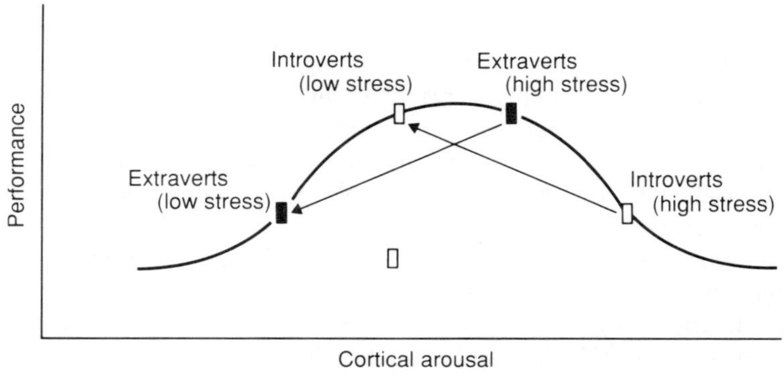

Figure 4.2 Arousal theory interpretation of interactive effects of extraversion and stress on performance.

Revelle *et al.* (1980) reported comparable effects of extraversion, time of day and caffeine in several studies of verbal intelligence test performance. In these studies, it was impulsivity rather than sociability which appeared to be responsible for the interaction. These data provide the empirical basis for Humphreys and Revelle's (1984) assertion that the key relationship between personality and arousal is a phase difference in circadian arousal rhythm between high and low impulsives.

If time of day is manipulated, a triple interaction among time of day, extraversion and arousal is frequently found (Matthews *et al.*, 1989; Revelle *et al.*, 1980), which may be described as the *modal interaction* for stress-dependent effects of extraversion. A typical example is shown in Figure 4.3 for missed targets in sustained attention, with arousal measured by self-report (Matthews, 1989b). Both Eysenck (1967) and Humphreys and Revelle (1984) assume the modal interaction is mediated by a causal chain such that personality affects arousal which in turn affects performance. However, there are two kinds of problem for this general, arousal–mediation explanation. Firstly, there is evidence inconsistent with the assumption that stress-dependent effects of extraversion are mediated by a correlation between extraversion and arousal. Secondly, although extraversion × arousal interactions

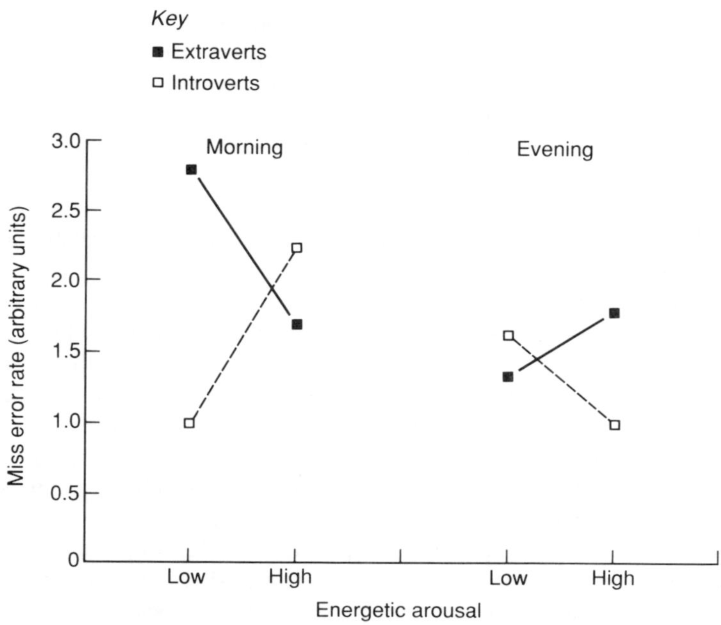

Figure 4.3 Missed target rate on the levels of control task as a function of time of day, extraversion, and arousal. (From Matthews, 1989b; © 1989 Elsevier Science Publishers BV.)

are commonly reported in the literature, they are not universal and appear to be specific to certain types of task. It is questionable whether arousal–mediation theories can account for this task-specificity of the interaction.

Problems of the mediating role of arousal

The mediating role of arousal in the modal interaction is challenged by studies which have taken a direct measure of arousal, usually by a validated self-report index. This procedure allows a direct test of underlying assumptions about the relationships among extraversion, arousal and performance. At one level these studies provide further evidence for the importance of arousal in explaining extraversion effects on performance because the majority show that extraversion interacts with directly measured arousal as it does with manipulated stressors. Studies which have manipulated time of day show the modal triple interaction for tasks such as intelligence test performance (Matthews, 1985), digit recall and five-choice serial reactions (Matthews *et al.*, 1989), and sustained attention (Matthews, 1989b). Careful consideration of these results raises two problems though. Firstly, the correlation between extraversion and arousal is frequently inconsistent with the observed interaction between the two variables. For example, Matthews (1987b) found that the interactive effect of impulsivity and self-report arousal on intelligence varied with time of day as in the Revelle *et al.* (1980) studies, but the impulsivity measure was negatively correlated with a composite measure of autonomic arousal at both morning and evening. In other studies, extraversion interacted with self-report arousal even though extraversion and arousal were unrelated (e.g. Matthews, 1985, 1986), or even positively correlated at both times of day (Matthews, 1989b, Matthews *et al.*, 1989).

A second problem is that interactions between extraversion and self-report arousal imply that extraversion affects performance even when subject groups are equated for arousal. This proposition is not consistent with any theory which proposes that extraversion affects performance via its correlation with arousal. Instead, the assumption of arousal–mediation of extraversion effects may be invalid. The data are more readily explained if it is assumed that the relationship between arousal and performance is qualitatively different in extraverted and introverted groups, as shown in Figure 4.4 (which may be contrasted with Figure 4.2). For example, the self-report arousal data just described suggest that in the morning there is a positive association between arousal and performance in extraverts, but a negative association in introverts, with these relationships reversing in the evening. In other words, any correlation between extraversion and arousal may simply be irrelevant to the interactive effect of the two variables on performance. As discussed previously,

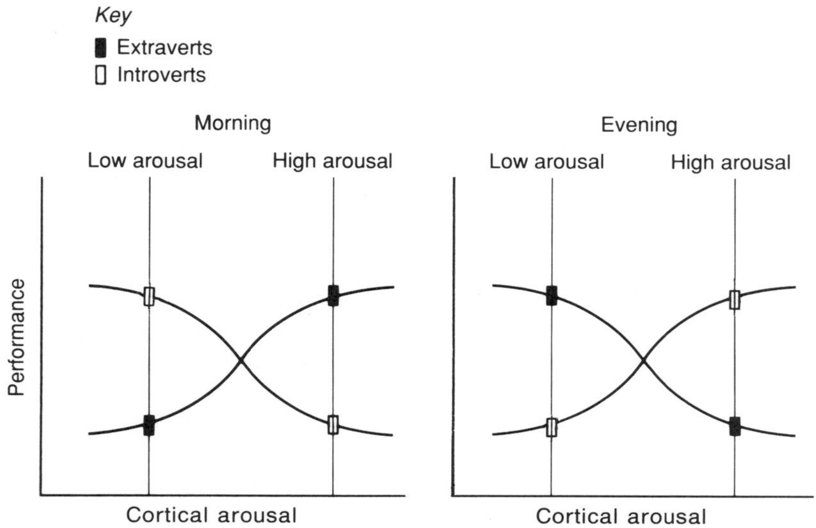

Figure 4.4 Hypothetical arousal–performance relationships in extraverted and introverted subjects in the morning and evening.

simple effects of extraversion on performance also do not seem to be contingent on the existence of an extraversion–arousal correlation.

Task-specificity of the modal interaction

Studies described previously (e.g. Eysenck and Eysenck, 1979; Dunne and Hartley, 1985) show main effects of extraversion in the absence of an extraversion × arousal interaction. We can then ask which parameters of tasks control whether an interactive effect of extraversion and arousal is found. It is difficult to identify relevant task attributes from studies of manipulated arousal because few studies systematically vary task parameters. Several studies of vigilance, for example, show the effect whereas others do not (e.g. McKeown *et al.*, 1986), but it is unclear which task parameters are critical. In studies of noise (the most commonly used stressor for this research), extraverts' tendency to perform better under noise generalizes across a variety of tasks, including both symbolically (Davies and Hockey, 1966) and physically encoded tasks (Geen *et al.*, 1985; Gupta and Nicholson, 1987). With other types of task, there are too few studies to assess the role of task parameters.

Matthews has recently conducted a series of studies of interactions between extraversion and self-report arousal, in which information processing demands of tasks were systematically manipulated. Matthews *et al.* (1989) suggested that those attentional tasks that require rapid but routine stimulus encoding are most sensitive to the modal interaction, such as five-choice serial reaction (Matthews *et al.*, 1989), and letter detection (Matthews, 1989b; Matthews and Chappelow, 1986). Matthews (1989b) showed that extraversion and arousal affected only 'low level' detection errors associated with easily perceived, single-letter targets, but not 'high level' errors associated with failing to apply a rule to switch targets. Matthews and Chappelow (1986) used a selective attention paradigm, where relevant and irrelevant information was distinguished by either spatial location or category membership. However, the presence or absence of irrelevant stimuli had little effect on the typical interactive effect of extraversion and arousal on detection accuracy found. Error rates in all these attentional tasks were low (less than five per cent). However, more demanding and probably more resource-dependent tasks (such as high event-rate, sustained attention tasks, and controlled visual and memory search) do not show the typical interactive effect of extraversion and arousal (Matthews *et al.*, 1990a,b) although they may be sensitive to linear effects of these variables, as discussed above. If undemanding, low error rate attentional tasks are more sensitive to the modal interaction than demanding, resource-limited tasks, it is unlikely that the modal interaction is mediated by individual differences in resource availability.

Extraversion, arousal and spreading activation

Matthews *et al.* (1989) noted that a number of tasks requiring semantic processing seemed to be particularly sensitive to the modal interaction in studies of both manipulated and directly measured arousal, such as verbal intelligence (Revelle *et al.*, 1980; Matthews, 1985), verbal fluency and flexibility (Matthews, 1986), proof-reading (Anderson and Revelle, 1982) and retrieval from semantic memory (Eysenck, 1981). They suggested that the modal interaction might be associated with individual differences in speed of spreading activation within a semantic network. Matthews and Harley (1989) tested this hypothesis within two studies of semantic priming of lexical decision, which showed that the extraversion × arousal interaction affected priming magnitude more reliably than unprimed lexical decision, as predicted. The effect was not sensitive to pattern masking of the primes, suggesting that it was not simply a perceptual effect. Moreover, it was similar at both short and long stimulus onset asynchronies, implying that both 'controlled' and 'automatic' priming routes (see Neely, 1977) were affected fairly equally. Harley and Matthews (see Matthews, in press) have used a computer simulation of an interactive activation network similar to that described by McClelland and Rumelhart (1981) to explore how individual differences in network parameters may affect lexical decision speed. They suggest that the observed pattern of data is consistent with extraversion and arousal interactively affecting the level of random noise within the network.

Extraversion appears to have an indirect, higher-order effect on processing, modifying the relationship between cortical arousal and cognitive activation.

Individual differences in noise within an interactive activation network might affect a wide variety of simple tasks such as vigilance and continuous performance, accounting for some of the range of tasks sensitive to the modal interaction. However, there are two problems for the network hypothesis. Firstly, the modal interaction affects not only simple attentional and encoding tasks but also complex tasks such as intelligence test performance (e.g. Matthews, 1985), and short-term memory tasks such as serial digit recall (Matthews *et al.*, 1989) and working memory (Matthews, 1987a). These effects may reflect the importance of simple encoding processes in these tasks. For example, Dempster (1981) attributes individual differences in serial recall to encoding processes. Intelligence test items sensitive to the modal interaction appear to be easy, 'speed' items, rather than difficult 'power' items (see Matthews and Harley, 1989), and so probably depend largely on a correct encoding of the problem. Matthews (1987a) used a working memory task in which the information to be remembered is embedded in sentences and which must be processed semantically. Although a typical extraversion × arousal interaction was found, there was no further interaction with articulatory suppression or with a concurrent memory load, suggesting that the interaction was not associated with any of the specific stores affected by these manipulations (see Hitch, 1980). Instead, extraversion and arousal may have affected the initial encoding of the sentences.

A second problem is that sometimes extraversion and self-report arousal interactively affect speed–accuracy trade-off or response criteria rather than efficiency of performance (Matthews *et al.*, 1990a). In the morning, increasing arousal increases the responsiveness of extraverts but not of introverts. However, this kind of effect is more typically found with tasks dependent on strategy use or resource availability, such as visual search, rather than with those dependent on routine encoding. This arousal-dependence of extraversion effects on responsivity offers a further explanation for the inconsistency of extraversion effects on speed–accuracy trade-off and response criteria noted in the previous section.

Explaining the modal interaction of extraversion and arousal

Both the Eysenck (1967) and Humphreys and Revelle (1984) theories are unsatisfactory because they assume that the interactive effects of extraversion and arousal are mediated by a correlation between extraversion and arousal, which may or may not vary with time of day. However, the evidence shows that the modal interaction does not appear to be contingent on any particular association between extraversion and arousal. The Eysenck (1967) theory is, in addition, flawed because it cannot account for the apparent restriction of the modal interaction to tasks with a routine encoding component, because it has little to say about information processing. The task-specificity of the interactive effect is also inconsistent with the Humphreys and Revelle (1984) theory. It predicts the interaction should be restricted to resource-limited tasks, but in fact such tasks are unlikely to show the effect. More specifically, Humphreys and Revelle (1984) state that the inverted U relationship between arousal and performance is confined to tasks requiring both SIT and STM resources, such as, in their opinion, intelligence tests. It is then difficult to see why purely attentional tasks such as vigilance and serial reaction should show the interactive effect when the underlying regression of performance on arousal is theoretically monotonic. In those studies where increased arousal merely raises extraverts' performance to that of introverts' (e.g. Davies and Hockey, 1966) it may be that introverts' performance is already data-limited and cannot benefit any more from increased arousal. However, there are several instances where increased arousal is actually detrimental to performance of introverts in the morning or extraverts in the evening (e.g. Matthews *et al.*, 1989), which cannot be explained on this basis.

The Matthews and Harley (1989) hypothesis avoids these problems by proposing a cognitive mechanism consistent with the observed task-specificity of the modal interaction, and by rejecting the correlation between extraversion and arousal as irrelevant to the interaction between the two variables. However, more detailed specification of the model is necessary, and it needs to be tested in studies using manipulations of arousal as well as self-report measures. Empirical evidence for the hypothesis is also strongly dependent on the validity of self-report measures of arousal for between-subjects comparisons, an issue discussed in detail by Matthews *et al.* (1989, 1990a).

EXTRAVERSION AND SENSITIVITY TO REWARD AND PUNISHMENT SIGNALS

Gray's (1981) theory of extraversion

A further psycho-biological theory of extraversion (Gray, 1981) relates extraversion to individual differences in susceptibility to signals of reinforcement. However, like Humphreys and Revelle (1984), Gray questions the causal status of extraversion. His proposal is that Eysenck's principal axes of personality, extraversion and neuroticism, should be rotated in factor space to give two new orthogonal dimensions of impulsivity and anxiety. These dimensions are associated with two neural systems, the behavioural activation system (BAS) and the behavioural inhibition system (BIS) respectively. Extraversion is then a mixture of high impulsivity and low anxiety, introversion is low impulsivity and high anxiety. Gray proposes that impulsivity is related to sensitivity to signals of reward, and neuroticism to sensitivity to signals of punishment and non-reward. Extraversion is thus associated with the balance of susceptibility to reward and punishment signals. The extravert is more sensitive to reward signals but less sensitive to punishment signals. These predictions are most directly testable in studies of conditioning: Gray (1981) and Eysenck and Eysenck (1985) disagree on the interpretation of the relevant evidence.

Experimental studies of extraversion and motivation

Generating predictions about task performance from Gray's (1981) theory is not straightforward. It is unclear whether increased sensitivity to reinforcement signals should distract from performance, or motivate the subject to perform better. A further complication is that the BIS and BAS have a variety of effects when activated, such as, in the case of the BIS, increased arousal, increased attention to environmental stimuli and inhibition of ongoing behaviour. Even if the BIS is more highly activated in introverts than in extraverts when punishment signals are delivered, the consequences for individual differences in performance are likely to be complex.

Empirically, extraversion interacts with manipulations of motivation and reinforcement in a manner broadly consistent with Gray's (1981) theory. There seem to be at least two distinct effects. Firstly, extraversion interacts with the general motivational context, such that extraverts perform better in rewarding compared with punishing conditions. Interactions of this kind are reported for pursuit rotor learning (Seunath, 1975), learning mathematics in the classroom (McCord and Wakefield, 1981), visual target location and digit recoding (Boddy *et al.*, 1986), and visual pattern matching (Nichols and Newman, 1986). Reinforcement in these studies is generally manipulated through verbal statements, or through monetary gains and losses. Secondly, at the level of individual trials, extraverts appear to speed up following punishment but not following reward, in conditions where both reward and punishment may be delivered (Nichols and Newman, 1986; Derryberry, 1987). Nichols and Newman (1986) propose modifications to Gray's (1981) theory to account for such data. Extraverts are not so much insensitive to punishment as unable to suppress a dominant but punished response, an effect demonstrated by Newman *et al.* (1985).

Conclusions

Overall, Gray's (1981) theory has provided a valuable stimulus to research, but the data are only partially consistent with prediction. Further problems are the lack of psychometric support for the rotation of personality axes suggested by Gray (1981), and possible confounding of manipulations of motivation and motivational signals with arousal changes (Eysenck and Eysenck, 1985). Pearce-McCall and Newman (1986) and Zinbarg and Revelle (1989) suggest that personality effects may be mediated by cognitive expectations of success, as well as by sensitivity of neural systems. There is also a potentially important parallel between the trial-to-trial effects of extraversion and findings from serial reaction time paradigms which suggest that following an error subjects voluntarily adjust their speed–accuracy trade-off (Rabbitt, 1979). Possibly, effects of extraversion on response speed on the trial following negative feedback reflect individual differences in the control processes which regulate speed–accuracy trade-off rather than in susceptibility to reinforcement signals *per se*. In summary, Gray (1981) has indicated an important empirical area of research, which requires theoretical integration with studies of arousal and of information processing and cognition.

CONCLUSIONS

A diversity of fairly replicable effects of extraversion on performance has been found. Compared with introverts, extraverts are poorer at some vigilance tasks and long-term memory but superior at a range of demanding attentional and STM tasks. Extraverts also tend to adopt a lower response criterion. Relationships between extraversion and task performance vary with time of day, arousal level and motivational variables. Research on extraversion thus provides a reasonably clear picture of the cognitive patterning associated with extraversion, and with its interactions with arousal, although there are a number of uncertainties over extraversion effects within specific paradigms. Table 4.1 sketches out patterns of performance change associated with simple effects of extraversion, and with extraversion × arousal interaction. To the five key aspects of performance identified by Hockey and Hamilton (1983), a further performance indicator of 'attentional resources', referring to performance on attentionally demanding tasks, has been added. Alertness is

Table 4.1 Patterns of performance change associated with simple and arousal-dependent effects of extraversion

			Fast responding			
	Alertness	*Selectivity*	*Speed*	*Accuracy*	*STM*	*Attentional resources*
Extraversion	–	0	+	–	+	+
Extraversion × arousal	+	0	+	+	+	0

indexed by the traditional, low-event rate vigilance task. For the interaction effect, + means that aroused extraverts perform well in the morning on the performance indicator concerned. The cognitive patterning of the two kinds of extraversion effect is clearly distinct.

There are several problem areas towards which future research could be directed. In studies of vigilance, the task parameters controlling whether extraversion affects the overall level of performance, performance decrement or has no effect, remain uncertain. There is also a need for direct tests of the relationship between extraversion and availability of multiple resources. The specific processes or stores responsible for the association between extraversion and memory require investigation too. There has also been little systematic research on the possible role of task variables in modifying interactions between extraversion and motivational variables: the cognitive patterning of this type of interaction cannot even be guessed at.

Theories of extraversion and performance have, at most, partial success in explaining the cognitive patterning of extraversion, and its interactions with arousal and motivation. The Eysenck (1967) theory successfully predicts several of the broad trends described: the tendency for extraverts to perform better on more difficult tasks, the behavioural impulsivity of extraverts, and the superiority of extraverts under arousing or stressful conditions during the morning. The historical importance of the Eysenck (1967) theory in stimulating research on extraversion and performance is indisputable. However, direct tests of the role of arousal in mediating correlations between extraversion and performance, using psycho-physiological or self-report indices of arousal, have been almost uniformly unsuccessful. The role of time of day is also unexplained by the theory. Given the theory's rather crude assumptions about the determinants of performance, it is not surprising that it cannot explain the more subtle effects of task parameters on the relationship between extraversion and performance. For example, task difficulty provides only a rough indication of whether extraverts are likely to out-perform introverts. The Humphreys and Revelle (1984) theory is difficult to evaluate because so few studies have manipulated or even controlled for time of day. Relevant evidence is patchy and comprises evidence both consistent and inconsistent with the main tenets of the theory. The main difficulties for the theory appear to be the lack of evidence for mediation of extraversion/impulsivity effects by arousal, and its inability to explain task parameter effects on the incidence of the modal interaction. As Revelle (1987) acknowledges, the theory provides only a partial account of extraversion effects in any case. Other theories (e.g. Dickman and Meyer, 1988; Nichols and Newman, 1986; Matthews and Harley, 1989) explain only limited parts of the data. However, progress made in relating extraversion to information processing mechanisms is a source of optimism although theory may have to accommodate effects of extraversion on several independent psychological mechanisms.

REFERENCES

Amelang, M., Wendt, W. and Fründt, H. (1977) Zum Einfluss von Extraversion/Introversion auf Konsolidierungsprozesse beim Behalten verbalen Materials. *Zeitschrift für Experimentelle und Angewandte Psychologie* **24**: 525–45.

Amelang, M. and Ullwer, U. (in press) Correlations between psychometric measures and psychophysiological as well as experimental variables in studies on extraversion and neuroticism. In *Explorations in Temperament*, edited by J. Strelan and A. Angleitner. New York: Plenum.

Anderson, K.J. and Revelle, W. (1982) Impulsivity, caffeine, and proof-reading: a test of the Easterbrook hypothesis. *Journal of Experimental Psychology: Human Perception and Performance* **8**: 614–24.

Bakan, P. (1959) Extroversion–introversion and improvement on an auditory vigilance task. *British Journal of Psychology* **50**: 325–32.

Barrett, E.S. (1987) Impulsiveness and anxiety: information processing and electro-encephalograph topography. *Journal of Research in Personality*, **21**: 453–63.

Bermudez, J., Perez, A.M. and Padilla, M. (1988) Extraversion and task properties as determinants of incidental recall. *European Journal of Personality* **2**: 57–66.

Blake, M.J.F. (1971) Temperament and time of day. In *Biological Rhythms*, edited by W.P. Colquhoun. New York and London: Academic Press.

Boddy, J., Carver, A. and Rowley, K. (1986) Effects of positive and negative verbal reinforcement on performance as a function of extraversion–introversion: some tests of Gray's theory. *Personality and Individual Differences* **7**: 81–8.

Brand, C.R. (1984) Personality dimensions: an overview of modern trait psychology. In *Psychology Survey 5*, edited by J. Nicholson and H. Beloff. Leicester: BPS.

Brebner, J. and Cooper, C. (1985) A proposed unified model of extraversion. In *Motivation, Emotion and Personality*, edited by J.T. Spence and C.E. Izard. Amsterdam: North-Holland.

Brebner, J. and Flavel, R. (1978) The effect of catch-trials on speed and accuracy among introverts and extraverts in a simple RT task. *British Journal of Psychology* **69**: 9–15.

Carr, G.D. (1969) Introversion–extraversion and vigilance performance. PhD thesis, Tufts University.

Colquhoun, W.P. (1960) Temperament, inspection efficiency, and time of day. *Ergonomics* **3**: 377–8.

Corcoran, D.W.J. (1972) Studies of individual differences at the Applied Psychology Unit. In *Biological Bases of Individual Behaviour*, edited by V.D. Nebylitsyn and J.A. Gray. New York and London: Academic Press.

Costa, P.T., Jr, McCrae, R.R. and Arenberg, D. (1983) Recent longitudinal research on personality and aging. In *Longitudinal Studies of Aging*, edited by K.W. Schaie. New York: Guildford Press.

Craig, M.J., Humphreys, M.S., Rocklin, T. and Revelle, W. (1979) Impulsivity, neuroticism and caffeine: do they have additive effects on arousal? *Journal of Research in Personality* **13**: 404–19.

Danzinger, P.R. and Larsen, J.D. (1989) Personality dimensions and memory as measured by signal detection. *Personality and Individual Differences* **10**: 809–12.

Davies, A.D.M. (1967) Temperament and narrowness of attention. *Perceptual and Motor Skills* **24**: 42.

Davies, D.R. and Hockey, G.R.J. (1966) The effects of noise and doubling the signal frequency on individual differences in visual vigilance performance. *British Journal of Psychology* **57**: 381–9.

Davies, D.R. and Parasuraman, R. (1982) *The Psychology of Vigilance*. New York and London: Academic Press.

Derryberry, D. (1987) Incentive and feedback effects on target detection: a chronometric analysis of Gray's model of temperament. *Personality and Individual Differences* **8**: 855–66.
Dempster, F.N. (1981) Memory span: sources of individual and developmental differences. *Psychological Bulletin* **89**: 63–100.
Dickman, S. (1985) Impulsivity and perception: individual differences in the processing of the local and global dimensions of stimuli. *Journal of Personality and Social Psychology* **48**: 133–49.
Dickman, S.J. and Meyer, D.E. (1988) Impulsivity and speed–accuracy trade-offs in information processing. *Journal of Personality and Social Psychology* **54**: 274–90.
Dunne, M.P. and Hartley, L.R. (1985) The effects of scopolamine upon verbal memory: Evidence for an attentional hypothesis. *Acta Psychologica* **58**: 205–17.
Easterbrook, J.A. (1959) The effect of emotion on cue utilization and the organization of behaviour. *Psychological Review* **66**: 183–201.
Edman, G., Schalling, D. and Levander, S.E. (1983) Impulsivity and speed and errors in a reaction time task: a contribution to the construct validity of the concept of impulsivity. *Acta Psychologica* **33**: 1–8.
Eysenck, H.J. (1967) *The Biological Basis of Personality*. Springfield: Thomas.
Eysenck, H.J. (1981) General features of the model. In *A Model for Personality*, edited by H.J. Eysenck. New York: Springer.
Eysenck, H.J. and Eysenck, M.W. (1985) *Personality and Individual Differences: A Natural Science Approach*. New York: Plenum.
Eysenck, M.W. (1974) Extraversion, arousal, and retrieval from semantic memory. *Journal of Personality* **42**: 319–31.
Eysenck, M.W. (1976) Extraversion, verbal learning, and memory. *Psychological Bulletin* **83**: 75–90.
Eysenck, M.W. (1977) *Human Memory: Theory, Research and Individual Differences*. Oxford: Pergamon.
Eysenck, M.W. (1981) Learning, memory and personality. In *A Model for Personality*, edited by H.J. Eysenck. New York: Springer.
Eysenck, M.W. (1982) *Attention and Arousal: Cognition and Performance*. New York: Springer.
Eysenck, M.W. and Eysenck, M.C. (1979) Memory scanning, introversion–extraversion, and levels of processing. *Journal of Research in Personality* **13**: 305–15.
Fagerstrom, K.O. and Lisper, H.O. (1977) Effects of listening to car radio, experience, and personality of the driver on subsidiary reaction time and heart rate in a long-term driving task. In *Vigilance*, edited by R.R. Mackie. New York: Plenum.
Fowles, D.C., Roberts, R. and Nagel, K. (1977) The influence of introversion/extraversion on the skin conductance response to stress and stimulus intensity. *Journal of Research in Personality* **11**: 129–46.
Gale, A. (1981) EEG studies of extraversion–introversion: What's the next step? In *Dimensions of Personality: Papers in Honour of H.J. Eysenck*, edited by R. Lynn. Oxford: Pergamon.
Gale, A., Bull, R., Penfold, V., Coles, M. and Barraclough, R. (1972) Extroversion, vigilance performance, and physiological arousal: failure to replicate traditional findings. *Psychonomic Science* **29**: 1–5.
Gange, J.J., Geen, R.G. and Harkins, S.G. (1979) Autonomic differences between extraverts and introverts during vigilance. *Psychophysiology* **16**: 392–7.
Geen, R.G., McCown, E.J. and Broyles, J.W. (1985) Effects of noise on sensitivity of introverts and extraverts to signals in a vigilance task. *Personality and Individual Differences* **6**: 237–41.
Giambra, L.M., Quilter, R.E. and Phillips, P.B. (1988) The relationship of age and extraversion to arousal and performance on a sustained attention task: A cross-sectional investigation using the Mackworth clock-test. *Personality and Individual Differences* **9**: 225–30.
Gillespie, C.R. and Eysenck, M.W. (1980) Effects of introversion–extraversion on continuous recognition memory. *Bulletin of the Psychonomic Society*, **15**: 233–5.
Gray, J.A. (1981) A critique of Eysenck's theory of personality. In *A Model for Personality*, edited by H.J. Eysenck. New York: Springer.

Gunter, B. and Furnham, A. (1986) Sex and personality differences in recall of violent and non-violent news from three presentation modalities. *Personality and Individual Differences* **6**: 829–38.

Gunter, B., Furnham, A. and Jarrett, J. (1984) Personality, time of day and delayed memory for TV news. *Personality and Individual Differences* **5**: 35–9.

Gupta, S. and Nicholson, J. (1987) Vigilance, personality and strength of the nervous system. *Personality and Individual Differences* **8**: 867–78.

Gupta, U. (1988) Personality, caffeine and human cognitive performance. *Pharmacopsychoecologia* **1**: 79–84.

Harkins, S.G. and Geen, R.G. (1975) Discriminability and criterion differences between extraverts and introverts during vigilance. *Journal of Research in Personality* **9**: 335–40.

Hastrup, J.L. (1979) Effects of electrodermal lability and introversion on vigilance decrement. *Psychophysiology* **16**: 302–10.

Hitch, G.J. (1980) Developing the concept of working memory. In *Cognitive Psychology: New Directions,* edited by G. Claxton. London: Routledge.

Hockey, G.R.J. and Hamilton, P. (1983) The cognitive patterning of stress states. In *Stress and Fatigue in Human Performance,* edited by G.R.J. Hockey. Chichester Wiley.

Humphreys, M.S. and Revelle, W. (1984) Personality, motivation and performance: a theory of the relationship between individual differences and information processing. *Psychological Review* **91**: 153–84.

Humphreys, M.S., Lynch, M.J., Revelle, W. and Hall, J.W. (1983) Individual differences in short-term memory. In *Individual Differences in Cognition,* Vol. 1, edited by R.F. Dillon and R.R. Schmeck. New York and London: Academic Press.

Imam, A. (1974) Extraversion and incidental learning. *Pakistani Journal of Psychology* **7**: 41–54.

Jones, B.M. (1974) Cognitive performance of introverts and extraverts following alcohol ingestion. *British Journal of Psychology* **65**: 35–42.

Klapp, S.T. and Netick, A. (1988) Multiple resources for processing and storage in short-term working memory. *Human Factors* **30**: 617–32.

Kumar, D. and Kapila, A. (1987) Problem solving as a function of extraversion and masculinity. *Personality and Individual Differences* **8**: 129–32.

Mangan, G.L. and Hookway, D. (1988) Perception and recall of aversive material as a function of personality type. *Personality and Individual Differences* **9**: 289–95.

Matthews, G. (1985) The effects of extraversion and arousal on intelligence test performance. *British Journal of Psychology* **76**: 479–93.

Matthews, G. (1986) The interactive effects of extraversion and arousal on performance: are creativity tests anomalous? *Personality and Individual Differences* **7**: 751–61.

Matthews, G. (1987a) Extraversion, self report arousal and performance: the role of task factors. Paper presented to the Third Meeting of the International Society for the Study of Individual Differences, Toronto, Canada.

Matthews, G. (1987b) Personality and multidimensional arousal: a study of two dimensions of extraversion. *Personality and Individual Differences* **8**: 9–16.

Matthews, G. (1988) Morningness–eveningness as a dimension of personality: trait, state and psychophysiological correlates. *European Journal of Personality* **2**: 277–93.

Matthews, G. (1989a) The factor structure of the 16PF: twelve primary and three secondary factors. *Personality and Individual Differences* **10**: 931–40.

Matthews, G. (1989b) Extraversion and levels of control of sustained attention. *Acta Psychologica* **70**: 129–46.

Matthews, G. (in press) Extraversion, arousal and levels of control of attention. In *Frontiers in Cognitive Science,* edited by Y. Hakoda. Tokyo: Science Company.

Matthews, G. and Chappelow, J. E. (1986) Effects of extraversion and arousal on selective attention. Paper presented to the British Psychological Society Cognitive Section Third Annual Conference, Oxford, England.

Matthews, G. and Harley, T.A. (1989) Extraversion, arousal and attention: a spreading activation model. Paper presented to the Fourth Meeting of the International Society for the Study of Individual Differences, Heidelberg, West Germany.

Matthews, G., Jones, D.M. and Chamberlain, A.G. (1989) Interactive effects of extraversion and arousal on attentional task performance: multiple resources or encoding processes? *Journal of Personality and Social Psychology* **56**: 629–39.

Matthews, G., Davies, D.R. and Lees, J.L. (1990a) Arousal, extraversion, and individual differences in resource availaility. *Journal of Personality and Social Psychology* **59**: 150–68.

Matthews, G., Davies, D.R. and Holley, P.J. (1990b) Extraversion, arousal and visual sustained attention: the role of resource availability. *Personality and Individual Differences* **11**: 1159–73.

Matthews, G., Davies, D.R. and Westerman, S.J. (1990c) Self-report arousal as a predictor of individual differences in attention. Paper presented to the 22nd IAAP International Congress of Applied Psychology, Kyoto, Japan.

Matthews, G., Jones, D.M. and Chamberlain, A.G. (in press) Predictors of individual differences in mail coding skills, and their variation with ability level. *Journal of Applied Psychology*.

McClelland, J.L. and Rumelhart, D.E. (1981) An interactive model of context effects in letter perception. Part I: An account of basic findings. *Psychological Review* **88**: 375–407.

McCord, R.R. and Wakefield, J.A. (1981) Arithmetic achievement as a function of introversion–extraversion and teacher presented reward and punishment. *Personality and Individual Differences* **2**: 145–52.

McCrae, R.R. and Costa, P.T., Jr (1987) Validation of the five-factor model of personality across instruments and observers. *Journal of Personality and Social Psychology* **52**: 81–90.

McKeown, J.F., Weaver, S.M. and Empson, J.A.C. (1986) Heart rate in a vigilance task: The effects of social presence and personality. *Biological Psychology* **23**: 67.

Murphy, J.A. and McKelvie, S.J. (1984) Extraversion and Stroop test performance. *Perceptual and Motor Skills* **58**: 882.

Neely, J.H. (1977) Semantic priming and retrieval from lexical memory: roles of inhibitionless spreading activation and limited-capacity attention. *Journal of Experimental Psychology (General)* **106**: 226–54.

Newman, J.P., Widom, C.S. and Nathan, S. (1985) Passive avoidance in syndromes of disinhibition: Psychopathy and extraversion. *Journal of Personality and Social Psychology* **48**: 1316–27.

Nichols, S.L. and Newman, J.P. (1986) Effects of punishment on response latency in extraverts. *Journal of Personality and Social Psychology* **50**: 624–30.

Parasuraman, R., Warm, J.S. and Dember, W.N. (1987) Vigilance: taxonomy and utility. In *Ergonomics and Human Factors: Recent Research*, edited by L. Mark, J.S. Warm and R.L. Huston. New York: Springer.

Pearce-McCall, D. and Newman, J.P. (1986) Expectation of success following punishment in introverts and extraverts: *Journal of Personality and Social Psychology* **50**: 439–46.

Puchalski, M. (1988) Impulsivity, time of day, and retention interval: the effect on cognitive performance. Doctoral dissertation, Northwestern University.

Rabbitt, P. (1979) Current paradigms and models in human information processing. In *Human Stress and Cognition: An Information Processing Approach*, edited by V. Hamilton and D.M. Warburton. Chichester: Wiley.

Revelle, W. (1987) Personality and motivation: sources of inefficiency in cognitive performance. *Journal of Research in Personality* **21**: 436–52.

Revelle, W., Amaral, P. and Turriff, S. (1976) Introversion–extraversion, time stress, and caffeine: the effect on verbal performance. *Science, New York* **192**: 149–50.

Revelle, W., Humphreys, M.S., Simon, L. and Gilliland, K. (1980) The interactive effect of personality, time of day and caffeine: a test of the arousal model. *Journal of Experimental Psychology (General)* **109**: 1–31.

Robinson, T.N., Jr and Zahn, T.P. (1988) Preparatory interval effects on the reaction time performance of introverts and extraverts. *Personality and Individual Differences* **9**: 749–62.

Schwartz, S. (1975). Individual differences in cognition: some relationships between personality and memory. *Journal of Research in Personality* **9**: 217–25.
Schwartz, S. (1979) Differential effects of personality on access to various long-term memory codes. *Journal of Research in Personality* **13**: 396–403.
Seunath, O.M. (1975) Personality, reinforcement and learning. *Perceptual and Motor Skills* **41**: 459–63.
Singh, I.L. (1989) Personality correlates and perceptual detectability of locomotive drivers. *Personality and Individual Differences* **10**: 1049–54.
Shigehisa, T. and Simons, J.R. (1973) Effects of intensity of visual stimulation on auditory sensitivity in relation to personality. *British Journal of Psychology* **64**: 205–13.
Stein, S.H. and Harrison, R.H. (1967) Conscious and preconscious influences on recall: a reassessment and extension. *Psychological Reports* **20**: 963–74.
Stelmack, R.M. (1981) The psychophysiology of extraversion and neuroticism. In *A Model for Personality*, edited by H.J. Eysenck. New York: Springer.
Stelmack, R.M. (1990) Biological bases of extraversion: psychophysiological evidence. *Journal of Personality* **58**: 293–311.
Tiggemann, M., Winefield, A.H. and Brebner, J. (1982) The role of extraversion in the development of learned helplessness. *Personality and Individual Differences* **3**: 27–34.
Vidacek, S., Kaliterna, L., Radosevic-Vidacek, B. and Folkard, S. (1988) Personality differences in the phase of circadian rhythms: a comparison of morningness and extraversion. *Ergonomics* **31**: 873–88.
Walker, E.L. (1958) Action decrement and its relation to learning. *Psychological Review* **65**: 129–42.
Wallace, J.F. and Newman, J.P. (1990) Differential effects of reward and punishment cues on response speed in anxious and impulsive individuals. *Personality and Individual Differences* **11**: 999–1010.
Weinman, J., Elithorn, A. and Cooper, R. (1985) Personality and problem solving: the nature of individual differences in planning, scanning and verification. *Personality and Individual Differences* **6**: 453–60.
Wickens, C.D. (1984) *Engineering Psychology and Human Performance*. Columbus, Ohio: Merrill.
Zinbarg, R. and Revelle, W. (1989) Personality and conditioning: a test of four models. *Journal of Personality and Social Psychology* **57**: 301–14.

5

Anxiety and Performance

J.H. MUELLER

As a feature of everyday human experience, 'anxiety' is a condition we are unlikely to escape. Sometimes the circumstances eliciting anxiety are clear to us, such as a job interview, whereas at other times the causal agent is more difficult to identify. The condition may be short-lived, perhaps especially when the eliciting agent is well-defined and some coping action can be taken, or the condition can be more enduring. Whatever the origin or lifespan, the commonplace expectation is probably that anxiety will hinder our performance.

However, closer inspection of such everyday ideas challenges them as over-simplifications. Just as the theoretical origins seem more complex and elusive than our daily experience of the emotion itself, so too the easy generalization about an anxiety–performance deficit appears to need qualification. The purpose of this chapter is to provide a summary of some of the evidence bearing on this point, and review some of the theoretical mechanisms that have been invoked to explain the effects. We will start by noting a sample of the methods that have been developed to define and quantify the experience of anxiety.

DEFINING ANXIETY

At one level, anxiety is somewhat difficult to operationalize because it seems to be a part of many other psychological experiences. Though this may be perceived as indicative of some central significance for the concept of anxiety, it does seem to preclude finding a singular technique to measure anxiety, certainly not a method independent of several other personality scales. As a

HANDBOOK OF HUMAN PERFORMANCE
VOLUME 3 ISBN 0-12-650353-2

result of this complexity a variety of methods for assessing anxiety have evolved. For our purpose, a reasonable working definition of anxiety might be as follows: '[an] unpleasant emotional state or condition which is characterized by subjective feelings of tension, apprehension, and worry, and by activation or arousal of the autonomic nervous system' (Spielberger, 1972, p. 482). This specifies both a psychological or cognitive component and a physiological aspect, and that provides a useful organizational scheme for classifying instruments to assess anxiety.

Physiological approaches

One subset of procedures has focused on physiological techniques such as electro-dermal responses, heart rate, respiration rate, pupillary dilation, and so forth. This strategy has appeal given that such dimensions are fairly clear-cut in terms of quantification, although they are occasionally cumbersome to assess. In addition, the experience of anxiety often coincides with the casual introspective judgement that we are physiologically aroused, presumably a mobilization in response to a perceived threat that may even be construed as having had survival significance.

Unfortunately, on closer inspection it appears that this desirable connection between physiological arousal and the psychological experience of anxiety is problematic. It does seem to be the case that the results obtained by comparing high and low arousal conditions on some performance measure often yield the same pattern of results as are obtained when comparing high and low anxiety subjects. This allows the findings in one area to serve as a stimulus for thinking in the other, though not always as a direct substitute in terms of conclusions. However, a number of efforts have shown that the physiological measures are often poorly intercorrelated themselves, and, furthermore, self-reported anxiety levels do not correlate very highly with the physiological measures, certainly not as well as might be expected or desired (e.g. Hodges, 1976; Bernstein *et al.*, 1986).

To date, then, the desired strong connections between the physiological condition, the phenomenological state, and the behaviours associated with anxiety have been hard to establish. This may reflect inadequacies in the phenomenal reports (including faulty emotional attributions about perceived arousal, e.g. Schacter, 1964, 1966), problems with the physiological measures, or even the conceptual link between arousal and anxiety. Although resolution of the connection between phenomenal experience and physiological measures will continue to be a matter of concern, investigators interested primarily in an index of anxiety to be used in a performance study have generally turned away from physiological measures.

However, other approaches present some problems as well. For example, one alternative is to induce anxiety in experimental subjects, perhaps by making (false) threats, for example, but this increasingly raises many ethical concerns, particularly when it is done at levels high enough to achieve ecological validity. To circumvent this issue, it may be possible to take opportunistic advantage of naturalistic variation in anxiety levels, such as often occur in the context of public speaking or other performances (e.g. Idzikowski and Baddeley, 1983; Steptoe and Fidler, 1987), trips to the dentist (e.g. Kent, 1989) or blood bank (e.g. Toglia *et al.*, 1989), or prior to voluntary hazardous activities, such as parachute jumping (e.g. Idzikowski and Baddeley, 1987). However, the opportunistic incidence and possible specificity of such naturalistic developments limits the utility of that strategy. Instead, most research on anxiety and performance has used some general self-report measure, typically derived from a written questionnaire.

Psychological inventories

TRAIT–ANXIETY ASSESSMENT

A major stimulus to research on anxiety came with the development of the manifest anxiety scale (MAS; Taylor, 1953). This was a fifty-item true–false inventory abstracted from the Minnesota Multiphasic Personality Inventory. Most importantly, the MAS was readily linked conceptually to the then-dominant theoretical framework of Hullian 'drive theory' (*cf.* Spence and Spence, 1966). In fact, this was the original stimulus for the development of the MAS as a measure of chronic individual differences in emotion-based motivation more than 'anxiety' *per se*. This connection with drive theory assured a number of testable hypotheses, and the MAS was a widely used measure of individual differences in anxiety during this period. However, this degree of attention inevitably led to the identification of some problems with the MAS, and this in conjunction with increased awareness of the complexity of the concept of anxiety sparked the development of other self-report instruments (e.g. McReynolds, 1968; Tasto, 1977).

STATE–ANXIETY ASSESSMENT

The next generation of self-report instruments began to distinguish between *trait* anxiety, characterized as an individual's enduring level of anxiety, and *state* anxiety, which is the more transitory experience triggered by some current environmental stimulus (e.g. Cattell and Scheier, 1961; Spielberger, 1966). The MAS was typically used to study the effects of anxiety on performance by comparing subjects who score at one or the other extreme on the questionnaire. This strategy presumed that high scorers, as chronically anxious people, would always be different from low scorers. However, evidence began to accrue indicating that although trait measures like the

MAS did assess anxiety-proneness, these predispositions to be anxious would be realized only when the appropriate environmental stressor was present. In other words, high scoring MAS subjects would actually experience anxiety during the experiment only if an explicit threat was apparent. Although high scorers may be inclined to perceive a greater variety of circumstances as threatening, and react more intensely to a stressor, nonetheless high trait anxiety would not guarantee high state anxiety. (In fact, the state–trait distinction can be extended to other emotional states as well, such as anger, e.g. Spielberger *et al.,* 1983.) Thus the MAS did not directly address the current anxiety level, nor do several other indices, such as the anxiety scale questionnaire developed by Cattell and Scheier (1963), the stimulus–response inventory of anxiety developed by Endler and Okada (1975), and the affect adjective checklist developed by Zuckerman (1960), though instructions for the latter can be altered to address current experiences, and mood checklist methodologies are becoming increasingly sophisticated (e.g. Matthews *et al.,* 1990).

Although the state–trait distinction was occasionally noted in earlier literature, it was only recently that instruments were developed to classify subjects in terms of both trait anxiety and situational or state anxiety. A major effort in this direction was the state–trait anxiety inventory (STAI; Spielberger *et al.,* 1970). This instrument assesses both general anxiety and current anxiety, using twenty self-report items for each, with scaled answers reflecting the degree of anxiety at four levels rather than just presence or absence. It was assumed that state anxiety scores would vary over time, as a function of when the person felt threatened by the environment, whereas trait anxiety would be more stable. High trait scorers would be vulnerable to a wider array of stressors as well as being more reactive to threats in general, and thus likely more often to display high state anxiety scores as well compared with low-trait scorers. Thus trait anxiety was the enduring, nominal level of anxiety, and state anxiety was the extent to which those predispositions to be anxious were being realized in a given situation at a specific moment in time.

The STAI was initially developed with careful attention to desirable psychometric properties, but it has continued to be thoroughly examined since its inception (e.g. Spielberger *et al.,* 1980). It was recently revised to reflect findings from research applications, to replace item content that overlapped with other emotional states such as depression, and to accommodate cultural shifts in linguistic connotations (Spielberger, 1983). At this point, after more than twenty years of extensive use, the STAI has established its value and underlined the importance of the distinction between state and trait anxiety. Consequently, laboratory studies comparing high and low anxiety subjects generally include some stressor in order to be sure the expected difference in anxiety is present, and verify its presence by collecting a state anxiety score at some point(s) during the experimental session. The evidence seems to validate this approach, particularly when the stressor involves psychological tension, such as instructions involving the subject's ego, as opposed to physical threat (e.g. Spielberger, 1977), most likely because the item content of the STAI addresses psychological stress rather than physical concerns.

SITUATIONAL ANXIETY INDICES

Another approach to increasing the predictive value of a general trait anxiety measure is to narrow the assessment to a well-defined target fear or threatening situation. By defining the stressor, subjects can presumably be more accurately classified in terms of the probable level of state anxiety that will be experienced during a future encounter with that type of situation. For example, one common experience in our modern world is explicit performance evaluation on a job (e.g. typing speed), or being tested implicitly on some skill (as during a concert performance). Although a person might not score especially high on some open-ended omnibus measure of anxiety, they might score high if the assessment focused on evaluative situations. Thus *test anxiety* as a trait could be determined, and because the context is well-defined the experimenter might be more confident in making inferences about the extent to which state anxiety levels would emerge on some future test. As a result, several indices of test anxiety have been developed, and three of these have seen fairly widespread use: the achievement anxiety test (AAT; Alpert and Haber, 1960), the test anxiety scale (TAS; Sarason, 1978), and the test anxiety inventory (TAI; Spielberger, 1980).

Because the typical laboratory study has many features of an evaluation, and because the workplace increasingly requires some covert or overt monitoring of performance, the evaluation component of trait anxiety has received increased attention in recent years, in fact serving as a model for anxiety research in some respects (*cf.* Schwarzer *et al.*, 1989a). Many of the general issues involved in studying the effect of test anxiety on performance date from an article by Mandler and Sarason (1952). Initially, they proposed that high anxiety during a test elicits task-irrelevant responses that interfere with on-task behaviours. Illustrative of these intefering responses would be thinking about the consequences of failure and engaging in assorted self-deprecating evaluations. This component of test anxiety has come to be called 'worry' to distinguish it from the arousal or 'emotionally' component, with the general assumption that the deleterious effects of test anxiety follow primarily from high levels of worry or cognitive interference (Liebert and Morris, 1967; Morris *et al.*, 1981a).

A direct test of this hypothesis requires the identification of scores for the worry aspect separate from a global measure of test anxiety, and it was for this reason that instruments such as the TAI (Spielberger, 1980) were developed. The AAT does have two subscales, debilitating and facilitating, but these do not correspond to the cognitive and physiological components just described. The TAS yields a single score, with item content almost entirely concerning the cognitive or 'worry' component, and thus it cannot be used to test predictions of differential effects for the cognitive and physiological components. The TAI is composed of twenty items, each answered on a four-level scale, with eight items focusing specifically on worry and eight other items comprising the emotionality subscale. Studies using the TAI have produced substantial evidence supporting the notion that worry scores are good predictors of performance deficits, particularly when global measures of learning are used (e.g. grade point averages). Studies using other assessments of 'worry' also seem generally consistent with this conclusion (e.g. Matthews, 1986). Some large-scale reviews have recently documented these conclusions (e.g. Hembree, 1988), with meta-analyses indicating that the predictive value of anxiety for academic performance is commonly about −0.21. The significance of the meta-analysis strategy in this domain has been reviewed by Schwarzer (1990), who further notes that the relationship between anxiety and performance in the meta-analyses seems to be stronger for females than for males.

Similar concerns with the interfering consequences of off-task thoughts has also led to the development of other inventories that try to separate further merely irrelevant thoughts (i.e. simple failure to concentrate, or distractibility) from *bona fide* worry (i.e. self-critical or task-deficiency concerns), such as the reactions to tests (Sarason, 1984) and cognitive interference questionnaires (Sarason *et al.*, 1990). Of course, it is possible to go beyond this basic distinction in self-attentive content and to consider more than a dichotomy of thoughts. For example, Heckhausen (1982) used ten categories of cognitions and found that the motivational state during the examination (success or failure orientation) also is relevant to whether specific cognitions are harmful.

Furthermore, considerable attention is being given to the feedback relationship between poor performance and test anxiety, that is, the extent to which poor performance follows or precedes high levels of worry (e.g. Everson *et al.*, 1989; Tobias, 1985; Hodapp, 1989). In contrast to the conventional view that high-anxiety causes poor performance in otherwise prepared and capable subjects, it may be that poor preparation will lead to justifiable fear of failure, largely independent of anxiety, so that the perception of probable failure by unprepared subjects during a task would escalate anxiety and further degrade performance. In simplest terms, this analysis puts the interpretation. In the latter case, test anxiety is an after-effect of poor preparation, not a prior handicap leading to poor performance by otherwise capable students.

There is some evidence that can be construed in this way (e.g. Zeidner, 1991), but given the history of outcomes on research in this area it would probably be overly optimistic to expect that the answer is as simple as just poor preparation by anxious students. In particular, recent studies by Naveh-Benjamin *et al.* (1987) considered competence in study skills along with individual differences in test anxiety. Test-anxious subjects with good study skills performed quite well in non-evaluative settings, but still suffered in an evaluative setting relative to their low-anxiety counterparts, whereas test-anxious subjects with poor study skills showed a performance deficit in both evaluative and non-evaluative settings.

Thus, although study skills appear to play a role, it appears that even with good preparation assured, anxious students may have problems in the typical evaluative setting. To complete this picture, it must be kept in mind that 'study skills' are not identical to 'test-taking skills'. The latter, training in 'test wiseness', has also been shown to reduce the cognitive aspects of test anxiety (Kalechstein *et al.,* 1988). This reinforces the notion that some of the effect of test anxiety derives from storage processes and some from retrieval processes. Although this complicates things somewhat, it actually allows therapy to be targeted better to fit the individual problem. A recent study by Naveh-Benjamin (1991) quite nicely shows that desensitization treatment was effective for those subjects who had primarily a retrieval problem (i.e. good study skills), whereas study skills training was beneficial for those anxious subjects who have more general problems.

Further refinements

As work continues on the assessment issues, we can identify increased efforts to pinpoint the critical situational determinants and components of anxiety. For example, it may be that even test anxiety is *domain specific,* at least for some people, as in 'mathematics anxiety' (e.g. Benson and Bandalos, 1989; Schwarzer *et al.,* 1989b). Schwarzer (1990) noted that this refinement from general anxiety to test anxiety to mathematics (or sport, etc.) anxiety typically does not substantially improve the degree of relationship between anxiety and performance according to patterns obtained in the meta-analyses. However, it seems useful to continue this line of work for the near future at least, and other variants that challenge the uni-dimensional view of anxiety, such as the multi-dimensional anxiety scales (Endler *et al.,* 1989).

Likewise, it may be empirically possible or even theoretically necessary to extract a *'social anxiety'* component in text anxiety (e.g. Morris *et al.,* 1981b; Sarason *et al.,* 1990; Schwarzer, 1990; Schwarzer and Quast, 1985). It is clear that self-focusing occurs during some anxious moments, but the extent to which it is a separate reaction is still at issue, as is the extent to which it is an antecedent or causal agent as opposed to being a by-product or non-causal correlated phenomenon (e.g. Bandura, 1988). It has otherwise been productive to distinguish self-awareness as a state from self-consciousness as a trait, and further to distinguish private and public components of each (e.g. Buss, 1980). Further assessment of the 'presence of others' component of anxiety, especially test anxiety, should be as useful as assessing differences between mere mind-wandering cognitions and self-critical cognitive content.

In addition, procedures such as overt thought-listing should enhance our understanding of the apparently critical role of self-preoccupation in evaluative settings (e.g. Blankenstein and Flett, 1990). Furthermore, investigators continue to be concerned about the relationship between anxiety and other personality dimensions and emotions. Although some efforts have targeted aspects such as neuroticism and impulsivity (Eysenck and Eysenck, 1977; Gray, 1981; Revelle, 1987), considerable attention is now being given to the connection between anxiety and depression (e.g. Clark *et al.*, 1990; Hedl and Bartlett, 1990; Mook *et al.*, 1990; Richards and French, 1990) and repression-sensitization (Eysenck *et al.*, 1987).

In sum, it seems clear that such efforts will enhance our ability to operationalize the construct of anxiety. It may be that specialized instruments or procedures other than those highlighted here will have unique value in some clinical settings (*cf.* Bernstein *et al.*, 1986), but laboratory research on the effects of anxiety on performance by otherwise normal subjects has made good progress using direct self-report assessment tools such as the STAI and other self-report indices of anxiety. We turn now to a selective survey of some of those data and the explanations of such effects.

ANXIETY AND PERFORMANCE: BASIC FINDINGS AND VARIABLES

The notion that anxiety invariably hinders performance clearly seems overly simplistic. A number of variables qualify that conclusion. Over the years, a large number of variables have been examined in a variety of tasks and paradigms. It is not possible to review all of these in detail here, and fortunately there are some extensive surveys and reviews already published (e.g. Broadbent, 1971; Eysenck, 1977, 1982; Kahneman, 1973; Spence and Spence, 1966). Instead, we focus on a limited number of factors to highlight and integrate some of the findings on problems that have continued to attract attention. In particular, two key variables will be examined in representative situations: task difficulty and retention interval.

Task difficulty

Among the earliest and most basic observations about the effect of anxiety on performance is that it is the extremes of the experience that are most troublesome. In everyday terms, too little anxiety implies that we may not attend or persevere sufficiently, whereas too much means we are vulnerable to the pitfalls of 'trying too hard' or 'spinning our wheels'. In the research literature on arousal and anxiety, this pattern of results is generally referred to as an 'inverted U' effect, to acknowledge that optimal performance will be achieved at some intermediate level of anxiety, with poorer performance at each extreme. This relationship between anxiety level and performance has most often been explored in conjunction with what appears to be a critical qualifying variable, namely task difficulty. The empirical relationship between arousal level, task difficulty and performance proficiency is typically referred to as the Yerkes–Dodson law (Yerkes and Dodson, 1908; Broadhurst, 1959). The most important feature of this principle is that task difficulty can be incorporated as a qualifying factor, by noting that the level of arousal that is optimal for performance is lower for difficult tasks than for easy tasks. In general terms, there is evidence in support of the outcome for a variety of definitions of arousal, including anxiety assessment, and for a variety of characterizations of difficulty.

RESPONSE STRENGTH

Yerkes and Dodson used electric shock to create differential levels of arousal in rats, and a simplistic brightness discrimination task was used to establish task difficulty. Subsequently, much of the early work on anxiety and task difficulty followed the drive theory analysis (Spence and Spence, 1966), and typically used the MAS and some verbal learning paradigm, often a paired associate task. In this case, task difficulty could be manipulated by, for example, having the to-be-learned pairs composed of dominant or non-dominant word associates (e.g. table–chair versus table–floor), thus matching the drive theory conception of strong and weak responses as high or low in a habit hierarchy. Drive theory argued that increasing drive energized all habits, both correct and incorrect. When the task was easy, the correct response was dominant at the outset, so that although increasing drive would strengthen both the desired and undesired responses, it would nonetheless strengthen the correct response more, thus correct performance would increase as drive increased (subject perhaps to some ceiling on correct response strength, e.g. physiological capacity). However, in the difficult task, where the correct response was by definition initially lower in the hierarchy, it was expected that drive increments would serve to energize already dominant error tendencies early in learning, and thus slow acquisition compared with low drive. The evidence from these habit-strength experiments was generally in accord with the notion that anxious subjects could out-perform low-anxiety subjects on the easy task but would be worse than low-anxiety subjects on a difficult task (at least in the early stages of acquisition).

COMPLEX ACTIVITIES

There are, of course, other definitions of difficulty. One general approach takes a conceptual leap and simply substitutes 'complex learning' for 'difficult' where concept learning or an intelligence test, for example, might serve as the difficult task. The presumption then is that anxiety will be more clearly harmful for these higher-order skills than for more routine tasks, whatever the difficulty of the latter in terms of correct-response position in the habit hierarchy.

Although the extension is certainly plausible at an intuitive level, this approach does break with the readily operationalized habit hierarchy definition of difficulty. Of course, that discontinuity may be perceived as much a virtue as a shortcoming, but in any event it means the outcomes of such experiments must be evaluated and interpreted separately. There is a further potential problem of being unable to define 'complex' *a priori* and independent of outcome. That is, failures to find anxiety harmful on a task intuitively defined as complex are vulnerable to a question-begging redefinition of difficult: the task was not complex enough because performance was not hindered. Nonetheless, when difficulty is construed in this way, complex tasks often do seem to be hindered by high anxiety, though there are exceptions. For example, Matthews (1986) found that although high anxiety hindered performance on a creativity task, it was not a factor for scores on an intelligence test.

When difficulty is defined in terms of a complex task, it is particularly helpful to identify the components that are involved. Not only does this help keep the definition of task difficulty at a more rigorous level, but it also makes it possible to determine whether anxiety has the same effect on each component across experimental settings. For example, in a study of reasoning from narrative text, Darke (1988a) observed that anxiety level was not a factor in drawing necessary inferences, but it did affect unnecessary inferences. Essential inferences may occur automatically without demanding much in the way of processing resources in working memory, but the unnecessary inferences do make demands on working memory, and thus the anxious subject is at a disadvantage. This outcome is consistent with the general argument that automatic or highly over-learned operations will be essentially unaffected by arousal level, whereas operations requiring rehearsal will be hindered by arousal because arousal will usurp some of the limited processing capacity (e.g. Hasher and Zacks, 1979). There are other ways to decompose task difficulty (e.g. by using something like Sternberg's (1977) componential analysis, or perhaps Gagne's (1985) hierarchy of learning types), though relatively little systematic work has been done along such lines involving individual differences in anxiety.

PROCESSING DEMANDS

Another approach to defining difficulty identifies a task as difficult if it requires considerable *effort*, or more specifically, if the task makes considerable demands on the processing resources or capacity of working memory. Effort then is readily operationalized here by the imposition of a concurrent secondary task that must be performed at the same time as the main task. The logic of much of this research derives in part from conceptions such as that proposed by Baddeley and Hitch (1974; see also Baddeley, 1986), who argued that 'short-term memory' could be characterized as consisting of a limited-capacity, modality-free central processor plus an articulatory loop, either of which might be selectively required or disrupted by tailoring a secondary task accordingly. Thus in a given situation 'difficulty' might be defined as either greater demands on the limited-capacity processor or by more interference with the articulatory rehearsal loop.

If anxiety has its effect on working memory capacity, then high- and low-anxiety subjects might differ especially on measures of capacity. Studies directly measuring simple memory span have been somewhat mixed in terms of showing anxious subjects to have significantly smaller digit spans, though the rank-order advantage does generally go to low-anxiety subjects. However, simple span measures at best assess capacity, and do not necessarily reflect demands made on the activities of the central processor component. As discussed later in the chapter, other evidence about resources in short-term memory using the dual-task methodology seems quite consistent with the idea that anxious subjects have fewer resources available for processing. This matches readily with the idea that some of the fixed capacity of working memory is inappropriately allocated to off-task activities, including inner-directed self-rumination and externally-directed threat monitoring.

Having acknowledged that the Yerkes–Dodson law has considerable support, it must be noted that the actual extent of supporting evidence is somewhat modest compared with the degree of acceptance of the idea (*cf.* review by Eysenck, 1982). Of course, some experiments, especially the earlier ones, are lacking in power or they are simply inconclusive given that they address only two levels of arousal, whereas at least three (or preferably more) must be examined to test for a curvilinear relationship. There also seems to be greater support for the outcome when arousal is induced by aversive experiences, including anxiety, than for incentive manipulations. In addition, it is perhaps prudent to evaluate the task-difficulty component separate from the general inverted-U outcome, and keep in mind that difficulty has been defined in various ways, not all of which are interchangeable.

CATASTROPHE

Nonetheless, the idea continues to generate some controversy (*cf.* Anderson, 1990) and stimulate alternative conceptions. Among the more novel recent efforts to recast the relationship between arousal level and performance is the catastrophe model proposed by Hardy and Parfitt (1991). This model was stimulated specifically by some apparent problems with the Yerkes–Dodson law in the domain of competitive sports. Catastrophe theory provides a way of conceptualizing outcomes when the relationships involve both continuous and discontinuous outcomes, that is when outcomes are described by smooth linear or curvilinear changes in the dependent variable over part of the range of manipulation of the independent variable(s), but also with some outcomes that defy such tidy inclusion. A complete treatment of such models or even this particular effort goes beyond the space available here (e.g. see Stewart and Peregoy, 1983), but Figure 5.1 presents the essence of their analysis of arousal and performance as a case of the cusp variety of catastrophe models.

Hardy and Parfitt (1991) incorporate both physiological and cognitive arousal in their model (through the latter may not correspond precisely to the 'worry' construct discussed earlier), so the result is a three-dimensional summary of performance, physiological arousal and cognitive arousal. The critical feature is the performance or behavioural surface, which in the three-dimensional summary resembles a wave breaking on the ocean or an overlapping fold in a tablecloth or blanket. For some combinations of physiological and cognitive arousal this produces a smooth and continuous change, so that when cognitive arousal is low and physiological arousal increases we get the venerable inverted U effect at the very back edge of Figure 5.1 (the $x-z$ 'wall') as a special case. However, as the situation also begins to incorporate cognitive arousal (as at the front edge or the intermediate line on the behaviour surface in Figure 5.1), then increases in physiological arousal will yield smooth performance gains up to a point, but then a 'catastrophic' or sudden and large decline occurs rather than a slow and gradual decline.

Their experiment produced some results in accord with the catastrophe characterization, though as usual there were some problems. It remains to be

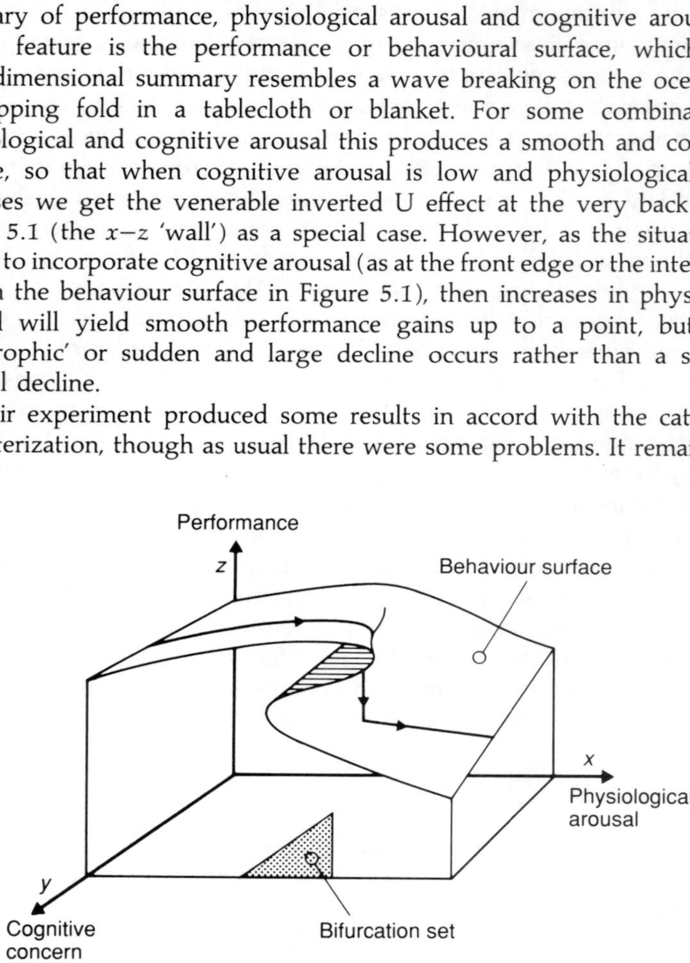

Figure 5.1 A catastrophe (cusp) model of the relationship between anxiety level and performance (adapted from Hardy and Parfitt, 1991).

seen how well such a model or some variant will generalize to other situations. As will be argued below, studying experienced subjects as well as inexperienced subjects is a desirable strategy, thus the use of well-practised participants in competitive sports has many attractions as a way to examine some aspects of the relationship between arousal and performance. However, a complete explanation must encompass the full range of capabilities and task features, and we will have to wait and see how well the catastrophe model(s) work in the broader scheme of anxiety research. Furthermore, catastrophe models are essentially descriptive (as is the basic Yerkes–Dodson law), and would still leave us in need of explanatory mechanisms that account for the performance changes. Nonetheless, such models certainly provide a new stimulus for thinking in this area, and may ultimately help resolve the mixed results ostensibly covered by the Yerkes–Dodson law.

Retention interval

Are anxious subjects always at risk, given that the task is difficult enough by some definition, or do other variables mitigate the handicap? A number of other variables have been considered, but several perspectives have an interest in whether performance may be especially disrupted when the test occurs soon after learning or at some more distant point in time.

TRACE CONSOLIDATION

Aside from task difficulty, considerable attention has been directed to retention interval, or the effect of anxiety on delayed tests as opposed to immediate tests. Historically, interest in the effect of arousal on delayed tests was stimulated by Walker's (1958) *action-decrement theory*. According to this view, the presence of arousal at the time of study prolongs the period of time that an event would be 'active'. This would enhance its prospects for storage and delayed retention, but perhaps interfere with the availability of the memory trace during the period of ongoing consolidation immediately following the study experience. Early research using item-content (e.g. provocative versus neutral words) to index arousal often produced supportive results (e.g. Kleinsmith and Kaplan, 1963), though there were a number of exceptions (*cf.* Eysenck, 1977). Somewhat more successful have been the efforts which examine the general idea by using arousal differences associated with extraversion–introversion. Eysenck (1967) argued that trace consolidation will take longer for introverts, leading to worse performance by introverts at short delays but better performance on long delayed tests, and evidence generally in accord with this expectation has been noted in a variety of contexts (e.g. Gunter *et al.*, 1984).

On the other hand, some investigators have recently argued that arousal will always benefit retention, that is at both short and long retention intervals, by focusing attention and strengthening storage rather than disrupting it. Phaf and Wolters (1986) used pupillary dilation to index arousal, and found that arousal led to better incidental short-term recall. Whatever the ultimate resolution of this issue in terms of arousal, neither pattern of results conforms to that generally obtained for anxiety, a case in point in terms of the occasional divergence of findings within the 'arousal complex' of constructs. However, there are other reasons to be interested in the effect of retention interval, and some of these accommodate the anxiety data fairly well.

ENCODING VARIATION

There are reasons other than consolidation duration to expect some encoding differences due to anxiety level on delayed tests that may not appear on immediate tests. For example, it has been proposed that arousal leads to a relative emphasis on processing superficial physical features at the expense of deeper, semantic processing (e.g. Schwartz, 1975). This leads to the expectation that, although shallow processing might be sufficient for an immediate test, the difference between high and low arousal conditions would be increasingly apparent on delayed tests, with aroused subjects retaining less than low-arousal subjects. Although delayed superiority for aroused subjects may be the case when arousal is defined in terms of extraversion, it does not seem to be so for anxiety. That is, relative to low-anxiety subjects, anxious subjects generally function at a deficit on both immediate and delayed tests (e.g. Mueller and Courtois, 1980), contrary to the consolidation view, and at least in accord with some version of the levels or breadth of processing interpretation.

STUDY-TEST CONGRUENCE

Another reason that the retention interval might be of some interest has to do with the considerable body of evidence that indicates optimal performance is achieved when the storage conditions match the test conditions. This congruence effect has been demonstrated for a variety of circumstances, and it goes by a variety of labels (e.g. encoding specificity, state-dependent learning, etc.). This outcome is best demonstrated when the study and test phases are discrete and clearly separated in time. Otherwise mismatched study and test conditions are difficult to construct for comparison to the matched conditions. Therefore, something other than an immediate test or ongoing assessment of performance is probably required.

Context-dependent retrieval is shown when performance is hindered because some study cues are missing at the time of a subsequent retrieval effort. To the extent that anxiety level functions as a part of the internal stimulus context, it can be asked whether performance is 'anxiety-dependent'. That is, would we obtain worse performance on a delayed test just because the internal anxiety experience shifts from one time (study) to another (test)?

An answer to this question requires a delayed test, where anxiety level can be induced or at least assessed separately for the study and test phase. By this analysis (e.g. Mueller *et al.*, 1989), it might be expected that subjects who are low in trait-anxiety would be low on both occasions, whereas the anxious subjects would experience a study–test mismatch, being perhaps more relaxed during study than on the test. Although this is a plausible notion, mood-dependent retrieval has been difficult to obtain consistently for other moods (*cf.* Bower and Mayer, 1989; Mueller *et al.*, 1991). To this point, the research is quite limited, but anxiety-dependence appears to be problematic as well (e.g. Foa *et al.*, 1989). This could be attributed to the fact that, in general, cognitive concerns seem more predictive of the anxiety deficit than emotionality, implying that without special efforts to the contrary situations may be matched in terms of study–test emotionality without being matched in terms of study–test worry, for example. It may well be that the self-attention component is the aspect that most needs to be present at both study and test.

In sum, with regard to retention interval, it appears that anxiety differs somewhat from the other variables in the 'arousal complex'. Whereas arousal may have long-term benefits for retention when operationalized in some ways, that appears not to be the case for anxiety, as anxious subjects generally do worse on both immediate and delayed tests. This may indicate that the effect of anxiety on storage is better understood in terms of a reduced number of features encoded, fewer high quality features being rehearsed, fewer associative links established during storage, or even shifted study–test context, rather than trace strength *per se*. In the next section, we will examine some of these theoretical mechanisms that have been implicated in explaining the anxiety deficit.

EXPLANATORY MECHANISMS

One way to conceptualize just how anxiety has its effect on performance would be to frame the question in terms of whether the effect occurs as a result of some process operative only during the test or whether the performance deficit is carried over from some earlier stage in learning, in other words, a by-product of differential original learning attributable to rehearsal or pre-rehearsal selection processes. Cognitive psychologists have come to accept that our memories may be affected by processes that occur during encoding as well as by retrieval conditions, and that optimal performance generally requires a close match of the study and test states. Memory research paradigms have been developed to allow variables to separately affect storage and retrieval, and this strategy seems applicable to the anxiety–performance question as well.

If we adopt this strategy, it becomes clear that a number of mechanisms have been proposed to explain the performance deficit that may emerge under conditions of high anxiety, and a provisional summary is shown in Figure 5.2. The advantage of using this organizational scheme is partly didactic, but it also accommodates better the growing judgement that no single process can account for all of the effects of anxiety on performance. In other words, this multi-stage approach incorporates several mechanisms as complementary, and this is likely to be more productive than artificially setting one explanation against another in a simplistic 'winner take all' format. For example, Everson

STUDY

Range of cue utilization: anxious subjects attend to fewer environmental features
Depth of encoding: anxious subjects focus on superficial or physical attributes
Breadth of processing: anxious subjects do not seek connections between aspects
Rehearsal style: anxious subjects are less flexible at using alternative strategies
Study skills: anxious subjects are deficient in the amount or quality of preparation
Threat monitoring: anxious subjects examine all events for danger potential
Self-image: anxious subjects see themselves as poor learners, study less

TEST

Response competition: anxious subjects must contend with irrelevant behaviours
Range of cue utilization: anxious subjects attend to fewer environmental features
Cognitive interference: anxious subjects think about task-irrelevant aspects
Self-focusing: anxious subjects are self-preoccupied
Resource overload: anxious subjects lose working memory capacity by worrying
Threshold fluctuation: anxious subjects need more information to respond or decide
Test-wiseness: anxious subjects are less knowledgeable about taking tests
Threat monitoring: anxious subjects examine all events for danger potential
Attributional style: anxious subjects accept failure and discount success
Self-image: anxious subjects see themselves as poor learners, expend less effort
Incongruent context: anxious subjects are less able to restore study cues at retrieval

Figure 5.2 A partial summary of the theoretical processes identified as underlying the effect of anxiety on performance, arranged by the primary locus of the effect of each in terms of the storage and retrieval components of learning.

et al. (1989) concluded that both test anxiety and study skills were needed to determine test performance more fully.

However, it must be acknowledged that the data obtained from previous laboratory experiments do not always tidily fit into just storage or just retrieval interpretations. That is, relatively little of the laboratory research on the effects of anxiety has systematically assessed its role at study versus at testing. Instead, a given level of anxiety typically has been present (absent) at both the time of storage and during attempted retrieval. This is because the study and test phases of, for example, paired associate learning, occur in a very compressed time frame in a typical laboratory learning experiment. Therefore, unless some long-term delayed test is used, the anxiety level during the test was also present during study. This is not so much a call for ecologically valid field experiments as it is a reminder that we can and should perhaps control this aspect in the laboratory, or at least acknowledge that anxiety may otherwise vary from study to test (and even at critical points near the test, e.g. Zeidner, 1991).

In spite of research paradigms that have often confounded the study–test locus of anxiety differences, it is possible to classify the theoretical interpretations of the outcome in terms of a process occurring at either the time of the test or during the study phase. We will examine the test-deficit view, first, that being perhaps the intuitively obvious locus of performance problems. For the sake of discussion, test-deficit processes can be loosely grouped into those dealing more with response execution versus those implicating response selection differences as a function of anxiety level.

Retrieval-based explanations

RESPONSE COMPETITION

The drive theory view (Spence and Spence, 1966) would be difficult to surpass as a retrieval explanation of the anxiety performance deficit. Subjects who are anxious at testing will experience the activation of various incorrect responses that will compete with successful performance of the desired behaviour, the main question being the initial relative placement of the correct and incorrect responses in the habit hierarchy (i.e. whether the task is easy or difficult). In the conventional conditioning and verbal learning experiments, studying (acquisition) and testing (performance) both occur with very little temporal separation, certainly not with a time interval long enough that it would be reasonable to assume the dissipation of arousal. Thus comparable anxiety will be present at each phase, but the basis for the anxiety deficit is clearly said to be at retrieval, that is, getting the correct response to be output, rather than storing it in the first place. When the acquisition or learning phase is clearly separated in time from the test phase, the explanatory burden placed on anxiety level at retrieval just becomes more obvious.

COGNITIVE INTERFERENCE

A case can also be made that, using this classification, most of the test anxiety explanations that derive from Mandler and Sarason's (1952) analysis also emphasize a retrieval-based process, albeit of a different type, where generally self-oriented cognitive concerns interfere with performance. That is, a learner is appraising performance, anticipating failure and loss of status, and so forth, while taking a test. Consequently, this self-preoccupation can be construed as a handicap that occurs during retrieval, in fact leading to the name of the construct, 'test' or retrieval/performance anxiety. In this case, though, it is necessary to acknowledge that in the typical laboratory situation such task-irrelevant thinking will likely have an impact on storage as well, given that study and test phases occur so close together in time. Outside the laboratory, such as perhaps in the case of a semester-long university course, the final examination will be well separated in time from at least some of the study activities. In such cases it seems unlikely that self-evaluative thinking occurs with the same frequency or intensity during the earlier study sessions that may characterize its occurrence at exam time. Thus the effect of self-absorbed, task-irrelevant thinking or worrying will occur primarily during the retrieval phase in such cases, whereas in laboratory studies cognitive concerns may often affect encoding as well as retrieval.

As should be apparent, these retrieval-based analyses, especially the latter, would also be well-suited to many non-academic everyday situations where job performance is monitored. In such cases, a skilled craftsman, for example, has long since acquired or stored all of the requisite behaviours, so there is little basis for assuming encoding differences or lack of learning. Nonetheless, when a periodic job review or opportunity for a promotion occurs, anxiety-prone individuals can be expected to have more trouble than less anxious people, presumably because they will tend to engage in off-task self-monitoring during the test or interview, quite aside from whether it was ever present during training. Another good example of this argument is in the performance of highly trained athletes under different anxiety levels (e.g. Heckhausen and Strang, 1988).

In addition, some procedure to identify everyday cognitive failures (e.g. Broadbent *et al.*, 1982) may provide another suitable format in which to study the effects of stress on behaviours that have already been well-established. It seems clear that cognitive failures occur outside the laboratory during periods of self-focused attention (e.g. Houston, 1989; Martin, 1983; Matthews and Wells, 1988), though a selective attention component may also be implicated (e.g. Tipper and Baylis, 1987) in addition to a retrieval failure, and further attention to the role of anxiety here would be quite useful. This would blend nicely with some systematic attention to comparisons of novices and experts in various domains in regard to anxiety effects on retrieval or performance or over-learned skills or knowledge, even including semantic memory paradigms from cognitive psychology experiments.

EVALUATIVE DEMANDS

Another set of circumstances where the retrieval interpretation is well-suited would be those situations where subjects are allowed to retake an exam without penalty or under some other unthreatening or non-evaluative conditions. Hypothetically, test-anxious subjects may know the material but be unable to perform on the typical test when there is no prospect for recovering from a mistake. Improved performance for anxious subjects under such no-penalty conditions speaks to the existence of a retrieval or 'blockage' component in the anxiety deficit (e.g. Covington and Omelich, 1987), though it may be that only the truly prepared anxious subjects would benefit (*cf.* Naveh-Benjamin *et al.,* 1987).

Other efforts to clarify the role of retrieval in the anxiety deficit have sometimes utilized different test procedures specifically designed to eliminate or minimize retrieval in some way, thus bypassing both response competition and self-focused distraction. One strategy is to compare recognition test results to recall data, working in part on the premise that whereas failure on a recall test may reflect either storage or retrieval problems, recognition failure should not reflect a retrieval problem. Differences due to anxiety level may be reduced on a recognition test, but differences generally remain, presumably because there are various storage processes which are affected by anxiety level as well as output processes (e.g. Hedl and Bartlett, 1989).

More recently, the form of the memory test has again become of interest in terms of how directly the test format requires information to be supplied. This interest has been motivated by the finding that information may appear to be lost when the test requires explicit performance, but that information shows its influence on an indirect or implicit memory test (e.g. Roediger, 1990). For example, amnesics may be unable to supply certain information when queried directly, whether the test is free recall or recognition (e.g. Which of these words was in the preceding study set: universe or computer?). However, these subjects may well answer correctly when given an indirect test involving, for example, completing a word given a fragment (U_I_E_ _ _) or answering some general knowledge question (What did the Big Bang create?). This implies that the information has not been forgotten, in that it can be used under some circumstances, but successful performance requires an indirect test rather than an on-demand assessment.

Is it possible that the anxiety deficit could be alleviated like the amnesic deficit by using an implicit test rather than an explicit test? To some extent, this would be consistent with the improvement by anxious subjects when they are allowed to retake an examination without penalty (e.g. Covington and Omelich, 1987), though that still involves an on-demand or direct test. One perspective (e.g. Mandler, 1980) on the difference between indirect and direct tests is that one memory process (implicit memory) is essentially the automatic strengthening of a mental representation, so that accessibility is enhanced without any necessary gain in retrievability, whereas another process (explicit memory) involves elaboration of the representation that is activated and strategic linking of it with other representations. It seems clear that anxious subjects do often have trouble with deep or elaborative rehearsal (e.g. Mueller, 1978), though again that evidence has been obtained only with direct tests so far.

A better answer would require a comparison of direct and indirect tests with high- and low-anxiety subjects. The research to date is quite limited, and somewhat inconclusive because it was conducted to test a somewhat different hypothesis (i.e. threat monitoring by anxious subjects). Mathews *et al.* (1989a) compared cued recall (explicit memory) and word completion performance (implicit memory) in clinically anxious subjects and normal subjects, using both threatening and non-threatening words. Considering just the neutral content in their study (which may correspond best to the more general concern with poorer performance by anxious subjects), currently anxious subjects seemed to do somewhat worse on both explicit and implicit tests, that is anxious subjects did not recover 'lost' information in the same way that amnesics often do on an indirect test. For the threatening material, currently anxious and normal subjects did not differ in terms of the direct test (cued recall), whereas the anxious subjects were clearly better than normals on the indirect test (word completion). Richards and French (1991) replicated the general finding of a dissociation between implicit and explicit memory tests, but on closer inspection the pattern was not quite the same as that found by Mathews *et al.* (1989a) and varied for different encoding conditions.

In sum, the type of material being recalled may make some difference in terms of whether or not the anxiety deficit can be eliminated by an indirect test, yet in neither case was the pattern precisely what an ideal result would be to conclude that an indirect test effectively revealed material blocked by a direct query, the counterpart to the early amnesia studies of implicit memory. That is, such a pattern would require high-anxiety subjects to do worse than normals on the direct test, then do as well on the indirect test. It could be that the results obtained by Mathews *et al.* (1989a) depart from this ideal because of complexities associated with the use of clinically anxious subjects, but that seems unlikely to be the sole factor because Richards and French (1991) used anxious normal subjects. It could be that the mixture of neutral and threatening material in the study set is the critical factor, but that will have to be determined by subsequent research. Thus the data are not yet definitive in terms of the basic question of whether the anxiety deficit can be resolved like the amnesic deficit simply by using an indirect test, but direct and indirect tests do seem to produce somewhat different patterns of performance for anxious subjects, and this strategy certainly seems to warrant further examination in the study of test anxiety and other mood states (e.g. depression) that involve apparent deficits on direct tests.

Storage-based explanations

CUE UTILIZATION

In contrast to test-activated processes that hinder performance even when storage actually did occur, acquisition *per se* could be affected if it occurs in the presence of high anxiety. The roots of many study-deficit explanations can be found in the cue-utilization hypothesis advanced by Easterbrook (1959). Easterbrook distinguished between task-relevant and task-irrelevant cues, and then argued that increments in drive would reduce a subject's range of cue utilization. Starting at relatively low levels of anxiety, the initial effect of a reduced range of cue utilization would be inattention to cues that are peripheral or functionally irrelevant to the task at hand, thus enhancing performance on the intentional task. However, continued increases in anxiety would eventually result in the exclusion of task-relevant cues as well, and at that point proficiency on the target task would begin to suffer. Assuming that difficult (i.e. complex) tasks involve processing and integrating more relevant features, the point at which a diminished range of attention would start to eliminate relevant cues would occur at lower anxiety levels as difficulty increases, thus providing a general theoretical explanation for the Yerkes–Dodson effect in terms of acquisition or encoding problems instead of retrieval processes. (Of course, a task could be difficult because just a few features are relevant, but a restricted range of attention would still be detrimental in terms of lowering the probability of sampling the pertinent feature in a large pool.)

The extent to which subjects attend to irrelevant content can be assessed in a variety of ways. One procedure uses some form of incidental content in conjunction with the primary task, and then observes performance on the target task as a function of the nature or compatibility of the added information. For example, Zaffy and Bruning (1966) added relevant or irrelevant serial order information as an incidental cue, and found that, for anxious subjects, learning of the target material was hindered less by irrelevant cues and helped less by relevant ones, compared with low anxiety subjects. This presumably occurred because the reduced range of attention for anxious subjects kept extraneous conflicting content from interfering, though by the same token the benefit of a helpful redundancy was missed as well.

Instead of observing effects on learning the target material, other studies have measured the subject's ability to recall the irrelevant *content per se* following passive exposure to it. Yet other procedures actually imposed and monitored an active secondary *task* along with the target task, assuming anxious subjects would not perform as well on the secondary task because their restricted range of cue utilization precludes attending to both the primary and secondary task content. A thorough review of early research using various methods to test Easterbrook's hypothesis indicated that high anxiety hindered performance on the secondary component in roughly 75 per cent of the cases (Eysenck, 1982), though interference with the primary task was less commonly found. Viewed at a distance, this is substantial support for a psychological hypothesis, but closer inspection reveals some troublesome details: different stressors yield somewhat different patterns of support; interpretive puzzles also abound. For example, the results obtained by Zaffy and Bruning (1966) can be construed as reflecting inattention to irrelevant material when anxious; however, in that procedure such a result also implies reduced distractibility under high anxiety, a condition that belies the reports by anxious subjects that they have trouble concentrating (Deffenbacher, 1978) and other data suggesting greater distractibility instead of less for anxious subjects.

In short, it seems fair to conclude that the evidence broadly indicates that anxiety affects what the subject attends to, but probably not as uniformly nor so inexorably as proposed by Easterbrook. In addition, Easterbrook saw anxiety as a unitary construct, whereas it now seems clear that there are generally different effects of the emotionality and worry components. From this over-simplified beginning then, we must work out the details of such attentional selectivity. Because the interest is in a finer-grain analysis of encoding, the tasks that have emerged as useful typically have a minimal retrieval component, but the implication is that if such anxiety-level encoding differences can be established then some effect will probably carry over to subsequent recall performance. In fact, the results seem to indicate more than one aspect of stimulus processing is affected by anxiety. A recent proposal by Eysenck (1988) sketches out a framework that shows the complexity of the problem, and the interrelatedness of the various components that seem to be involved. In this scheme, at least four possible components may be involved in attentional differences as a function of anxiety level: content, distraction, selection *per se* and capacity.

THREAT MONITORING

In terms of *content*, it appears that anxious subjects are more prone to attend to emotional stimuli, or to examine all stimuli in terms of their threat potential, compared with low-anxiety subjects (*cf.* review by Mathews, 1991). For example, irrelevant threat stimuli command processing resources even when present in a second task (e.g. Mathews and MacLeod, 1986). Furthermore, ambiguous stimuli may be more readily seen as threatening by anxious subjects (Mathews *et al.*, 1989b). Thus selective attention under high anxiety does not include all experiences equally, but shows a specific bias to find danger in external cues whether those are task-relevant or not. This seems to be an enduring aspect of the behaviour of the trait-anxious subject (e.g. Mathews *et al.*, 1990), that is a general vulnerability rather than just a reaction triggered by emotions aroused by current conditions.

Interestingly though, this increased vigilance toward threat cues does not always lead to enhanced free recall of such events; in fact, anxious subjects may recall non-threat items better than threat items (e.g. Mogg *et al.*, 1987). This is at odds with the mood congruence phenomenon in memory discussed earlier. For example, happy subjects tend to recall more happy experiences than sad ones, and vice versa for sad subjects, leading to the expectation that anxious subjects would remember more anxiety-provoking content than nonemotional content. Ingram *et al.* (1987) did find some results consistent with mood-congruent retention (in the form of self-referent specificity), but neither Mogg *et al.* (1987) nor Foa *et al.* (1989) found this, nor were the data of Mueller and Thompson (1984) generally consistent with mood-congruent recall. Some of the data obtained by Mathews *et al.* (1989a) were more in accord with mood congruence, but only with an indirect memory test. The explanation for some of the inconsistency on mood congruence may be that, for anxious subjects, the effort at detection is followed by disengagement or at least by efforts to evade the event tagged as a threat (e.g. Carver *et al.*, 1983), with the result that less elaborative encoding occurs.

In any event, the result suggests a somewhat different anxiety effect on processing from what seems to occur in the case of depression (where a depressive schema may be associated with some early attention bias), and following detection the depressed subject seems to continue to contemplate the depression-related material. The result with depressives then is that the depressive content is recalled better (e.g. Greenberg and Beck, 1989), whether or not it is perceived differentially from non-depressive content. It appears that anxious subjects attend more to emotional or threat material, even endorse it as self-descriptive (Mueller and Thompson, 1984), but are not necessarily able to remember it better relative to neutral content. In general, this would also seem inconsistent with the argument of Phaf and Wolters (1986) that arousal defined otherwise yields a strong memory trace. The substantial evidence that the anxiety experience involves considerable internal self-directed monitoring may help to explain the apparent ineffectiveness of mood congruence, in that the external monitoring occurs along with internal monitoring.

CONCENTRATION

Distractibility is, loosely speaking, the inability to concentrate on the target task when irrelevant stimulation is present. If anxious subjects are preoccupied with self-monitoring of performance, then it is not surprising that they have trouble concentrating in this sense, and there seems to be ample evidence that they engage in various forms of self-directed, task-irrelevant attention. In addition, if, as noted above, anxious people are constantly vigilant to detect environmental threats, then they will be easily directed off-task by external events as well. Although some evidence can be construed as indicating reduced distractibility under high anxiety (e.g. Zaffy and Bruning, 1966), the preponderance of evidence seems in accord with increased distractibility at high anxiety levels.

ATTENTION

In considering *general selectivity* among those signals that are attended to, we acknowledge the basic thrust of the original Easterbrook hypothesis whereby anxiety is associated with generally reduced utilization of peripheral cues. When peripheral cues are irrelevant to the task, this should be beneficial, but performance will eventually suffer when the reduction begins to drop out some of the salient information. At this point, additional factors could become involved in the selection process, as anxious subjects may begin to select specific stimulus dimensions for processing. One relevant dimension for anxious subjects may be the perceived threat significance of a stimulus, but even in the absence of a threat it may be that anxious subjects process differently from low-anxiety subjects. For example, Schwartz (1975, 1979) proposed that aroused subjects would engage in shallow or superficial processing, such as attending to orthographic or acoustic features, as opposed to deeper semantic encoding, with the result that long-term retention by anxious subjects would suffer whether short-term performance did or not. There is evidence that this happens under some circumstances, though it often can be interpreted as also involving a high-anxiety deficit in elaborative rehearsal as much as simply attending to shallow features (Mueller, 1978). It seems clear that anxious subjects do less processing of the deeper features and less elaborative rehearsal relative to low-anxiety subjects, with the expected problems that that creates for long-term retention. They may also do less shallow processing or less maintenance rehearsal as well, at least under some circumstances (e.g. Darke, 1988b).

Another approach to looking at how stimuli are detected and utilized considers not just the breadth of attention, but the *threshold* or criterion used to decide that an event has occurred or that a response should be made. This criterion viewpoint argues that, in signal detection terms, anxious subjects set a higher or more stringent decision criterion with regard to reporting the occurrence of a signal. Therefore, the poorer performance of anxious subjects may reflect not differential sensitivity or detection of the signal *per se*, but simply greater caution in reporting. Much of the more recent work on this general viewpoint derives directly or indirectly from Broadbent's (1971) landmark analysis of stress and arousal effects on simple vigilance tasks. Unfortunately, although there has been considerable work on other indices of arousal in vigilance, relatively little has been done in terms of the effects of anxiety.

The essential argument would be that anxious subjects may be more cautious about responding, in effect gathering additional evidence before responding, and thus they appear to be either inattentive, unaware or distracted by inference from lower performance levels, but in fact the non-responses are attributable to decision criteria different from those of low-anxiety subjects. Geen (1985) found evidence consistent with this criterion-difference viewpoint in a study of test-anxious subjects performing on a conventional vigilance task. That is, test-anxious subjects did not differ from low-anxiety subjects in terms of signal identification (d'), but anxious subjects did show higher criterion levels (β). This outcome can be understood in terms of strategies for coping with the fear-of-failure component of test anxiety, namely that when it is not possible to avoid the test *per se*, at least try to avoid failing by adopting a cautious strategy to minimize incorrect responding.

The argument for greater caution by anxious subjects is bolstered by data from tasks quite different from simple signal detection. For example, Goulet and Mazzei (1969) found that anxious subjects seemed to take longer to begin emitting responses in paired associate learning, a finding that is contrary to drive theory but consistent with the interpretation that anxious subjects wanted to be confident before overtly responding whereas low-anxiety subjects were willing to respond on the basis of less associative strength. More recently, Mikulincer *et al.* (1990) examined natural categorization by anxious and normal subjects, and found that anxious subjects were less inclusive of atypical instances of a category, and otherwise behaved as if they were being more cautious about what qualified an object for category membership.

Nichols-Hoppe and Beach (1990) have extended the more-cautious logic to a complex decision-making task. Their procedure had subjects selecting apartments, based on differences in rent, size, noise level and other attributes. The task required subjects to decide among various options, while allowing the researchers to assess the amount of information (i.e. criterion level) considered by high- and low-anxiety subjects and to track their tendencies to reinspect information. High test-anxious subjects not only inspected more information than their low-anxiety counterparts, they also reinspected more information. Importantly, these differences did not seem merely derivative of differences in short-term memory capacity *per se* as assessed by digit span tests. Of course, as the task became more complex, even low-anxiety subjects began to have similar difficulties.

In sum, it seems that anxious subjects may be more cautious and process more information before rendering a decision. However, it is not yet clear that the quality of the decisions they reach are acceptable or equivalent to those of the low-anxiety subjects even after the extra effort, so this is a viewpoint that requires further work. The approach seems promising though, because it extends the threshold-difference rationale of the detection task to more complex situations which allow us to examine how information is detected and applied in a realistic manner. At this level of complexity, of course, the processes involved in the anxiety deficit may include retrieval as well as storage differences.

COMPENSATORY EFFORT

Although reduced cue utilization was conceived as an automatic process by Easterbrook, it increasingly seems more likely that focused attention reflects in part a more deliberate effort to cope with the limited processing resources that remain when some capacity in working memory is allocated to task-irrelevant behaviours such as monitoring external threats and/or internal self-recriminations. Of course, one understandable but ultimately maladaptive strategy to cope with the competing demands for processing resources would indeed be to avoid or reduce the more time-consuming endeavours of analysing deep features or encoding elaboratively. Although this has long-term negative consequences, such retrenchment can often be at least partially effective in the immediate present.

An alternative coping strategy would be to increase the 'effort' allocated to the task. It seems clear that one of the results of subjects being confronted with a challenging task is an increment in some measures of arousal (e.g. Kahneman, 1973), and several theorists have argued that this may reflect heightened efforts to compensate for these task demands (e.g. Eysenck, 1979; Hamilton, 1975). In other words, 'performance efficiency' (objective behavioural measures of task mastery) may not always show the effects of anxiety because subjects can to some extent compensate by adjusting their commitment or 'processing effectiveness', under-estimating the adverse effects of anxiety. This is just a subset of a larger concern with the point at which some compensatory process will neutralize interference and eliminate a distraction effect at the level of performance. In such research, compensation both seems more likely and more successful for easy tasks, and, when the distracting material is dissimilar to the target material (e.g. Graydon and Eysenck, 1989), quite consistent with anxiety research on these factors. Thus increased distractibility when anxiety increases would seem the likely result for complex tasks, whereas for simple tasks increasing anxiety would have either no effect or perhaps yield some benefit (reduced distractibility).

In the context of anxiety, however, one additional factor may affect whether anxious subjects persist with or fail to expend extra effort on a task. It has been argued that anxious subjects should have an *attributional style* of explaining their successes (and failures) that differs from the style of low-anxiety subjects (e.g. Arkin *et al.*, 1983). Specifically, anxious subjects fail to attribute success to their own ability (e.g. passing it off as lucky, an atypical result, etc.), but they do self-critically accept their failures as due to general lack of ability, whereas low-anxiety subjects attribute causes to outcomes in a more completely self-serving manner, viewing success as derived from ability and explaining failure in terms other than personal ability. Although the evidence for this is limited, Hedl (1990) and Schwarzer (1990) have also reported evidence in accord with this general expectation. It seems reasonable to believe that compensatory effort will result when subjects perceive they can claim the credit for success, so it seems important to establish just when anxious subjects can accept that commitment and when they will otherwise opt out of expending more effort. Thus Schwarzer's (1990) call for greater attention to the mitigating effects of contextual features, such as, the extent of the teacher's focus on time management, incentive systems, and so forth (*cf.* Helmke, 1988) seems quite appropriate.

INPUT LIMITS

The final feature of this storage-oriented analysis of anxiety effects considers individual differences in the size of the short-term storage system. Reduced capacity in immediate memory under high anxiety seems well-established, whether capacity is conceived in terms of a spatial or size dimension or conceptualized in more strategic or operational terms as resource allocation. For example, Darke (1988b) reported two experiments comparing high and low test-anxious subjects, one using the traditional digit span procedure and another using a sentence verification measure to assess working memory capacity. The research was conceived in the context of Baddeley's (1986) characterization of immediate memory, whereby there is an articulatory rehearsal loop as well as an executive component coordinating the operations. The digit span task merely requires the information in working memory to be maintained in serial order, without any comprehension or integration of the information. Thus it reflects primarily the articulatory loop component rather than processing capacity. As has been found by others, anxious subjects had smaller digit spans than low-anxiety subjects. The other capacity measure required subjects to verify sentences while also recalling a word from the sentences. Performance on this task requires more than mere maintenance of information, though ultimately it still reflects output from working memory. This measure also showed reduced working memory capacity for anxious subjects, in fact the deficit seemed somewhat greater even than with the digit span task. Thus it seems clear that anxiety handicaps at least the operation of the articulatory loop, and possibly the operation of the central executive as well.

Another perspective on the question of resource allocation is provided by Revelle and his colleagues (e.g. 1987). They distinguish tasks in terms of the extent to which *sustained information transfer* (SIT) is involved, as distinct from the amount of storage required. In other words, tasks that require subjects to maintain a readiness to respond (such as vigilance tasks) are high in SIT, whereas letter cancellation would be low. In this view, reduced capacity can be a factor, but just as critical is whether the same content must remain in working memory for a prolonged period of time. Anxious subjects confront a number of options within this framework, but in general the expectation is that arousal will facilitate the SIT component, though further reducing the capacity component. For example, given their proclivity to engage in off-task behaviour and their relatively greater sensitivity to failure, it is not surprising that in terms of the speed–accuracy trade-off, anxious subjects often sacrifice speed to try to increase accuracy. Furthermore, they may in general simply seek less challenging endeavours than do low-anxiety subjects as a way of managing information overloads in a limited-capacity system. This viewpoint provides yet another reason to believe that high anxiety may hinder processing efficiency, whether or not that effect always shows up in diminished performance efficiency.

CONCLUSIONS

When examined in the laboratory, the effect of anxiety on performance is not just a generalized hindrance. Furthermore, the effect of anxiety appears to be considerably more complex than implied in the drive theory analysis that seemed so promising in the 1960s (*cf.* Spence and Spence, 1966). This appears to be the reward for the degree of attention devoted to this area in the interim, that is, learning the boundary conditions within which drive theory applies, more than any outright rejection of a role for response competition. In the synopsis presented above, a number of findings have been reviewed that seem to require more than a retrieval conflict for their explanation, and others that implicate an output problem but not competing response systems. Therefore, understanding the effect of anxiety on performance requires specifying additional processes. Convenient as it might be, it is not possible at this point to propose an integrated scheme fitting all these new ideas together. Nonetheless, a number of conclusions can be drawn from the database that has accumulated.

Firstly, anxiety cannot be construed as a unitary construct. Not only must trait (dispositional) anxiety be differentiated from state (situational) anxiety, but the experience of anxiety seems to involve at least two components that correspond to arousal and irrelevant cognitive concerns. In general, the evidence indicates that the latter is more predictive of an effect of anxiety on performance, specifically a detrimental effect. This appears to hold whether the cognitions are self-focused or directed to external events, though it may be the case that the nature of the most harmful cognitive activity can be more clearly specified. Furthermore, the assessment of the effect of anxiety may be enhanced by attention to situational constraints. For example, test anxiety has become a particularly useful model for research, perhaps because of the extent to which evaluation is defined as a part of the general experience of anxiety, perhaps because evaluation triggers concern with appearance to others and thus self-focusing, or because it illustrates a particular and readily identifiable source of threat. How much added benefit is to be obtained by pursuing domain-specific indices of anxiety remains to be determined.

Secondly, it seems clear that examination of the nature of self-attentive activities will continue to contribute to our understanding of the effects of anxiety. Although self-focusing may or may not be diagnostically different from one emotional state to another (*cf.* Ingram, 1990), it does nonetheless have a prominent role in anxiety assessment and thus our characterization of whether anxiety will hinder performance or not. Determining the extent to which this is provoked by the presence of others' promises to help the development of self-report measures of anxiety as well.

Thirdly, it seems clear that anxiety can affect storage processes as well as retrieval processes, and affect storage somewhat differently provided the study phase is clearly separated from the actual performance evaluation. This may include generally reduced cue utilization, differences in the type of material attended to (e.g. threatening or non-threatening, its physical or semantic features), poor study skills (defined in terms of rehearsal style, or more global academic preparation strategies), or perhaps diminished effort due to self-image or confidence deficits. It does seem that the encoding phase is one aspect where anxiety differs from 'arousal' defined otherwise, in that there is no consistent evidence that studying while anxious yields enhanced long-term recall, and the evidence rather consistently shows high-anxiety deficits for both short and long retention intervals. In addition, these storage differences set the stage for potentially mismatched contextual cues of a physiological or psychological nature when the study and test phases are clearly separated, especially when the study phase does not involve as much apprehension as the test will.

Lastly, response competition during the test phase hinders anxious subjects, particularly at high levels of anxiety and on difficult tasks, even when the material has been learned or even over-learned. This handicap may take the form of associative or output interference, or it may derive from cognitive activities that usurp capacity or resources in working memory. The extent to which training in taking tests can help is of interest, as are other ways of working around the blockage by disguising the evaluative threat in the situation.

REFERENCES

Alpert, R. and Haber, R.N. (1960) Anxiety in academic achievement situations. *Journal of Abnormal and Social Psychology* **61**: 207–15.

Anderson, K.J. (1990) Arousal and the inverted-U hypothesis: a critique of Neiss's 'Reconceptualizing arousal'. *Psychological Bulletin* **107**: 96–100.

Arkin, R.M., Kolditz, T.A. and Kolditz, K.K. (1983) Attributions of the test-anxious student: self-assessments in the classroom. *Personality and Social Psychology Bulletin* **9**: 271–80.

Baddeley, A.D. (1986) *Working Memory*. Oxford University Press.

Baddeley, A.D. and Hitch, G. (1974) Working memory. In *The Psychology of Learning and Motivation*, Vol. 8, edited by G.H. Bower. New York and London: Academic Press, pp. 47–89.

Bandura, A. (1988) Self efficacy conception of anxiety. *Anxiety Research*, **1**: 77–98.

Benson, J. and Bandalos, D. (1989) Structural model of statistics test anxiety in adults. In *Advances in Test Anxiety Research*, Vol. 6, edited by R. Schwarzer, H.M. van der Ploeg and C.D. Spielberger. Lisse: Swets and Zeitlinger, pp. 137–51.

Bernstein, D.A., Borkovec, T.D. and Coles, M.G.H. (1986) Assessment of anxiety. In *Handbook of Behavioral Assessment*, edited by A.R. Ciminero, K.S. Calhoun and H.E. Adams. New York: Wiley, pp. 353–403.

Blankenstein, K.R. and Flett, G.L. (1990) Cognitive components of test anxiety: a comparison of assessment and scoring methods. *Journal of Social Behavior and Personality* **5**: 187–202.

Bower, G.H. and Mayer, J.D. (1989) In search of mood-dependent retrieval. *Journal of Social Behavior and Personality* **4**: 121–56.

Broadbent, D.E. (1971) *Decision and Stress*. New York and London: Academic Press.

Broadbent, D.E., Cooper, P.F., FitzGerald, P. and Parkes, K.R. (1982) The Cognitive Failures Questionnaire (CFQ) and its correlates. *British Journal of Psychology* **21**: 1–16.

Broadhurst, P.L. (1959) The interaction of task difficulty and motivation: The Yerkes–Dodson law revived. *Acta Psychologica* **16**: 321–38.

Buss, A.H. (1980) *Self-consciousness and Social Anxiety*. San Francisco: W.H. Freeman.

Carver, C.S., Peterson, L.M., Follansbee, D.J. and Scheier, M.F. (1983) Effects of self-directed attention on performance and persistence among persons high and low in text anxiety. *Cognitive Therapy Research* **7**: 333–54.

Cattell, R.B. and Scheier, H. (1961) *The Meaning and Measurement of Neuroticism and Anxiety*. New York: Ronald Press.

Cattell, R.B. and Scheier, H. (1963) *Handbook for the IPAT Anxiety Scale*. Champaign, Ill.: Institute for Personality and Ability Testing.

Clark, D.A., Beck, A.T. and Stewart, B. (1990) Cognitive specificity and positive–negative affectivity: complementary or contradictory views on anxiety and depression? *Journal of Abnormal Psychology* **99**: 148–55.

Covington, M. and Omelich, C.L. (1987) 'I know it cold before the exam': a test of the anxiety-blockage hypothesis. *Journal of Educational Psychology* **79**: 393–400.

Darke, S. (1988a) Effects of anxiety on inferential reasoning task performance. *Journal of Personality and Social Psychology* **55**: 499–505.

Darke, S. (1988b) Anxiety and working memory capacity. *Cognition and Emotion* **2**: 145–54.

Deffenbacher, J.L. (1978) Worry, emotionality, and task-generated interference in test anxiety: An empirical test of attentional theory. *Journal of Educational Psychology* **70**: 248–54.

Easterbrook, J.A. (1959) The effect of emotion on cue utilization and the organization of behavior. *Psychological Review* **66**: 183–201.

Endler, N.S and Okada, M. (1975) A multidimensional trait measure of anxiety: the S–R inventory of general trait anxiousness. *Journal of Consulting and Clinical Psychology* **43**: 319–29.

Endler, N.S., Edwards, J.M., Vitelli, R. and Parker, J.DA. (1989) Assessment of state and trait anxiety: Endler Multidimensional Anxiety Scales. *Anxiety Research* **2**: 1–14.

Everson, H., Millsap, R.E. and Browne, J. (1989) Cognitive interference or skills deficit: an empirical test of two competing theories of test anxiety. *Anxiety Research* **1**: 313–25.

Eysenck, H.J. (1967) *The Biological Basis of Personality*. Springfield, Ill.: Thomas.

Eysenck, M.W. (1977) *Human Memory: Theory, Research, and Individual Differences*. New York: Pergamon.

Eysenck, M.W. (1979) Anxiety, learning, and memory: a reconceptualization. *Journal of Research in Personality* **13**: 363–385.

Eysenck, M.W. (1982) *Attention and Arousal: Cognition and Performance*. New York: Springer.

Eysenck, M.W. (1988) Anxiety and attention. *Anxiety Research* **1**: 9–15.

Eysenck, M.W., MacLeod, C. and Mathews, A. (1987) Cognitive functioning and anxiety. *Psychological Research* **49**: 189–195.

Eysenck, S.B.G. and Eysenck, H.J. (1977) The place of impulsiveness in a dimensional system of personality description. *British Journal of Social and Clinical Psychology* **16**: 57–68.

Foa, E.B., McNally, R. and Murdock, T.B. (1989) Anxious mood and memory. *Behavior Research and Therapy* **27**: 141–7.

Gagne, R.M. (1985) *The Conditions of Learning and Theory of Instruction*, 4th edn. New York: Holt, Rinehart and Winston.

Geen, R.G. (1985) Test anxiety and visual vigilance. *Journal of Personality and Social Psychology* **49**: 963–70.

Goulet, L.R. and Mazzei, J. (1969) Verbal learning and confidence thresholds as a function of test anxiety, intelligence and stimulus similarity. *Journal of Experimental Research in Personality* **3**: 247–252.

Gray, J.A. (1981) A critique of Eysenck's theory of personality. In *A Model for Personality*, edited by H.J. Eysenck. New York: Springer, pp. 246–76.

Graydon, J. and Eysenck, M.W. (1989) Distraction and cognitive performance. *European Journal of Cognitive Psychology* **1**: 161–79.

Greenberg, M.S. and Beck, A.T. (1989) Depression versus anxiety: a test of the content-specificity hypothesis. *Journal of Abnormal Psychology* **98**: 9–13.

Gunter, B., Furnham, A. and Jarrett, J. (1984) Personality, time of day, and delayed memory for TV news. *Personality and Individual Differences* **5**: 35–9.

Hamilton, V. (1975) Socialization anxiety and information processing: a capacity model of anxiety-induced performance deficits. In *Stress and Anxiety*, Vol. 2, edited by I.G. Sarason and C.D. Spielberger. New York and London: Academic Press.

Hardy, L. and Parfitt, G. (1991) A catastrophe model of anxiety and performance. *British Journal of Psychology* **82**: 163–178.

Hasher, L. and Zacks, R.T. (1979) Automatic and effortful processes in memory. *Journal of Experimental Psychology (General)* **108**: 356–88.

Heckhausen, H. (1982) Task-irrelevant cognitions during an exam. In *Achievement, Stress, and Anxiety*, edited by H.W. Krohne and L. Laux. Washington, DC: Hemisphere.

Heckhausen, H. and Strang, H. (1988) Efficiency under record performance demands: Exertion control – an individual difference variable? *Journal of Personality and Social Psychology* **55**: 489–98.

Hedl, J.J. (1990) Test anxiety and causal attributions: some evidence toward replication. *Anxiety Research* **3**: 73–84.

Hedl, J.J. and Bartlett, J.C. (1989) Test anxiety, sentence comprehension, and recognition memory. *Anxiety Research* **1**: 269–79.

Hedl, J.J. and Bartlett, J.C. (1990) Depression and test anxiety in comprehension and memory: Independent effects? In *Cross-cultural Anxiety*, Vol. 4, edited by C.D. Spielberger, R. Diaz-Guerro and J. Strelau. New York: Hemisphere, pp. 87–105.

Helmke, A. (1988) The role of classroom context factors for the achievement-impairing effect of test anxiety. *Anxiety Research* **1**: 37–52.

Hembree, R. (1988) Correlates, causes, effects, and treatment of test anxiety. *Review of Educational Research* **58**: 47–77.

Hodapp, V. (1989) Anxiety, fear of failure, and achievement: Two path-analytic models. *Anxiety Research* **1**: 301–312.

Hodges, W.F. (1976) The psychophysiology of anxiety. In *Emotion and Anxiety: New Concepts, Methods, and Applications*, edited by M. Zuckerman and C.D. Spielberger. Hillsdale, NJ.: L. Erlbaum, pp. 175–94.

Houston, D.H. (1989) The relationship between cognitive failure and self-focused attention. *British Journal of Clinical Psychology* **28**: 85–6.

Idzikowski, C. and Baddeley, A.D. (1983) Waiting in the wings: apprehension, public speaking

and performance. *Ergonomics* **26**: 575–83.
Idzikowski, C. and Baddeley, A.D. (1987) Fear and performance in novice parachutists. *Ergonomics* **30**: 1463–74.
Ingram, R.E. (1990) Self-focused attention in clinical disorders: review and a conceptual model. *Psychological Bulletin* **107**: 156–76.
Ingram, R.E., Kendall, P.C., Smith, T.W., Donnell, C. and Ronan, K. (1987) Cognitive specificity in emotional distress. *Journal of Personality and Social Psychology* **53**: 734–42.
Kahneman, D. (1973) *Attention and Effort*. Englewood Cliffs, NJ: Prentice Hall, Inc.
Kalechstein, P.B.W., Hocevar, D. and Kalechstein, M. (1988). Effects on test-wiseness training on test anxiety, locus of control and reading achievement in elementary school children. *Anxiety Research* **1**: 247–61.
Kent, G. (1989) Memory of dental experiences as related to naturally occurring changes in state anxiety. *Cognition and Emotion* **3**: 45–53.
Kleinsmith, K.L. and Kaplan, S. (1963) Paired-associate learning as a function of arousal and interpolated interval. *Journal of Experimental Psychology* **65**: 190–3.
Liebert, R.M. and Morris, L.W. (1967) Cognitive and emotional components of test anxiety: a distinction and some initial data. *Psychological Reports* **20**: 975–8.
Mandler, G. (1980) Recognizing: the judgment of previous occurrence. *Psychological Review* **87**: 252–71.
Mandler, G. and Sarason, S.B. (1952) A study of anxiety and learning. *Journal of Abnormal and Social Psychology* **47**: 166–73.
Martin, M. (1983) Cognitive failure: everyday and laboratory performance. *Bulletin of the Psychonomic Society* **21**: 97–100.
Mathews, A. (1991) Anxiety and the processing of emotional infomation. In *Progress in Experimental Personality and Psychopathology Research: Models and Methods of Psychopathology*, edited by L.J. Chapman, J.P. Chapman and D. Fowles. New York: Springer.
Mathews, A. and MacLeod, C. (1986) Discrimination of threat cues without awareness in anxiety states. *Journal of Abnormal Psychology* **95**: 131–8.
Mathews, A., Mogg, K., May, J. and Eysenck, M.W. (1989a) Implicit and explicit memory bias in anxiety. *Journal of Abnormal Psychology* **98**: 236–40.
Mathews, A., Richards, A. and Eysenck, M.W. (1989b) Interpretation of homophones related to threat in anxiety states. *Journal of Abnormal Psychology* **98**: 31–4.
Mathews, A., May, J., Mogg, K. and Eysenck, M.W. (1990) Attentional bias in anxiety: selective search or defective filtering? *Journal of Abnormal Psychology* **99**: 166–73.
Matthews, G. (1986) The effects of anxiety on intellectual performance: when and why are they found? *Journal of Research in Personality* **20**: 385–401.
Matthews, G. and Wells, A. (1988) Relationships between anxiety, self-consciousness, and cognitive failure. *Cognition and Emotion* **2**: 123–32.
Matthews, G., Jones, D.M. and Chamberlain, A.G. (1990) Refining the measurement of mood: the UWIST Mood Adjective Checklist. *British Journal of Psychology* **81**: 17–42.
McReynolds, P. (1968) The assessment of anxiety: a survey of available techniques. In *Advances in Psychological Assessment*, Vol. 1, edited by P. McReynolds. Palo Alto, Ca.: Science and Behavior Books.
Mikulincer, M., Kedem, P. and Paz, D. (1990) The impact of trait anxiety and situational stress on the categorization of natural objects. *Anxiety Research* **2**: 85–101.
Mogg, K., Mathews, A. and Weinman, J. (1987) Memory bias in clinical anxiety. *Journal of Abnormal Psychology* **96**: 94–8.
Mook, J., van der Ploeg, H.M and Kleijn, W.C. (1990) Anxiety, anger, and depression relationships at the trait level. *Anxiety Research* **3**: 17–31.
Morris, L.W., Davis, M.A. and Hutchings, C.H. (1981a) Cognitive and emotional components of anxiety: Literature review and a revised worry-emotionality scale. *Journal of Educational Psychology* **73**: 541–55.
Morris, L.W., Harris, E.W and Rovins, D.S. (1981b) Interactive effects of generalized and situational expectancies on the arousal of cognitive and emotional components of social

anxiety. *Journal of Research in Personality* **15**: 302–11.

Mueller, J.H. (1978) The effects of individual differences in test anxiety and type of orienting task on levels of organization in free recall. *Journal of Research in Personality* **12**: 471–80.

Mueller, J.H. and Courtois, M.R. (1980) Test anxiety and breadth of encoding experiences in free recall. *Journal of Research in Personality* **14**: 458–466.

Mueller, J.H. and Thompson, W.B. (1984) Test anxiety and distinctiveness of personal information. In *Advances in Test Anxiety Research*, Vol. 3, edited by H.M. van der Ploeg, R. Schwarzer and C.D. Spielberger. Lisse: Swets and Zeitlinger, pp. 21–37.

Mueller, J.H., Lenhart, K. and Gustavson, K. (1989) Study habits and contextual dependency as a function of test anxiety level. In *Advances in Test Anxiety Research*, Vol. 6, edited by R. Schwarzer, H.M. van der Ploeg and C.D. Spielberger. Lisse: Swets and Zeitlinger, pp. 77–85.

Mueller, J.H., Grove, T.R. and Thompson, W.B. (1991) Mood dependent retrieval and mood awareness. *Cognition and Emotion* **5**: 331–49.

Naveh-Benjamin, M. (1991) A comparison of training programs intended for different types of test-anxious students: further support for an information-processing model. *Journal of Educational Psychology* **83**: 134–9.

Naveh-Benjamin, M., McKeachie, W.J. and Lin, Y.G. (1987) Two types of test anxious students: support for the information processing model. *Journal of Educational Psychology* **79**: 131–6.

Nichols-Hoppe, K.T. and Beach, LR (1990) The effects of test anxiety and task variables on predecisional information search. *Journal of Research in Personality* **24**: 163–72.

Phaf, R.H. and Wolters, G. (1986) Induced arousal and incidental learning during rehearsal. *American Journal of Psychology* **99**: 341–54.

Revelle, W. (1987) Personality and motivation: sources of inefficiency in cognitive performance. *Journal of Research in Personality* **21**: 436–52.

Richards, A. and French, C.C. (1990) Central versus peripheral presentation of stimuli in an emotional Stroop task. *Anxiety Research* **3**: 41–9.

Richards, A. and French, C.C. (1991) Effects of encoding and anxiety on implicit and explicit memory performance. *Personality and Individual Differences* **12**: 131–9.

Roediger, H.L. (1990) Implicit memory: retention without remembering. *American Psychologist* **45**: 1043–56.

Sarason, I.G. (1978) The test anxiety scale: concept and research. In *Stress and Anxiety*, Vol. 5, edited by C.D. Spielberger and I.G. Sarason. New York and London: Academic Press, pp 193–216.

Sarason, I.G. (1984) Stress, anxiety and cognitive interference. *Journal of Personality and Social Psychology* **46**: 929–38.

Sarason, I.G., Sarason, B.R. and Pierce, G.R. (1990) Anxiety, cognitive interference, and performance. *Journal of Social Behavior and Personality* **5**: 1–18.

Schacter, S. (1964) The interaction of cognitive and physiological determinants of emotional states. In *Psychobiological Approaches to Social Behavior*, edited by P.H. Leiderman and D. Shapiro. Stanford, Ca.: Stanford University Press, pp. 138–73.

Schacter, S. (1966) The interaction of cognitive and physiological determinants of emotional state. In *Anxiety and Behavior*, edited by C.D. Spielberger. New York and London: Academic Press, pp. 193–224.

Schwarzer, R. (1990) Current trends in anxiety research. In *European Perspectives in Psychology*, Vol. 2, edited by P.J.D. Drenth, J.A. Sergeant and R.J. Takens. Chichester: Wiley, pp. 225–44.

Schwarzer, R. and Quast, H. (1985) Multidimensionality of the anxiety experience: evidence for additional components. In *Advances in Test Anxiety Research*, Vol. 4, edited by H.M. van der Ploeg, R. Schwarzer and C.D. Spielberger. Lisse: Swets and Zeitlinger, pp. 3–14.

Schwarzer, R., van der Ploeg, H.M. and Spielberger, C.D. (eds) (1989a) *Advances in Test Anxiety Research*, Vol. 6. Lisse: Swets and Zeitlinger.

Schwarzer, R., Seipp, B. and Schwarzer, C. (1989b) Mathematics performance and anxiety: a meta-analysis. In *Advances in Test Anxiety Research*, Vol. 6, edited by R. Schwarzer, H.M. van der Ploeg and C.D. Spielberger. Lisse: Swets and Zeitlinger, pp. 105–19.

Schwartz, S. (1975) Individual differences in cognition: some relationships between personality and memory. *Journal of Research in Personality* **9**: 217–25.

Schwartz, S. (1979) Differential effects of personality on access to various long-term memory codes. *Journal of Research in Personality* **13**: 396–403.

Spence, J.T. and Spence, K.W. (1966) The motivational components of manifest anxiety: drive and drive stimuli. In *Anxiety and Behavior,* edited by C.D. Spielberger. New York and London: Academic Press, pp. 291–326.

Spielberger, C.D. (1966) Theory and research on anxiety. In *Anxiety and Behavior,* edited by C.D. Spielberger. New York and London: Academic Press, pp. 3–20.

Spielberger, C.D. (1972) Conceptual and methodological issues in anxiety research. In *Anxiety: Current Trends in Theory and Research,* Vol. 2, edited by C.D. Spielberger. New York and London: Academic Press, pp. 481–93.

Spielberger, C.D. (1977) Anxiety: Theory and research. In *International Encyclopedia of Neurology, Psychiatry, Psychoanalysis, and Psychology,* edited by B.B. Wolman. New York: Human Sciences Press.

Spielberger, C.D. (1980) *Preliminary Professional Manual for the Test Anxiety Inventory.* Palo Alto, Ca.: Consulting Psychologists Press.

Spielberger, C.D. (1983) *Manual for the State–Trait Anxiety Inventory.* Palo Alto, Ca.: Consulting Psychologists Press.

Spielberger, C.D., Gorsuch, R.D. and Lushene, R.D. (1970) *STAI Manual for the State–Trait Anxiety Inventory.* Palo Alto, Ca.: Consulting Psychologists Press.

Spielberger, C.D., Vagg, P.R., Baker, L.R., Donham, G.W. and Westberry, L.G. (1980) The factor structure of the state–trait anxiety inventory. In *Stress and Anxiety,* Vol. 7, edited by I.G. Sarason and C.D. Spielberger. Washington, DC: Hemisphere, pp. 95–109.

Spielberger, C.D., Jacobs, G., Russell, S. and Crane, R.S. (1983) Assessment of anger: the state–trait anger scale. In *Advances in Personality Assessment,* Vol. 2, edited by J.N. Butcher and C.D. Spielberger. Hillsdale, NJ: L. Erlbaum, pp. 159–87.

Steptoe, A. and Fidler, H. (1987) Stage fright in orchestral musicians: a study of cognitive and behavioral strategies in performance anxiety. *British Journal of Psychology* **87**: 241–9.

Sternberg, R.J. (1977) *Intelligence, Information Processing, and Analogical Reasoning.* Hillsdale, NJ: Erlbaum.

Stewart, I.N. and Peregoy, P.L. (1983) Catastrophe theory modeling in psychology. *Psychological Bulletin* **94**: 336–62.

Tasto, D.L. (1977) Self-report schedules and inventories. In *Handbook of Behavioral Assessment,* edited by A.R. Chiminero, K.S. Calhoun and H.E. Adams. New York: Wiley.

Taylor, J.A. (1953) A personality scale of manifest anxiety. *Journal of Abnormal and Social Psychology* **41**: 81–92.

Tobias, S. (1985) Test anxiety: interference, defective skills, and cognitive capacity. *Educational Psychologist* **20**: 135–42.

Tipper, S.P. and Baylis, G.C. (1987) Individual differences in selective attention: the relation of priming and interference. *Personality and Individual Differences* **8**: 667–75.

Toglia, M.P., Payne, D.G., Nightingale, N.L. and Ceci, S.J. (1989) Event memory under naturalistic stress. *Bulletin of the Psychonomic Society* **27**: 405–8.

Walker, E.L. (1958) Action decrement and its relation to learning. *Psychological Review* **65**: 129–42.

Yerkes, R.M. and Dodson, J.D. (1908) The relation of strength of stimulus to rapidity of habit-formation. *Journal of Comparative Neurology and Psychology* **18**: 459–82.

Zaffy, D.J. and Bruning, J.L. (1966) Drive and the range of cue utilization. *Journal of Experimental Psychology* **71**: 382–4.

Zeidner, M. (1991) Test anxiety and aptitude test performance in an actual college admissions testing situation: temporal considerations. *Personality and Individual Differences* **12**: 101–9.

Zuckerman, M. (1960) The development of an affect adjective check list for the measurement of anxiety. *Journal of Consulting Psychology* **24**: 457–62.

6

Mood

G. MATTHEWS

STRUCTURE AND ASSESSMENT OF MOOD

Definitions of mood

In everyday parlance, mood refers to a pervasive and relatively mild emotional state. In psychological use, the term is distinctly fuzzy. Mayer (1986) defines mood as an emotion-like experience lasting for at least several minutes. Mood is to be distinguished from specific cognitive evaluations, despite their role in the aetiology of affective states. Mood-states are more persistent over time than the transient emotional reactions generated by evaluations. Another defining property of moods is their lack of reference to specific objects, in contrast to motivational states, such as hunger, and emotions such as suspicion and fear (Mackay, 1980). There are few fundamental moods (Thayer, 1989), in contrast to emotion, whose structure may be quite elaborate (e.g. Ortony *et al.*, 1987). Theories of affect deal primarily with emotion rather than mood, so some reference to theories of emotion will be necessary in considering possible causal relationships between mood and performance. It is also difficult to distinguish moods and emotions empirically, particularly as one of the causes of moods may be after-effects of emotions (Frijda, 1986).

Psychometric models of mood

The structure and dimensionality of mood have been widely debated. Mackay (1980) and Thayer (1989) review the various mood dimensions proposed to

HANDBOOK OF HUMAN PERFORMANCE
VOLUME 3 ISBN 0-12-650353-2

account for the psychometric structure of responses on questionnaires composed of items concerning current mood-state, or on adjective checklists, on which the respondent indicates how well mood descriptors apply to their mood. Nowlis's (1965) pioneering research identified twelve monopolar dimensions of mood. Some of the Nowlis factors are highly specific, such as nonchalance, defined by 'nonchalant' and 'leisurely', and subsequent structural models of mood have usually been more parsimonious. One popular contemporary model of mood posits two bipolar, orthogonal dimensions. The first dimension contrasts feelings of vigour and energy with tiredness and fatigue; the second, tension and anxiety with relaxation and calmness. These twin aspects of mood have been variously termed energetic and tense arousal (Thayer, 1989), positive and negative affect (Watson and Tellegen, 1985), and arousal and stress (Cox and Mackay, 1985). In fact, both dimensions correlate positively with indices of autonomic arousal (Thayer, 1978). Rotation of the two dimensions through approximately forty-five degrees gives dimensions of pleasure–displeasure and general arousal (Russell, 1979), or of frequency and intensity of affect (Diener *et al.*, 1985). A viable alternative is a three-factor model of the kind originally proposed by Wundt (1905), on the basis of introspection, with dimensions of pleasant–unpleasant, aroused–subdued and tense–relaxed. Matthews *et al.* (1990a) pointed out that the factor analyses purporting to support the two-factor model are often flawed, particularly by use of inaccurate criteria for deciding the number of factors to extract. Their own analysis used a valid number-of-factors criterion and obtained three factors corresponding to those of Wundt (1905), labelled hedonic tone, energetic arousal and tense arousal respectively. Sjoberg *et al.* (1979) and Thayer (1978) obtained similar factor solutions: Sjoberg *et al.* also indicate the importance of distinguishing mood-states from social orientations. Mackay (1980), Sjoberg *et al.* (1979), Matthews *et al.* (1990a) and Watson (1988) discuss a variety of psychometric issues concerned with the measurement of

Table 6.1 Correspondences between reference mood dimensions and other structural models of mood

	Energetic arousal	*Tense arousal*	*Hedonic tone*	*General arousal*
Thayer, 1989	Energy	Tension	–	–
Cox and Mackay, 1985	Arousal	Stress	–	–
Watson and Tellegen, 1985	Positive affect	Negative affect	–	–
Russell, 1979	–	–	Pleasure/ displeasure	Arousal
Diener *et al.*, 1985	–	–	Frequency of affect	Intensity of affect
Sjoberg *et al.*, 1979	Activation	Tension	Pleasantness	–

mood, such as the influence of response formats and response sets, and the utility of factor analysis.

The use of various alternative descriptive schemes for mood is confusing. For comparative purposes this chapter uses a frame of reference based on the work of Thayer (1989) and Matthews *et al.* (1990a). Correspondences between the four aspects of mood described by Matthews *et al.* (1990a) and other commonly used descriptive schemes are shown in Table 6.1. Hedonic tone (pleasure–displeasure) is moderately positively correlated with energy (around +0.3), and negatively correlated with tension (around −0.3). Measures of general arousal are likely to be quite strongly correlated with both energy and tension but independent of hedonic tone.

Mood and personality

Another important psychometric issue is the distinctiveness of mood states from more enduring personality traits. If mood and personality measures cannot be psychometrically discriminated, we must conclude that moods are simply another expression of personality. Cattell (1973) reasons that mood dimensions should be identified through the factor analysis of mood difference scores across two or more occasions, to discriminate moods from traits and trait changes. The eight state questionnaire (Curran and Cattell, 1974) was developed on this principle, although it appears to be rather over-factored (Matthews *et al.*, 1990a). Somewhat less rigorously, we can attempt to demonstrate that (1) traits have greater temporal stability than states, and (2) trait–state correlations are relatively low. The first point is not seriously disputed, but there is some controversy over the strength of the relationship between traits and states. Watson (1988) suggests that the positive affect (i.e. energy) is strongly related to the extraversion personality trait, and negative affect (tension) to neuroticism. However, there are three respects in which these simple equivalences may be misleading. Firstly, correlations between extraversion, neuroticism and mood are quite small in magnitude, typically 0.2 — 0.4 (Emmons and Diener, 1986; Williams, 1989; Matthews *et al.*, 1990a). Secondly, hedonic tone is also related to extraversion (positively), and to neuroticism (negatively) (Williams, 1989), although these correlations may be statistically dependent on the interrelationship of hedonic tone with energy and tension (Matthews *et al.*, 1990a). Thirdly, state–trait correlations are likely to vary with situations. Extraverts' preference for greater levels of stimulation, relative to introverts (Eysenck and Eysenck, 1985), should be reflected in variation in extraversion–mood correlations with ambient stimulation. Relationships between trait and state anxiety measures vary with type and level of environmental stress (Endler, 1983). Moods also correlate modestly with other, more specific personality traits, and with intra-individual variability of mood (Thayer, 1989). In summary, traits and states are not strongly correlated in most circumstances, and, in performance research, it is necessary to discriminate the two kinds of construct.

EXPLAINING RELATIONSHIPS BETWEEN MOOD AND PERFORMANCE

Relationships between mood and performance can be investigated within both experimental and correlational studies. In either case, we must identify the underlying causal pathways responsible for the observed mood–performance relationship. Ideally, theories of mood would suggest plausible hypotheses, but, unfortunately, there is no consensus on the aetiology of mood states. Most empirical work on mood (see Thayer, 1989, for a comprehensive review) relates loosely to one of two general themes. Firstly, affective states may be an expression of brain states (e.g. Gray, 1987), so that performance effects are driven by the neural antecedents of mood. Secondly, affect may result primarily from cognitive appraisal of the person's transactions with the physical and social environment (Lazarus *et al.*, 1970). The remainder of this section describes studies of psychobiological and cognitive influences on mood in more detail, and assesses their relevance to performance studies. Many of these studies are concerned with discriminating influences on different aspects of mood, so that specific dimensions of mood, such as energy and tension, may be linked to specific neural or cognitive antecedents.

Psychobiology of mood

BIOLOGICAL INFLUENCES ON MOOD

The most direct experimental evidence for biological influences on mood comes from pharmacological and psychophysiological studies of mood (Thayer, 1989). Drug studies can be used to test for correspondences between mood states and the neurotransmitter whose action is modified by the drug. Thayer (1989) reviews studies showing that drugs differ in their effects on energy, tension and hedonic tone. Pharmacological evidence links a variety of neurotransmitters to arousal states, particularly acetylcholine and the monoamines noradrenaline, dopamine and serotonin (Mason, 1984; Robbins, 1986). Likewise, pleasurable mood has been linked to endogenous opioid peptides, or endorphins (Panksepp, 1986). Unfortunately, drugs frequently affect more than one dimension of mood simultaneously, and there appears to be no simple mapping of mood-states onto neurotransmitters. For example, monoamines have been implicated in the pleasantness of mood, as well as in subjective arousal level (Mason, 1984). A number of physiological correlates of mood have been reported (Thayer, 1989), but different dimensions of mood are not clearly differentiated by physiological measures.

Other empirical studies show mood change resulting from more indirect biological manipulations such as food intake and level of gross activity. Thayer (1989) reviews evidence suggesting that energy at first rises and then declines following carbohydrate ingestion, whereas tension shows an increase of longer latency. Mild exercise, such as a brisk walk, reliably raises energy and decreases tension (Thayer, 1989). Sleep deprivation has the opposite effect: reducing energy and raising tension (Johnson, 1982), whereas deep muscle relaxation reduces tension without significantly affecting energy (Matthews *et al.*, 1990a). Circadian rhythms have stronger effects on energy than on tension, but the menstrual cycle is associated with variation in both energy and tension (Thayer, 1989). As with drug studies, such evidence suggests that the biological antecedents of energy and tension may differ, but the data are too complex to infer underlying neural mechanisms. In any case, cognitive appraisal of these manipulations is usually not controlled.

NEURAL THEORIES OF MOOD

There have been several attempts to relate affect or moods to neural systems defined by anatomical substrate and function. Gray (1987) distinguishes three systems: reward, fight/flight and behavioural inhibition, and speculates that they are related to positive affective states, active negative states (e.g. anger) and passive negative states (anxiety, depression) respectively. Similarly, Clark and Watson (1988) relate positive and negative affect (energy and tension) to neural systems associated with sensitivity to reward and punishment signals. They propose that positive affect is primarily sensitive to pleasant events, such as enjoyable social interaction, whereas negative affect is more sensitive to unpleasant events and stress. Thayer (1989) suggests that energetic and tense arousal are controlled by the reticular activating system and the limbic system respectively. By and large, energy is more sensitive to manipulations of motor activity and physiological energy mobilization, whereas tense arousal is primarily sensitive to stress and emotion-inducing stimuli.

These theories are all somewhat speculative, because of the difficulties of investigating neural correlates of mood within human subjects. These difficulties may be essentially methodological. Drug studies may fail to distinguish the neurotransmitters with specific moods for several reasons. Firstly, drugs frequently affect two or more neurotransmitters, and there may be several discrete functional systems associated with each neurotransmitter (see, for example, Robbins and Everitt, 1982). Secondly, subjective arousal may be driven by overall cortical arousal, rather than by the more differentiated systems which cause cortical arousal. Cortical arousal may be generated by either aminergic or cholinergic afferents (Vanderwolf and Robinson, 1981), but, conceivably, the two kinds of cortical arousal are subjectively equivalent.

A third difficulty is controlling for interaction between neural systems, such as that between noradrenergic and dopaminergic systems, for example (Robbins, 1986). Thayer (1989) suggests that neural interactions may be responsible for a reciprocal relationship between energetic and tense arousal sometimes observed at high levels of arousal. Alternatively, even within essentially psychobiological models, there may genuinely be no simple correspondence between neural and subjective states, because brain states and information processing may conjointly affect mood. For example, output from Gray's (1987) behavioural inhibition system depends both on the activity levels in ascending afferent pathways to the system, and on the processing of information within the system.

Cognitive and social influences on mood

An alternative approach to explaining mood states is to identify the dominant causal process as the person's cognitive appraisal of their environment, its personal significance, and the opportunities for action which it affords. The importance of appraisal is demonstrated empirically by studies showing that mood is affected by a variety of suggestive techniques, such as hypnosis, discussed in a following section. Lazarus and Folkman (1984) relate affect to primary appraisal, evaluation of the implications for personal well-being of an event. Benign-positive appraisals are mainly associated with pleasurable emotions, harm/loss with unpleasant emotion, threat with anxiety and anger, and challenge with eagerness and excitement. There is little direct evidence on the relationship between appraisal and mood, although Ferguson and Cox (1991) found partial support for the Lazarus and Folkman hypotheses. Secondary appraisal, evaluation of ability to cope with or act within the situation, and the specific coping strategies adopted, may also influence emotion, independently of primary appraisal (Folkman and Lazarus, 1988). A special case of appraisal is the perception of bodily activity, which influences the effect associated with physiological arousal (Schachter and Singer, 1962), although direct pharmacological effects on affect may sometimes override appraisal effects (Marshall and Zimbardo, 1979). Lazarus and Folkman (1984) also describe social influences on affect, mediated by appraisals of match or mismatch between individual and social identities, of socially normative expectations about behaviour in relation to family and work roles, and of social change. The social environment also affects secondary appraisal through, for example, the perceived availability of social support.

There are a limited number of experimental studies which distinguish cognitive influences on different aspects of mood (Thayer, 1989). The general trend is for tense arousal to be the mood dimension most sensitive to psychological stressors such as examination anxiety, noise (Thayer, 1978), and threatening films and music (e.g. Matthews *et al.*, 1990a). Hedonic tone also tends to be sensitive to such influences, although there are differences in detail between stressor effects on tension and hedonic tone (Matthews *et al.*, 1990a). In contrast, energetic arousal is relatively insensitive to cognitive manipulations, although there are a few reports of effects (Thayer, 1989). Thayer and Moore (1972) found that both tension and tiredness were altered by anxiety-inducing instructions. Several longitudinal studies of the influence of daily events on mood have also been interpreted within the cognitive–social perspective (e.g. Eckenrode, 1984).

Mood, performance and causality

CAUSAL STATUS OF MOOD

All three primary mood dimensions are sensitive in some degree to both biological and cognitive manipulations, which poses something of a problem for explaining performance effects. As we have seen, theories of emotion often view affect primarily as a by-product of either neural processes or cognitive appraisal. We may ask why performance researchers should be concerned with mood at all. If, for example, the main causal influence on behaviour is appraisal, why not study effects of appraisal on performance directly, without reference to mood? There are both pragmatic and theoretical reasons why mood effects on performance are worth studying. Although mood states may correlate with psychophysiological measures (Thayer, 1989), and with measures of cognitive activity such as task-irrelevant thoughts (Sarason *et al.*, 1986), correlations fall considerably short of unity. On pragmatic grounds, then, although moods may ultimately be reducible to biological and/or cognitive antecedents, stronger performance data may be obtained by measuring mood directly.

At a theoretical level, it may be incorrect to see mood as simply an epiphenomenon to neural and/or cognitive processes: some causal models see affect as a direct cause of behaviour. Zajonc (1984) suggests that affect and cognition constitute interacting but separate systems, such that affect can be generated directly by neural mechanisms without cognitive involvement. Lazarus (1984) provides a rejoinder to this view, but such chicken-and-egg arguments are notoriously difficult to resolve. More generally, affective states may have a conceptual status distinct from their antecedents, if they indicate a specific functional state of the mind. Several cognitive scientists have suggested that affect may be an emergent property of complex information processing systems operating with limited knowledge and capacity, and multiple goals (see Oatley, 1987). Affect may be a part of a more complex system for goal-setting and action, whose function is to bias the system towards affect-compatible goals (Oatley and Johnson-Laird, 1987). In similar vein, Simon (1982) suggests a possible basis for distinguishing emotion and mood. Emotion is affect associated with the interruption and redirection of attention, and somatic arousal, whereas mood provides a diffuse context which influences cognitive activity without interrupting it. Unfortunately, such approaches have stimulated little work on affect and performance, although they have obvious relevance to studies of strategy and goal selection.

MECHANISMS FOR MOOD EFFECTS ON PERFORMANCE

In practice, three distinct types of general mechanism have been proposed to explain effects of moods on performance: *energy, interference* and *cognitive bias* mechanisms. The assumption of energetic interpretations of mood effects is that mood affects the efficiency or speed of information processing. The attentional resource metaphor, the idea that there is a pool of energy or fuel for processing (Hirst and Kalmar, 1987), is particularly apt for describing such effects. I posit that resource availability is particularly sensitive to energetic arousal (e.g. Matthews *et al.*, 1990b), although hedonic tone may also affect processing efficiency. *Interference* theories assume that affect has detrimental effects on performance through generating task-irrelevant cognitions which divert processing resources or structures from the task at hand (e.g. Wine, 1982). Such theories have been applied primarily to anxiety, and so will not be discussed in detail (see Mueller, this volume). *Cognitive bias* theories propose that moods affect selectivity of processing of affect-related material. Bias may operate at various stages of processing. For example, an unhappy person may selectively perceive negatively-toned material, retrieve negative material from long-term memory, and respond to negative rather than positive stimuli. Bias models have been applied primarily to states of pleasant and unpleasant affect (e.g. Bower, 1981). All three mechanisms are very general, in that they could be associated with either lower-level 'automatic' or higher-level 'controlled' processes, and be driven by either neural or other cognitive processes.

Manipulation and measurement of mood in performance studies

TECHNIQUES FOR MOOD MANIPULATION

The two principal techniques for studies of mood and performance are the manipulation of mood and the measurement of individual differences in naturally occurring normal and pathological mood-states. Mood may be manipulated directly by auto-suggestion or hypnosis. For example, the popular Velten procedure requires subjects to read a graded sequence of self-descriptive statements characteristic of the desired mood state (Velten, 1968). Hasher *et al.* (1985) list several difficulties associated with procedures of this kind, notably their demand characteristics, which may influence subsequent performance, and the possibility that the materials they use will activate personal memories which may then bias or prime subsequent responding independently of affective state. There are also considerable individual differences in response, which vary systematically with traits such as basal depression and neuroticism (Blackburn *et al.*, 1990). In defence of induction techniques, Velten induction is effective in some subjects even when the instruction is to pretend to feel the mood (Polivy and Doyle, 1980), and induced moods may persist even when the subject is instructed that the experiment is over (see Ellis *et al.*, 1985).

The role of demand characteristics may be reduced by exposing the subject to emotion-inducing stimuli without specific instructions. Film and music manipulations, for example, are effective in eliciting both positive and negative emotions (Lazarus *et al.*, 1970; Thayer, 1989). Mood manipulations may also be covert: Isen and Levin (1972), for example, allowed subjects to 'find' a coin in the return slot of a telephone; Laird *et al.* (1982) manipulated facial expression, and Erlichman and Halpern (1988) inflicted odours of varying pleasantness on subjects. These indirect methods carry the risk, to varying degrees, of confounding the mood change with other effects of the manipulation used. For example, two films which differ in affective content may also differ in the quantity and type of cognitions they evoke. There may also be individual differences in affective response to manipulations. Another difficulty is that manipulations frequently affect more than one dimension of mood independently (see Thayer, 1989), complicating the interpretation of results. Matthews *et al.* (1990a) suggest that some rather strong stressors such as sleep deprivation evoke a generalized state of emotional stress associated with increased tension, decreased energy and poorer hedonic tone.

INDIVIDUAL AND GROUP DIFFERENCES IN MOOD

Naturally occurring moods are investigated experimentally in two guises. The most direct method is to measure individual differences in pre-task mood, typically by adjective checklist, and correlate mood with performance. The assumption here is that variation in mood reflects a wide range of causal influences, such that, typically, no single influence accounts for a high proportion of the variation. It is, of course, important to control experimentally or statistically for major influences on mood, such as time of day and personality. Another difficulty is that between-subjects comparisons in mood may be confounded by individual differences in basal mood. Perhaps a person reporting high arousal is only aroused relative to their characteristic mood: Matthews *et al.* (1990b) discuss this issue in detail. Mood may also be affected by anticipation and appraisal of success on the task, which complicates interpretation of results. Matthews (1986) showed that a positive association between hedonic tone and creativity test performance increased with time on task, suggesting an effect of performance on mood, rather than vice versa. In addition, performance correlates of chronic abnormal mood, such as depression, may be investigated. Mild depression has been studied within normal populations, and severe depression through using clinical patients. However, such evidence is of subsidiary importance for mood research since depressives and controls appear to differ in the structure of their cognitions as well as in affect (e.g. Ingram, 1984). There is also extensive confounding of depression with other cognitive and affective variables in such studies (Ingram, 1989). Matthews and Southall (1991) showed that clinical depression is associated with lowered energy and increased tension, as well as with lowered hedonic tone (state depression). Hence, both experimental and correlational methods have their respective strengths and weaknesses. Experimental manipulation is likely to provoke a variety of cognitive and affective changes which differ from person to person, whereas unmanipulated moods are likely to be confounded with a variety of antecedent causes and other individual difference factors.

EFFICIENCY OF INFORMATION PROCESSING AND ENERGETIC AROUSAL

The hypothesis that energetical states such as affective arousal have a causal influence on performance has traditionally been expressed in terms of the Yerkes–Dodson law (Mueller, this volume). The contribution of mood studies to research on energetics and performance was first identified by Thayer (e.g. 1978, 1989). Since both experimental and correlational studies show that energetic and tense arousal are related to physiological energy mobilization and expenditure, self-report measures can be used to test whether pre-task arousal predicts subsequent performance. Thayer (1978) reviews several early studies of this type, which suggest that energy, but not tension, predict reaction time, verbal learning and examination performance.

This section reviews a systematic programme of research on energetic arousal and performance which Matthews and his colleagues at Aston University have conducted to assess the relationship between energy and attention on a variety of tasks. (Tension did not reliably predict performance in these studies.) The research literature on stress and performance provided several bases for prediction. The Yerkes–Dodson law predicts inverted U relationships between arousal and performance, with the optimal level of arousal inversely related to task difficulty. However, in line with recent critiques of traditional arousal theory (see Hockey *et al.*, 1986), no trace of these relationships was found in any study, and the Yerkes–Dodson law was rejected as a useful description of the phenomena. Studies of stress and information processing (Hockey, 1984) suggest that arousal effects should vary with task parameters. Although specific stressors tend to cause specific changes in the patterning of cognitive performance, arousing agents do have some effects common to the majority of manipulations. Some of these effects may be characterized as changes in the efficiency of components of performance others as strategy shifts. The research reviewed focused on four elements of performance which may be sensitive to arousal effects: attentional resource availability, attentional selectivity, readiness to respond, and short-term or working memory. Humphreys and Revelle (1984) suggest that arousal affects the efficiency of performance, increasing availability of resources for sustained information transfer and attention, and reducing resources for short-term memory (STM). In contrast, Hockey's (1984) review of stress effects emphasizes strategy shifts in arousal. The majority of arousing stressors increase attentional selectivity and shift response strategy towards speed and inaccuracy on tasks requiring fast responding.

Performance of single attentional tasks

SUSTAINED ATTENTION

Studies of sustained attention suggest that task versions made demanding by means of high event rates, degraded stimuli, working memory loads and other task manipulations are prone to show perceptual sensitivity decrements over time (Davies and Parasuraman, 1982). This effect can be attributed to depletion of attentional resources resulting from prolonged work (Parasuraman *et al.*, 1987). Parasuraman (1985) used a secondary probe reaction time (RT) task to show directly that perceptual sensitivity decrements in detection of degraded digits are mediated by resource availability. The first series of studies used a task similar to Parasuraman's (1985) to test the relationship between pre-task energetic arousal and resource availability. Subjects were required to detect the digit 0 in a sequence of single digits presented at an event rate of one / second. Typical results are shown in Figure 6.1: the dependent variable is a non-parametric measure of perceptual sensitivity, Pollack and Norman's (1964) estimate of $P(\mathrm{A})$. Energetic arousal interacted synergistically with the task parameters of degradation and time on task, such that low energy subjects were lower in $P(\mathrm{A})$ than high energy subjects when stimuli were degraded, with the magnitude of the energy effect increasing with time at work. Subsequent studies have shown that the effect generalizes to detection of differences in line length, a task using physical rather than symbolic stimuli (Matthews *et al.*, 1990c). Moreover, stimulus degradation is neither a necessary nor a sufficient condition for facilitative effects of energy on sustained attention. Matthews *et al.* (1990b) showed that energy predicted efficiency of detection on a self-paced task version, using undegraded digits, on which subjects themselves made the task demanding by spontaneously adopting a risky speed–accuracy trade-off. Less demanding but still degraded versions of the task showed neither a perceptual sensitivity decrement nor any sensitivity to energy (Matthews *et al.*, 1989, 1990c). Performance on these tasks was

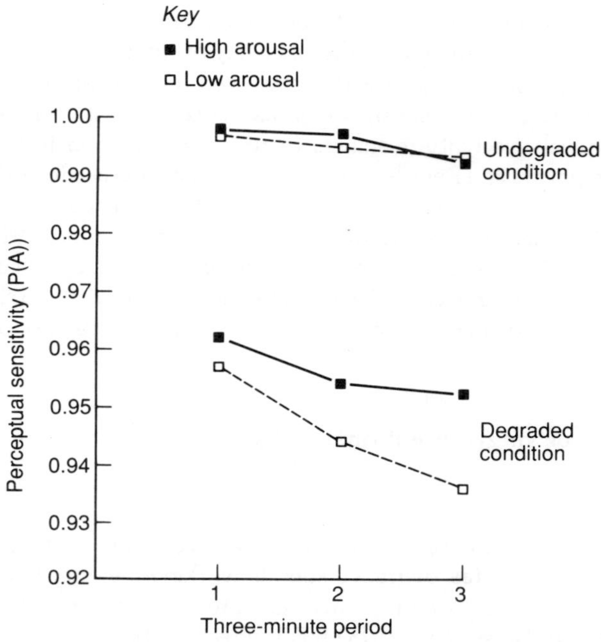

Figure 6.1 Perceptual sensitivity (P(A)) in sustained attention as a function of stimulus degradation, task period and level of energetic arousal. (Data from Matthews *et al.*, 1990b; figure from Matthews *et al.*, 1990c, © 1990 Pergamon Press plc.)

presumably limited by data quality rather than resource supply. Matthews *et al.* (1990c) summarized these studies as showing a strong association between the incidence of a perceptual sensitivity decrement, and the incidence of facilitatory (and linear) effects of energy on sensitivity. Extrapolating from existing theory (Parasuraman *et al.*, 1987), the data imply that energetic arousal is positively correlated with attentional resource availability, as the Humphreys and Revelle (1984) resource theory predicts.

SEARCH AND OTHER TASKS

Further studies attempted to assess the generality of the energy effect on qualitatively different tasks. Matthews *et al.* (1990b) tested the association between energy and speed of visual search, using Schneider and Shiffrin's (1977) task. The target is varied from trial to trial, such that on variably mapped (VM) trials targets and distractors are interchanged at random, whereas on consistently mapped trials (CM) targets and distractors constitute separate, easily distinguished sets, such as digit targets and consonant distractors. According to Schneider and Shiffrin (1977), processing on VM trials requires slow, serial, resource-limited, demanding controlled processing, whereas target detection on CM trials is fast, parallel and 'automatic'. Matthews *et al.* (1990b) found that energy was unrelated to automatic CM search, and to VM search within a single-item display. However, energy was strongly positively related to speed of search within a four-item display. As in the studies of sustained attention, energetic arousal appeared to facilitate performance of more demanding, resource-limited task conditions only. A further study (Matthews *et al.*, 1990b) showed that energy was positively and linearly related to speed of letter transformation, where letters must be recoded by counting forward through the alphabet (e.g. the answer to A + 3 is D), irrespective of memory load or transformation difficulty.

Other studies identified a set of focused and sustained attention tasks which were insensitive to simple effects of energy, such as five-choice serial reaction, self-paced detection of infrequent letters, and selective attention to single character targets (see Matthews *et al.*, 1989). These tasks were characterized by low error rates (less than 5 per cent); by comparison, error rates on the resource-limited sustained attention and search tasks were typically 5–15 per cent. The resource hypothesis is further strengthened by the failure of these relatively undemanding attentional tasks to show the facilitative effects of energy characteristic of more demanding tasks. (Low error rate attentional tasks are sensitive to disordinal interactions of energy with extraversion, which appear to reflect a separate mechanism, as discussed by Matthews, chapter 4, this volume.)

Working memory and short-term memory

There are two ways of testing Humphreys and Revelle's (1984) second hypothesis that arousal decreases availability of STM resources: by use of attentional tasks which impose a load on STM, and by use of direct measures of short-term retention. The role of memory load has been investigated in several studies. The general prediction from the Humphreys and Revelle (1984) theory is that adding a memory load to an attentionally demanding task should replace the positive, monotonic arousal–performance curve with an inverted U regression. Matthews *et al.* (1990c) tested memory load effects in sustained attention, with tasks described by Davies and Parasuraman (1982) as *successive tasks*, where information must integrate across trials. An example would be the detection of three successive odd digits in a digit sequence. In contrast, the sustained attention tasks previously described are *simultaneous tasks*, in which all the information necessary for deciding whether stimuli are targets is present on each individual trial. Results were complex. A successive line detection task showed the same linear, facilitative effects of energy as for the simultaneous equivalent task. Two studies of a successive digit detection task showed that high energy impaired performance in the morning but facilitated it in the afternoon. A study of controlled memory search demonstrated that energy was unrelated to simple memory search, but was related by a U-shaped curve to combined visual and memory search (Matthews *et al.*, 1990b). Another study of memory loaded visual search failed to show any effect of energetic arousal (Matthews *et al.*, 1989). Overall, effects of memory load on the arousal–performance regression were either non-existent or highly task-specific.

Possibly, memory loads in these studies were insufficient to test the Humphreys and Revelle hypotheses, although most of the within-subjects memory load manipulations effected substantial changes in performance level. Other experiments have specifically investigated short-term retention for larger sets of items. Matthews *et al.* (1989) failed to find any linear or curvilinear effect of energetic arousal on ordered recall of nine-digit strings. Matthews (1987) obtained a similar null effect on ordered recall of words, using Baddeley *et al.*'s (1985) working memory task, in which words must be entered into STM during sentence processing. On a second task, free, non-ordered recall of unrelated word lists, energy enhanced retention of the later, 'recency' items, but had no effect on earlier 'pre-recency' items, as shown in Figure 6.2. The effect of energy was similar when subjects' subvocal articulation was suppressed, and when a secondary memory load was imposed. This study appears to narrow down deleterious effects of energy on memory to the specific memory store responsible for short-term recency effects. Hitch (1980) terms this store the verbal input register and suggests that it affords relatively

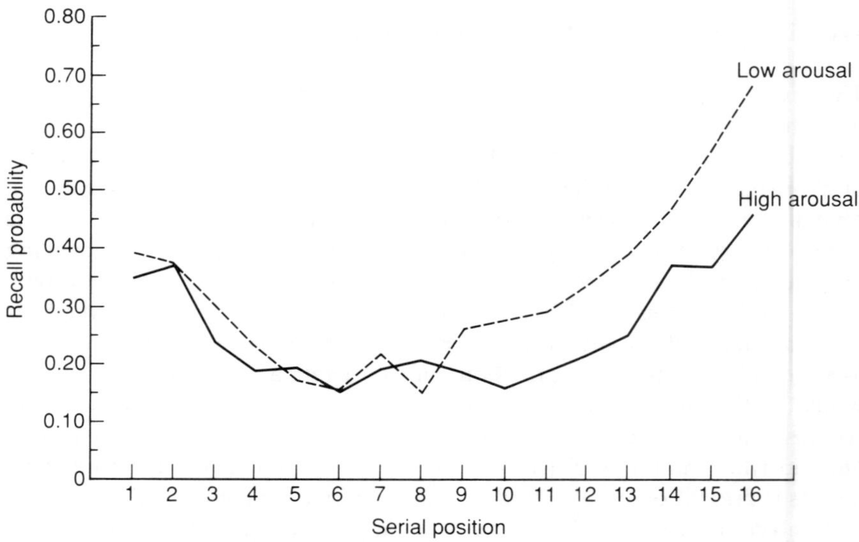

Figure 6.2 Free recall as a function of serial position and level of energetic arousal. (From Matthews, 1987.)

passive storage of the last few verbal chunks of information. Although evidence is limited, these studies suggest that energy is related to a specific verbal store rather than more general resources for STM.

Dual-task performance and task strategy

The importance of dual-task studies is that they allow effects on strategy and efficiency to be distinguished. If energy is associated with increased resource availability, dual-task performance, being more strongly resource-limited, should be more sensitive to energy facilitation than single-task performance. Conversely, if energy acts primarily to increase the selectivity of attention, the reverse effect will be obtained. Energy effects should also vary with task priorities if these are manipulated.

DUAL-TASK SUSTAINED ATTENTION

Matthews *et al.* (1991) conducted four dual-task studies of sustained attention, to digit and line stimuli. Three studies used the secondary probe RT technique (Parasuraman, 1985), with an auditory or visual stimulus presented in close temporal proximity to the primary stimuli of the sustained attention task. Surprisingly, no effects of energy on secondary RT were found. Moreover, presentation of the secondary probe stimuli blocked the normally reliable facilitative effects of energy on more demanding task versions. In the fourth study, task stimuli were alternated, rather than presented at almost the same time. Various combinations of sustained attention tasks were used, with equal priority assigned to each of the tasks paired together. The two task parameters were whether the task was simultaneous or successive, and whether the task was performed singly or in combination with a second task. Stimuli were undegraded, so effects on single task performance were not expected to be strong. Results showed that energy enhanced perceptual sensitivity only when the task was successive, and when it was performed together with a second task. Since successive tasks appear to be more resource-demanding than simultaneous tasks (Parasuraman *et al.*, 1987), results are consistent with the resource hypothesis.

DUAL-TASK CONTROLLED SEARCH

A further study by Matthews and Margetts (1991) investigated controlled semantic category search: the subject must search a display of words for a category exemplar. In dual-task conditions, the subject was required to search independent sets of simultaneously displayed green and blue words, with the priorities assigned to each colour of word varied. It is assumed that subjects

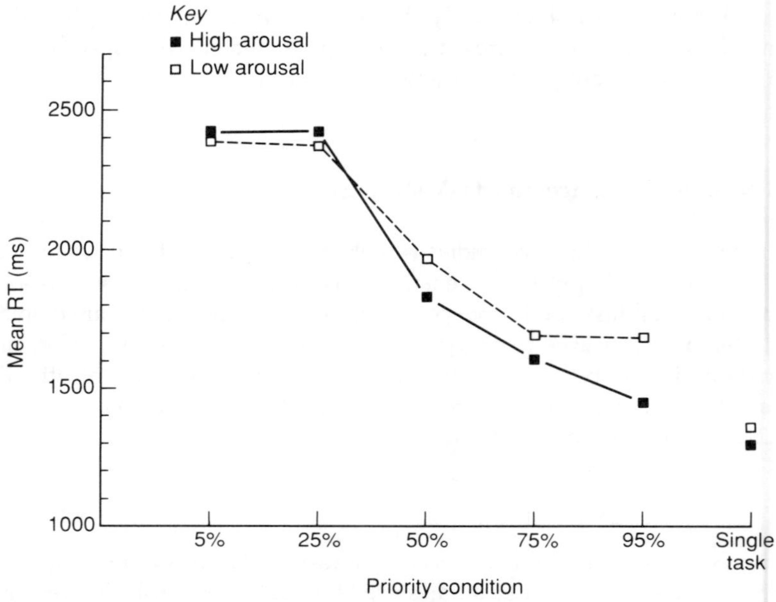

Figure 6.3 Speed of controlled category search as a function of task priority and level of energetic arousal. (From Matthews and Margetts, 1991, © 1991 Lawrence Erlbaum Associates, Inc.)

adopt a predominantly serial search strategy in both single- and dual-task conditions. There were two main results. Firstly, energy was more strongly positively related to speed of search in dual-task search relative to single-task search. Secondly, the effect of energy varied with the notional priority of the two elements of dual-task search as shown in Figure 6.3. The facilitative effect of energy increased progressively with priority, and energy was actually non-significantly negatively related to search speed for the two lowest priority task conditions. These results imply that although energy is positively related to resource availability, the additional resources are deployed only to relatively high priority task components, including the condition where each of two components is assigned equal priority.

Energy and attention: theoretical issues

The data reviewed may be summarized as showing that energy has straightforward facilitative effects on performance efficiency on resource-limited attentional tasks in many circumstances, but has only rather task-specific effects on short-term retention. Consistent with attentional resource theories, energy effects on performance are found with tasks placing high demands on both encoding processes (detection of degraded digits and lines), and on semantic or central processing (category search and letter transformation). However, the dual-task studies appear to identify two constraints on the incidence of the energy effect: low task priority and parallel processing. The role of task priority is probably associated with choice of strategy for resource deployment. It is unclear whether the blocking of the energy effect by parallel processing is related to strategy or to the benefits of high energy being cancelled out by energy impairing parallel processing. Other strategic effects of arousal identified in Hockey's (1984) review were not found. The studies reviewed checked the effects of energy on response criterion, and on speed–accuracy trade-off for self-paced tasks, with generally negative results (Matthews *et al.*, 1990b). Energy also had no effect on rule-driven target switching (Matthews, 1989), or on goodness of fit of performance to a serial search strategy (Matthews and Margetts, 1991). Hence, at a descriptive level, the strongest effect of energy is on performance efficiency: strategic effects of energy were restricted to attentional selectivity changes in the Matthews and Margetts (1991) study. Next, consideration is given to the comparability of energy and manipulated arousal effects on performance, and the nature of the underlying causes of the association between energy and resource availability.

ENERGY AND STRESSOR EFFECTS

Energy effects on attention closely resemble those of external stressors which affect energy. For example, the stimulant drugs amphetamine and caffeine appear to increase perceptual sensitivity or reduce perceptual sensitivity decrement, while sleep deprivation has adverse effects on vigilance (Davies and Parasuraman, 1982). Interestingly, noise, which has stronger effects on tension than on energy (Thayer, 1989) has rather weak effects on vigilance (Davies and Parasuraman, 1982). Fisk and Scerbo (1987) claim that controlled processing is more sensitive than automatic processing to manipulated stress. The priority dependence of the energy effect (Matthews and Margetts, 1991) is also consistent with research on a variety of arousers (Eysenck, 1982). It is difficult to draw such close parallels for the memory data: for example, although caffeine is said to impair working memory (Humphreys and Revelle, 1984), amphetamine effects on STM are inconsistent (Warburton and Wesnes, 1984). It may be possible to use mood measures to categorize stress states, to clarify their effects on performance. Different aspects of stress-driven state change may mediate different aspects of performance change. For example, the facilitative effects of caffeine on attention may be mediated by increased energy, whereas its deleterious effects on working memory may be mediated by increased tension.

CAUSAL EXPLANATIONS FOR ENERGY EFFECTS

In principle, both biological and cognitive explanations of the energy–performance association can be imagined. Energy may be related to a neural system whose activity affects resource availability, or, alternatively, to appraisals of the task as challenging or rewarding, which in turn would affect motivation (see Weiner, 1985). There is no direct evidence for or against mediation of effects by cognitive appraisal. However, there are some intriguing parallels between energy effects and effects of nicotine, reviewed by Warburton (1986) and Wesnes and Parrott (1992). Like increased energy, nicotine improves the overall level of vigilance, and reduces perceptual sensitivity decrement. Nicotine also enhances dual-task performance, but the effect may be modified by task instructions, as in the Matthews and Margetts (1991) study. Nicotine tends to raise energy (Thayer, 1989), and cholinergic antagonists such as scopolamine reduce energy (Dunne and Hartley, 1985). These comparisons imply possible cholinergic mediation for energy–performance correlations. Beatty (1986) suggests that cholinergic projections from brain stem to cortex can be identified with Moruzzi and Magoun's (1949) brain stem reticular formation, which Thayer (1989) identifies as a possible neural substrate for energy. Beatty (1986) also reviews evidence suggesting that acetylcholine increases the signal-to-noise ratio of the selective response to visual stimuli of single cells. Other neurotransmitter systems may also be implicated. For example, activating the dorsal noradrenergic bundle also appears to increase the cellular response to attended inputs (Mason, 1984). Dopamine release is strongly implicated in the behavioural effects of stimulant drugs such as amphetamine (Iversen and Iversen, 1981). However, according to Robbins (1986), dopamine systems primarily affect speed and probability of responding rather than perceptual efficiency, a very different pattern of performance change from that associated with individual differences in energy.

Hedonic tone and performance efficiency

Positive hedonic tone may also be associated with greater efficiency of information processing. A related idea is the Pollyanna hypothesis that positive material is preferentially and more efficiently processed (Matlin and Stang, 1978). Ellis and Ashbrook (1988) review a series of studies of induced mood and performance which show that both encoding and retrieval from memory for neutral stimulus materials are impaired in depressed or unpleasant mood states. However, many studies of mood and memory fail to show the effect (Mayer, 1986). Ellis and Ashbrook (1988) reason that the effect is more reliable for tasks whose encoding requires effort: for example, retention of highly structured material such as prose is insensitive to depressed mood. Depressed mood reduces attentional resource availability because resources are diverted to processing of self-related and other task-irrelevant information. Task performance will be impaired if the mood is strong and the task is sufficiently demanding. It is a considerable weakness of the theory that the evidence for it comes mainly from studies of memory, in which the role of resource allocation is unclear. Depressed mood might well affect strategy rather than capacity. For example, the failure of depressed subjects to benefit from elaborative information (Ellis *et al.*, 1984) could result from their choosing not to encode the additional information rather than from an inability to do so. Performance facilitation from induced positive moods has also been demonstrated in studies of decision making (Isen and Means, 1983) and creativity (Isen *et al.*, 1987). It is unclear in these studies whether mood is affecting strategy or efficiency. Another possible mechanism is self-focus of attention. Negative mood-states and self-focus appear to be positively and reciprocally related (Wood *et al.*, 1990), and self-focused attention may impair task performance, through an interference mechanism (Carver *et al.*, 1983; Wells, 1989).

Studies of naturally occurring depressive moods, particularly in depressed patients show a wider range of performance deficits in attention and memory (Johnson and Magaro, 1987; Williams *et al.*, 1988). Johnson and Magaro (1987) suggested that such deficits in memory may be attributed to lack of effort and motivation. Again, there is little direct evidence on whether lack of effort leads to ineffective strategy use or to lack of attentional resources available for task performance. Johnson and Magaro review several studies showing that depressive patients adopt more conservative, cautious strategies for response. The most rigorous investigation of this issue (Griffin *et al.*, 1986), which used a sustained attention task, concluded that mildly depressed students were not deficient in resources. However, failure of these subjects to react to probability information suggested a motivational deficit. In summary, hedonic tone may affect performance efficiency, but it is unclear whether the mechanism is one of energization or of interference. There are some indications that the effect may be mediated by choice of resource allocation strategy rather than through variation in resource availability, as in the case of energy effects.

HEDONIC TONE AND COGNITIVE BIAS

The principal affective biasing of cognition is *mood-congruence* in processing (Bower, 1981): a mood-state facilitates processing of state-congruent material, and impairs processing of incongruent material. There are two main areas of empirical research: mood-congruence in perception and judgement, and mood-congruence in memory. There are only a few instances of research on mood-induced bias in response selection and execution. Subjects tend to choose prototypical category exemplars congruent with their mood (Mayer, 1986), for example. More subtly, positive mood increases caution in decision making under risk or uncertainty, through increasing the aversiveness or negatively utility of losses (Isen *et al.*, 1988). Moods may also bias social responding, in that positive moods reliably increase helping behaviour (Carlson *et al.*, 1988), although negative moods have more complex effects (Clark, 1986). Theories of mood-congruence are considered following the review of data.

Perception and attention

SIMPLE ENCODING PROCESSES

Effects of induced mood on simple processes of perception and attention appear to be weak. Bower (1987) reviews four studies which failed to find any effect of induced mood on tasks using emotional verbal stimuli, such as tachistoscopic recognition thresholds, colour naming on the Stroop task, and lexical decision. Two further studies of visual recognition thresholds (Small, 1985; Small and Robins, 1988) obtained more positive results. In both studies, a mood-congruence effect was found for depression-related words, which were recognized at briefer exposures when a depressed mood was induced than when a neutral mood was induced. Small and Robins (1988) obtained the additional, paradoxical effect that elated content words were also recognized more easily in depressed mood. The authors suggest that the negative mood primes positive as well as negative emotional concepts. In another study demonstrating mood-congruence, Izard *et al.* (1965) reported that mood biased which of two stereoscopically presented faces, one happy and one angry, was perceived in a binocular conflict situation.

Studies of chronically depressed subjects provide somewhat more consistent results. Even mildly depressed undergraduates, selected by questionnaire, show slower colour naming of mood-congruent words on the Stroop test (Gotlib and McCann, 1984). However, a subsequent study of mildly depressed subjects failed to show mood congruence of selective attention to word pairs (Gotlib *et al.*, 1988). Gotlib *et al.* suggest that non-depressives show an attentional bias towards positive material, whereas depression is associated with more evently distributed attention. Clinically depressed patients consistently show greater Stroop interference when processing negative material (Gotlib *et al.*, 1988). Further studies have suggested, conflictingly, that the amount of affect-related interference in patient groups increases with level of current depressed mood (Williams and Broadbent, 1986), and is more strongly related to previous than current depression (Williams and Nulty, 1986). Depressed patients are also slower to make lexical decisions on neutral words, relative to positive and negative words, but fail to show greater semantic priming of emotional word recognition (Matthews and Southall, 1991).

COMPLEX STIMULUS EVALUATION

Mood effects on more complex evaluations of stimuli are rather more robust. The world, the self and others are appraised as generally more positive when one is in a pleasant mood. Mood-congruent bias resulting from induced mood has been demonstrated for ratings of satisfaction with possessions (Isen *et al.*, 1978), task performance (Wright and Mischel, 1982), and with life as a whole (Schwartz and Clore, 1983). Mood also biases judgements of self-efficacy and assessments of other people (Bower, 1981, 1987). Schwartz and Clore (1983) suggest these biases are associated with misattributions of mood: bias is reduced when subjects are alerted to likely causes of their mood. Probability judgements of the likelihood of pleasant or unpleasant events are similarly affected by mood (Mayer, 1986). Mood-congruent biases in judgement and evaluation are also found in mild and clinical depression (Williams *et al.*, 1988). Of particular interest is 'depressive realism' on tasks where the subject must judge whether or not they can control a desired outcome. Controls tend falsely to believe that they have control when in fact they do not, but depressed students are more accurate in detecting lack of contingency between outcome and their own responses (Alloy and Abramson, 1988). Alloy and Abramson suggest that depressed persons are more realistic and even-handed in their processing of positive and negative self-referent information. In other words, level of depression is associated with a trade-off between accuracy of self-perception and positive self-appraisal. There has been some debate over the generality and implications of the depressive realism effect (e.g. Williams *et al.*, 1988).

Memory

There is an extensive literature on affect-related bias in memory, which is not reviewed in detail here: the reader is referred to Blaney (1986), Williams *et al.* (1988) and Ucros (1989). I summarize here the principal findings from the two main task paradigms used: *mood-state-dependent* memory (MSD), and *mood-congruent* memory (MC) for experimental materials and real-life events. In experiments on MSD, the aim is to demonstrate an interaction between input and output moods: retention should improve as the match between input and output moods increases. Experiments on MC aim to demonstrate interaction between mood and the affective valence of material learned or retrieved. Unhappy subjects should preferentially learn items associated with sadness, and so forth.

METHODOLOGICAL PROBLEMS

Various methodological difficulties have surfaced in the context of memory research. One problem is that lack of precise control of subjects' emotions and strategies impedes classification of effects. It is difficult to demonstrate MC at input because mood may affect the time spent examining stimuli of differing emotional content, rather than encoding (Blaney, 1986). It is also unclear whether MSD and MC at output constitute distinct phenomena. Ucros (1989) suggests that output MC may be an instance of MSD, if affectively-toned items affect mood as they are encoded. A depressed person recalling an unhappy event is retrieving an item which was probably encoded in an unhappy mood. It is uncertain whether single words presented in laboratory contexts have much effect on mood, though. Blaney (1986) discusses in detail the difficulties in distinguishing between MSD and output MC. A second problem is that the reliability of MC effects varies with a wide range of method factors (Ucros, 1989). Some of these factors probably influence the strength of mood-states. Ucros's review shows that MSD and output MC effect sizes were greater when subjects were selected for hypnotizability, or, *post hoc*, for success of the mood manipulation. In addition, contrasts between positive and negative moods give stronger effects than contrasts between emotional and neutral moods, as might be expected. We have seen previously that subjects' sensitivity to mood manipulation depends on personality traits of neuroticism and depression (Blackburn *et al.*, 1990). This finding suggests potentially serious state–trait confounding in studies using subjects selected for mood change. Successful mood-congruence studies may, in fact, be those selecting trait depressives or neurotics.

MOOD-STATE DEPENDENT MEMORY

State-dependent effects on memory of external environments and of internal states induced by drugs are generally reliable (Eich, 1980). It is believed that the effect results from the dependence of retrieval on overlap between contextual cues present at input and output (Tulving, 1983). In mood research, the issue is whether mood is a sufficiently strong influence on the internal context to generate the effect. Bower (1981) reviewed some early studies from his laboratory showing MSD in which mood was manipulated by hypnosis. Subjects learnt two lists of words, one list in a happy mood, the other in a sad mood. After a varying retention interval, they then free-recalled one of the two lists in either of the two moods. Recall was better when output and input moods matched, as expected. More recent reviews of the MSD literature (e.g. Blaney, 1986; Bower, 1987) tend to stress failures to replicate the effect, which Bower describes as a capricious will-of-the-wisp. There has been little MSD research using clinical patients, presumably because of the difficulty of manipulating mood in these groups. Weingartner *et al.*

(1977) report an interesting study of bipolar manic depressives, in which there was an MSD effect related to the subjects' natural variations in mood.

The inconsistency of the effect may reflect the role of task factors, in addition to the methodological factors described previously. For example, Bower (1981) suggested that MSD is more likely when the subject learns two lists in different moods, so that mood can subsequently be used as a retrieval cue to reduce inter-list interference. A meta-analysis conducted by Ucros (1989) investigates task factors in detail, although in most cases the variation of effect size with task factors is averaged across MSD and MC designs. Ucros's meta-analysis confirms that interference designs, in which mood is manipulated at input within-subjects, give somewhat larger effect sizes than designs where input mood is constant for each subject. Other relevant task factors were types of encoding and retrieval: larger effect sizes for MSD were associated with intentional learning relative to incidental learning, and free recall relative to cued recall and recognition. Bower (1987) has proposed that to generate MSD the subject must causally attribute his or her emotional state to the material encoded in order for the mood to aid subsequent retrieval. This criterion may be too restrictive; nevertheless, it is likely that stronger MSD effects will be found when mood and stimulus material are actively inter-associated at encoding.

MOOD-CONGRUENT MEMORY

Experiments on MC take three typical forms: experimental studies of input MC and output MC, using artificial materials such as word lists varying in affective content, and studies of bias in autobiographical or naturalistic memory in different mood-states. Most reviewers consider that MC is a more reliable phenomenon than MSD (e.g. Bower, 1987): Ucros's (1989) meta-analysis shows that the average effect size for output MC is indeed larger than for MSD (0.51 versus 0.33), but the difference only approached significance ($p < 0.10$). Input and output MC effects appear to be of roughly comparable reliability. A few studies (see Blaney, 1986) have manipulated mood at both input and output, allowing a direct comparison, but results are inconclusive. The majority of studies of MC, such as Bower's initial demonstrations of the effect, have used free-recall tasks, but the effect does not appear to generalize to recognition (Bower and Cohen, 1982). Studies of real-life memory typically require the subject to recall events in response to a cue, such as a recent or childhood event (Gilligan and Bower, 1984), or a neutral word may be used to prime retrieval (Teasdale and Fogarty, 1979). Such studies show somewhat stronger MC effects than studies of experimental material (Ucros, 1989), although confounding of material recalled with mood at encoding is a serious problem for this design.

Experimental studies have also capitalized on naturally occurring moods in normal and patient groups. Blaney (1986) reviews several studies of recall of self-referent statements: depressives tend to over-recall negative statements and/or under-recall positive ones. Several of these studies showed that MC was stronger when a self-reference set was induced, with subjects required to focus on the personal relevance of the statements. Depressed patients also show MC in verbal learning, although the effect is partially attributable to response bias (Williams *et al.*, 1988; Matthews and Southall, 1991). Comparison of mildly depressed undergraduates with controls does not appear to be an effective method for demonstrating MC (Blaney, 1986). Blaney also points out that in a number of studies of both clinical depressives and mood induction, MC is primarily due to a bias towards positive material in a positive mood state, rather than a negative bias in negative mood. MC for retrieval of real-life events has also been demonstrated in clinically depressed patients, but this result is difficult to interpret because depressives may have experienced more genuinely unpleasant events than non-depressives, and they may also re-interpret neutral events as being negative (Blaney, 1986; Williams *et al.*, 1988). Clark and Teasdale (1982) used a sample of depressives whose mood varied with time of day, and showed that affective valence of personal memories varied appropriately with mood.

Theories of mood-congruence

The data reviewed show that mood-congruence is a pervasive effect affecting a wide variety of tasks, from simple visual recognition thresholds to social evaluations. Theory must explain not just the existence of mood-congruence, but also its variation with task factors. In particular, induced moods appear to have rather weak effects on simple perceptual tasks, but more reliable effects on more complex evaluations, and on memory. Within studies of memory, the strength of effects appears to be enhanced by tasks which encourage active processing, such as intentional rather than incidental learning, and recall rather than recognition. Stronger effects on both judgement and memory have generally been obtained when processing is self-referent, particularly in patient groups (Blaney, 1986). It is unclear whether this effect results from the special status of the self or whether self-reference is just one of several ways of increasing elaboration of processing with respect to contextual cues such as mood. Differences in bias between induced moods and moods associated with clinical syndromes such as depression pose special problems because they could be attributed either to greater strength of mood in clinical groups or to differential effects of state mood and affect-related traits. Theories of depressed mood and performance are firmly cognitive in orientation, and tend to assume that changes in information processing are caused by the characteristic appraisals and knowledge structures associated with depression (Beck *et al.*, 1979). The possible role of neural processes in generating cognitive bias has been rather neglected. In this section, two theories of normal mood and performance are outlined, and explanations for differences between normal and abnormal mood-states are discussed.

BOWER'S (1981, 1987) NETWORK THEORY

In a classic paper, Bower (1981) proposed that emotions were represented cognitively as nodes within a semantic network. Emotions constitute special kinds of concepts or knowledge, integrated within the information processing system. Emotion nodes may be directly activated by appraisals, or through reciprocal excitation between emotion nodes and expressive behaviours and autonomic arousal. Emotion nodes are associatively linked with specific concepts and memories, so that emotion nodes and associated concepts will tend to be mutually excitatory through the automatic, unconscious spread of activation from one associated node to another. Inducing emotion causes a whole range of associated concepts to be partially activated, increasing their probability of entering awareness. Further papers (see Bower, 1987) have elaborated the basic theory to account for intensity of emotion, distinctions between names, concepts and referents, and complex emotional reactions. The network theory predicts that mood-congruence effects should be found across a wide range of tasks. If a person feels happy, their memories for pleasant events will be partially activated, making them easier to access. Likewise, positive attributes of stimuli will be more salient because of pre-existing activation of the nodes for positive qualities. The contrast between activation patterns in positive and negative mood is likely to be enhanced by mutually inhibitory associations between incompatible emotions such as happiness and sadness.

Bower (1987) provides a rather pessimistic appraisal of the success of the theory. This pessimism may be misplaced given that many of the predictive failures may be attributed to methodological problems such as failure to induce strong moods (see Ucros, 1989). More seriously, there are a number of theoretical difficulties also for network theory. Firstly, Bower (1981) attributes mood-congruence to an automatic spread of activation between nodes, but it is possible that the effect also results from voluntary strategy implementation. Bower (1981) himself indicates that mood affects elaborations and inferences, but does not make explicit which mood-congruence effects result directly from the spread of activation and which depend on subsequent strategic, interpretative processes. Blaney (1986) outlines several possible strategies which may contribute to mood-congruence. Unhappy people may, for example, selectively attend to negative material because they are trying to rebut a negative self-image or overcome their own weaknesses. Congruence may also result from subject compliance, or from subjects' attempts to find a causal explanation for their moods. Secondly, Williams *et al.* (1988) suggest the network model is more successful as a general framework than as a detailed theory. They describe a number of specific problems, such as neglect of the role of retrieval processes in memory, which may explain the failure to find mood-congruence in recognition paradigms, and of differences between general, specific, and self-relevant memories. Similarly, Bower (1987) indicates that more attention should be paid to the role of encoding processes in establishing associative links between emotion nodes and episodic memories. Thirdly, the model has never been represented as a computer simulation, which is a weakness because interactive activation networks may have unexpected properties which can only be identified through simulation (Matthews and Southall, 1991).

THE WILLIAMS *ET AL.* (1988) FRAMEWORK

Williams *et al.* attempt to provide a framework allowing distinctions between anxiety and depression effects, and between state and trait effects. They propose two stages of processing: an automatic pre-attentive stage controlling resource allocation to encoding, succeeded by a strategic stage controlling elaboration processes. Anxiety primarily affects the first stage, depression the second. Within the elaboration stage, there is an affective decision mechanism which assesses the negativity of input, and a mechanism which controls facilitation or inhibition of elaboration of input items. State depression (or unpleasant mood) makes affective decisions more negative, whereas trait depression is associated with a permanent bias in resource allocation towards negative items. The framework thus deals with some issues neglected by Bower (1981, 1987), including the role of elaboration in retrieval. Mood-congruence in memory results from increased elaboration of congruent items, at either input or input. This hypothesis explains why, empirically, active processing of material increases the strength of MC effects. Williams *et al.* (1988) differ sharply from Bower (1981) in attributing depression effects mainly to strategic rather than automatic processes, although there is little direct evidence either way. There are also some general theoretical difficulties with the Williams *et al.* (1988) framework. They appear to confound early and late processing with automatic and strategic processing, which is not a necessary correspondence (see, for example, Norman and Shallice, 1985). The mechanism for state depression effects on mood-congruence in non-clinical subjects also seems problematic, since state mood affects only evaluation of negativity but not elaboration as such.

MODELS FOR CLINICAL DEPRESSION EFFECTS ON PERFORMANCE

The Williams *et al.* (1988) model represents one approach to distinguishing between state mood and clinical depression. Other theories of clinical depression and cognition are too numerous to describe here. Ingram's (1984) review of the area presents a synthesis which identifies many of the distinctive features of clinical depression. Ingram starts from a network model similar to

Bower's (1981), within which depression is associated with activation of a depression-emotion node. In the clinical depressive, activation of the node is maintained by the recycling of activation through a 'loss-associated cognitive network' composed of network nodes associated with the events, memories and beliefs related to the depressing situation. This network or loop serves to elaborate depression-related cognitions in a fairly automatic way. It may be interrupted by voluntary control processes, and inability to do so may relate to severity of depression. Most theories of clinical depression emphasize the importance of beliefs or schemas relating to the self. Within Ingram's (1984) model, this results from the incorporation of nodes relating to the self within the loss-associated network, which explains the dependence of mood-congruence on self-relevant material. Self-relevant stimuli are more likely to activate the loss-associated network than, for example, experimental negative word lists.

CONCLUSIONS

The studies of mood reviewed suggest that there are least two areas of performance research where consistent mood effects have been demonstrated: energy effects on attentional efficiency, and hedonic tone effects on mood congruence in a variety of tasks. The broad comparability of effects of energy and manipulated arousers, and of hedonic tone and natural depressed mood demonstrates the value of mood studies in investigating effects of stress and psychopathology on performance. The review also shows the importance of careful attention to methods and task factors in studies of both energy and hedonic tone. Energy does not correlate with performance of all difficult attentional tasks: performance must be resource-limited to be energy-sensitive. Likewise, in studies of mood-congruence, it is essential that induced or natural moods are sufficiently strong, and that several specific task parameters are set appropriately. Future mood research should also strive to eliminate confounding of mood with other affective and cognitive variables.

As described previously, there are two levels at which theories of mood and performance may be developed: the detailed description of mood correlates of information processing, and causal theories of mood–performance associations. The first type of explanation is more advanced than the second. At a descriptive level, energy effects are compatible with resource models of performance, and hedonic tone effects with interactive activation network or other information-processing models. One of the major concerns in this context is the *level of control* of effects. Are moods associated with changes in the function of lower-level, stimulus-driven 'automatic' processing, making few capacity demands, or with an upper level, capacity-limited and driven by voluntary plans and strategies? Simple effects of energy appear to be confined to the efficiency of upper-level functioning (although energy and extraversion may interactively affect lower-level processes: see Matthews, chapter 4, this volume). Expression of these effects in performance changes may be modified by task strategy, but, to date, there is little evidence that energy directly affects strategy. There is still confusion over the level of hedonic tone effects on cognitive bias. Mood-congruent responses may be preferentially activated by the automatic spread of activation, or by voluntary strategy for elaboration of input, or both. Surprisingly, there has been little empirical research directed towards this issue, which remains an important task for the future. Another aim for future research is the integration of mood studies with cognitive science approaches to affect. Simon's (1982) view that mood constitutes a diffuse background context for information-processing appears to be compatible with the energy data, but the position regarding mood-congruence effects is less clear. Mood-congruence might result from either the chronic activation of individual items of mood-congruent knowledge, or from bias in activation of goals and plans.

Causal theories of mood effects on performance are largely a matter for speculation at present. As described, we may construct plausible biological and cognitive explanations for energy and hedonic tone effects respectively. However, nothing in the data precludes a cognitive explanation for energy effects or a biological mechanism for mood-congruence. Nor are cognitive and biological explanations necessarily incompatible. Multivariate research simultaneously manipulating both cognitive and biological influences on mood may be necessary for further progress. Lastly, research of this kind must beware of excessively linear causal models. Although the present review has emphasized that mood may cause performance changes, or correlate with causes of performance, there is undoubtedly feedback from perceived performance and success to affect, which implies a need for more cyclical, closed-loop models for the relationships between mood and processes of cognition, neural systems and performance.

REFERENCES

Alloy, L.B. and Abramson, L.Y. (1988) Depressive realism: four theoretical perspectives. In *Cognitive Processes in Depression*, edited by L.B. Alloy. New York: Guilford.

Baddeley, A., Logie, R. and Nimmo-Smith, I. (1985) Components of fluent reading. *Journal of Memory and Language* **24**: 119–31.

Beatty, J. (1986) Computation, control and energetics: a biological perspective. In *Energetics and Human Information Processing*, edited by G.R.J. Hockey, M.G.H. Coles and A.W.K. Gaillard. Dordrecht: Martinus Nijhoff.

Beck, A.T., Rush, A.J., Shaw, B.F. and Emery, G. (1979) *Cognitive Therapy of Depression*. New York: Guilford.

Blackburn, I.M., Cameron, C.M. and Deary, I.J. (1990) Individual differences and response to the Velten Mood Induction Procedure. *Personality and Individual Differences* **11**, 725–31.

Blaney, P.H. (1986) Affect and memory: a review. *Psychological Bulletin* **99**: 229–46.
Bower, G.H. (1981) Mood and memory. *American Psychologist* **36**: 129–48.
Bower, G.H. (1987) Commentary on mood and memory. *Behaviour Research and Therapy* **25**: 443–55.
Bower, G.H. and Cohen, P.R. (1982) Emotional influences in memory and thinking: data and theory. In *Affect and Social Cognition,* edited by S. Fiske and M. Clark. Hillsdale, NJ: Erlbaum.
Carlson, M., Charlin, V. and Miller, N. (1988) Positive mood and helping behavior: a test of six hypotheses. *Journal of Personality and Social Psychology* **55**: 211–29.
Carver, C.S., Peterson, L.M., Follansbee, D.J. and Scheier, M.F. (1983) Effects of self-directed attention on performance and resistance among persons high and low in test-anxiety. *Cognitive Therapy and Research* **7**: 333–54.
Cattell, R.B. (1973) *Personality and Mood by Questionnaire.* New York: Jossey-Bass.
Clark, D.M. and Teasdale, J.D. (1982) Diurnal variations in clinical depression and accessibility of memories of positive and negative experience. *Journal of Abnormal Psychology* **91**: 87–95.
Clark, L.A. and Watson, D. (1988) Mood and the mundane: relations between daily life events and self-reported mood. *Journal of Personality and Social Psychology* **54**: 296–308.
Clark, M.S. (1986) Some effects of everyday moods and possible individual differences in these effects. In *Energetics and Human Information Processing,* edited by G.R.J. Hockey, M.G.H. Coles and A.W.K. Gaillard. Dordrecht: Martinus Nijhoff.
Cox, T. and Mackay, C. (1985) The measurement of self-reported stress and arousal. *British Journal of Psychology* **76**: 183–6.
Curran, J.P. and Cattell, R.B. (1974) *The Eight State Questionnaire.* Champaign, Ill.: IPAT.
Davies, D.R. and Parasuraman, R. (1982) *The Psychology of Vigilance.* New York and London: Academic Press.
Diener, E., Larsen, R.J., Levine, S. and Emmons, R.A. (1985) Intensity and frequency: dimensions underlying positive and negative affect. *Journal of Personality and Social Psychology* **48**: 1253–65.
Dunne, M.P. and Hartley, L.R. (1985) The effects of scopolamine upon verbal memory: evidence for an attentional hypothesis. *Acta Psychologica* **58**: 205–17.
Eckenrode, J. (1984) Impact of chronic and acute stressors on daily reports of mood. *Journal of Personality and Social Psychology* **46**: 907–18.
Eich, J.E. (1980) The cue dependent nature of state dependent retrieval. *Memory and Cognition* **8**: 157–73.
Ellis, H.C. and Ashbrook, P.W. (1988) Resource allocation model of the effects of depressed mood states on memory. In *Affect, Cognition and Social Behavior,* edited by K. Fiedler and J. Forgas. Toronto: Hogrefe.
Ellis, H.C., Thomas, R.L. and Rodriguez, I.A. (1984) Emotional mood states and memory: elaborative encoding, semantic processing and cognitive effort. *Journal of Experimental Psychology (Learning, Memory and Cognition)* **10**: 470–82.
Ellis, H.C., Thomas, R.L., McFarland, A.D. and Lane, J.W. (1985) Emotional mood states and retrieval in episodic memory. *Journal of Experimental Psychology (Learning, Memory and Cognition)* **11**: 363–70.
Emmons, R.A. and Diener, E. (1986) Influence of impulsivity and sociability on subjective well-being. *Journal of Personality and Social Psychology* **50**: 1211–5.
Endler, N.S. (1983) Interactionism: a personality model but not yet a theory. In *Nebraska Symposium on Motivation. Personality 1982: Current Theory and Research,* edited by M.M. Page and R. Dienstbier. University of Nebraska Press.
Erlichman, H. and Halpern, J.N. (1988) Affect and memory: effects of pleasant and unpleasant odors on retrieval of happy and unhappy memories. *Journal of Personality and Social Psychology* **55**: 769–79.
Eysenck, H.J. and Eysenck, M.W. (1985) *Personality and Individual Differences: A Natural Science Approach.* New York: Plenum.
Eysenck, M.W. (1982) *Attention and Arousal: Cognition and Performance.* London: Springer.

Ferguson, E. and Cox, T. (1991) The nature and measurement of primary appraisal. University of Nottingham.

Fisk, A.D. and Scerbo, M.W. (1987) Automatic and control processing approach to interpreting vigilance performance: a review and reevaluation. *Human Factors* **29**: 653–660.

Folkman, S. and Lazarus, R.S. (1988) Coping as a mediator of emotion. *Journal of Personality and Social Psychology* **54**: 466–75.

Frijda, N.H. (1986) *The Emotions*. Cambridge University Press.

Gilligan, S.G. and Bower, G.H. (1984) Cognitive consequences of emotional arousal. In *Emotions, Cognition and Behavior*, edited by C.E. Izard, J. Kagan and R.B. Zajonc. Cambridge University Press.

Gotlib, I.H. and McCann, C.D. (1984) Construct accessibility and depression: An examination of cognitive and affective factors. *Journal of Personality and Social Psychology* **47**: 427–39.

Gotlib, I.H., McLachlan, A.L. and Katz, A.N. (1988) Biases in visual attention in depressed and nondepressed individuals. *Cognition and Emotion* **2**: 185–200.

Gray, J.A. (1987) *The Psychology of Fear and Stress*, 2nd edn. Cambridge University Press.

Griffin, J.A., Dember, W.N. and Warm, J.S. (1986) Effects of depression on expectancy in sustained attention. *Motivation and Emotion* **10**: 195–205.

Hasher, L., Rose, K.C., Zacks, R.T., Sanft, H. and Doren, B. (1985) Mood, recall, and selectivity effects in normal college students. *Journal of Experimental Psychology (General)* **114**: 104–8.

Hirst, W. and Kalmar, D. (1987) Characterizing attentional resources. *Journal of Experimental Psychology (General)* **116**: 68–81.

Hitch, G.J. (1980) Developing the concept of working memory. In *Cognitive Psychology: New Directions*, edited by G. Claxton. London: Routledge.

Hockey, G.R.J. (1984) Varieties of attentional state: the effects of the environment. In *Varieties of Attention*, edited by R. Parasuraman and D.R. Davies. New York and London: Academic Press.

Hockey, G.R.J., Coles, M.G.H. and Gaillard, A.W.K. (eds) (1986) *Energetics and Human Information Processing*. Dordrecht: Martinus Nijhoff.

Humphreys, M.S. and Revelle, W. (1984) Personality, motivation and performance: a theory of the relationship between individual differences and information processing. *Psychological Review* **91**: 153–84.

Ingram, R.E. (1984) Toward an information-processing analysis of depression. *Cognitive Therapy and Research* **8**: 443–78.

Ingram, R.E. (1989) Affective confounds in social–cognitive research. *Journal of Personality and Social Psychology* **57**: 715–22.

Isen, A.M. and Levin, P.F. (1972) The effect of feeling good on helping: cookies and kindness. *Journal of Personality and Social Psychology* **21**: 384–8.

Isen, A.M. and Means, B. (1983) The influence of positive affect on decision making strategy. *Social Cognition* **2**: 18–31.

Isen, A.M., Shalker, T., Clark, M. and Karp, L. (1978) Affect, accessibility of material in memory and behaviour: a cognitive loop? *Journal of Personality and Social Psychology* **36**: 1–12.

Isen, A.M., Daubman, K.A. and Nowicki, G.P. (1987) Positive affect facilitates creative problem solving. *Journal of Personality and Social Psychology* **52**: 1122–31.

Isen, A.M., Nygren, T.E. and Ashby, F.G. (1988) Influence of positive affect on the subjective utility of gains and losses: it is just not worth the risk. *Journal of Personality and Social Psychology* **55**: 710–7.

Iversen, S.D. and Iversen, L.L. (1981) *Behavioral Pharmacology*, 2nd edn. Oxford University Press.

Izard, C.E., Wehmer, G.M., Livsey, W. and Jennings, J.R. (1965) Affect, awareness, and performance. In *Affect, Cognition, and Personality*, edited by S.S. Tomkins and C.E. Izard. New York: Springer.

Johnson, L.C. (1982) Sleep deprivation and performance. In *Biological Rhythms, Sleep, and Performance*, edited by W.B. Web. Chichester: Wiley.

Johnson, M.H. and Magaro, P.A. (1987) Effects of mood and severity on memory processes in depression and mania. *Psychological Bulletin* **101**: 28–40.

Laird, J.D., Wagener, J.J., Halal, M. and Szegda, M. (1982) Remembering what you feel: effects of emotion on memory. *Journal of Personality and Social Psychology* **42**: 646–57.

Lazarus, R.S. (1984) On the primacy of cognition. *American Psychologist* **37**: 1019–24.

Lazarus, R.S. and Folkman, S. (1984) *Stress, Appraisal and Coping*. New York: Springer.

Lazarus, R.S., Averill, J.R. and Opton, E.M., Jr (1970) Toward a cognitive theory of emotion. In *Feelings and Emotions*, edited by M. Arnold. New York and London: Academic Press.

Mackay, C.J. (1980) The measurement of mood and psychophysiological activity using self-report techniques. In *Techniques of Psychophysiology*, edited by I. Martin and P.H. Venables. New York: Wiley.

Marshall, G.D. and Zimbardo, P.G. (1979) Affective consequences of inadequately explained physiological arousal. *Journal of Personality and Social Psychology* **37**: 970–88.

Mason, S.T. (1984) *Catecholamines and Behaviour*. Cambridge University Press.

Matlin, M.W. and Stang, D.J. (1978) *The Pollyanna Principle*. Cambridge, Ma.: Schenkman.

Matthews, G. (1986) The interactive effects of extraversion and arousal on performance: are creativity tests anomalous? *Personality and Individual Differences* **7**: 751–61.

Matthews, G. (1987) Extraversion, self-report arousal and performance: the role of task factors. Paper presented to the Third Meeting of the International Society for the Study of Individual Differences, Toronto, Canada.

Matthews, G. (1989) Extraversion and levels of control of sustained attention. *Acta Psychologica* **70**: 129–146.

Matthews, G. and Margetts, I. (1991) Self-report arousal and divided attention: A study of performance operating characteristics. *Human Performance* **4**: 107–25.

Matthews, G. and Southall, A. (1991) Depression and the processing of emotional stimuli: a study of semantic priming. *Cognitive Therapy and Research* **15**: 283–302.

Matthews, G., Jones, D.M. and Chamberlain, A.G. (1989) Interactive effects of extraversion and arousal on attentional task performance: multiple resources or encoding processes? *Journal of Personality and Social Psychology* **56**: 629–39.

Matthews, G., Jones, D.M. and Chamberlain, A.G. (1990a) Refining the measurement of mood: the UWIST mood adjective checklist. *British Journal of Psychology* **81**: 17–42.

Matthews, G., Davies, D.R. and Lees, J.L. (1990b) Arousal, extraversion, and individual differences in resource availability. *Journal of Personality and Social Psychology* **59**: 150–68.

Matthews, G., Davies, D.R. and Holley, P.J. (1990c) Extraversion, arousal and visual sustained attention: the role of resource availability. *Personality and Individual Differences* **11**: 1159–73.

Matthews, G., Davies, D.R. and Westerman, S. (1991) Self-report arousal and dual-task performance: efficiency or selectivity? Paper presented to the Annual Conference of the British Psychological Society.

Mayer, J.D. (1986) How mood influences cognition. In *Advances in Cognitive Science*, Vol. 1, edited by N.E. Sharkey. Chichester: Ellis Horwood.

Moruzzi, G. and Magoun, E.W. (1949) Brain-stem reticular formation and activation of the EEG. *Electroencephalography and Clinical Neurophysiology* **1**: 455–73.

Norman, D.A. and Shallice, T. (1985) Attention to action: willed and automatic control of behaviour. In *Consciousness and Self-Regulation: Advances in Research*, Vol. 4, edited by R.J. Davidson, G.E. Schwartz and D. Shapiro. New York: Plenum.

Nowlis, V. (1965) Research with the mood adjective check list. In *Affect, Cognition and Personality*, edited by S.S. Tomkins and C.E. Izard. New York: Springer.

Oatley, K. (ed.) (1987) Cognitive science and the understanding of emotions. *Cognition and Emotion* **1**: 209–347 (special issue).

Oatley, K. and Johnson-Laird, P. (1987) Towards a cognitive theory of emotions. *Cognition and Emotion* **1**: 29–50.

Ortony, A., Clore, G.L. and Foss, M.A. (1987) The referential structure of the affective lexicon.

Cognitive Science **11**: 361–84.
Panksepp, J. (1986) The neurochemistry of behavior. *Annual Review of Psychology* **37**: 77–107.
Parasuraman, R. (1985) Vigilance: a multifactorial approach. In *Attention and Performance*, Vol. 11, edited by M.I. Posner and O.S.M. Marin. Hillsdale, NJ: Erlbaum.
Parasuraman, R., Warm, J.S. and Dember, W.N. (1987) Vigilance: taxonomy and utility. In *Ergonomics and Human Factors: Recent Research*, edited by L. Mark, J.S. Warm and R.L. Huston. New York: Springer.
Polivy, J. and Doyle, C. (1980) Laboratory induction of mood states through the reading of self-referent mood statements: affective changes or demand characteristics. *Journal of Abnormal Psychology* **89**: 286–90.
Pollack, I. and Norman, D.A. (1964) A nonparametric analysis of recognition experiments. *Psychonomic Science* **1**: 125–6.
Robbins, T.W. (1986) Psychopharmacological and neurobiological aspects of the energetics of information processing. In *Energetics and Human Information Processing*, edited by G.R.J. Hockey, M.G.H. Coles and A.W.K. Gaillard. Dordrecht: Martinus Nijhoff.
Robbins, T.W. and Everitt, B.J. (1982) Functional studies of the central catecholamines. *International Review of Neurobiology* **23**: 303–65.
Russell, J.A. (1979) Affective space is bipolar. *Journal of Personality and Social Psychology* **37**: 345–56.
Sarason, I.G., Sarason, B.R., Keefe, D.E., Hayes, B.E. and Shearin, E.N. (1986) Cognitive interference: situational determinants and traitlike characteristics. *Journal of Personality and Social Psychology* **51**: 215–26.
Schachter, S. and Singer, J.E. (1962) Cognitive, social, and physiological determinants of emotional state. *Psychological Review* **69**: 379–99.
Schneider, W. and Shiffrin, R.M. (1977) Controlled and automatic human information processing. I: Detection, search and attention. *Psychological Review* **84**: 1–66.
Schwartz, N. and Clore, G.L. (1983) Mood, misattribution, and judgments of well-being: Informative and directive functions of affective states. *Journal of Personality and Social Psychology* **45**: 513–23.
Simon, H.A. (1982) Comments. In *Affect and Cognition*, edited by M.S. Clark and S.T. Fiske. Hillsdale, NJ: Erlbaum.
Sjoberg, L., Svensson, E. and Persson, L.-O. 1979) The measurement of mood. *Scandinavian Journal of Psychology* **20**: 1–18.
Small, S.A. (1985) The effect of mood on word recognition. *Bulletin of the Psychonomic Society* **23**: 453–55.
Small, S.A. and Robins, C.J. (1988) The influence of induced depressed mood on visual recognition thresholds: predictive ambiguity of associative network models of mood and cognition. *Cognitive Research and Therapy* **12**: 295–304.
Teasdale, J.D. and Fogarty, S.J. (1979) Differential effects of induced mood on retrieval of pleasant and unpleasant events from episodic memory. *Journal of Abnormal Psychology* **88**: 248–57.
Thayer, R.E. (1978) Toward a psychological theory of multidimensional activation (arousal). *Motivation and Emotion* **2**: 1–34.
Thayer, R.E. (1989) *The Biopsychology of Mood and Arousal*. Oxford University Press.
Thayer, R.E. and Moore, L.E. (1972) Reported activation and verbal learning as a function of group size (social faciliatation) and anxiety-inducing instructions. *Journal of Social Psychology* **88**: 277–87.
Tulving, E. (1983) *Elements of Episodic Memory*. Oxford University Press.
Ucros, C.G. (1989) Mood state-dependent memory: a meta-analysis. *Cognition and Emotion* **3**: 139–67.
Vanderwolf, C.H. and Robinson, T.E. (1981) Reticulo-cortical activity and behavior: a critique of the arousal theory and a new synthesis. *Behavioral and Brain Sciences* **4**: 459–514.

Velten, E.C. (1968) A laboratory task for induction of mood states. *Behaviour Research and Therapy* **6**: 473–82.

Warburton, D.M. (1986) A state model for mental effort. In *Energetics and Human Information Processing*, edited by G.R.J. Hockey, A.W.K. Gaillard and M.G.H. Coles. Dordrecht: Martinus Nijhoff.

Warburton, D.M. and Wesnes, K. (1984) Drugs and human information processing. In *Psychology Survey*, Vol. 5, edited by J. Nicolson and H. Beloff. Leicester: British Psychological Society.

Watson, D. (1988) The vicissitudes of mood measurement: effects of varying descriptors, time frames, and response formats on measures of positive and negative affect. *Journal of Personality and Social Psychology* **55**: 128–41.

Watson, D. and Tellegen, A. (1985) Toward a consensual structure of mood. *Psychological Bulletin* **98**: 219–35.

Weiner, B. (1985) An attributional theory of achievement motivation and emotion. *Psychological Review* **92**: 548–73.

Weingartner, H., Miller, H. and Murphy, D.L. (1977) Mood-state dependent retrieval of verbal associations. *Journal of Abnormal Psychology* **86**: 276–284.

Wells, A. (1989) Self-attention and anxiety. Paper presented to the World Congress of Cognitive Therapy, Oxford University.

Wesnes, K.A. and Parrott, A.C. (1992) Smoking, nicotine and human performance. In *Handbook of Human Performance*, Vol. 2, edited by D.M. Jones and A.P. Smith. New York and London: Academic Press, chapter 5.

Williams, D.G. (1989) Personality effects in current mood: pervasive or reactive? *Personality and Individual Differences* **10**: 941–8.

Williams, J.M.G. and Broadbent, D.E. (1986) Distraction by emotional stimuli: use of a Stroop task with suicide attempters. *British Journal of Clinical Psychology* **25**: 101–10.

Williams, J.M.G. and Nulty, D.D. (1986) Construct accessibility, depression and the emotional Stroop task: transient mood or stable structure. *Personality and Individual Differences* **7**: 485–91.

Williams, J.M.G., Watts, F.N., MacLeod, C. and Mathews, A. (1988) *Cognitive Psychology and Emotional Disorders*. Chichester: Wiley.

Wine, J.D. (1982) Evaluation anxiety: a cognitive-attentional construct. In *Achievement, Stress and Anxiety*, edited by H.W. Krohne and L. Laux. Washington, DC: Hemisphere.

Wood, J.V., Saltzberg, J.A. and Goldsamt, L.A. (1990) Does affect induce self-focused attention? *Journal of Personality and Social Psychology* **58**: 899–908.

Wright, J. and Mischel, W. (1982) Influence of affect on cognitive special learning person variables. *Journal of Personality and Social Psychology* **43**: 901–14.

Wundt, W. (1905) *Grundriss der Psychologie*. Leipzig: Engelmann.

Zajonc, R.B. (1984) On the primacy of emotion. *American Psychologist* **39**: 117–23.

7

Effects of Sleep and Circadian Rhythms on Performance

S.S. CAMPBELL

INTRODUCTION

The relationship between the quality of a night's sleep and performance efficiency on the following day has probably been understood, at least at an intuitive level, since the first humans went to bed early in anticipation of the next day's hunting expedition. Notwithstanding the more recent tradition of undertaking 'all-nighters' in preparation for an important exam, the vast majority of people would undoubtedly agree that one is likely to perform better after a good night's sleep.

As early as the 1800s, attempts to quantify this relationship were under way using a behavioural equivalent of the time-honoured procedure of organ extirpation to determine function (Kleitman, 1963). In the first series of sleep deprivation studies in humans, Patrick and Gilbert (1896) found that ninety consecutive hours without sleep resulted in significant performance deficits, including reduced sensory acuity, slowed reaction time and motor speed, and declines in the capacity to memorize simple information. In contrast, subsequent experiments found no detrimental effects on measures of performance following sixty-five hours (Robinson and Hermann, 1922) and twenty-four hours (Robinson and Richardson-Robinson, 1922) of sleep deprivation. These studies may have been the first, but certainly were not the last, to report contradictory findings concerning the seemingly simple link between sleep and performance.

Indeed, the modern era of sleep research brought with it several developments that further complicated understanding of the relationship between sleep and the ability to perform. Perhaps the most important of

HANDBOOK OF HUMAN PERFORMANCE
VOLUME 3 ISBN 0-12-650353-2

these developments concerned the growing integration of sleep research with the field of human chronobiology. With the growing interest in the study of sleep and waking over multiple twenty-four hour periods, it soon became clear that sleep propensity was determined not only by the amount of prior wakefulness, but also (and perhaps *more so*) by an internal clock that governed the timing of virtually every other function in the human body—including performance efficiency (Aschoff, 1965). Thus, such factors as time on shift, chronic sleep debt and prior sleep history became complicated by their interactions with circadian factors. Moreover, examination of the relationship between sleep and performance became more difficult, since both variables covaried as a function of time of day.

This chapter examines the effects of sleep on performance within the general framework of chronobiology. Firstly, we explore the relationship between performance efficiency and various aspects of major sleep episodes. We then address some of the implications of these findings from both a theoretical and an applied perspective. However, before examining the relationship between circadian aspects of sleep and their influence on performance efficiency, we review the nature of human sleep from the general perspective of biological rhythms.

AN OVERVIEW OF HUMAN SLEEP AND CIRCADIAN RHYTHMS

In response to the earth's rotation, virtually all species have developed endogenously mediated rhythms with frequencies close to twenty-four hours. The pervasive nature of such rhythmic components in physiology and behaviour suggests that this circadian (from the Latin *circa* about, *dies* day; Halberg, 1959) temporal organization is vital to the overall well-being of the organism. Among the numerous systems and functions mediated by the circadian timing system are hormonal output, body core temperature, rest and activity, sleep and wakefulness, and motor and cognitive performance. In all, literally hundreds of circadian rhythms in mammalian species have been identified (see, for example, Aschoff, 1981; Conroy and Mills, 1970), and Aschoff (1965) has noted that 'there is apparently no organ and no function in the body which does not exhibit a similar daily rhythmicity'.

Because of the predominance of rhythms recurring about once a day, biological rhythms with longer or shorter frequencies have typically been classified as infradian, or ultradian rhythms, respectively. An example of an infradian rhythm is the human menstrual cycle. An example of an ultradian rhythm is the recurrence of dream sleep (REM sleep) about every ninety minutes throughout a normal night's sleep. It is rhythms in the circadian range, and to a lesser extent the ultradian range, that are of primary relevance to this chapter. Most performance measures show oscillations in the twenty-four hour range, though considerable evidence suggests shorter-term fluctuations, as well. Likewise, the human sleep/wake cycle, which so profoundly influences performance, is primarily a circadian system, but with important ultradian components.

Sleep as a biological rhythm

In the early 1960s, Aschoff and co-workers began studies which, over the next twenty years, would lay the foundation for much of what we know today about the human circadian system (for a summary of much of this work, see Aschoff and Wever, 1981; Wever, 1979). Most studies were conducted in an underground laboratory consisting of two studio apartments that were free of all environmental clues to time of day. The laboratory was heavily sound-dampened and the timing and intensity of illumination could be controlled from outside the apartments by the experimenters. In addition, subjects were studied in isolation in order to eliminate possible time clues provided by social contact.

The first experiments conducted in this environment (Aschoff, 1965) demonstrated that adult humans exhibit 'free-running' rhythms of rest and activity averaging slightly longer than twenty-five hours (Figure 7.1). That is, a subject's average 'day' continued for about an hour longer than the natural day, though in some people the subjective day continued for a substantially longer period (up to fifty hours). Thus, subjects who thought that they had been in the time-free environment for, say, three weeks were often quite surprised when they were informed that a month or more had elapsed.

Further investigations of many other systems confirmed that endogenous daily rhythms tended to free-run at frequencies slightly longer than twenty-four hours, and that all such rhythms typically stayed synchronized with one another (for a complete review, see Moore-Ede *et al.*, 1982). This internal organization among rhythms is seen clearly in the usual relationship between the sleep/wake system and the rhythm of body temperature. In the time-free environment, major sleep episodes tend to be initiated around the low point (nadir) of the temperature rhythm and are terminated several hours after the nadir (see Figure 7.1). Aschoff and Wever observed remarkable inter-individual precision in the period length of the sleep/wake rhythm under these conditions. The average twenty-five hour rhythms deviated only about one half-hour between individuals (Wever, 1979).

For any single individual, however, the day-to-day flexibility of the circadian system is both obvious and well-documented (Webb and Agnew, 1978). We are not suddenly overcome with sleep at a particular point in our temperature rhythm, nor are we startled awake each morning by a biological alarm clock

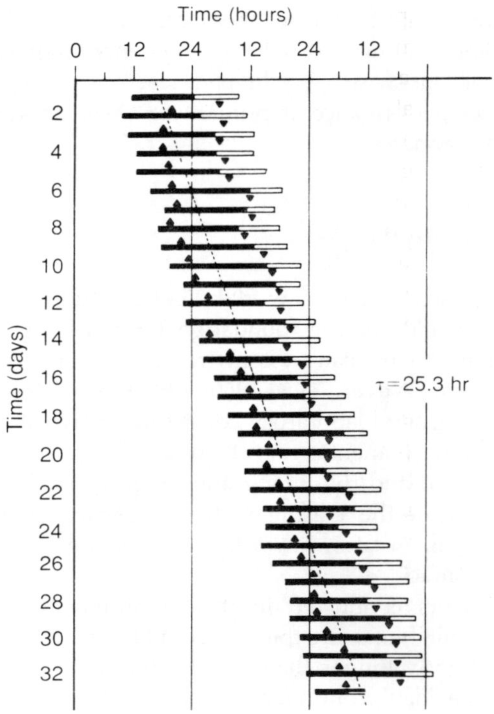

Figure 7.1 Free-running rhythm of a subject living in an environment without time cues. Rest (white bars) and activity (black bars) are presented as a function of time of day for successive subjective days of the study. The daily maximum (▲) and minimum (▼) of body core temperature are also shown. (From Wever, 1979.)

tied to the temperature cycle. Rather, we routinely shift our bedtimes and waking up times to accommodate changes in our daily schedules. At the level of individual behaviour, then, the human circadian system is a 'sloppy' system (Campbell, 1984; Campbell and Zulley, 1988). It is this inherent flexibility in the system that allows our free-running endogenous rhythms to be synchronized, or entrained, by the numerous environmental, behavioural and social cues that provide the structure of our daily lives.

Napping as a biological rhythm

Because most adult humans exhibit a strong propensity to obtain their daily sleep quotas in one nightly episode, the human sleep system has traditionally been considered to be monophasic in nature. As illustrated in Figure 7.1, this assumption seems to be borne out in traditional time-free studies. Although subjects free-run with a period slightly longer than twenty-four hours, they nevertheless maintain a monophasic sleep/wake organization, with one sleep episode per subjective day. Yet, the extent to which such a pattern of sleep and wakefulness is mediated by biology and to what degree it is dictated by societal (or experimental) demands has been questioned (Campbell and Zulley, 1985; Dinges and Broughton, 1989). If the human sleep system is, in fact, monophasic, it would stand as the soul exception to an apparent phylogenetic rule of polyphasic sleep (Campbell and Tobler, 1984). There is now quite convincing evidence, however, that this is not the case. Rather, human sleep is more appropriately viewed as a polyphasic system, with at least two 'preferred' phase positions for the occurrence of sleep within the twenty-four hour day.

In the traditional time-free environment, subjects are instructed to lead a 'regular' life: that is, to eat three meals in normal sequence, *not* to nap after lunch, but rather to sleep only when they are certain that their major sleep period is commencing (see, for example, Aschoff, 1965; Weitzman *et al.*, 1982). In response to such instructions, compliant, well-motivated subjects exhibit monophasic, circadian sleep patterns. However, only minor changes in experimental instructions result in significant alterations in sleep patterns. Figure 7.2 shows the frequency of occurrence of sleep episodes taken by a group of subjects living under identical time-free conditions for seventy-two

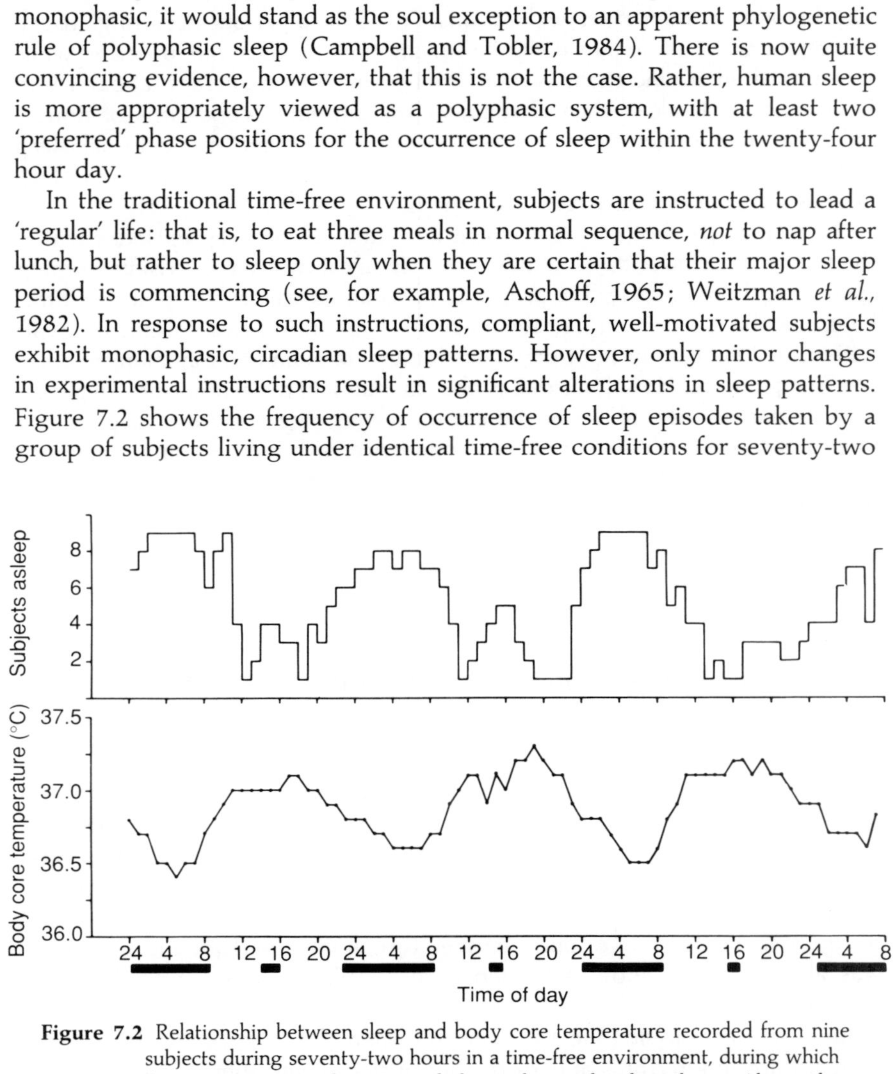

Figure 7.2 Relationship between sleep and body core temperature recorded from nine subjects during seventy-two hours in a time-free environment, during which they were permitted to eat and sleep when inclined to do so. Above the group temperature curve is a summation histogram of the number of subjects asleep during a given hour of the study. Black bars are average onsets and durations of major sleep episodes and naps. (From Campbell and Zulley, 1985.)

continuous hours, but given the instruction to eat and sleep whenever inclined to do so. Major sleep episodes continue to show a strong propensity to occur in association with the trough of body core temperature. In addition, under these conditions there is a marked tendency for a second interval of sleep to occur around the maximum of body core temperature. These sleep episodes are differentiated not only by their placement within the twenty-four hour day, but also by their average durations. Those sleep periods occurring around the temperature minimum continue for an average of about 8 hours, while those initiated around the maximum are terminated, on average, about 1.5–2 hours later. It is clear, then, that under the entrained conditions of normal daily life, the longer sleep episodes correspond to major, nocturnal sleep periods and the shorter sleep episodes correspond to the afternoon sleep periods that we typically refer to as naps.

To summarize, both the placement and duration of sleep episodes within the twenty-four hour day are influenced significantly by the circadian timing system. Although, under the proper circumstances we can sleep at any time, humans exhibit a pronounced tendency to sleep during two specific intervals within the twenty-four hour day, tied to the maximum and minimum of body core temperature. How long one is able to maintain a sleep episode depends, in large part, on the phase of the circadian cycle the episode is begun. The longest sleep episodes occur in correspondence with the declining portion of the circadian rhythm in body core temperature, the shortest with the rising portion. Under normal, entrained conditions, these times correspond to night and day, respectively.

BIOLOGICAL RHYTHMS AND PERFORMANCE

Following the initial discovery of rhythmicity in numerous physiological systems, it was soon ascertained that many human psychological processes and mental functions exhibited fluctuations across the day, as well. These included subjective assessments of alertness and mood and objectively measured efficiency in a wide range of performance tasks. And, just as the sleep/wake system was found to be synchronized to the circadian rhythm of body temperature, human performance efficiency was also found to show a tendency to parallel the rise and fall of the temperature rhythm. (It should be emphasized that no causal relationship is implied, nor should one be inferred, when the temporal link between temperature and rhythms of performance or sleep/wakefulness is considered. Rather, body temperature is a convenient and traditional 'marker' of the endogenous circadian clock against which to reference other variables showing systematic changes as a function of time of day, particularly psychological measures such as performance efficiency and mood (Monk, 1989).)

Methodological considerations

Several difficulties inherent in the study of rhythmic aspects of performance must be considered prior to a discussion of the findings (for a full discussion of these points, see Colquhoun, 1981; Folkard and Monk, 1985). Firstly, and perhaps most importantly, performance tasks are performed voluntarily. As such, unlike physiological processes, performance efficiency may be dictated in part or wholly by motivation of the subject. The question must be asked, then, is an observed 'rhythm' in task performance an actual reflection of time-of-day changes in cognitive efficiency or simply a reflection of fluctuations in motivation to perform? On the other hand, if a periodicity in performance is not observed, does this mean a rhythm does not exist, or simply that changes in motivation across the day have effectively masked, or 'washed out', the underlying rhythm? These often become critical issues when attempting to apply the results of laboratory studies to the workplace, since motivational components of the two setting may differ significantly.

It is also important to keep in mind the obvious fact that performance is a waking behaviour. Performance efficiency cannot be assessed when the subject is asleep. Thus, the approximately eight-hour interval of the twenty-four hour day usually spent in sleep must be filled either by waking subjects periodically through the sleep period to do performance tasks, or by extending, or displacing, the usual waking period. All of these procedures (sleep interruption, sleep deprivation, sleep displacement) are likely to influence the results. Because of such limitations, Colquhoun (1981) has emphasized that, with respect to the evaluation of temporal components of performance efficiency, the focus is more specifically on 'time-of-(waking)day effects'.

Circadian components

Early studies confirmed that, in general terms, performance measures show gradually increasing levels of efficiency in association with the rising portion of the body core temperature cycle. Under the entrained conditions of daily life this corresponds to the interval beginning at roughly 7 a.m. and ending with a peak in performance in the early evening. The trough in such measures of performance was reported to occur in the very early hours of the morning (approximately 2–6 a.m.), in association with the minimum portion of the body temperature cycle (for reviews, see Colquhoun, 1971; 1972; Kleitman, 1963).

Subsequent, and inevitably more refined, experiments led to the identification of several important qualifications to the general finding of 'performance paralleling temperature'. Firstly, the nature of the task to be performed was found to be of considerable importance. Many of the procedures employed in the early studies consisted of relatively boring vigilance tasks, requiring little in the way of higher level cognitive functioning or mental processing. As a greater range of cognitive skills was tested by a larger variety of performance tasks it became apparent that factors such as perceptual involvement, memory load and type (short- or long-term) and amount of logical reasoning required all were important in determining the exact course of performance efficiency across the day (see, for example, Folkard *et al.*, 1976). Moreover, the nature of the measure chosen in evaluating the results was found to have a significant impact on the time-of-day effects observed. For example, Monk and Leng (1982) found that if performance efficiency on a search task was evaluated in terms of speed of response, the usual relationship with temperature was observed: subjects became faster across the day. However, if accuracy of response, rather than speed, was the critical measure, then an opposite relationship was observed.

It has been suggested that these different relationships observed between the circadian course of body core temperature and the circadian variation in various performance tasks may reflect the differential control of the performance rhythms by either the 'strong oscillator' presumed by some to govern body core temperature, or the 'weak oscillator' presumed responsible for the timing of sleep/wake behaviour (Monk *et al.*, 1983). Alternatively, the existence of one or more 'performance oscillators' has even been proposed, with at least one of these oscillators having an endogenous period of about twenty-one hours (Folkard *et al.*, 1983, 1985).

Such conclusions are based on findings from a small number of subjects, studied for extended periods in time-free environments, under conditions of 'forced internal desynchronization'. This experimental approach involves forcing a split between expression of the two putative oscillators by extending or shortening the sleep/wake cycle such that its period falls outside the range of entrainment of the 'strong oscillator' (see Wever, 1979, for a further description of this experimental strategy). By so doing, and then examining the circadian course of performance on various tasks, it is theoretically possible to identify the controlling oscillator for a particular task.

Using this procedure in a single subject, Monk and co-workers (1983) concluded that performance on a manual dexterity task (Purdue pegboard test) was governed by the same oscillator controlling body core temperature whereas performance on a verbal reasoning task (a modification of the Baddeley test) was influenced by both sleep/wake and temperature oscillators. Employing the same technique in seven subjects, Folkard and co-workers (1983) found that performance on a simple letter cancellation task closely followed the circadian rhythm of body core temperature, and for four of the subjects, the same was true for a more complex verbal reasoning task. However, three subjects exhibited circadian performance rhythms for the more complex task with a period of twenty-one hours, clearly different from both temperature and sleep/wake rhythms. The authors conclude from these findings that memory-loaded performance tasks are controlled by an 'underlying oscillator with an autonomous period of about 21 hours' (p. 225). They fail however, to explain the possible adaptive significance of such an 'oscillator'. In summary, in light of the remarkably small number of subjects involved in these studies, conclusions drawn from this experimental paradigm must be interpreted with extreme caution.

Individual differences

Common experience tells that there are considerable individual differences in the ability to perform across the twenty-four hour day. Although a number of factors have been examined in this regard (see, for example, Davies, 1985) probably the two most important determinants of when an individual is likely to exhibit optimum performance are age and where he or she falls on a 'morningness–eveningness' continuum (Monk, 1990). An individual's morningness is typically derived from the outcome of a self-assessment questionnaire that evaluates behavioural patterns and preferences relative to time of day (Horne and Östberg, 1976). As might be expected, extreme morning types have been reported to have more difficulty adapting to (night) shift work, whereas extreme evening types may perform poorly in the early morning. Age may play an important role, in as much as people tend to exhibit a greater degree of 'morningness' as they grow older (Monk, 1990).

To summarize, the various qualifications and caveats notwithstanding, there is considerable evidence to indicate that performance efficiency and other psychological processes such as arousal and mood are subject to significant circadian fluctuations. While many performance tasks are closely tied to the rise in body core temperature across the daytime hours, there are clearly measures that deviate from such a relationship. Indeed, in certain cases (e.g. those involving short-term memory processes), the relationship between daytime temperature and performance efficiency is an inverse one (Folkard and Monk, 1980; Laird, 1925). However, regardless of the course across the daytime hours, the evidence is overwhelming that performance efficiency declines to minimum levels during the night-time hours (i.e. the time associated with the trough of body temperature). To the extent that individuals differ in the timing of their circadian rhythms (i.e. extreme morning and evening types), individual differences may play a roll in the timing of optimum performance, as well.

SLEEP AND PERFORMANCE

From the foregoing discussion it is logical to assume that optimal levels of performance are achieved during the daytime, immediately following a good night's sleep of normal duration. After all, under these conditions, both the sleep period and the performance interval occur at their appropriate circadian phases.

If this is the case, then several obvious questions arise regarding alterations in the usual relationship between sleep and performance. For example, can we continue to perform well when our sleep is truncated? If not, at what level of sleep restriction is performance efficiency compromised? On the other hand, can extended sleep lead to even better performance? Can we 'bank' sleep, thereby providing a reserve to be used at a later time? Can a short nap enhance performance? If so, to what extent? Is a consolidated sleep period more beneficial for subsequent performance than the same amount of sleep obtained in two or more episodes?

Questions such as these are of considerable interest to investigators in human performance since numerous settings require workers to perform in the face of restricted sleep over both short and long intervals. At the root of virtually all of these questions, then, is the issue of sleep deprivation. An enormous amount of research has addressed the specific issue of performance and total sleep deprivation, and chapter 9 in this volume is dedicated to that topic. As such, the next section does not address the issue of total sleep deprivation, but focuses instead on the issue of partial sleep deprivation, or sleep restriction.

Restricted sleep

Based on the premise that optimal performance should follow a normal night's sleep, one might expect a simple, linear relationship between the degree of sleep restriction and subsequent performance efficiency. However, experimental findings do not present a consistent picture in this regard (Johnson, 1974). One of the first studies to examine the impact on performance of partial sleep loss found no effect of shortening average sleep time by two hours per night for one week (Laird and Wheeler, 1926). In fact, the three subjects performed a mental multiplication task more rapidly, and with no loss of accuracy, following the shortened sleep regimen than at baseline.

Webb and Agnew (1965) found that a reduction in sleep to three hours per night for eight consecutive days resulted in marginal deteriorations in performance (an addition task, an auditory vigilance task and a visual vigilance task), but only on the last two days of the study. Even then, 'these decrements were neither uniform nor fully consistent', with large inter- and intra-individual differences. Likewise, restricting the normal sleep length of eight subjects by forty per cent, to an average of 4.6 hours per night, for five consecutive nights, resulted in only subtle performance decrements on one task (card sorting), and actual improvement on another (anagrams) (Herscovitch *et al.*, 1980).

In contrast to these findings, Wilkinson and co-workers have reported decrements in vigilance performance following two consecutive nights of sleep restriction to five hours, and impairment on an addition task following two nights in which sleep was reduced to three hours per night (Wilkinson *et al.*, 1966). In a further study, this group reported cumulative deficits in vigilance and addition speed across four nights in which sleep was restricted to four hours per night (Hamilton *et al.*, 1972). However, performance on a digit span task was enhanced following the four-hour sleep restriction. Tilley and Wilkinson (1984) reported poorer performance on an unprepared simple reaction time task following only one night of sleep restriction of similar magnitude (from a baseline of 8–8.5 hours down to 4 hours). Moreover, they found further impairment following a second night of restriction.

Likewise, Clodore and co-workers (1987) used a series of short-term memory tasks to assess the relative effects of restricting sleep by either delaying bedtime by two hours, or by advancing awakening by two hours (both resulting in reductions of total sleep time from about eight to six hours). There was no effect of such sleep displacement on the easiest memory task, but accuracy declined significantly on the most difficult task when subjects were required to rise two hours earlier than normal.

These last results notwithstanding, Webb (1969) has noted an important limitation of most partial sleep loss studies: 'they are restricted in the length of time during which the partial regimen [is] imposed'. As such, it is impossible to determine the extent to which the effects of restricted sleep might be cumulative. Johnson and Macleod (1973) attempted to address this methodological problem by studying two subjects over a period of five months during which sleep was gradually reduced (by 0.5 hours every two weeks) from baseline levels (7.85 and 7.77 hours) to 4 hours per day. Subjects' performance was assessed during the second week of the 5.5 hour sleep period and again during the last week of the 4 hour sleep period, using a memory task, an addition task and a reading comprehension task. Both subjects showed 'relatively mild' performance decrements on the memory and comprehension tasks at 4 hours of sleep, though the actual degree of deficit is not stated. The addition task was little affected, however, even at 4 hours of sleep. As in the study by Webb and Agnew (1965) there were substantial differences between the subjects in the degree of performance decrement observed. An added indication of the negligible impact sleep restriction had on performance, at least from the subjects' point of view is the fact that both reported voluntary reductions in sleep lengths of 1–1.5 hours (compared with pre-study averages) a full eight months after the study ended.

This was also the case for a group of eight subjects studied by Friedmann and co-workers (1977) who continued to show reduced total sleep times a year after completing the study. In this study, sleep was restricted to 4.5–5.5 hours per night, for up to eight months. Performance measures (auditory vigilance, word memory, digit span, rapid alternation) remained essentially unaffected throughout the study. Only at the lowest sleep level was there evidence of impairment in the form of increased variability in response times.

Webb and Agnew (1974) published the results of a similar study, in which they restricted the sleep of fifteen subjects to 5.5 hours per night for sixty consecutive days. As in the Johnson and Macleod study, no significant changes were found on a number of performance indices, including an addition task, a word memory test and a test of grip strength. Slight decrements were observed on a vigilance task, thought to be most sensitive to effects of sleep loss. However, the authors concluded that 'subjects' vigilance did not materially decline, but rather their willingness to perform declined' (p. 271).

Concerned that practice effects may have confounded the results of these studies, Horne and Wilkinson (1985) examined the effects of two months' sleep restriction (to six hours from the norm of eight) and compared the results with a non-restricted control group. Again, using a one hour auditory vigilance task, they found no significant difference between the restricted and control groups over the six-week experimental period.

In contrast to the large proportion of negative laboratory findings, there is some real-world evidence that even less pronounced sleep restriction, maintained over relatively extended intervals, may result in reduced performance efficiency. After reviewing reports and related information on the relationship between sleep and human error catastrophes (such as industrial and vehicular accidents), the Committee on Catastrophes, Sleep and Public Policy of the Association of Professional Sleep Societies concluded that 'inadequate sleep, even as little as 1 or 2 h less than usual sleep, can greatly exaggerate the tendency for error *during the time zones of vulnerability*' (emphasis added) (Mitler *et al.*, 1988). These 'zones of vulnerability' correspond to the two phases of high sleep propensity (circa 1 a.m.–8 a.m. and 2 p.m.–6 p.m.). Likewise, Akerstedt (1988) has suggested that performance deficits associated with shift work (particularly the nightshift) are, in large part, the consequence of chronic sleep restriction associated with trying to sleep at an inappropriate circadian phase.

Taken together, these findings indicate that restricted sleep *per se* probably does not significantly compromise performance efficiency, at least in the short term. Although some effects have been observed in response to approximately forty per cent reductions in normal sleep length, those effects are remarkably subtle, quite inconsistent and, therefore, difficult to measure and virtually impossible to characterize. However, several investigators have reported much more robust effects on performance of similar sleep restriction, when that sleep is shifted to a different circadian phase. This, combined with the real-world experience mentioned above, suggests that *placement* of restricted sleep periods within the twenty-four hour day may be an important factor in terms of their effects on subsequent performance.

Sleep at the inappropriate phase

The widespread and growing dependence on round-the-clock operations, in virtually every area of industry and commerce, has made it necessary for relatively large segments of the population to obtain daily sleep quotas throughout the twenty-four hour day. In addition, the growing ease and availability of transmeridian travel makes sleep displacement as a consequence of time zone shifts an ever-increasing problem. Because of this relevance to real-world situations, the issue of sleep period time displacement has received increased attention in recent years.

In a study to examine purely the effects of displaced sleep (as opposed to displaced and restricted sleep) Taub and Berger (1974) permitted ten subjects their usual 7–8 hours of sleep, but shifted the time of night during which the subjects could obtain the sleep. On four consecutive weeks, bedtimes were either advanced or delayed by two or four hours. Deficits in performance on a calculation task, as well as on a vigilance task, were observed following all shifted sleep conditions when compared with baseline sleep (midnight to 8 a.m.). There were no significant differences between conditions in performance nor in total sleep obtained.

These findings are in sharp contrast to those of Nicholson *et al.* (1985), who also allowed the full quota of daily sleep but at displaced times. In that study, subjects permitted to obtain four hours of sleep between 6 p.m. and 10 p.m. and an additional four hours between 8 a.m. and 12 a.m. performed no worse on the following day (digit symbol substitution, symbol copying, letter cancellation) than when they were allowed to obtain their sleep in one normal consolidated night-time sleep episode.

In a follow-up to their study, Taub and Berger (1976) tested effects on performance of manipulating both the phase *and* duration of sleep. They either extended/restricted habitual sleep length by three hours, or delayed/advanced habitual sleep by three hours, in subjects whose normal sleep length was 9.5–10.5 hours (i.e. habitual long sleepers). All manipulations caused decrements in both speed and accuracy on the vigilance task relative to performance following habitual sleep. The authors concluded from these results that 'maintenance of accustomed sleep schedules is equal to or greater in importance for the integrity of most waking behavioral functions than obtaining some invariant amount of sleep'.

Similar results have been reported by investigators who have studied effects of sleep period displacement associated with transmeridian travel. For example, Klein and Wegmann (1974) found that a sleep period time displacement of six hours (associated with air travel between the US and Germany) resulted in deficits in performance (reaction time, symbol cancellation, addition) following the first day of displaced sleep. There was no difference between east- and westbound travel (i.e. between advanced and delayed sleep displacement), and the deficits disappeared within three to five days. Elsewhere, these authors have reported that the declines in psycho-motor performance associated with transmeridian flights are equivalent to the deficits observed in subjects with blood-alcohol concentrations of 0.05 per cent (Wegmann and Klein, 1985).

Despite difficulties with learning effects, impairment was also observed in the laboratory as a consequence of a simulated jet lag protocol, in which sleep times were advanced six hours (Monk *et al.*, 1988). These investigators reported a significant slowing in the ability to perform a verbal reasoning task in seven of the eight subjects studied. As in the study of Klein and Wegmann, such decrements were observed for only the first three days following sleep displacement.

It is clear from these examples that displaced sleep, whether truncated or not, is associated with deficits, sometimes quite severe, in the ability to perform a wide range of tasks. When examining the relationship between displaced sleep and subsequent performance, it is important to keep in mind that most of these manipulations necessarily alter the phase of performance testing as well, not to mention a host of other physiological and psychological indices that show circadian cycles. Therefore, when performance deficits are observed, it is virtually impossible to determine the relative contributions of displaced sleep *per se*.

It is safe to assume, however, that altering one's sleep time does play a critical role in the observed impairments. To the shift worker and to many, if not most, investigators, sleep disturbance associated with the displacement of major sleep episodes is *the* major factor contributing to compromised performance (see, for example, Akerstedt, 1988; Folkard and Monk, 1985). If this is the case then the question must be asked, what is it about such displaced sleep episodes that contributes to the observed performance decrements? It is well known that displaced sleep is characterized by greater disruption and fragmentation than sleep taken at the usual time (see, for example, Webb and Agnew, 1971; Weitzman and Kripke, 1981). The following section examines the effects of this disrupted sleep on performance.

Sleep disruption

Bonnet has conducted an elegant series of studies designed to examine the effects of disrupted nocturnal sleep on subsequent performance (1985, 1986a, 1986b, 1987, 1989a, 1989b; Downey and Bonnet, 1987). In the first investigation, subjects' nocturnal sleep episodes were disrupted following each minute of sleep, for two consecutive nights. Upon final morning awakening, performance was assessed using an addition task, a simple reaction time test, and a digit symbol substitution task.

All three measures of performance were significantly impaired following the second night of sleep disruption, and the addition task was significantly worse following both nights. In fact, deficits on the addition task were equivalent to those seen following one night of total sleep deprivation, or following two nights of sleep reduction to less than three hours per night (Wilkinson *et al.*, 1966). This, despite the fact that such sleep disruption resulted in a total sleep time of only about one hour less than that obtained on the baseline night.

In a similar study, Bonnet (1986a) compared the effects on performance of awakenings each minute (as above), every ten minutes, or each minute, after two and a half hours of uninterrupted sleep. Subjects performed best following the two and a half hour sleep episode and in an intermediate fashion following the ten minute condition. As in the first study, performance following awakenings each minute was no better than total sleep deprivation.

From these results, Bonnet (1985) speculated that 'the fragmentation [of sleep] itself may somehow interfere with the sleep restorative process' and that sleep must continue undisturbed for at least 10 minutes for it to be restorative. Yet, in these studies, he was unable to reject the possibility that the observed impairment was the result of slow wave sleep (SWS) deprivation rather than sleep disruption. In an effort to address this issue more closely, Bonnet conducted a study in which he disrupted sleep in a manner that either preserved, or deprived, substantial amounts of SWS (1986b). While both conditions resulted in performance deficits relative to baseline measures, no differences in the degree of impairment were observed between the two disruption conditions. Clearly, then, it was sleep fragmentation, and not SWS restriction, that was related to reduced daytime function. A subsequent experiment (Bonnet, 1989a) confirmed the finding that at least ten minutes of uninterrupted sleep are required for the restorative value of sleep to be evident in performance efficiency.

Taken together, the results of these studies indicate that there is a direct relationship between the period of consolidated sleep and the amount of performance impairment on the following day. Given an equivalent total sleep time, sleep must occur in uninterrupted bouts of between twenty and forty minutes in order to maintain performance levels associated with a normal night's sleep. In other words, *sleep continuity* appears to be a critical factor in determining the value of a sleep episode relative to subsequent performance. A number of investigations have demonstrated that displaced sleep is characterized by a significant degree of fragmentation when compared with normal night-time sleep. Such truncated, disrupted sleep, in conjunction with performance intervals that are often displaced, may explain in large part the significant performance decrements observed following sleep period time displacement.

Sleep inertia

Immediately following awakening from night-time sleep, a hangover effect, or 'sleep inertia' effect, has been observed by many investigators. This post-sleep decrement in performance, often accompanied by confusion and dysphoria, has been recognized for many years (Kleitman, 1963; Langdon and Hartman, 1961) and detrimental effects on a large number of tasks have been documented (for reviews see Dinges *et al.,* 1985; Naitoh and Angus, 1989). In general, the effects of sleep inertia are transient, typically lasting for less than twenty minutes in well-rested subjects. However, the effects may be longer lasting and more severe in subjects who have been sleep-deprived for extended periods prior to the nap (Akerstedt and Gillberg, 1979; Dinges *et al.,* 1981).

There is some evidence that structural components of sleep episodes may also play a role in subsequent levels of sleep inertia. The stage of sleep out of which a subject is awakened may be related to the severity of sleep inertia effects. For example, Dinges and co-workers (1981) found that subjects awakened from slow wave sleep (stage 4) showed the most severe decrements on a reaction time task. Similarly, the composition of the preceding sleep period may also be important with respect to the degree of sleep inertia observed. The more slow wave sleep obtained, the more severe the subsequent sleep inertia effect is likely to be (Dinges *et al.,* 1985; Naitoh and Angus, 1989). Because structural components of sleep are intimately related to the time of day of occurrence, circadian effects are also likely to affect the degree of sleep inertia observed.

Sedatives and hypnotics

Sleep inertia effects may be exacerbated by the use of sleeping pills. Despite the recent development of short-acting hypnotics, hangover effects continue to represent a potentially serious problem (Gorenstein and Gentil, 1983). For example, symptoms including memory loss, psycho-motor deficits and general malaise have been reported on the day following triazolam administration (Borbely *et al.,* 1983; Hindmarch and Clyde, 1980; Morgan *et al.,* 1984; Nicholson and Stone, 1980; Ogura *et al.,* 1980). Although a full discussion of this issue is beyond the scope of this chapter, it should be pointed out that virtually all hypnotics, at some therapeutic doses, result in performance decrements on the following day (see Johnson and Chernik, 1982; Koelega, 1989, for reviews).

SUMMARY AND IMPLICATIONS

The data reviewed here indicate that human performance is quite tolerant to significant manipulations in the duration of preceding sleep episodes. Even when daily sleep quotas are curtailed by as much as forty or fifty per cent for as long as several months, a wide range of cognitive and psycho-motor performance tasks are only marginally affected. Such evidence supports the notion, most strongly put forth by Horne (1985, 1988), that human sleep is composed of two distinct types of sleep, only one of which is required for 'brain restitution' and, presumably, optimal waking performance. This 'obligatory sleep' comprises approximately the first five hours of a night's sleep, a time during which slow wave sleep is predominant. Horne refers to the rest of the night's sleep as facultative sleep. Under the assumptions of this model, facultative sleep does not contribute to brain restitution, but rather, is used to 'occupy the unproductive hours of darkness' (1985, p. 54). As such, humans are capable of maintaining normal performance levels, even when sleep is substantially restricted.

Performance capacity appears to be less tolerant with respect to manipulations of sleep placement within the twenty-four hour day. This is probably the result of an interaction between two, well-established characteristics of the human circadian timing system. Firstly, such displacement of sleep within the circadian day is likely to result in substantial disruption of the normal sleep process. Sleep at the inappropriate circadian phase is generally more difficult to maintain, and therefore, more fragmented, shallower and less restful. This reduction in sleep continuity appears to be particularly detrimental to subsequent performance. Thus, *sleep continuity, and not sleep duration* is the key factor in determining the extent to which a sleep episode will enhance subsequent performance.

Secondly, manipulations of sleep placement are typically associated with displacement of the timing of performance, as well. The well-documented circadian variations in performance efficiency make it likely that impairments would be observed regardless of prior sleep history. There is little question that such manipulations of circadian rhythms in performance *per se* exacerbate the negative effects on performance of fragmented sleep. From a theoretical perspective, then, these results underline the critical influence imposed on human sleep and performance by the endogenous circadian system. There is a substantial cost involved with sleeping and performing at the inappropriate circadian phase.

The findings (particularly the sleep disruption studies) further suggest that the mechanism by which sleep restores cognitive performance requires durations on the order of minutes, rather than hours, in order to be effective. Bonnet (1985) has suggested several possible mechanisms by which sleep fragmentation may interfere with this restorative process. It has been proposed for example, that protein synthesis may play a crucial role in the restorative capacity of sleep. Since protein synthesis proceeds over a period of minutes, but is disrupted by exercise, it is possible that increased metabolism associated with very frequent arousals may reduce the restorative capacity of sleep. On the other hand, less frequent arousals, i.e. brief bouts of consolidated sleep, would permit protein synthesis to proceed unhampered. Similarly, growth hormone secretion has been implicated in the sleep restorative process and sleep disruption may inhibit GH secretion, as well.

From a practical perspective, the finding that we can continue to function quite well on restricted 'sleep diets' is good news for many of us, who are able to perform (read: work) during the interval at which our circadian rhythms dictate that such behaviour is likely to be optimal (read: daytime). It means that, if necessary (or even desired), we can add several hours of productive wakefulness to our lives, for months at a time, without significant impairment.

Yet, for a large subset of the population (some 20 million people in the US alone), this information is of little comfort. Rotating shift workers and permanent night workers, must contend with a different reality. Because these individuals must typically sleep at an inappropriate circadian phase, their sleep is not only truncated but also fragmented, often to a significant degree. As such, the 'sleep diet' imposed on shift workers is likely to be less 'nutritious' than that of day workers. Moreover, because they must work at inappropriate circadian phases, shift and night workers' performance would probably remain suboptimal, even if quality sleep could be achieved. The data reviewed here make it clear that the most pernicious schedules are those which induced short and fragmented sleep *and* results in displaced work hours. These are the very conditions with which shift workers must contend.

What can be done to alleviate such problems? A number of strategies have been tested, including shift schedule manipulations, drug interventions, napping strategies, behavioural controls and, most recently, timed exposure to bright light. All such approaches have been reported to be successful, to greater or less extents, and further research will undoubtedly enhance the effectiveness of many interventions. Regardless of the approach taken, however, it must be kept in mind that evolution has dictated that we are diurnal animals, always have been, always will be. As such, no matter what the countermeasure, it is certain that significant deviations from natural circadian placement will be accompanied by disturbed sleep and impaired performance.

REFERENCES

Akerstedt, T. (1988) Sleepiness as a consequence of shift work. *Sleep* **11**(1): 17–34.

Akerstedt, T. and Gillberg, M. (1979) Effects of sleep deprivation on memory and sleep latencies in connection with repeated awakenings from sleep. *Psychophysiol* **16**: 49–52.

Aschoff, J. (1965) Circadian rhythms in man: a self-sustaining oscillator with an inherent frequency underlies human 24-hour periodicity. *Science, New York* **148**: 1427–32.

Aschoff, J. (ed.) (1981) *Handbook of Behavioral Neurobiology, Vol. 4, Biological Rhythms.* New York: Plenum.

Aschoff, J. and Wever, R. (1981) The circadian system of man, In *Handbook of Behavioral Neurobiology, Vol. 4, Biological Rhythms,* edited by J. Aschoff. New York: Plenum.

Bonnet, M. (1985) Effect of sleep disruption on sleep, performance and mood. *Sleep* **8**(1): 11–19.

Bonnet, M. (1986a) Performance and sleepiness as a function of frequency and placement of sleep disruption. *Psychophysiology* **23**(3): 263–71.

Bonnet, M. (1986b) Performance and sleepiness following moderate sleep disruption and slow wave sleep deprivation. *Physiol Behav* **37**: 915–8.

Bonnet, M. (1987) Sleep restoration as a function of periodic awakening, movement, or electroencephalographic change. *Sleep* **10**(4): 364–73.

Bonnet, M. (1989a) Infrequent periodic sleep disruption: effects on sleep, performance and mood. *Physiol Behav* **45**: 1049–55.

Bonnet, M. (1989b) The effects of sleep fragmentation on sleep and performance in younger and older subjects. *Neurobiol Aging* **10**: 21–5.

Borbely, A., Loepfe, M., Mattmann, P. and Tobler, I. (1983) Midazolam and triazolam: hypnotic action and residual effects after a single bedtime dose. *Arzneim.-Forsch.* **33**: 1500–2.

Campbell, S. (1984) Duration and placement of sleep in a 'disentrained' environment. *Psychophysiology* **21**(1): 106–13.

Campbell, S. and Tobler, I. (1984) Animal sleep: a review of sleep duration across phylogeny. *Neurosci Biobehav Rev* **8**: 269–300.

Campbell, S.S. and Zulley, J. (1985) Ultradian components of human sleep/wake patterns during disentrainment. In *Ultradian Rhythms in Physiology and Behavior,* edited by H. Schulz and P. Lavie. Berlin: Springer.

Campbell, S. and Zulley, J. (1988) Napping as a biological rhythm: disentrainment of the human sleep/wake system. In *Sleep '86,* edited by W.P. Koella, F. Obal, H. Schulz *et al.* New York: Gustav Fischer.

Clodore, M., Benoit, O., Foret, J., Touitou, Y., Touron, N., Bouard, G. and Auzeby, A. (1987) Early rising or delayed bedtime: which is better for a short night's sleep? *Eur J Appl Physiol* **56**: 403–11.

Colquhoun, W.P. (ed.) (1971) *Biological Rhythms and Human Performance.* New York and London: Academic Press.

Colquhoun, W.P. (ed.) (1972) *Aspects of Human Efficiency: Diurnal Rhythms and Loss of Sleep.* London: English Universities Press.

Colquhoun, W.P. (1981) Rhythms in performance. In *Handbook of Behavioral Neurobiology, Vol. 4, Biological Rhythms,* edited by J. Aschoff. New York: Plenum.

Conroy, R.T. and Mills, J.N. (eds) (1970) *Human Circadian Rhythms.* Baltimore: Williams and Wilkins.

Davies, D. (1985) Individual and group differences in sustained attention. In *Hours of Work: Temporal Factors in Work Scheduling,* edited by S. Folkard and T. Monk. New York: Wiley.

Dinges, D., Orne, E., Evans, F. and Orne, M. (1981) Performance after naps in sleep-conducive and alerting environments. In *The Twenty-four Hour Workday: Proceedings of a Symposium on Variations in Work–Sleep Schedules,* edited by L. Johnson, D. Tepas, W. Colquhoun and M. Colligan. US Dept Health and Human Services, Cincinnati.

Dinges, D., Orne, M. and Orne E. (1985) Assessing performance upon abrupt awakening from naps during quasi-continuous operations. *Behav Res Meth, Instr & Comp* **17**(1): 37–45.

Dinges, D., Orne, M., Whitehouse, W. and Orne, E. (1987) Temporal placement of a nap for alertness: contributions of circadian phase and prior wakefulness. *Sleep* **10**(4): 313–29.

Dinges, D. and Broughton, R. (eds) (1989) *Sleep and Alertness: Chronobiological, Behavioral and Medical Aspects of Napping.* New York: Raven Press.

Downey, R. and Bonnet, M. (1987) Performance during frequent sleep disruption. *Sleep* **10**(4): 354–63.

Folkard, S. and Monk, T.H. (1980) Circadian rhythms in human memory. *British Journal of Psychology* **71**: 295–307.

Folkard, S. and Monk, T.H. (eds) (1985) *Hours of Work: Temporal Factors in Work Scheduling*. New York: Wiley.

Folkard, S., Knauth, P., Monk, T. and Rutenfranz, J. (1976) The effect of memory load on the circadian variation in performance efficiency under a rapidly rotating shift system. *Ergonomics* **19**(4): 479–88.

Folkard, S., Wever, R. and Wildgruber, C. (1983) Multi-oscillatory control of circadian rhythms in human performance. *Nature, London* **305**: 223–6.

Folkard, S., Marks, M., Minors, D. and Waterhouse, J. (1985) Circadian rhythms in human performance and affective state. *Acta Psychiat Belg* **85**: 568–81.

Friedmann, J., Globus, G., Huntley, A., Mullaney, D., Naitoh, P. and Johnson, L. (1977) Performance and mood during and after gradual sleep reduction. *Psychophysiology* **14**(1): 245–50.

Gorenstein, C. and Gentil, V. (1983) Residual and acute effects of fluazepam and triazolam in normal subjects. *Psychopharmacol* **80**: 376–9.

Halberg, F. (1959) Physiologic 24-hour periodicity: general and procedural considerations with reference to the adrenal cycle. *Zeitschrift fuer Vitamin-, Mormon- und Fermentforschung* **10**: 225–96.

Hamilton, P., Wilkinson, R. and Edwards, R. (1972) A study of four days partial sleep derivation. In *Aspects of Human Efficiency*, edited by W. Colquhoun. London: English Universities Press.

Herscovitch, J., Stuss, D. and Broughton, R. (1980) Changes in cognitive processing following short-term cumulative partial sleep deprivation and recovery oversleeping. *J Clin Neuropsychol* **2**(4): 301–19.

Hindmarch, I. and Clyde, C. (1980) The effects of triazolam and nitrazepam on sleep quality, morning vigilance and psychomotor performance. *Arzneim.-Forsch.* **30**: 1163–6.

Horne, J. (1985) Sleep loss: underlying mechanisms and tiredness. In *Hours of Work: Temporal Factors in Work Scheduling*, edited by S. Folkard and T. Monk. New York: Wiley.

Horne, J. (1988) *Why We Sleep: The Functions of Sleep in Humans and Other Mammals*. New York: Oxford University Press.

Horne, J. and Östberg, O. (1976) A self-assessment questionnaire to determine morningness-eveningness in human circadian rhythms. *Int J Chronobiol* **4**: 97–110.

Horne, J. and Wilkinson, S. (1985) Chronic sleep reduction: daytime vigilance performance and EEG measures of sleepiness, with particular reference to 'practice' effects. *Psychophysiol* **22**(1): 69–78.

Johnson, L. (1974) The effect of total, partial and stage sleep deprivation on EEG patterns and performance. In *Behavior and Brain Electrical Activity*, edited by N. Burch and H. Altshuler. New York: Plenum.

Johnson, L. and Macleod, W. (1973) Sleep and awake behavior during gradual sleep reduction. *Perceptual and Motor Skills* **36**: 87–97.

Johnson, L. and Chernik, D. (1982) Sedative-hypnotics and human performance. *Psychopharmacology* **76**: 101–13.

Klein, K. and Wegmann, H. (1974) The resynchronization of human circadian rhythms after transmeridian flights as a result of flight direction and mode of activity. In *Chronobiology*, edited by L. Scheving, F. Halberg and J. Pauly. Tokyo: Igaku Shoin.

Kleitman, N. (1963) *Sleep and Wakefulness*. University of Chicago Press.

Koelega, H. (1989) Benzodiazepines and vigilance performance: a review. *Psychopharmacology* **98**: 145–56.

Laird, D.A. (1925) Relative performance of college students as conditioned by time of day and day of week. *Journal of Experimental Psychology* **8**: 50–63.

Laird, D. and Wheeler, W. (1926) What it costs to lose sleep. *Industrial Psychology* **1**: 694–6.

Langdon, D. and Hartman, B. (1961) *Performance Upon Sudden Awakening*. SAM Report 62-17, USAF School of Aeronautic Medicine, Brooks AFB, Texas.

Mitler, M., Carskadon, M., Czeisler, C., Dement, W., Dinges, D. and Graeber, R. (1988) Catastrophes, sleep and public policy: consensus report. *Sleep* **11**(1): 100–9.

Monk, T.H. (1989) Circadian rhythms in subjective activation, mood, and performance efficiency. In *Principles and Practice of Sleep Medicine*, edited by M.H. Kryger, T. Roth and W.C. Dement. Philadelphia: W.B. Saunders.

Monk, T.H. (1990) The relationship of chronobiology to sleep schedules and performance demands. *Work and Stress* **4**(3): 227–36.

Monk, T.H. and Leng, V.C. (1982) Time of day effects in simple repetitive tasks. *Acta Psychologia* **51**: 207–21.

Monk, T., Weitzman, E., Fookson, J., Moline, M., Kronauer, R. and Gander, P. (1983) Task variables determine which biological clock controls circadian rhythms in human performance. *Nature, London* **304**: 543–5.

Monk, T., Moline, M. and Graeber, R. (1988) Inducing jet lag in the laboratory: patterns of adjustment to an acute shift in routine. *Aviat Space Environ Med* **59**(8): 703–10.

Moore-Ede, M.C., Sulzman, F.M. and Fuller, C.A. (1982) *The Clocks That Time Us*. Cambridge, Ma.: Harvard University Press.

Morgan, K., Adam, K. and Oswald, I. (1984) Effects of loprazolam and triazolam on psychological functions. *Psychopharmacol.* **82**: 386–8.

Naitoh, P. (1981) Circadian cycles and restorative power of naps. In *Biological Rhythms and Shift Work*, edited by L.C. Johnson, D.J. Tepas, W.P. Colquhoun and M.J. Colligan. New York: Spectrum.

Naitoh, P. and Angus, R. (1989) Napping and human functioning during prolonged work. In *Sleep and Alertness: Chronobiological, Behavioral and Medical Aspects of Napping*, edited by D. Dinges and R. Broughton. New York: Raven.

Nicholson, A. and Stone, B. (1980) Activity of the hypnotics flunitrazepam and triazolam in man. *British Journal of Clinical Pharmacology* **9**: 187–94.

Nicholson, A., Pascoe, P., Roehrs, T., Roth, T., Spencer, M., Stone, B. and Zorick, F. (1985) Sustained performance with short evening and morning sleeps. *Aviation, Space and Environment Medicine* **56**: 105–14.

Patrick, G. and Gilbert, J. (1896) On the effects of loss of sleep. *Psychological Review* **3**: 469–83.

Robinson, E. and Hermann, S. (1922) Effects of loss of sleep. I. *Journal of Experimental Psychology* **5**: 19–32.

Robinson, E. and Richardson-Robinson, F. (1922) Effects of loss of sleep. II. *Journal of Experimental Psychology* **5**: 93–100.

Taub, J. and Berger, R. (1974) Effects of acute shifts in circadian rhythms of sleep and wakefulness on performance and mood. In *Chronobiology*, edited by L. Scheving, F. Halberg and J. Pauly. Tokyo: Igaku Shoin.

Taub, J. and Berger, R. (1976) The effects of changing the phase and duration of sleep. *J Exp Psychol: Hum Percept Perform* **2**(1): 30–41.

Tilley, A. and Wilkinson, R. (1984) The effects of a restricted sleep regime on the composition of sleep and performance. *Psychophysiology* **21**(4): 406–12.

Webb, W. (1969) Partial and differential sleep deprivation. In *Sleep: Physiology and Pathology*, edited by A. Kales. Philadelphia: J.P. Lippincott.

Webb, W. and Agnew, H. (1965) Sleep: effects of a restricted regime. *Science, New York* **150**: 1745–7.

Webb, W. and Agnew, H. (1971) Effect on sleep of a sleep period time displacement. *Aerospace Med* **42**(2): 152–5.

Webb, W. and Agnew, H. (1974) The effects of a chronic limitation of sleep length. *Psychophysiology* **11**(3): 265–74.

Webb, W. and Agnew, H. (1978) Effects of rapidly rotating shifts on sleep patterns and sleep structure. *Aviation, Space and Environmental Medicine* **49**(2): 384–9.

Wegmann, H. and Klein, K. (1985) Jet-lag and aircrew scheduling. In *Hours of Work: Temporal Factors in Work Scheduling*, edited by S. Folkard and T. Monk. New York: Wiley.

Weitzman, E.D. and Kripke, D.F. (1981) Experimental 12-hour shift of the sleep–wake cycle in man: effects on sleep and physiologic rhythms. In *Biological Rhythms and Shift Work,* edited by L.C. Johnson, D.J. Tepas, W.P. Colquhoun and M.J. Colligan. New York: Spectrum.
Weitzman, E., Moline, M., Czeisler, C. and Zimmermann, J. (1982) Chronobiology of aging: temperature, sleep–wake rhythms and entrainment. *Neurobiol Aging* **3**: 299–309.
Wever, R.A. (1979) *The Circadian System of Man.* New York: Springer.
Wilkinson, R., Edwards, R. and Haines, E. 1966) Performance following a night of reduced sleep. *Psychonomic Science* **5**: 471.

8

Time of Day and Performance

A.P. SMITH

INTRODUCTION

People's ability to perform efficiently is not constant but shows temporal variation. This chapter describes how our ability to carry out different activities changes over the normal working day. It is essential to know and understand the relationship between time of day and performance for this will allow us to structure hours of work to increase productivity, safety and cost-effectiveness, and to improve the quality of life of the workforce.

The effects of time of day on performance have been studied extensively (see Colquhoun, 1981; Folkard, 1983; Folkard and Monk, 1985; and Smith, 1989a, for reviews). First of all, a brief account of early research is given, and this is followed by more detailed coverage of studies and approaches which are not included in earlier reviews.

Time of day effects in human performance may reflect endogenous rhythms (see Campbell, this volume) or they may be produced by external factors which occur at particular times (e.g. meals: see Smith and Kendrick, 1992). Most laboratory studies of time of day effects have been confined to the 'normal day' (9 a.m. to 11 p.m.), and have usually involved short periods of testing. Such studies avoid the problems of sleep deprivation (see Tilley and Brown, this volume), and fatigue due to prolonged work is not an issue in the experiments (see Craig, this volume). There have, however, been applied studies of the effects of abnormal living routines produced by shiftwork or time-zone transitions. In between these two types of study are experimental studies of night work (see Tilley and Brown, this volume) and prolonged working hours. Recent studies of the

HANDBOOK OF HUMAN PERFORMANCE
VOLUME 3 ISBN 0-12-650353-2

combined effects of environmental stress and nightwork show that researchers are aware that it is a mistake to consider time of day in isolation. Indeed, if one wants to make practical recommendations about temporal factors in the workplace one has to consider the effects of other factors which may be present, and are described elsewhere in this series (e.g. noise: see Smith and Jones, 1992).

Early research

Much of the early research was concerned with applied problems such as which time of day is best for teaching different subjects. Freeman and Hovland (1934) reviewed this early research and concluded that there is little agreement over experiments about the effects of time of day on mental performance. This partially reflects the fact that researchers often based their conclusions on the average of many tasks, although the individual tasks often showed a pattern quite different from the average trend. The importance of the nature of the task is returned to later in this chapter. These early results were explained either in terms of a progressive recovery from the effects of sleep (if performance was better later in the day: see Gates, 1916) or to an increase in fatigue (if performance was worse later in the day: see Laird, 1925).

Kleitman (1963) suggested that there was a parallelism between time-of-day effects in the performance of simple tasks and the circadian rhythm of body temperature (which shows a consistent twenty-four hour periodicity with a peak around 9 p.m. and a trough at 4 a.m.). This is illustrated in Figure 8.1, which shows results from four experiments on time of day and visual search, and also the diurnal trend in sublingual temperature.

Research in the 1960s continued to study time of day and simple tasks, although a causal relationship between performance and temperature was rejected, and a basic arousal rhythm postulated as the crucial mediating factor. Arousal was assumed to increase over the waking day to reach a peak in the early evening, and simple tasks were assumed to be performed more efficiently when arousal was high. Other tasks were assumed to be performed most efficiently at lower levels of arousal, which accounted for the results (see Figure 8.2) showing that tasks involving immediate memory are generally performed better earlier in the day (when arousal is low: see Blake, 1967; Baddeley *et al.*, 1970; and Hockey *et al.*, 1972). The arousal model of time-of-day effects could also explain the interactions between time of testing and other agents thought to influence arousal (e.g. noise: see Blake, 1971).

However, the arousal model has several problems. Firstly, it is unclear what one should use as an index of arousal. If one takes body temperature as the index one would argue that arousal increases over the day. However, when subjective rating of alertness is used as the index of arousal one finds that it peaks in the late morning (see Figure 8.3).

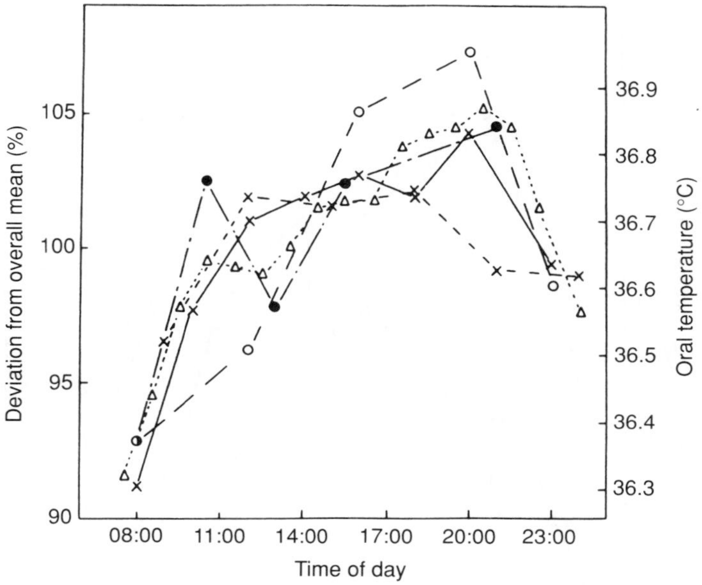

Figure 8.1 Diurnal variation in serial visual search performance (after Blake, 1967 ●–·–●; Klein *et al.*, 1977 ×–––×; Fort and Mills, 1976 ×——×; Hughes and Folkard, 1976 ○–––○). Also shown is the trend in oral temperature (after Colquhoun *et al.*, 1968 △–––△).

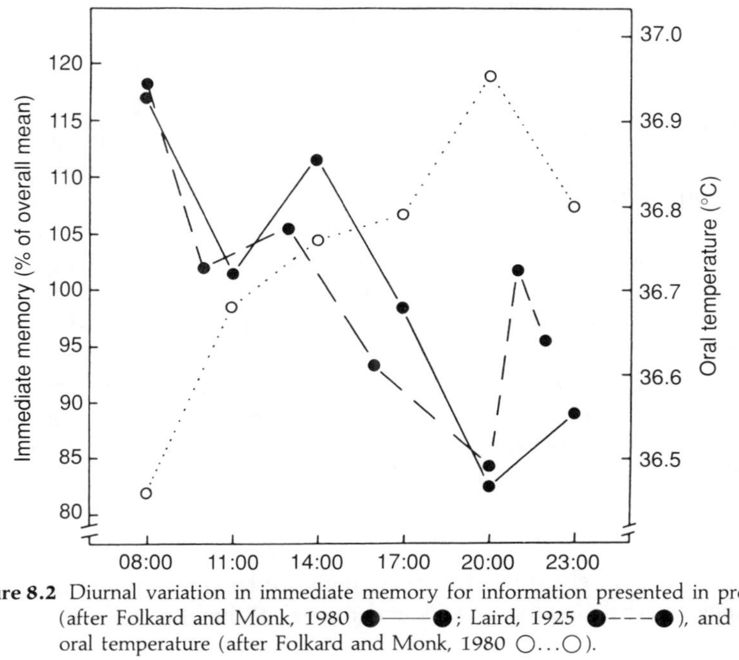

Figure 8.2 Diurnal variation in immediate memory for information presented in prose (after Folkard and Monk, 1980 ●——●; Laird, 1925 ●–––●), and in oral temperature (after Folkard and Monk, 1980 ○...○).

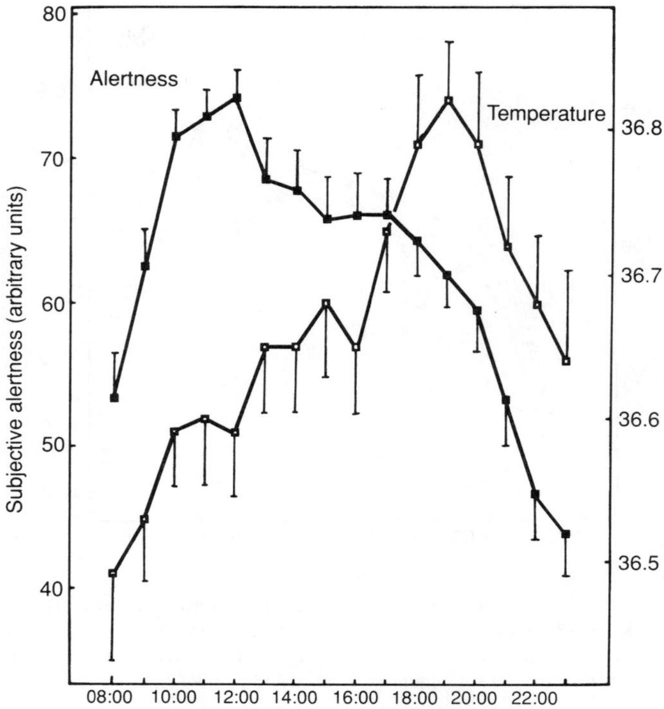

Figure 8.3 Diurnal variation in subjective alertness and oral temperature (plotted together with ± 1 standard error). After Monk *et al.* (1983).

A second problem for arousal theory is that it is difficult to test and falsify (see Folkard, 1983). Also, research on a variety of factors thought to alter arousal suggests that a uni-dimensional model of arousal is inadequate and that distinct activation states must be considered (see Smith, 1987a). Recent experimental results also suggest that time of day does not always interact with other factors thought to influence arousal. Indeed, as early as 1971 Broadbent suggested that noise and time of day influence different mechanisms. This view has been supported by results which have failed to find interactions between the two factors (e.g. Smith, 1987a, 1989b; Smith and Miles, 1985, 1986a, 1987a). Another problem for arousal theory is that the effect of time of day on performance varies depending on characteristics of the person doing the task or the strategy used. These last points can be illustrated by considering the effects of time of day on memory tasks.

TIME OF DAY AND WORKING MEMORY

The two most widely studied working memory tasks in time-of-day research have been verbal reasoning tasks and mental arithmetic tasks. Laird (1925)

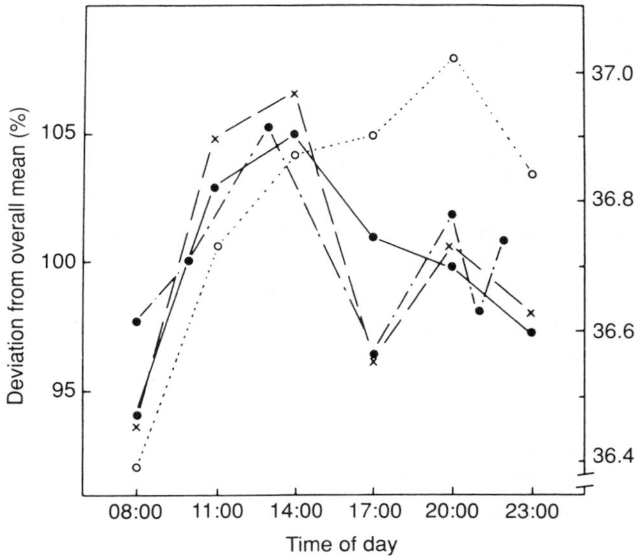

Figure 8.4 Diurnal variation in working memory performance speed (after Folkard, 1975 ×–––× and ●——●, and Laird, 1925 ●–·–●), and in oral temperature (after Folkard, 1975 ○...○).

found that performance of these tasks reached a peak at midday, and this has been confirmed by Folkard (1975). These data are shown in Figure 8.4.

Other studies have shown that performance of such tasks shows different trends depending on the ability or level of practice of the subject. Rutenfranz and Helbruegge (1957) found that schoolchildren's performance on mental arithmetic tasks peaked early in the day, whereas Blake found that sailors who were highly practised at the tasks showed a late peak. Monk and Leng (1986) also found that performance of a logical reasoning task showed a significant interaction between time of day and morningness, with the morning types being best at 8 a.m. and evening types showing a later peak.

STRATEGIES OF MEMORY AT DIFFERENT TIMES OF DAY

Folkard (1979) presents evidence that subjects carry out more 'maintenance processing' in the morning but more 'elaborative encoding' in the afternoon. One could, therefore, account for the decrease in immediate memory for short strings of items (e.g. digit span type tasks) over the day in terms of reduced use of subvocal rehearsal. Indeed, Oakhill (1988) has recently shown that the superior immediate recall of text in the morning can be attributed to better verbatim memory at this time.

There is other evidence to support the view that more elaborative processing occurs later in the day. Marks and Folkard (1988) found that presentation of text in the early evening was associated with better delayed recall of important information than was morning presentation. This effect appeared to be due to an improvement later in the day in the subjects' ability to construct a representation of the material which incorporated the text's hierarchical structure. Similarly, Oakhill (1988) found that subjects tested in the afternoon integrated the text as they were reading it, so that they had an enduring memory for the theme of the text but not for the exact meaning.

If some time-of-day effects depend on the strategy used to do the task then it should be possible to alter the effects by eliminating or replacing the strategy used at a particular time of day. This has been confirmed by Folkard and Monk (1979), who showed that articulatory suppression reduced immediate recall of pre-recency items in the morning but not in the afternoon. Similarly, Folkard (cited by Folkard and Monk, 1985) found that neither an acoustically confusable verbal reasoning task nor a visuo-spatial memory task showed a reliable trend over the day. All this suggests that diurnal variations in working memory performance may be limited to tasks that normally rely on the use of the articularltory loop.

A profile of the effects of time of day on different aspects of performance

Previous accounts of the effects of time of testing on performance have generally concluded that the speed of performing perceptual–motor tasks is quicker later in the day, whereas immediate memory shows the opposite trend. Working memory tasks often peak in the middle of the day and delayed recall is better when initial learning occurs in the afternoon rather than in the morning (see Folkard *et al.*, 1977). The previous section suggested that the effects of time of testing on working memory tasks and recall of text reflect the use of different strategies at different times. One must now consider whether this view is also supported in studies of other types of function.

PERCEPTUAL–MOTOR TASKS

Early research on simple motor tasks (e.g. card sorting) demonstrated a similar diurnal trend to that observed for serial search. However, other experiments have shown that performance of motor tasks peaks in the middle of the day (see Monk and Leng, 1982, for a review). Monk and Leng suggest that time-of-day effects in motor tasks can be attributed to a change in strategy over the day. They present data which show that people become faster and less accurate later in the day. If one is performing a motor task such as the pegboard task, there will be a point where reduced accuracy also reduces speed (e.g. if pegs are fumbled or dropped). This would plausibly explain why performance on such tasks slows down later in the day.

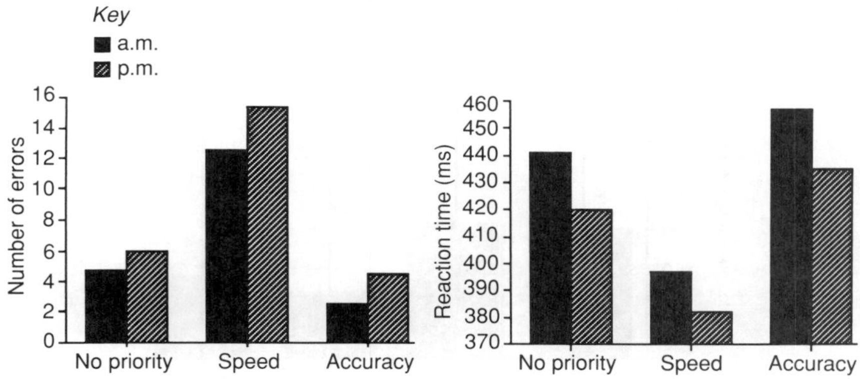

Figure 8.5 Effects of time of day and instructions on speed and accuracy.

There is other evidence showing that perceptual–motor tasks are performed faster but less accurately as the day progresses (see Blake, 1971; Craig and Condon, 1984, 1985). This confirms the view that time-of-day effects in performance reflect differences in the way tasks are performed rather than changes in the efficiency of processes. One must now consider whether the changes in strategy are under voluntary control or reflect passive biases induced by particular states. The results of Folkard and Monk (1979) show that eliminating a strategy removes the time-of-day effect observed in immediate recall. Smith (1991a) examined whether the speed–accuracy trade-off observed in time of day experiments could be altered by getting the subject to give priority to speed or accuracy. Subjects carried out a serial response task and each subject performed three conditions. In the first, subjects were given the usual instruction to 'respond as quickly and accurately as possible'. In the other conditions, either speed or accuracy was emphasized. The results are shown in Figure 8.5.

Performance was faster but less accurate in the early evening compared with the early morning and this was observed in all conditions (even though the instructions modified performance). This shows that the speed–accuracy trade-off which occurs over the day is not due to subjects choosing to adopt a particular strategy at a given time.

The next sections consider aspects of performance which have not been reviewed in detail before, namely semantic memory, selective and sustained attention.

SEMANTIC MEMORY TASKS

Millar *et al.* (1980) examined the effects of time of testing on recognition of dominant and non-dominant instances of categories. The results showed that

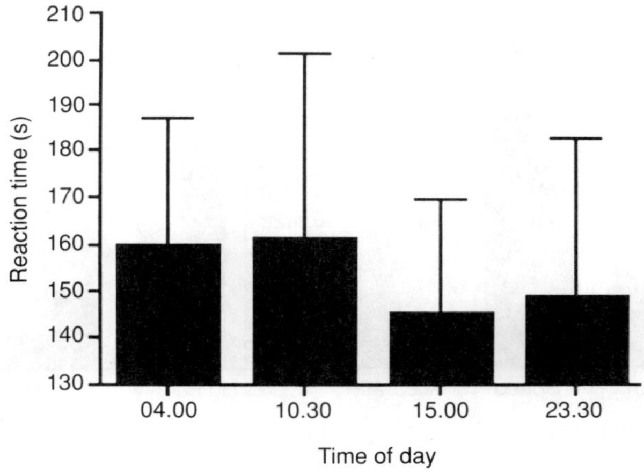

Figure 8.6 Time of day and speed of semantic processing. (Scores are the mean times in seconds to verify 100 sentences; from Smith, 1987a.)

responses were quicker later in the day and that this was entirely due to responses to non-dominant instances. Tilley and Warren (1983) found that retrieval from semantic memory was faster later in the day, and again the largest difference between morning and evening was found with low-dominance items.

Smith (1987a) used a category instance retrieval task where the subject was shown the category name and a letter and had to produce an instance beginning with the letter. The category–letter combinations were arranged to produce either dominant or non-dominant instances. Performance of the task was quicker later in the day but no interaction was obtained between time of day and dominance. Further evidence that retrieval from semantic memory is quicker later in the day comes from studies using Baddeley's semantic processing task which have shown that semantic verification is quicker in the late afternoon than in the early morning (Smith, 1987a, 1989b). Indeed, the circadian trend for semantic memory tasks is similar to that observed for perceptual–motor tasks, and this is illustrated by the data collected in an experimental night work study (Smith, 1987a) and shown in Figure 8.6.

It should also be noted that there is evidence from semantic memory tasks that changing the way of doing the task alters the time-of-day effect. Smith (1987a) found that performance of a category instance task was quicker later in the day when subjects were given separate lists of dominant and non-dominant instances. However, when the two types of instance were in the same list, and the subjects had continually to change retrieval strategies, then the effect of time of day was removed.

SELECTIVE AND SUSTAINED ATTENTION

Easterbrook (1959) explained the relationship between arousal and performance in terms of changes in selectivity. On the basis of Easterbrook's theory one would expect selectivity to be greater later in the day. Selectivity in memory and attention can be examined in several ways. The first approach described here is concerned with examining diurnal biases towards dominant, salient, high priority or high probability sources. One task used to examine this topic has been the Stroop colour word test. In one condition of this test the subject has to name the colour of the ink in which an irrelevant colour word is printed. Hartley and Shirley (1976) showed that interference increased over the day to peak at 8 p.m., which is the opposite to what one would have predicted on the basis of arousal theory. Smith and Miles (1987b) found no difference between late morning and early afternoon performance of the interference condition, and this has also been the case when early evening and early morning are compared (Smith, 1992). However, the last study did find changes in the control conditions of the Stroop tasks, with patches of colour being named more rapidly in the morning and colour names being read more quickly in the afternoon.

Another method of examining selectivity is to have a dual task where one component has a higher priority than the other. Smith (1992) had subjects recall the order of a list of words (the high priority task) and then recall which location they had been presented in (the low priority task). Unlike other factors such as noise, time of day did not interact with priority. Another technique used to examine selectivity involves making one signal source more probable than the others. Smith (unpublished) examined the effects of time of testing on a biased probability choice reaction time test and found that time of day did not interact with signal probability.

The general conclusion from the above studies is that selective attention does not differ in the early morning and early evening. Indeed, where differences in selectivity have been observed at different times of day, these have often been in the opposite direction from that predicted by arousal theory (see Hartley and Shirley, 1976; Millar *et al.*, 1980; Tilley and Warren, 1983). However, reliable time-of-day effects have been observed with serial search tasks, which clearly involve selective attention. These effects may reflect the changes in the speed–error trade-off function which have already been described. However, time-of-day effects are not observed in free-search tasks where the subject can scan the material in any way (Monk and Leng, 1982). This suggests that there may be changes in the focusing of attention over the day, with information being sampled from a wider angle later in the day. This could explain why colour patches are named more quickly in the morning (when attention is focused), whereas reading words, where the eyes are focused on material ahead of the word being uttered, is better later in the day.

Broadbent *et al.* (1989) examined the effects of time of testing on performance of a focused attention task and category search task. The results showed that the Eriksen effect (a measure of the focusing of attention) was smaller later in the day, showing that attention moves from focused to wide angle as the day progresses. This has been replicated by Smith (1991b) and the data are shown in Figure 8.7.

One must now consider whether time of day influences the ability to sustain attention. Craig *et al.* (1981a) examined the influence of time of testing on auditory vigilance. Results from five studies showed that both hits and false alarms exhibited a fairly consistent tendency to be lowest early in the morning and increased in parallel over the day. However, these time-of-day effects were small, and significant in only a minority of analyses. Indeed, the effects were attributed to shifts in response criterion rather than to altered levels of signal detection. This view has been confirmed in other studies, with detection being faster, more confident, but less accurate later in the day (e.g. Craig, 1979; Craig and Condon, 1985).

More recent studies have examined memory-loaded detection tasks or 'cognitive vigilance' tasks (see Davies and Parasuraman, 1982). Davies *et al.* (1984) found that performance on a memory-loaded vigilance task was worse in the afternoon than in the morning. However, Gale *et al.* (1972) and Smith (1987b) found no effect of time of day on the Bakan vigilance task. These few results suggest that the effects of time of testing on sustained attention are still unclear. Much more definite effects have been obtained in studies of the 'post-lunch dip' and these are described in a later section and in Smith and Kendrick (1992).

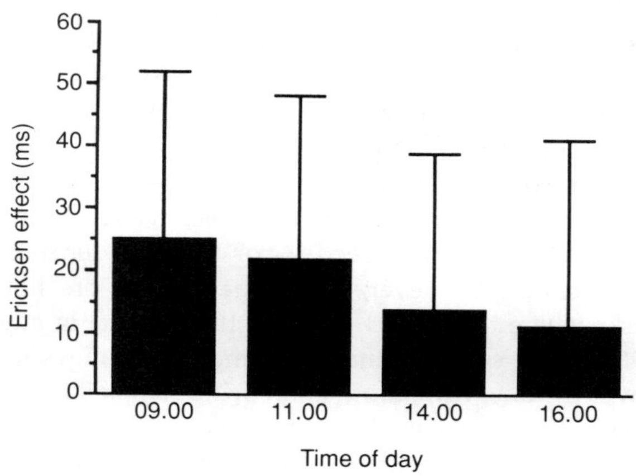

Figure 8.7 Diurnal variation in the size of the Eriksen effect (from Smith, 1991b). The bigger the Eriksen effect the more focused the person's attention (standard deviations shown as bars).

The sections so far have concentrated on the variation seen within different types of task over the day. The characteristics of the person performing the task may also be important: these are considered next.

Individual differences

Early experiments (e.g. Colquhoun, 1960; Colquhoun and Corcoran, 1964) found that introverts performed better than extraverts in the morning, whereas there was little difference between the two groups in the afternoon. Blake (1971) confirmed the superiority of introverts in the morning and also showed the reverse effect in the afternoon. However, the relationship between introversion and time of day may easily be modified by other factors. For example, Colquhoun and Corcoran (1964) found that introverts were only better than extraverts in the morning when subjects were tested in isolation, and the presence of other subjects improved the performance of extraverts tested in the morning. The above studies used simple performance tests; Revelle *et al.* (1980) used a cognitive task and found that it was the impulsivity component of the extraversion scale that was responsible for the time-of-day effects.

Another dimension which has been related to individual differences in time-of-day effects is morningness. Horne *et al.* (1980) found that morning types detected more targets in the morning whereas evening types were better later in the day. However, Monk and Leng (1982) found no interaction between morningness and time of day for perceptual–motor tasks, only for cognitive ones.

Possible reasons for diurnal variation in performance

The arousal theory of time-of-day effects has largely been rejected as a complete explanation of time-of-day effects. Even researchers who explain time-of-day effects in performance in terms of endogenous rhythms would argue that there are several rhythms or effects that interact to influence the individual's state and performance. For example, alertness is likely to be determined by the amount of time elapsed since waking, the temperature rhythm and the sleep–wake cycle. Even this model is likely to be too simplistic in that exogenous factors must also be considered. One possibility is that cumulative fatigue may influence performance later in the day. Indeed, the shift to risk observed at later times is similar to the criterion change produced by fatigue (see Craig, this volume).

Another dynamic influence on performance is motivation. Colquhoun (1981) has suggested that certain time-of-day effects may be produced by diurnal variation in motivation rather than by passive changes in the efficiency of psychological processes. Indeed, the late peak in performance observed by Blake (1967) may be due to a 'last test' or 'end spurt' effect. Motivation and time of day can be studied by measuring motivation at different times or by changing motivation and seeing what happens to the time-of-day effects.

Smith (1985) found that state anxiety was significantly higher in the afternoon. Furthermore, the early morning state is characterized by high levels of aspiration and low fear of failure, whereas in the late afternoon subjects put more effort into performance (but only if operations are likely to repay this investment to effort: see Smith, 1987b). This view is consistent with results obtained by Oakhill (1986b), which showed that subjects engaged in more effortful processing later in the day, but only when this enabled them to answer a subsequent question more rapidly. Similarly, Breen-Lewis and Wilding (1984) have reported results which can be interpreted as showing that subjects may adopt demanding processing strategies more readily later in the day.

An alternative way of examining motivation and time of day is to investigate whether changes in motivation alter time-of-day effects in performance. Blake (1971) showed that diurnal variations in performing a letter cancellation task could be removed by announcing each subject's score to the group being tested. Similarly, Chiles *et al.* (1968) found that increasing motivation removed the circadian variation found in a number of performance measures. These results show that time-of-day effects can be removed by changing motivation. Smith (1987b) has shown that time-of-day effects can be created by manipulating motivation. Subjects carried out the Bakan vigilance task in the early morning and late afternoon. The control group showed no difference in performance at these times. Another group of subjects were told that their results would be made public, thus increasing their anxiety. This increase was greater in the afternoon than in the morning and was associated with a greater improvement in performance. In other words, a time-of-day effect was produced because the manipulation of motivation had a greater effect in the afternoon than the morning. This shows that one must consider the impact of the 'whole test situation' when assessing the effects of time of day on performance. Indeed, one of the best examples of the impact of external influences associated with particular times is the post-lunch dip in performance. This is briefly described below and the reader is referred to Craig (1986) and the chapter by Smith and Kendrick (1992) for a more detailed account of this topic.

THE POST-LUNCH DIP

Post-lunch impairments have been found both in real-life jobs (Bjerner and Svensson, 1953; Hildebrandt *et al.*, 1974) and the laboratory (Blake, 1971;

Craig *et al.*, 1981b). Recent studies show that certain impairments, especially impairments of sustained attention, depend on consumption of lunch (see Smith and Miles, 1986b, 1987b). Other effects (e.g. movement time) may be observed even when lunch is not consumed. Folkard and Monk (1985) have reported that the strongest evidence for an endogenous component in the post-lunch dip comes from isolation studies where a dip in performance resembling the post-lunch dip is observed even though the performance rhythm is moving with a different period from that of food ingestion.

Short-duration tasks rarely show an effect of lunch ((Christie and McBrearty, 1979) unless they are part of a larger battery (Smith and Miles, 1986c, 1987a). This suggests that the local lunchtime effect is not the same as differences between early morning and late afternoon. Indeed, Smith (1988a) found that delayed recall of text was worse after lunch than before, but found no interaction between pre/post-lunch testing and the importance of the information to be recalled. In contrast, Oakhill (1986a), comparing early morning and evening, found an interaction between time of day and the importance of the information.

There is evidence that the effect of lunch depends on the nature of the meal, although the effects of nutrient content and size are small (see Smith *et al.*, 1988, 1990). Similarly, the characteristics of the person eating the meal are important, with low anxiety subjects typically showing a greater post-lunch dip (Craig *et al.*, 1981b; Smith and Miles, 1986a). The post-lunch dip can be removed by stimulant factors such as noise (Smith and Miles, 1986a) or caffeine (Smith *et al.*, 1990). This again shows that post-lunch effects are different from early morning/late afternoon differences, in that these are not affected by noise (Smith, 1989a) or caffeine (Smith *et al.*, 1991).

The results summarized above show that the pre/post-lunch differences are qualitatively different from those studied in many time-of-day experiments. One must now ask whether results obtained from studies looking at a wider range of times are consistent with the view of time-of-day effects based on studies carried out within the normal day.

EXPERIMENTAL STUDIES OF NIGHT-WORK

Kleitman and Jackson (1950) and Colquhoun *et al.* (1968) examined performance efficiency during four-hour duty spells like those used in rapidly rotating watch-keeping systems on ships. The results from the night watches showed that perceptual–motor tasks were impaired at this time. A different pattern emerges when one considers the effects of night work on cognitive tasks. Hughes and Folkard (1976) showed that performance of cognitive tasks adjusted more rapidly to an inverted routine, and this has been confirmed in a laboratory study of twenty-one consecutive nightshifts (Monk *et al.*, 1978).

Table 8.1 A summary of the performance tests used by Smith and Miles in the study of noise and night-work, the times at which they are performed, and the overall results

Battery 1 Times: 09.00, 10.00, 12.00, 13.30, 14.30, 16.30, 22.00, 23.00, 01.00, 02.30, 03.30, 05.30	
Pegboard test	Performed more slowly at night
Logical reasoning test	No effect of noise of night-work
Low memory-load search test	Performed more slowly in the second half of the night
High memory-load search test	1. Performed more slowly after meals both in the day and night 2. More errors in noise
Battery 2 Times: 09.30, 11.40, 14.00, 16.30, 22.30, 00.40, 03.00, 05.10	
Simple reaction time test	Reaction times slower at night
Bakan vigilance test	1. Less accurate after meals, both in the day and night 2. More errors in noise
Battery 3 Times: 10.30, 15.00, 23.30, 04.00	
Semantic processing test	Speed increased until the late evening then declined in the early hours of the morning
Digit symbol substitution	No effect of noise or night-work
Running memory test	Recent items recalled better at night, items further back recalled better in the day. Noise influenced the recall strategy
Serial reaction test (males only)	Errors increased after subjects had been in noise for some time
Free search test (females only)	No effect of noise or night-work

Folkard *et al.* (1976) examined the effects of a rapidly rotating shift system on performance of low, medium and high memory-load search tasks. The results showed that the more complex version was performed better at night.

Smith and Miles examined the effects of night-work on a range of tasks (see Smith, 1988b, 1990, 1991c; Miles and Smith, 1988; Smith and Miles, 1985, 1986a, 1986b, 1987a, 1987c). These results are summarized in Table 8.1.

Generally, the results confirm those from previous studies, with performance of perceptual–motor tasks being impaired in the latter part of the night shift, whereas performance on working memory tasks was not. Semantic memory tasks showed a similar trend to the perceptual–motor tasks.

One of the main aims of the Smith and Miles study was to examine possible interactions between night work and noise. The results showed that both factors influenced performance but that their effects were independent. This confirms results from recent studies using a more limited range of times, and argues against interpreting the effects of these factors in terms of a uni-dimensional theory of arousal.

CONCLUSIONS

The first conclusion to be drawn from the studies reviewed in this chapter is that performance of many tasks changes over the day. Such effects have been observed not only in the laboratory but also in a much smaller number of studies carried out in real-life settings (see Folkard and Monk, 1985). The performance changes are often large, with a change of ±15 per cent of the daily average frequently being observed.

The second conclusion is that the exact pattern of diurnal variation depends on the nature of the task. Indeed, where several tasks have to be carried out over the day, efficiency may be improved by scheduling certain topics in the morning and others in the afternoon. Time-of-day effects depend not only on the task but also on the way it is performed. Indeed, recent research suggests that many time-of-day effects do not reflect automatic changes arising from processing limitations, but are due to the adoption of different strategies over the course of the day. At the moment it is unclear whether the strategy changes observed over the day reflect endogenous rhythms or are attempts to maintain competent performance in a suboptimal state. Indeed, while it is at times useful to consider performance in relation to the physiological state of the individual, it is also important to consider the whole testing context. The roles of endogenous rhythms, exogenous factors and motivation have been discussed separately, and yet it is the combination of these factors and the individual's interpretation of them which determines the nature of the observed time-of-day effects in performance. This means that future studies must collect as much information as possible about all factors relevant to performance rather than considering just time of testing and the effect this has on general indicators of efficiency such as average speed or accuracy. This view applies not only to laboratory studies but to real-life performance at different times of day (see Folkard and Monk, 1980), and many of the factors that need to be considered are reviewed in this volume and the others in this series. Unfortuntely, most of the effects of different factors are examined in isolation, which means that it is difficult to assess the functional impact of combinations of them. Clearly, this must be attempted in the future, and such an approach will increase both the practical significance of the research and the sophistication of our models of the way different factors affect performance.

REFERENCES

Baddeley, A.D., Hatter, J.E., Scott, D. and Snashall, A. (1970) Memory and time of day. *Quarterly Journal of Experimental Psychology* **22**: 605–9.

Bjerner, B. and Svensson, A. (1953) Shiftwork and rhythm. *Acta Medica Scandinavica* **278**: 102–7.

Blake, M.J.F. (1967) Time of day effects on performance in a range of tasks. *Psychonomic Science* **9**: 345–50.

Blake, M.J.F. (1971) Temperament and time of day. In *Biological Rhythms and Human Performance*, edited by W.P. Colquhoun. New York and London: Academic Press.

Breen-Lewis, K. and Wilding, J. (1984) Noise, time of day and test expectations in recall and recognition. *British Journal of Psychology* **75**: 51–63.

Broadbent, D.E. (1971) *Decision and Stress.* New York and London: Academic Press.

Broadbent, D.E., Broadbent, M.H.P. and Jones, J.L. (1989) Time of day as an instrument for the analysis of attention. *European Journal of Cognitive Psychology* **1**: 69–94.

Chiles, W.D., Alluisi, E.A. and Adams, O. (1968) Work schedules and performance during confinement. *Human Factors* **10**: 143–96.

Christie, M.J. and McBrearty, E.M.T. (1979) Psychophysiological investigation of post-lunch state in male and female subjects. *Ergonomics* **22**: 307–23.

Colquhoun, W.P. (1960) Temperament, inspection efficiency and time of day. *Ergonomics* **3**: 377–8.

Colquhoun, W.P. (1981) Rhythms in performance. In *Handbook of Behavioural Neurobiology*, Vol. 4, edited by J. Aschoff. New York: Plenum.

Colquhoun, W.P. and Corcoran, D.W.J. (1964) The effects of time of day and social isolation on the relationship between temperament and performance. *British Journal of Social and Clinical Psychology* **3**: 226–31.

Colquhoun, W.P., Blake, M.J.F. and Edwards, R.S. (1968) Experimental studies of shift work. I: A comparison of 'rotating' and 'stabilized' 4-hour systems. *Ergonomics* **11**: 437–53.

Craig, A. (1979) Discrimination, temperature and time of day. *Human Factors* **21**: 61–8.

Craig, A. (1986) Acute effects of meals on perceptual and cognitive efficiency. *Nutrition Reviews* **44** (Supplement): 163–71.

Craig, A. and Condon, R. (1984) Operational efficiency and time of day. *Human Factors* **26**: 197–205.

Craig, A. and Condon, R. (1985) Speed–accuracy trade-off and time of day. *Acta Psychologica* **58**: 115–22.

Craig, A., Wilkinson, R.T. and Colquhoun, W.P. (1981a) Diurnal variation in vigilance efficiency. *Ergonomics* **24**: 641–51.

Craig, A., Baer, K. and Diekmann, A. (1981b) The effects of lunch on sensory–perceptual functioning in man. *International Archives of Occupational and Environmental Health* **49**: 105–14.

Davies, D.R. and Parasuraman, R. (1982) *The Psychology of Vigilance*. New York and London: Academic Press.

Davies, D.R., Parasuraman, R. and Toh, M.-Y. (1984) Time of day, memory load and vigilance performance. In *Trends in Ergonomics / Human Factors*, Vol. 1, edited by A. Mital. Amsterdam: Elsevier.

Easterbrook, J.A. (1959) The effect of emotion on cue utilization and the organization of behaviour. *Psychological Review* **66**: 183–201.

Folkard, S. (1975) Diurnal variation in logical reasoning. *British Journal of Psychology* **66**: 1–8.

Folkard, S. (1979) Time of day and level of processing. *Memory and Cognition* **7**: 247–52.

Folkard, S. (1983) Diurnal variation. In *Stress and Fatigue in Human Performance*, edited by G.R.J. Hockey. Chichester: Wiley.

Folkard, S. and Monk, T.H. (1979) Time of day and processing strategy in free recall. *Quarterly Journal of Experimental Psychology* **31**: 461–75.

Folkard, S. and Monk, T.H. (1980) Circadian rhythms in human memory. *British Journal of Psychology* **71**: 295–307.

Folkard, S. and Monk, T.H. (1985) Circadian performance rhythms. In *Hours of Work: Temporal Factors in Work Scheduling*, edited by S. Folkard and T.H. Monk. Chichester: Wiley.

Folkard, S., Knauth, P., Monk, T.H. and Rutenfranz, J. (1976) The effect of memory load on the circadian variation in performance efficiency under a rapidly rotating shift system. *Ergonomics* **19**: 479–88.

Folkard, S., Monk, T.H., Bradbury, R. and Rosenthall, J. (1977) Time of day effects in school children's immediate and delayed recall of meaningful material. *British Journal of Psychology* **68**: 45–50.

Fort, A. and Mills, J.N. (1976) Der Einfluss der Tageszeit und des vorhergehenden Schlaf-Wach-Musters auf die Liestungsfahigkeit unmittelbar nach dem Aufsteren. In *Biologische Rhythmen und Arbeit*, edited by G. Hildebrandt. Heidelberg: Springer.

Freeman, G.L. and Hovland, C.I. (1934) Diurnal variations in performance and related physiological processes. *Psychological Bulletin* **31**: 777–99.

Gale, A., Bull, R., Penfold, V., Coles, M. and Barraclough, R. (1972) Extraversion, time of day, vigilance performance and physiological arousal: failure to replicate traditional findings. *Psychonomic Science* **29**: 1–5.

Gates, A.I. (1916) Variations in efficiency during the day, together with practice effects, sex differences, and correlations. *University of California Publications in Psychology* **2**: 1–156.

Hartley, L. R. and Shirley, E. (1976) Color-name interference at different times of day. *Journal of Applied Psychology* **61**: 119–22.

Hildebrandt, G., Rohmert, W. and Rutenfranz, J. (1974) Twelve and 24 hour rhythms in error frequency of locomotive drivers and the influence of tiredness. *International Journal of Chronobiology* **2**: 97–110.

Hockey, G.R.J., Davies, S. and Gray, M.M. (1972) Forgetting as a function of sleep at different times of day. *Quarterly Journal of Experimental Psychology* **24**: 386–93.

Horne, J.A., Brass, C.G. and Pettit, A.N. (1980) Circadian performance differences between morning and evening 'types'. *Ergonomics* **23**: 129–36.

Hughes, D.G. and Folkard, S. (1976) Adaptation to an 8-h shift in living routine by members of a socially isolated community. *Nature, London* **264**: 232–4.

Klein, K.E., Herrmann, R., Kuklinski, P. and Wegman, H.M. (1977) Circadian performance rhythms: experimental studies in air operations. In *Vigilance: Theory, Operational Performance and Physiological Correlates,* edited by R.R. Mackie. New York: Plenum.

Kleitman, N. (1963) *Sleep and Wakefulness.* University of Chicago Press.

Kleitman, N. and Jackson, D.P. (1950) Body temperature and performance under different routines. *Journal of Applied Physiology* **3**: 309–28.

Laird, D.A. (1925) Relative performance of college students as conditioned by time of day and day of week. *Journal of Experimental Psychology* **8**: 50–63.

Marks, M. and Folkard, S. (1988) The effects of time of day on recall from expository text. In *Practical Aspects of Memory, Current Research and Issues,* Vol. 2, edited by M. Gruneberg, P. Morris and R. Sykes. Chichester: Wiley.

Millar, K., Styles, B.C. and Wastell, D.G. (1980) Time of day and retrieval from long-term memory. *British Journal of Psychology* **71**: 407–14.

Miles, C. and Smith, A.P. (1988) The combined effects of noise and nightwork on running memory. In *Practical Aspects of Memory: Current Research and Issues,* vol. 2, edited by M. Gruneberg, P. Morris and R. Sykes. Chichester: Wiley.

Monk, T.H. and Leng, V.C. (1982) Time of day effects in simple repetitive tasks: some possible mechanisms. *Acta Psychologica* **51**: 207–21.

Monk, T.H. and Leng, V.C. (1986). Interactions between inter-individual and inter-task differences in the diurnal variation of human performance. *Chronobiology International* **3**: 171–7.

Monk, T.H., Knauth, P., Folkard, S. and Rutenfranz, J. (1978) Memory based performance measures in studies of shiftwork. *Ergonomics* **21**: 819–26.

Monk, T.H., Leng, V.C., Folkard, S. and Weitzman, E.D. (1983) Circadian rhythms in subjective alertness and core body temperature. *Chronobiologia* **10**: 49–55.

Oakhill, J.V. (1986a) Effects of time of day and information importance on adults' memory for a short story. *Quarterly Journal of Experimental Psychology* **38A**: 419–30.

Oakhill, J.V. (1986b) Effects of time of day on the integration of information in text. *British Journal of Psychology* **77**: 481–8.

Oakhill, J.V. (1988) Effects of time of day on text memory and inference. In *Practical Aspects of Memory: Current Research and Issues,* Vol. 2, edited by M. Gruneberg, P. Morris and R. Sykes. Chichester: Wiley.

Revelle, W., Humphrey, M.S., Simon, L. and Gilliland, K. (1980) The interactive effects of personality, time of day and caffeine: a test of the arousal model. *Journal of Experimental Psychology (General)* **109**: 1–31.

Rutenfranz, J. and Helbruegge, T. (1957) Under Tageschwankungen de Rechengeschwindigkeit bei 11-jahrigen kinder. *Zeitschrift Kinderheilk* **80**: 65–82.

Smith, A.P. (1985) Diurnal variation in text anxiety and effort. In *Advances in Test Anxiety Research*, Vol. 4, edited by H. van der Ploeg, R. Schwarzer and C. Spielberger. Lisse: Swets and Zeitlinger.

Smith, A.P. (1987a) Activation states and semantic processing: a comparison of the effects of noise and time of day. *Acta Psychologica* **54**: 271–88.

Smith, A.P. (1987b) Task-related motivation and time of testing. In *Advances in Test Anxiety Research*, Vol. 5, edited by R. Schwarzer, H. van der Ploeg and C. Spielberger. Lisse: Swets and Zeitlinger.

Smith, A.P. (1988a) Effects of meals on memory and attention. In *Practical Aspects of Memory: Current Research and Issues*, Vol. 2, edited by M. Gruneberg, P. Morris and R. Sykes. Chichester: Wiley.

Smith, A.P. (1988b) Individual differences in the combined effects of noise and nightwork on human performance. In *Recent Advances in Researches on the Combined Effects of Environmental Factors*, edited by O. Manninen. Finland: Tampere.

Smith, A.P. (1989a) Diurnal variations in performance. In *The Acquisition and Performance of Cognitive Skills*, edited by A.M. Colley and J.R. Beech. Chichester: Wiley.

Smith, A.P. (1989b) Circadian variation in stress: the effects of noise at different times of day. In *Stress and Anxiety*, Vol. 12, edited by C.D. Spielberger and J. Strelau. New York: McGraw-Hill.

Smith, A.P. (1990) An experimental investigation of the combined effects of noise and nightwork on human function. In *Noise as a Public Health Problem, Vol. 5, New Advances in Noise Research, Part II*, edited by B. Berglund and T. Lindvall. Stockholm: Swedish Council for Building Research.

Smith, A.P. (1991a) Strategy choice and time of day. In *Contemporary Ergonomics 1991*, edited by E.J. Lovesey. London: Taylor and Francis.

Smith, A.P. (1991b) Noise and aspects of attention. *British Journal of Psychology* **82**: 313–24.

Smith, A.P. (1991c) The combined effects of noise, nightwork and meals on mood. *International Archives of Occupational and Environmental Health* **63**: 105–8.

Smith, A.P. (1992) The effects of time of day, introversion and neuroticism on selectivity in memory and attention. *Perceptual and Motor Skills* **74**: 851–60.

Smith, A.P. and Jones, D.M. (1992) Noise and performance. In *A Handbook of Human Performance*, Vol. 1, edited by D.M. Jones and A.P. Smith. New York and London: Academic Press.

Smith, A.P. and Kendrick, A. (1992) Meals and performance. In *A Handbook of Human Performance*, Vol. 2, edited by D.M. Jones and A.P. Smith. New York and London: Academic Press.

Smith, A.P. and Miles, C. (1985) The combined effects of noise and nightwork on human function. In *Contemporary Ergonomics 1985*, edited by D. Oborne. London: Taylor and Francis.

Smith, A.P. and Miles, C. (1986a) The combined effects of nightwork and noise on human function. In *Studies in Industrial and Organizational Psychology 3. Night and Shiftwork: Long-term Effects and their Prevention*, edited by M. Haider, M. Koller and R. Cervinka. Frankfurt: Peter Lang.

Smith, A.P. and Miles, C. (1986b) Effects of lunch on cognitive vigilance tasks. *Ergonomics* **29** 1251–61.

Smith, A.P. and Miles, C. (1986c) Acute effects of meals, noise and nightwork. *British Journal of Psychology* **77**: 377–89.

Smith, A.P. and Miles, C. (1987a) The combined effects of occupational health hazards: an experimental investigation of the effects of noise, nightwork and meals. *International Archives of Occupational and Environmental Health* **59**: 83–9.

Smith, A.P. and Miles, C. (1987b) Effects of lunch on selective and sustained attention. *Neuropsychobiology* **16**: 117–20.

Smith, A.P. and Miles, C. (1987c) Sex differences in the effects of noise and nightwork on performance. *Work and Stress* **1**: 333–9.

Smith, A.P., Leekam, S., Ralph, A. and McNeill, G. (1988) The influence of meal composition on post-lunch changes in performance efficiency and mood. *Appetite* **10**: 195–203.

Smith, A.P., Rusted, J.M., Eaton-Williams, P., Savory, M. and Leathwood, P. (1990) Effects of caffeine given before and after lunch on sustained attention. *Neuropsychobiology* **23**: 160–3.

Smith, A.P., Rusted, J.M., Savory, M., Eaton-Williams, P. and Hall, S.R. (1991) The effects of caffeine, impulsivity and time of day on performance, mood and cardiovascular function. *Journal of Psychopharmacology* **5**: 120–8.

Tilley, A. and Warren, P. (1983) Retrieval from semantic memory at different times of day. *Journal of Experimental Psychology (Learning, Memory and Cognition)* **9**: 718–24.

9

Sleep Deprivation

A. TILLEY & S. BROWN

The original purpose of sleep deprivation was to discover the functions of sleep. After almost one hundred years of research and over one hundred studies later, this Holy Grail of sleep deprivation research has still not been found but the quest has revealed some interesting findings along the way. In humans, the effects of sleep deprivation are largely observed in behaviour and performance, with few detectable physiological consequences, at least not in the short term. In other animals, however, the ultimate consequence is death.

While death in animals is an alarming outcome of long periods without sleep, and while the physiological changes preceding death are interesting because they may tell us more about the functions of sleep, from an applied viewpoint, it is the effects of one or two nights of sleep deprivation that are of most concern to humans. Losing a night's sleep happens to us all from time to time and to many of us (shiftworkers, jet-setters, sleep researchers, new parents) regularly. Fortunately, longer periods without sleep are seldom experienced outside the laboratory. Indeed, in the real world it is usually possible to take some sleep in the form of naps when normal sleep is prevented. Therefore, this chapter concentrates on the effects of short periods without sleep. It examines the lapse hypothesis as an explanation of how sleep deprivation impairs performance and what factors interact with loss of sleep to affect performance; it considers how much sleep and what kind of sleep humans need to keep body and soul together, and it discusses the effects of naps.

HANDBOOK OF HUMAN PERFORMANCE
VOLUME 3 ISBN 0-12-650353-2

THE EFFECTS OF SLEEP DEPRIVATION

Physiological and neurological effects

Sleep deprivation is ultimately lethal. However, there is some debate as to the cause of death. The earliest sleep deprivation experiments were performed on puppies, by Marie de Manacéine, back in 1894 (Manaceine, 1897). The puppies died within four to six days of being kept awake by continuous walking or handling, with the younger puppies dying first. The puppies developed severe hypothermia, had a lowered red cell count and lost weight. Post mortems revealed nothing particularly unusual except for many small cerebral haemorrhages. Although the death of these puppies strongly suggests that sleep deprivation is decidedly unhealthy, it is possible that the harsh procedures used to keep the animals awake and the constant activity may have contributed to their deaths.

Kleitman repeated Manacéine's study in 1927 (see Kleitman, 1963) at the University of Chicago, keeping puppies awake from two to seven days, but this time using milder deprivation procedures and including control puppies (littermates) who helped to keep the experimental animals awake by playing with them. Despite this relatively gentle regime, two of the twelve experimental puppies died in convulsions, curiously during 'recovery' sleep, and, like Manacéine's puppies, all showed a marked drop in red blood cell count and loss of appetite, but no hypothermia. Autopsies of the brains of all the puppies revealed clear abnormalities for both experimental and control animals but no differences between the two groups, which suggests that either the abnormalities were genetic in origin, which seems unlikely, or a result of the crude autopsies of the time.

Other early sleep deprivation studies on dogs (Tarozzi, 1899; Okazaki, 1928), rabbits (e.g. Crile, 1921; Bast, 1925; Leake *et al.*, 1927) and rats (e.g. Licklider and Bunch, 1946) also resulted in the death of the animals, after nine to seventy-seven days in the case of dogs, four to thirty-one days in the case of the rabbits, and three to fourteen days in the case of the rats. Histological findings of the dog studies were very inconsistent. As for the rabbits, they sometimes lost weight and developed severe hypothermia just before death. Post mortems revealed degenerative changes to the liver, adrenal glands, thyroid glands and brain, but again, the stressful sleep deprivation procedures and relatively crude autopsies may have been partly responsible for the findings. The only findings of note from Licklider and Bunch's study were that the rats became extremely irritable and died from bites inflicted on each other. Further investigation by these researchers found that only total sleep deprivation resulted in death. The rats could survive, if not thrive, on about one-third of their normal sleep time, although they also became irritable and their growth was stunted if the sleep restriction began in adolescence.

The most sophisticated and elaborate series of sleep deprivation studies ever performed on animals began in the early 1980s and were carried out by Alan Rechtschaffen and his team at the University of Chicago (see Rechtschaffen *et al.,* 1989). These studies, on rats, have revealed a distinct sleep deprivation syndrome over and above any effects due to other factors, such as activity or the stress of the deprivation procedures. Experimental rats are placed with a control in a carousel device surrounded by water (see Figure 9.1). Each animal has its EEG continuously monitored by a computer. Each time the experimental rat attempts to sleep, the floor is revolved and both rats have to move to avoid a bath. The control rat can sleep whenever the experimental rat is awake. After eleven to thirty-three days of this treatment, the experimental rats died. Before death, these rats became dishevelled and scrawny, developed ulcers and lesions on their tails and paws, lost weight despite eating more, increased their energy expenditure, developed hypothermia during the later stages of deprivation, and showed increased plasma norepinephrine and reduced plasma thyroxine (signs of metabolic stress). Apart from becoming debilitated and suffering some weight loss, the control rats all survived the ordeal. Surprisingly, post mortem examinations of the main organs (brain, liver, kidneys, lungs, etc.) detected no significant differences between the two groups of animals. Nevertheless, as both groups of rats were treated identically, the death of the experimental rats and the physiological changes that preceded death cannot be due to the deprivation procedure or activity and must, presumably, be attributed to sleep deprivation *per se.*

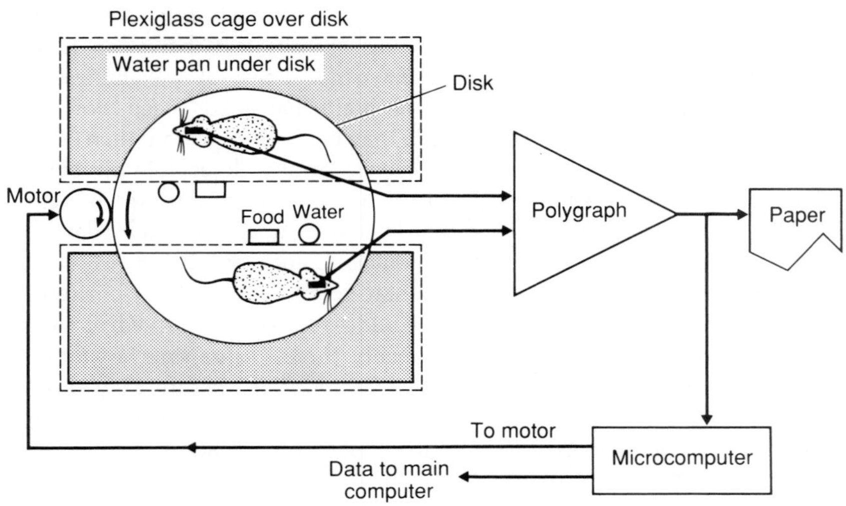

Figure 9.1 The carousel device used by the Chicago group to deprive rats of sleep. (Reproduced from Bergmann *et al.,* 1989.)

So what seems to be going wrong when animals are deprived of sleep and why do they die? The tentative conclusions of the Chicago group and others (e.g. Horne, 1988) is that loss of body heat and a breakdown of thermoregulation are the critical effects of sleep deprivation. Horne (1988) has speculated that these effects may be caused by loss of the deeper forms of non-REM sleep, which might be the equivalent of slow wave sleep (SWS) in humans (see Campbell, this volume, for details of the composition and structure of sleep). SWS may play an important role in the control, maintenance or integration of thermo-regulatory processes (see McGinty and Szymusiak, 1990). In particular, SWS may be a state of finely controlled exothermy and, when feverish, a state of antipyresis. Interestingly, humans undergoing sleep deprivation usually show a small drop in body temperature, often tend to eat rather a lot and wrap-up warm or turn up the heating (Horne, 1988). These effects and behaviours may be signs of, or responses to thermo-regulatory irregularity, threat or stress.

The physiological and neurological effects of sleep deprivation on humans are minor and certainly far less dramatic than those observed in other animals. The most common effects are nearly all of a neurological nature and include heightened sensitivity to pain, fine hand tremor, problems in controlling eye movements and focusing the eyes, drooping eyelids and slurred speech. Studies examining heart rate, blood pressure, respiration, skin conductance, galvanic skin response, body weight, blood and urine constituents have generally reported little or no change following sleep deprivation and, even where effects have been reported, they have always been minimal, falling well within a normal physiological range. As Horne (1988) has pointed out, the human body appears to be able to get along quite well without sleep. There is certainly no evidence from human studies to suggest that sleep is a vital restorative for the body, repairing the wear and tear of wakefulness. What evidence there is suggests that it is the brain that needs sleep, not the rest of the body and that some forms of sleep may be more important than others.

However, it is possible that the absence of any detectable physiological effects of sleep deprivation on humans is because humans are rarely deprived of sleep for more than two to three days at a time, with eight days being the longest period for a group of individuals. Using various indices (e.g. daily sleep amounts, life span, body mass, starvation times), Rechtschaffen *et al.* (1989) have estimated that humans would need to be deprived of sleep for at least twice as long as rats, and probably three to five times as long: that is, somewhere between sixty and one hundred days, before they died. If it is going to take up to one hundred days without sleep to kill a person and given that the sleep deprivation syndrome seen in rats largely manifests itself towards the end of the deprivation period, perhaps it is not too surprising that the physiological effects on humans in the first few days of deprivation are relatively minor.

The most telling physiological effects of sleep deprivation in humans are related to subsequent recovery sleep. Following four to eleven nights of total sleep deprivation (Berger and Oswald, 1962; Gulevich *et al.*, 1966; Kales *et al.*, 1970), about 40 per cent of the lost SWS and 30 per cent of the lost REM sleep are recovered over three recovery nights. Following one night (Berger *et al.*, 1971; Borbély *et al.*, 1981; Carskadon and Dement, 1985) or two nights (Williams *et al.*, 1964; Moses *et al.*, 1975a) of total sleep deprivation, up to 100 per cent of the lost SWS may be recovered over the next two nights, but less than 50 per cent of the lost REM sleep is usually recovered. In all studies, the recovery of SWS takes precedence over the recovery of REM sleep. The strong recovery of lost SWS and its precedence over REM recovery clearly suggests that SWS is the most important component of sleep, the dominant 'sleep drive', and probably vital for the brain.

The importance and predominance of SWS over all other forms of sleep is also reflected in the composition of sleep when sleep time is restricted. Providing sleep is not reduced below about four hours, SWS is preserved at or near normal amounts whereas REM sleep and the lighter forms of non-REM sleep (stages 1 and 2) are dramatically reduced (Webb and Agnew, 1965, 1974, 1975; Sampson, 1965; Dement and Greenberg, 1966; Johnson and Macleod, 1973; Taub and Berger, 1973, 1976; Mullaney *et al.*, 1977; Carskadon *et al.*, 1981; Carskadon and Dement, 1981; Tilley and Wilkinson, 1984; Tilley, 1985; Edinger *et al.*, 1990). This effect is largely an artifact of the temporal distribution of the sleep stages: that is, SWS is concentrated in the first half of the night or sleep period and REM, stage 2 and stage 1 in the second half. Therefore, any restriction on sleep time will naturally cut deeply into the time normally devoted to REM and the lighter fractions of non-REM sleep. SWS will remain relatively safe and intact until sleep time drops below about four hours, when SWS will be encroached upon. When the restriction on sleep time is lifted, SWS increases if there has been a loss, but there is only a limited recovery of the lost REM and lighter forms of non-REM sleep. Once again, then, the evidence suggests that SWS is the most important form of sleep. As far as possible, SWS is conserved or spared and does not get pushed aside by any need to recover REM or the lighter components of non-REM sleep, which appear to be expendable.

Behavioural effects

Although total sleep deprivation would probably kill you in the long run, it is extremely unlikely that you would go mad in the short run. Indeed, a night without sleep might actually do you some good if you happen to be suffering from clinical depression (Gillin, 1983; Kryger *et al.*, 1989). Reports of psychotic behaviour during sleep deprivation are extremely rare and usually occur only when the person has a history of abnormal behaviour (Katz and Landis, 1935; Tyler, 1955; Brauchi and West, 1959; Luby *et al.*, 1960; Koranyi and Lehmann,

1960). For most people, apart from sleepiness, the worst that can be expected over the first few days of sleep deprivation are visual and tactile misperceptions (not hallucinations), perseveration, mild disorientation, irritibility, short temper, lethargy, fatigue and negative mood-states. These unpleasant, sometimes miserable feelings, and experiences are again an indication that, first and foremost, sleep deprivation is affecting the brain.

Performance effects

Sleep deprivation impairs performance. In general, the performance of any task that is long, dull and boring, or that requires sustained concentration and vigilance, is almost guaranteed to deteriorate following loss of sleep. Examples of such tasks are monitoring equipment, such as radar screens and control panels, quality control, keyboard operations and driving. The performance of short (i.e. tasks that can be completed in less than a few minutes), interesting and stimulating tasks, on the other hand, is less susceptible to impairment by sleep deprivation. However, short duration tasks are not entirely immune to sleep deprivation (see Dinges and Kribb, 1991 for a review), especially if the task places heavy demands on working memory or calls for sustained attention, high response rates, reasoning, creativity or divergent thinking. For example, any task, however short, that requires mentally juggling a few numbers, processing large amounts of interdependent, sequential information or coming up with novel solutions to a problem is likely to be impaired by sleep deprivation.

The performance profile of a sleep-deprived person is typically characterized by intermittent periods of slow performance or non-responding which increase in frequency and duration as loss of sleep accumulates. The discovery of these periods of mental and motor 'gaps' or 'blocks' in performance, first noticed by Patrick and Gilbert in 1896 and subsequently confirmed by Warren and Clarke (1937), Bjerner (1949) and Bills (1958) sowed the seeds of the lapse hypothesis.

THE LAPSE HYPOTHESIS

The lapse hypothesis finally emerged from a series of sleep deprivation studies conducted at the Walter Reed Army Institute in Maryland during the late 1950s (Williams *et al.*, 1959). The lapse hypothesis is quite simple: sleep deprivation results in mental and motor lapses in performance. These lapses are probably brought on by short (one to two seconds), irresistible periods of sleep or microsleeps. In other words, the sleep-deprived person intermittently drops off to sleep for a moment or two during which time performance of a task is involuntarily suspended. The subject may perform normally between lapses, but as sleep loss increases, lapses occur more frequently and last longer. The result is that performance becomes increasingly uneven, with efficient performance alternating with faltering performance when the subject is drifting off to sleep, or no performance at all when the subject is technically asleep. This effect on performance is illustrated in Figure 9.2: as sleep loss increases, although the subject is periodically capable of responding just as quickly as normal, slow reaction times become slower and more frequent.

Williams and co-workers noticed that lapses not only increased in frequency and duration as sleep loss increased, but were also affected by such factors as the monotony and duration of the task. For example, under normal conditions, ten minutes on a monotonous vigilance test presented no problems, but performance began to deteriorate after seven minutes following one night without sleep and after two minutes following two nights of sleep deprivation (see Figure 9.3). They also noticed that in tasks where subjects were allowed to go at their own pace (subject paced tasks), while the time taken to complete the task increased due to lapses, errors remained few and far between. Errors only arose when the subjects were under some time constraint (work-paced tasks).

The basic tenets of the lapse hypothesis have remained virtually unchallenged and unchanged over the years. However, there has been one minor challenge and modification, by Kjellberg (1977a, b, c). Kjellberg's reservations about the lapse hypothesis lie in its restrictiveness. Kjellberg believes that the underlying effect of sleep deprivation is to lower arousal. He sees lapses as just the final, catastrophic and most dramatic product of lowered arousal.

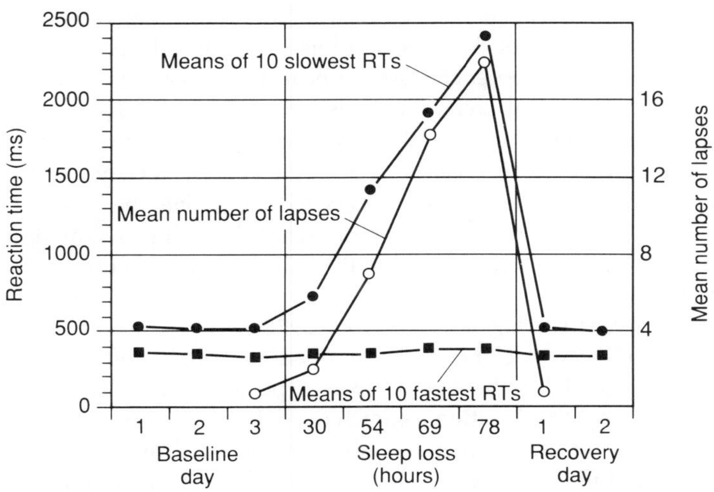

Figure 9.2 The effects of sleep deprivation on fast and slow reaction times and on the incidence of lapses. (Adapted from Williams *et al.*, 1959.)

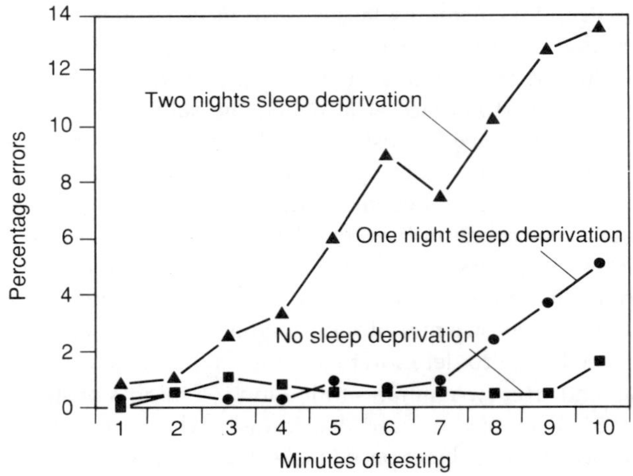

Figure 9.3 The effect of task duration and sleep deprivation on performance of a vigilance task. Performance deteriorates as time on task and sleep deprivation increase. (Adapted from Williams *et al.*, 1965.)

According to Kjellberg, the performance of the sleep-derived person is not essentially normal between lapses, as the lapse hypothesis would have us believe, but generally degraded. For example, close analysis of the changes in simple reaction time over a ten minute period shows that while responses may be as fast as normal at the very beginning of the task, all responses become slower towards the end (Lisper and Kjellberg, 1972).

This idea that the effects of sleep deprivation are mediated by low arousal is supported by studies of the effects of loud noise and sleep loss on selective attention. Loud noise, a potent arouser, appears to focus attention. For example, when performing a dual component task involving tracking a moving dot while monitoring lights in central or peripheral vision, loud noise produces faster reaction times to the centrally located lights (Hockey, 1970a). Sleep deprivation, on the other hand, appears to undermine the ability to focus attention in that reaction times to the centrally placed lights slow down soon after beginning the task (Hockey, 1970b). Sleep deprived subjects have also been shown to be easily distracted and to have difficulty maintaining focused attention in a card sorting task (Norton, 1970).

Further evidence that the sleep-deprived person is suffering from low arousal is provided by the EEG. When a person is in a state of relaxed wakefulness, the EEG is often characterized by alpha (8–10 Hz) activity. Alpha activity is reduced when a person is tired and drowsy, and disappears as the person drifts off to sleep. EEG recordings of sleep-deprived subjects while they are behaviourally awake show a reduction in alpha activity similar to that seen when someone is falling asleep. And when performing a task, failures to respond to a stimulus are often associated with reduced alpha (Williams *et al.*, 1959) or even slow waves (indicative of EEG defined deep sleep) during lapses in performance (Bjerner, 1949).

Another piece of EEG evidence suggesting that lapses are not the be all and end all of sleep deprivation is provided by the contingent negative variation (CNV) or expectancy wave. The CNV is a negative shift in the EEG which occurs between a warning stimulus and an imperative stimulus which requires the subject to make a response. After normal sleep, the amplitude of the CNVs associated with fast responses to the imperative stimulus are typically greater than those associated with slow responses (Papakostopoulos and Fenelon, 1975). After sleep deprivation, however, the relationship appears to be reversed, in that now it is the slower responses that are associated with the larger amplitude CNVs (Lister, 1981). Lister also found that the amplitude of the CNV gradually declined with time on task for auditory vigilance when subjects were sleep-deprived but increased under non-deprivation conditions. Overall, the EEG evidence suggests that the brain is in a chronically and qualitatively different electrophysiological state when sleep deprived and that lapses are but just one behavioural symptom of this state.

In conclusion, low arousal or sleepiness is the underlying cause of the performance decrements following sleep deprivation. A brain that is hovering on the verge of sleep is not in an optimum state to attend to, register, process and act upon incoming information. Attention is likely to wander or fade, registration may fail, information processing will be interrupted or degraded, and responses will slow, stall or be inappropriate.

MODIFIER VARIABLES

One of the most interesting and revealing features of the variations in performance associated with sleep deprivation are the effects of what Johnson (1982) refers to as modifier variables, many of which were first identified and elucidated by the Walter Reed group or by Wilkinson (1965). These modifier variables and their effects are listed in Table 9.1.

One of the key modifier variables is motivation. Given enough encouragement, incentive or threat (e.g. competition, the lure of large amounts of cash, or loss of life and limb) the sleep-deprived person can usually pull themselves together, shrug off sleepiness and perform more or less normally for a while. This feat appears to be achieved by concentrating harder on the task in hand and applying more (compensatory?) effort. The ability to increase concentration and try harder when the need arises is probably the reason many short duration tasks appear to be immune from the effects of sleep deprivation and why the best laid plans and expectations of many a sleep deprivation researcher

Table 9.1 Modifier variables and their effects during sleep deprivation

Type of variable	*Effect on performance decrement during sleep deprivation*	*Some references*
Task variables		Williams *et al.*, 1959; Wilkinson, 1965; Johnson, 1982
Duration	Increased by increasing task duration	Heslegrave and Angus, 1985
Pacing	Omission error rate will increase if pacing out of subjects control (i.e. work-paced tasks). Task will take longer for self-paced tasks, but errors will tend to be low	Williams *et al.*, 1965; Wilkinson, 1965; Johnson, 1982
Knowledge of results	Reduced by feedback of performance level	Wilkinson, 1961
Difficulty	Increases with increasing difficulty	Williams and Lubin, 1967
Complexity	Increases with increasing complexity	Wilkinson, 1965; Hockey, 1970b; Babkoff *et al.*, 1988
Interest value	Reduced if task interesting	Wilkinson, 1964
Memory load	Increases with increasing memory load	Heslegrave and Angus, 1985; Babkoff *et al.*, 1988
Proficiency level	Reduces with increasing proficiency level	Johnson, 1982
Non-task variables		Wilkinson, 1965; Johnson, 1982
Fatigue	Increased by increasing fatigue	Lubin, 1967; Craig (this volume)
Motivation/incentive	Reduced by increased motivation or incentive	Horne and Pettitt, 1985
Circadian rhythms	Modulated by circadian rhythm	Kleitman, 1963; Rutenfranz *et al.*, 1972; Åkerstedt and Gillberg, 1982; Tilley and Warren, 1984; Babkoff *et al.*, 1988
Exercise	Reduced if brief bout taken prior to testing or exercise moderate but increased if heavy and prolonged	Lybrand *et al.*, 1954; Hassleman *et al.*, 1960; Webb and Agnew, 1973; Lubin *et al.*, 1976; Angus *et al.*, 1985; Englund *et al.*, 1985; Tilley and Bohle, 1988
Experience of sleep deprivation	Increased by repeated experience	Wilkinson, 1961; Webb and Levy, 1984; Webb, 1985a
Noise	Reduces performance decrements	Corcoran, 1962; Wilkinson, 1963; Hartley and Shirley, 1977
Environmental temperature	Warm may increase, cold may decrease	Wilkinson *et al.*, 1964
Drugs	Reduced by stimulants, increased by depressants	Tyler, 1947; Kornetsky *et al.*, 1959; Laties, 1961
Stimulating activity	Increased and increases sleepiness	Horne, 1976; Horne and Minard, 1985
Individual differences	Decrements may be greater in elderly, extraverts or unfit	Corcoran, 1962; Webb and Levy, 1982; Webb, 1985a, 1985b; Pleban *et al.*, 1985

have been thwarted. However, increased concentration and effort will only overcome one or two nights of sleep deprivation. After three or more nights without sleep, no amount of extra effort will fend off sleepiness indefinitely and performance will eventually and inevitably collapse.

Another key modifier variable is circadian rhythms (see Campbell, this volume). The effects of sleep deprivation are typically more pronounced during the night, when the person would normally be asleep. Indeed, performance during the first night without sleep can often be worse than performance the next day when the number of hours awake is actually greater (Kleitman, 1963). However, this is not always the case, as a recent study conducted in our laboratory demonstrates. Subjects were required to perform a five minute, iterative, descending subtraction task (that is, starting with a random, three digit number, 850, for example, the subject mentally subtracts 9, announces the answer, '841', mentally subtracts 8, announces the answer, '833', and so on) once every hour over a 36 hour period without sleep, starting at 8 a.m. The task places a heavy demand on working memory and is a good example of the kind of information processing that is susceptible to disruption by sleep deprivation. As illustrated in Figure 9.4, subtraction rate initially increased to peak at around noon; this was followed by a steady decline until the early evening, after which there was a dramatic decline through the night. Performance began to pick up from about 6 a.m. onwards reaching a peak on day 2 at around noon, after which a decline set in again. Notice that although performance improved during the morning on day 2, peak performance was still well below peak performance on day 1. The performance profile for this task is one of a linear decline (dotted line in Figure 9.4) superimposed on a circadian rhythm. The linear decline is presumably the result of accumulating sleep loss whereas the non-linear trends are presumably due to an underlying circadian rhythm.

Babkoff *et al.* (1988) have reported similar effects during seventy-two hours without sleep for the performance of a short duration, variable memory-load, visual search task, with the greatest performance decrement being for the more complex levels of the task.

There is also evidence to suggest that long-term sleep deprivation or disruption, such as occurs during shift work, may affect the phase or amplitude of the circadian rhythm (Folkard *et al.*, 1976; Bugge *et al.*, 1979; Babkoff *et al.*, 1988; Mikulincer *et al.*, 1989; and see Smith, this volume). Even short-term sleep deprivation may affect rhythmical aspects of performance by modifying the temporal structure of daytime alertness and sleepiness (see Lavie, 1985).

The effects of many of these modifier variables are probably mediated via their influence on sleepiness. Variables that increase sleepiness, such as dull, protracted tasks, fatigue, circadian performance troughs or depressants, are likely to exacerbate the effects of sleep deprivation, whereas variables that reduce sleepiness and pep up the brain, such as interesting tasks, high motivation, brief bouts of moderate exercise prior to testing or stimulants, are likely to counteract the effects of sleep deprivation.

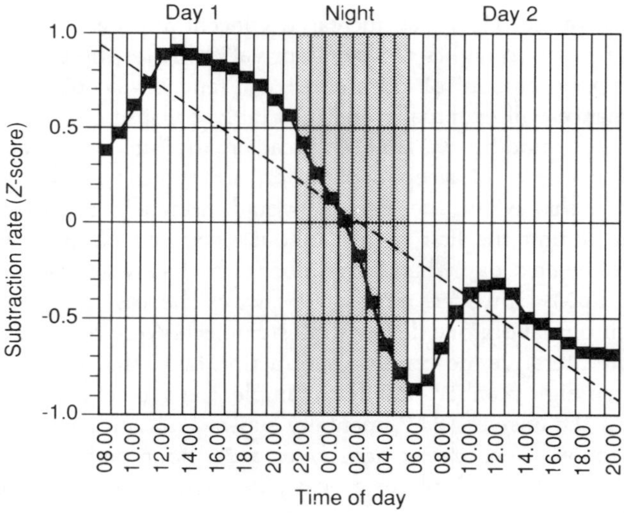

Figure 9.4 Subtraction rate as a function of time of day for a 5-minute, iterative, descending subtraction task during 36 hours without sleep. The function is a group average following smoothing and standardization of individual data.

SLEEP DEPRIVATION AND MEMORY PROCESSES

The lapse hypothesis can account for most of the effects of sleep deprivation on performance. However, it has difficulty explaining some of the memory deficits that accompany sleep deprivation, particularly long-term memory deficits.

Initially, Williams *et al.* (1959) thought that lack of stimulus registration caused by lapses during the verbal presentation of a twenty-five item list could account for the immediate recall deficits they observed. However it was subsequently discovered that immediate recall was still impaired even when subjects wrote each item down during list presentation (Williams *et al.*, 1966). If lapses are causing these deficits, then they must be disrupting subsequent encoding or rehearsal and not just preventing stimulus registration.

Two further studies (Elkin and Murray, 1974; Polzella, 1975) have attempted to pin down the locus and cause of the short-term memory deficits following sleep deprivation. Both used a probe recognition task. In the first study, subjects were required to write down a series of digit triplets which were followed by an immediate or delayed, by twenty seconds, triplet probe. Following fifty-five hours without sleep, subjects made more copying errors and showed poorer delayed recognition. So, both encoding and rehearsal appear to be impaired by sleep deprivation and both could be due to lapses.

In the second study, Polzella (1975) presented subjects with a series of digit or letter pairs followed by a probe. Following twenty-four hours without sleep, reaction times to the probe were slower and recognition impaired. Polzella believed that lapses were responsible for the slower reaction times and prevented the encoding of items in short-term memory. Unfortunately, however, because a check on sensory registration was not included in Polzella's study, it is not possible to specify at what stage of the memory processing chain the lapses occurred: registration, encoding or rehearsal.

In the realm of long-term memory, it is well established that sleep during a retention interval reduces forgetting (see Tilley *et al.*, 1991, for a review). Why it reduces forgetting is open to question. Nevertheless, if sleep reduces forgetting, then, if anything, sleep deprivation might be expected to increase forgetting.

Williams *et al.* (1966) demonstrated that forgetting was indeed increased by sleep deprivation if learning occurred after a night without sleep and testing was carried out the next day, following recovery sleep. And Tilley and Empson (1981) have shown that sleep deprivation increases forgetting if it occurs following learning, although here the effect may be related to retrieval difficulties at the time of recall because recognition was not impaired by sleep deprivation. These results suggest that sleep deprivation may be affecting memory processes that occur at some time between initial learning and recall (consolidation, for example) or affecting retrieval.

In a recent study in our laboratory, we found that sleep deprivation also increases proactive interference. Starting at 8.15 a.m. and following a night of sleep or sleep deprivation, subjects were placed on a learn–recall/learn–recall/learn–recall schedule with a three hour retention interval between learning and recall. At each learning session, subjects were presented with a randomized list of five letter nonsense words which they were required to learn to a two-thirds criterion level. As illustrated in Figure 9.5, the rate of increase in the amount of forgetting from one list to the next was significantly greater for sleep-deprived subjects. As the learning acquisition rates (i.e. trials to criterion) were the same for both groups, these results indicate that sleep deprivation is affecting memory processes that occur between learning and recall or at recall. For example, sleep deprivation could be impairing memory consolidation or it could be creating retrieval difficulties due to poor list differentiation, perhaps as a result of temporal disruption or confusion.

It is difficult to account for these long-term memory effects solely by recourse to the lapse hypothesis. It is unlikely that intermittent lapses or microsleeps are alone responsible for any disruption of long-term memory processes, such as consolidation, or for chronic retrieval difficulties at the time of recall. As mentioned earlier, sleep deprivation also induces a sleepy electrophysiological and psychological state, albeit one that waxes and wanes over the day, during which memory processes and functioning are probably generally impaired or less efficient. Although the brain can monitor and

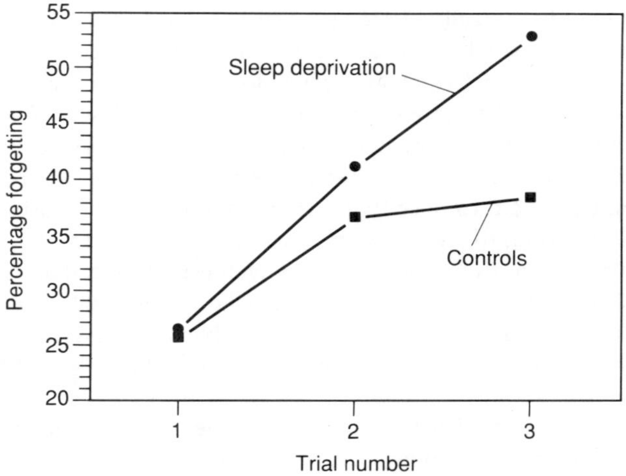

Figure 9.5 Changes in percent forgetting over three successive 3-hour retention intervals for sleep-deprived and control groups. The rate of increase is significantly greater for the sleep-deprived group.

respond to incoming information while it is asleep, stimulus thresholds are generally higher, information processing and immediate retrieval of the information is generally degraded, attenuated or truncated, and long-term recall highly improbable (for a review, see Bonnet, 1982). The sleep-deprived brain must to some extent be susceptible to, and labouring under, the same kinds of deficiency.

REDUCED SLEEP OR PARTIAL SLEEP DEPRIVATION

Most of the discussion has focused on the consequences of total sleep deprivation yet, in the real world, it is unusual for people to go without sleep for more than one night. On the other hand, it is relatively common for people to obtain less than a full night's sleep. So, how much sleep do we need for psychological performance to remain normal?

One of the first attempts to answer this question was made at the Medical Research Council's Applied Psychology Unit in Cambridge (Wilkinson *et al.*, 1966). In one of the most systematic studies of partial sleep deprivation ever conducted, a group of sailors had their sleep restricted to 0, 1, 2, 3, 5 or $7\frac{1}{2}$ hours for two consecutive nights. On three occasions during the daytime, the sailors performed Wilkinson's auditory vigilance task (a task that has similar demands to listening for unusual sonar signals), a simple addition task, and a coding task. Each task was well practised and lasted one hour. The most revealing effects were for the vigilance task (see Figure 9.6). Wilkinson found that after the first night of restricted sleep, performance dropped dramatically when the amount of sleep obtained fell below three hours. However, after two nights, the deterioration began at around the five hour per night mark. Thus, if sleep is restricted for more than one night, it appears that five hours sleep per night may be the minimum requirement to maintain performance at normal levels.

Although Wilkinson did not measure sleep EEGs, he speculated that the performance decrements may be due to lost stage 4 sleep. Performance is beginning to suffer at around the point where the capacity to obtain a full quota of stage 4 sleep in particular, and SWS in general, would be compromised. For a single night of restricted sleep, this would happen at around the three to four hour mark. For two nights in a row, however, this would begin to happen earlier because of the extended period of wakefulness prior to the second night of restricted sleep, which would increase SWS pressure, and the recovery of any lost SWS from the first night. Thus, Wilkinson's results suggest that obtaining a full quota of SWS may be necessary for the maintenance of normal performance capacity.

At around the same time that Wilkinson was running his restricted sleep experiments in Cambridge, Webb was conducting an experiment at the University of Florida in which sleep was restricted to three hours per night for eight consecutive nights (Webb and Agnew, 1965). Performance did not begin to deteriorate until the seventh day. This would seem to imply that three hours sleep per night is sufficient to maintain performance at respectable

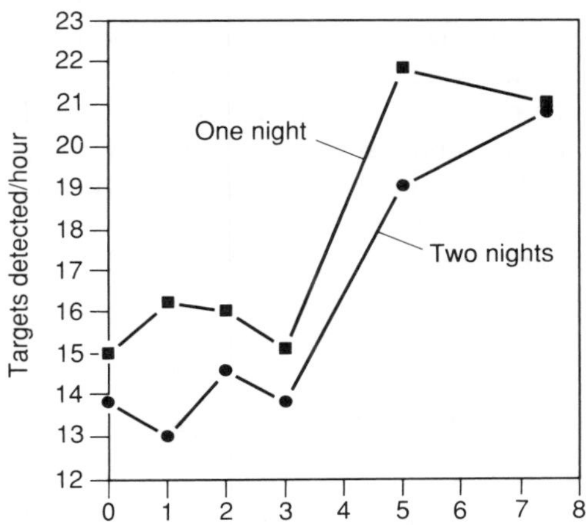

Figure 9.6 The effects of variable amounts of sleep per night on performance of an auditory vigilance task. (Adapted from Wilkinson *et al.*, 1966.)

levels and that five hours sleep per night may be more than enough. However, the tests used by Webb were much shorter than those used by Wilkinson and none involved detection. In other words, the tests may not have been sensitive enough to detect an earlier decline in performance.

If three hours sleep per night is too little and five hours too much, what about four hours? Back in Cambridge, a second study was conducted in which sleep was restricted to either 4, 6 or $7\frac{1}{2}$ hours per night for four days (Hamilton *et al.*, 1972). Four hours sleep per night appeared to maintain performance at rested levels on the Wilkinson auditory vigilance task, but an unexpected practice effect may have offset a decline in performance over the four day period. Therefore, four hours may be just under the minimum sleep requirement.

A subsequent study by Tilley and Wilkinson (1984) supports this conclusion. Performance of a less onerous twenty minute simple reaction time task was impaired after one night of restricted (four hours) sleep and deteriorated further after a second night. These findings and others (Rutenfranz *et al.*, 1972; Webb and Agnew, 1974; Friedman *et al.*, 1977) have indicated that, over the long term and apart from the odd very short sleeper (Jones and Oswald, 1968; Meddis *et al.*, 1973; Struss and Broughton, 1978), a reduction in sleep time to around five hours per night is about the minimum that most people can tolerate.

Although about five hours sleep per night is a desired minimum to prevent performance decrements, this may only apply to nocturnal sleep. Five hours sleep per day may be insufficient if it is taken during the daytime. For example, the shift worker on nights not only has to cope with a circadian performance trough at night but also has to try to catch up on lost sleep during the day, typically by going to bed in the morning. The problem here is that sleep is being attempted over an inappropriate phase of the circadian temperature rhythm (i.e. during an upswing). The result of trying to sleep at the 'wrong' time of day is that the shift worker's diurnal sleep is easily disturbed by noise and tends to be shorter, lighter and more fragmented than nocturnal sleep (Tilley *et al.*, 1982). Despite obtaining more than five hours sleep per day, there is a day-to-day build-up of partial sleep deprivation because daytime sleep quality is poor, and a night-to-night deterioration in performance (Tilley *et al.*, 1982).

THE EFFECTS OF NAPS

When nocturnal sleep is prevented, restricted or disturbed, dozing or napping tends to become the order of the day. Daytime naps, particularly afternoon naps, can assist in the reclamation of lost sleep, especially SWS (Benoit *et al.*, 1980; Naitoh, 1981; Åkerstedt and Gillberg, 1986; Tilley *et al.*, 1987), or even be utilized to gain SWS credit (Karacan *et al.*, 1970; Feinberg *et al.*, 1985), and a series of naps spread across the twenty-four hours can replace a single period of unbroken nocturnal sleep (Weitzman *et al.*, 1974; Carskadon and Dement, 1975; Moses *et al.*, 1975b), although this is generally considered to be a less efficient strategy for obtaining sleep because the quality and quantity of sleep is compromised by circadian factors (see Campbell, this volume). Naps can increase subsequent alertness or reduce sleepiness (Lumley *et al.*, 1986), and be beneficial in preserving task performance and mood or reversing the deficits inflicted by sleep deprivation.

Although a nap is generally beneficial in alleviating the deterioration in performance resulting from inadequate or insufficient sleep, the benefits are unlikely to be seen until at least two hours after the nap. Indeed, performance will usually be worse immediately after the nap, especially if the nap is taken at night, because of sleep inertia (see Campbell, this volume). For example, Naitoh (1981) found that, following forty-five hours of continuous work without sleep, a two hour early morning nap (4 a.m. to 6 a.m.) resulted in severe and prolonged (up to six hours) sleep inertia and performance deficits. The sleep inertia was shorter and less severe and performance subsequently improved if the nap was postponed until midday. Dinges *et al.* (1985) have also shown that night-time naps produce greater immediate performance decrements than daytime naps. The effects of a nap on performance will therefore depend upon when the nap is taken and how soon after the nap performance is tested.

The effects of a nap will also depend on the amount of sleep deprivation and the length of the nap. The greater the amount of sleep deprivation, the longer and more severe the sleep inertia (Dinges *et al.*, 1985) and the longer the nap will need to be to return performance to normal levels (Rosa *et al.*, 1983). After one night of sleep deprivation, a daytime nap of around one hour would appear to be the minimum duration to reduce subsequent sleepiness (Lumley *et al.*, 1986), but this still leaves a sleep debt.

CONCLUSIONS

Sleep deprivation is unpleasant and potentially harmful. It will make you sleepy and irritable; it will impair performance; it can disrupt circadian rhythms; it probably disturbs thermo-regulation; and, if prolonged, would probably kill you. The most important kind of sleep appears to be SWS. In the long term, five hours sleep per night is about the minimum most people need in order to obtain a full quota of SWS, to prevent daytime sleepiness and to prevent performance decrements. Anything less than five hours per night will probably need to be supplemented by a daytime nap. The recuperative power of a nap will depend upon its timing, its duration and the amount of sleep deprivation.

ACKNOWLEDGEMENTS

This chapter would have been far more difficult to write had it not been for the half dozen or so scholarly reviews of sleep deprivation that have appeared during the past twenty-five years. (e.g. Wilkinson, 1965; Lubin, 1967; Naitoh, 1976; Johnson, 1975, 1982; Horne, 1978, 1988; Dinges and Kribb, 1991). We are indebted to these authors.

REFERENCES

Åkerstedt, T. and Gillberg, M. (1982) Displacement of the sleep period and sleep deprivation. *Human Neurobiology* **1**: 163–71.

Åkerstedt, T. and Gillberg, M. (1986) A dose–response study of sleep loss and spontaneous sleep termination. *Psychophysiology* **23**: 293–7.

Angus, R.G., Heslegrave, R.J. and Myles, S.W. (1985) Effects of prolonged sleep deprivation, with and without chronic physical exercise, on mood and performance. *Psychophysiology* **22**: 276–82.

Babkoff, H., Mikulincer, M., Caspy, T. and Kempinski, D. (1988) The topology of performance curves during 72 hours of sleep loss: a memory and search task. *Quarterly Journal of Experimental Psychology* **40**: 737–56.

Bast, T.H. (1925) Morphological changes in fatigue. *Wisconsin Medical Journal* **24**: 271–2.

Benoit, O., Foret, J., Bouard, G., Merle, B., Landau, J. and Marc, M.E. (1980) Habitual sleep length and patterns of recovery sleep after 24 hour and 36 hour sleep deprivation. *Electroencephalography and Clinical Neurophysiology* **50**: 477–85.

Berger, R.J. and Oswald, I. (1962) Effects of sleep deprivation on behaviour, subsequent sleep, and dreaming. *Journal of Mental Science* **108**: 457–65.

Berger, R.J., Walker, J.M., Scott, T.D., Manguson, L.J. and Pollack, S.L. (1971) Diurnal and nocturnal sleep stage patterns following sleep deprivation. *Psychonomic Science* **23**: 273–5.

Bergmann, B.M., Kushida, C.A., Everson, C.A., Gilliland, M.A., Obermeyer, W. and Rechtschaffen, A. (1989) Sleep deprivation in the rat. II: Methodology. *Sleep* **12**: 5–12.

Bills, A.G. (1958) Studying motor functions and efficiency. In *Methods of Psychology*, edited by T.G. Andrews. New York: Wiley.

Bjerner, B. (1949) Alpha depression and lowered pulse rate during delayed actions in a serial reaction test. *Acta Physiologica Scandinavica* **19**: 93.

Bonnet, M. (1982) Performance during sleep. In *Biological Rhythms, Sleep, and Performance*, edited by W.B. Webb. Chichester: Wiley.

Borbély, A.A., Baumann, F., Brandeis, D., Strauch, I. and Lehmann, D. (1981) Sleep deprivation: effect on sleep states and EEG density in man. *Electroencephalography and Clinical Neurophysiology* **51**: 458–93.

Brauchi, J.T. and West, L.J. (1959) Sleep deprivation. *Journal of the American Medical Association* **171**: 11–4.

Bugge, J.F., Opstad, P.K. and Magnus, P.M. (1979) Changes in the circadian rhythm of performance and mood in healthy young men exposed to prolonged, heavy physical work, sleep deprivation, and caloric deficit. *Aviation, Space and Environmental Medicine* **50**: 663–8.

Carskadon, M.A. and Dement, W.C. (1975) Sleep studies on a 90-minute day. *Electroencephalograpy and Clinical Neurophysiology* **39**: 145–55.

Carskadon, M.A. and Dement, W.C. 1981) Cumulative effects of sleep restriction on daytime sleepiness. *Psychophysiology* **18**: 107–13.

Carskadon, M.A. and Dement, W.C. (1985) Sleep loss in elderly volunteers. *Sleep* **8**: 207–21.

Carskadon, M.A., Harvey, K. and Dement, W.C. (1981) Acute restriction on nocturnal sleep in children. *Perceptual and Motor Skills* **53**: 103–12.

Corcoran, D.W.J. (1962) Noise and loss of sleep. *Quarterly Journal of Experimental Psychology* **14**: 178–82.

Crile, G.W. (1921) Studies in exhaustion. *Archives of Surgery* **2**: 196–220.

Dement, W.C. and Greenberg, S. (1966) Changes in total amount of stage 4 sleep as a function of partial sleep deprivation. *Electroencephalography and Clinical Neurophysiology* **20**: 523–6.

Dinges, D.F. and Kribb, N.B. (1991) Performing while sleepy: effects of experimentally-induced sleepiness. In *Sleep, Sleepiness and Performance*, edited by T.H. Monk. Chichester: John Wiley and Sons.

Dinges, D.F., Orne, M.T. and Orne, E.C. (1985) Assessing performance upon abrupt awakening from naps during quasi-continuous operations. *Behavior Research Methods, Instruments, and Computers* **17**: 37–45.

Edinger, J.D., Marsh, G.R., McCall, W.V., Erwin, C.W. and Lininger, A.W. (1990) Daytime functioning and nighttime sleep before, during and after a 146-hour tennis match. *Sleep* **13**: 526–32.

Elkin, A.J. and Murray, D.J. (1974) The effects of sleep loss on short-term recognition memory. *Canadian Journal of Psychology* **28**: 192–8.

Feinberg, I., March, J.D., Floyd, T.C., Jimison, R., Bossom-Demitrack, L. and Katz, P.H. (1985) Homeostatic changes during post-nap sleep maintain baseline levels of delta EEG. *Electroencephalography and Clinical Neurophysiology* **61**: 134–7.

Folkard, S., Knauth, P., Monk, T.H. and Rutenfranz, J. (1976) The effect of memory load on the circadian variation in performance efficiency under a rapidly rotating shift system. *Ergonomics* **19**: 479–88.

Friedmann, J., Globus, G., Huntley, A., Mullaney, D., Naitoh, P. and Johnson, L. (1977) Performance and mood during and after gradual sleep reduction. *Psychophysiology* **14**: 245–50.

Gillin, J.C. (1983) The sleep therapies of depression. *Progress in Neuropsychopharmacology and Biological Psychiatry* **7**: 351–4.

Gulevich, G., Dement, W.C. and Johnson L.C. (1966) Psychiatric and EEG observations on a case of prolonged (264 h) wakefulness. *Archives of General Psychiatry* **15**: 29–35.

Hamilton, P., Wilkinson, R.T. and Edwards, R.S. (1972) A study of four days partial sleep deprivation. In *Aspects of Human Efficiency*, edited by W.P. Colquhoun. London: English Universities Press.

Hartley, L.R. and Shirley, E. (1977) Sleep loss, noise and decisions. *Ergonomics* **20**: 481–9.

Hassleman, M., Schaff, G. and Metz, B. (1960) Influences respectives du travail, de la température ambiante et de la privation de sommeil sur l'excretion urinaire de catecholamioines chez l'homme normal. *Comptes Rendus des Seances de la Société de Biologie* **154**: 197–201.

Heslegrave, R.J. and Angus, R.G. (1985) The effects of task duration and work-session location on performance degradation induced by sleep loss and sustained cognitive work. *Behavior Research Methods, Instruments, and Computers* **17**: 592–603.

Hockey, G.R.J. (1970a) Effect of loud noise on attentional selectivity. *Quarterly Journal of Experimental Psychology* **22**: 28–36.

Hockey, G.R.J. (1970b) Changes in attention allocation in a multi-component task under loss of sleep. *British Journal of Psychology* **61**: 473–80.

Horne, J.A. (1976) Recovery sleep following different visual conditions during total sleep deprivation in man. *Biological Psychology* **4**: 107–18.

Horne, J.A. (1978) A review of the biological effects of total sleep deprivation in man. *Biological Psychology* **7**: 55–102.

Horne, J.A. (1988) *Why We Sleep*. Oxford: Oxford University Press.

Horne, J.A. and Minard, A. (1985) Sleep and sleepiness following a behaviourally 'active' day. *Ergonomics* **28**: 567–75.

Horne, J.A. and Pettitt, A.N. (1985) High incentive effects on vigilance performance during 72 hours of total sleep deprivation. *Acta Psychologica* **58**: 123–39.

Johnson, L.C. (1975) The effect of total, partial, and stage sleep deprivation on EEG patterns and performance. In *Behavior and Brain Electrical Activity*, edited by N. Burch and H.L. Altschuler. New York: Plenum.

Johnson, L.C. (1982) Sleep deprivation and performance. In *Biological Rhythms, Sleep, and Performance*, edited by W.B. Webb. Chichester: Wiley.

Johnson, L.C. and Macleod, W.L. (1973) Sleep and awake behaviour during gradual sleep reduction. *Perceptual and Motor Skills* **36**: 87–97.

Jones, H.W. and Oswald, I. (1968) Two cases of healthy insomnia. *Electroencephalography and Clinical Neurophysiology* **24**: 378–80.

Kales, A., Tan, T.L., Kollar, E.J., Naitoh, P., Preston, T.A. and Malmstrom, E.J. (1970). Sleep patterns following 205 hours of sleep deprivation. *Psychonomic Science* **32**: 189–200.

Karacan, I., Williams, R.L., Finley, W.W. and Hursch, C.J. (1970). The effects of naps on nocturnal sleep: influence on the need for stage-1 REM and stage 4 sleep. *Biological Psychiatry* **2**: 391–9.

Katz, S. and Landis, C. (1935) Psychologic and physiologic phenomena during a prolonged vigil. *Archives of Neurology and Psychiatry* **34**: 307–16.

Kjellberg, A. (1977a) Sleep deprivation and some aspects of performance. I: Problems of arousal changes. *Waking and Sleeping* **1**: 139–43.

Kjellberg, A. (1977b) Sleep deprivation and some aspects of performance. II: Lapses and other attentional effects. *Waking and Sleeping* **1**: 145–8.

Kjellberg, A. (1977c) Sleep deprivation and some aspects of performance. III: Motivation comment and conclusions. *Waking and Sleeping* **1**: 149–53.

Kleitman, N. (1963) *Sleep and Wakefulness*. University of Chicago Press.

Koranyi, E.K. and Lehmann, M.D. (1960) Experimental sleep deprivation in schizophrenic patients. *Archives of General Psychiatry* **2**: 534–44.

Kornetsky, C., Mirsky, A.F., Kessler, E.K. and Dorff, J.E. (1959) The effects of dextro-amphetamine on behavioral deficits produced by sleep loss in humans. *Journal of Pharmacology and Experimental Therapeutics* **127**: 46–50.

Kryger, M.H., Roth, T. and Dement, W.C. (1989) *Principles and Practice of Sleep Medicine*. New York: Saunders.

Laties, V.G. (1961) Modification of affect, social behavior and performance by sleep deprivation and drugs. *Journal of Psychiatric Research* **1**: 12–25.

Lavie, P. (1985). Ultradian cycles in wakefulness: possible implications for work–rest schedules. In *Hours of Work*, edited by S. Folkard and T.H. Monk. Chichester: Wiley.

Leake, C., Grab, J.A. and Senn, M.J. (1927) Studies in exhaustion due to lack of sleep. II. Symptomatology in rabbits. *American Journal of Physiology* **92**: 127–30.

Licklider, J.C.R. and Bunch, M.E. (1946) Effects of enforced wakefulness upon the growth and the maze-learning performance of white rats. *Journal of Comparative Psychology* **39**: 339–50.

Lisper, H.O. and Kjellberg, A. (1972) Effects of 24 hours sleep deprivation on rate of decrement in a 10-minute auditory reaction time task. *Journal of Experimental Psychology* **96**: 287–90.

Lister, S.G. (1981) A theoretical formulation of the effects of sleep loss. Doctoral thesis, University of Hull.

Lubin, A. (1967) Performance under sleep loss and fatigue. In *Sleep and Altered States of Consciousness*, edited by S.S. Kety, E.V. Evarts and H.L. Williams. Baltimore: Williams and Wilkins.

Lubin, A., Hord, D.J., Tracy, M.L. and Johnson, L.C. (1976) Effects of exercise, bedrest and napping on performance decrement during 40 hours. *Psychophysiology* **13**: 334–9.

Luby, E.D., Frohman, C.E., Grisell, J.L., Lenzo, J.E. and Gottlieb, J.S. (1960) Sleep deprivation: effects on behaviour, thinking, motor performance, and biological energy transfer systems. *Psychosomatic Medicine* **22**: 182–92.

Lumley, M., Roehrs, T., Zorick, F., Lamphere, J. and Roth, T. (1986) The alerting effects of naps in sleep-deprived subjects. *Psychophysiology* **23**: 403–8.

Lybrand, W.A., Andrews, T.G. and Ross, S. (1954) Systemic fatigue and perceptual organization. *American Journal of Psychology* **67**: 704–7.

Manacéine, M. de (1897) *Sleep: Its Physiology, Pathology, Hygiene and Psychology.* London: Walter Scott.

McGinty, D. and Szymusiak, R. (1990) Keeping fool: a hypothesis about the mechanisms and functions of slow-wave sleep. *Trends in Neuroscience* **12**: 480–7.

Meddis, R., Pearson, A.J.D. and Langford, G. (1973) An extreme case of healthy insomnia. *Electroencephalography and Clinical Neurophysiology* **35**: 213–4.

Mikulincer, M., Babkoff, H., Caspy, T. and Sing, H.C. (1989) The effects of 72 hours of sleep loss on psychological variables. *British Journal of Psychology* **80**: 145–62.

Moses, J.M., Johnson, L.C., Naitoh, P. and Lubin, A. (1975a) Sleep stage deprivation and total sleep loss: effects on sleep behaviour. *Psychophysiology* **12**: 141–6.

Moses, J., Hord, D.J., Lubin, A., Johnson, L.C. and Naitoh, P. (1975b) Dynamics of nap sleep during a 40 hour period. *Electroencephalography and Clinical Neurophysiology* **39**: 627–33.

Mullaney, D.J., Johnson, L.C., Naitoh, P., Friedman, J.K. and Globus, G.G. (1977) Sleep during and after gradual sleep reduction. *Psychophysiology* **14**: 237–44.

Naitoh, P. (1976) Sleep deprivation in human subjects: a reappraisal. *Waking and Sleeping* **1**: 53–60.

Naitoh, P. (1981) Circadian cycles and the restorative power of naps. In *Biological Rhythms, Sleep and Shift Work*, edited by L.C. Johnson, D.I. Tepas, W.P. Colquhoun and M.J. Colligan. New York: Spectrum.

Norton, R. (1970) The effects of acute sleep deprivation on selective attention. *British Journal of Psychology* **61**: 157–61.

Okazaki, S. (1928) An experimental study of the lack of sleep. *Psychological Abstracts* **2**: 628.

Papakostopoulos, D. and Fenelon, B. (1975) Spacial distribution of the contingent negative variation (CNV) and the relationship between CNV and reaction time. *Psychophysiology* **12**: 74–8.

Patrick, G.T. and Gilberg, J.A. (1896) On the effects of loss of sleep. *Psychological Review* **3**: 469–83.

Pleban, R.J., Thomas, D.A. and Thompson, H.L. (1985) Physical fitness as a moderator of cognitive work capacity and fatigue onset under sustained combat-like operations. *Behavior Research Methods, Instruments, and Computers* **17**: 86–9.

Polzella, D.J. (1975) Effects of sleep deprivation on short-term recognition memory. *Journal of Experimental Psychology* **104**: 194–200.

Rechtschaffen, A., Bergmann, B.M., Everson, C.A., Kushida, C.A. and Gilliland, M.A. (1989) Sleep deprivation in the rat: X. Integration and discussion of the findings. *Sleep* **12**: 68–87.

Rosa, R.R., Bonnet, M.H. and Warm, J.S. (1983) Recovery of performance during sleep following sleep deprivation. *Psychophysiology* **20**: 152–9.

Rutenfranz, J., Aschoff, J. and Mann, H. (1972) The effects of a cumulative sleep deficit, duration of preceding sleep period and body temperature on multiple choice reaction time. In *Aspects of Human Efficiency*, edited by W.P. Colquhoun. London: English Universities Press.

Sampson, H. (1965) Deprivation of dreaming sleep by two methods. *Archives of General Psychiatry* **13**: 79–86.

Struss, D. and Broughton, R. (1978) Extreme short sleep: personality profiles and a case study of sleep requirement. *Waking and Sleeping* **2**: 101–5.

Tarozzi, G. (1899) Sull' influenza dell' insonnia sperimentale sul ricambio materiale. *Rivista di Patologia Nervosa e Mentale* **4**: 1–23.

Taub, J.M. and Berger, R.J. (1973) Sleep stage patterns associated with acute shifts in the sleep-wakefulness cycle. *Electroencephalography and Clinical Neurophysiology* **35**: 613–9.

Taub, J.M. and Berger, R.J. (1976) The effects of changing the phase and duration of sleep. *Journal of Experimental Psychology: Human Perception and Performance* **2**: 30–41.

Tilley, A.J. (1985) Recovery sleep at different times of the night following loss of the last four hours of sleep. *Sleep* **8**: 129–36.

Tilley, A.J. and Bohle, P. (1988) Twisting the night away: the effects of all night disco dancing on reaction time. *Perceptual and Motor Skills* **66**: 107–12.

Tilley, A.J. and Empson, J.A.C. (1981) Picture recall and recognition following total and selective sleep deprivation. In *Sleep 1980: Circadian Rhythms, Dreams, Noise and Sleep,* edited by W.P. Koella. Basel: Krager.

Tilley, A.J. and Warren, P.S.G. (1984) Retrieval from semantic memory during a night without sleep. *Quarterly Journal of Experimental Psychology* **36**: 281–9.

Tilley, A.J. and Wilkinson, R.T. (1984) The effects of a restricted sleep regime on the composition of sleep and on performance. *Psychophysiology* **21**: 406–12.

Tilley, A.J., Wilkinson, R.T., Warren, P.S.G., Watson, W.B. and Drud, M. (1982) The sleep and performance of shiftworkers. *Human Factors* **24**: 629–41.

Tilley, A.J., Donohoe, F. and Hensby, S. (1987) Homeostatic changes in slow wave sleep during recovery sleep following sleep loss and partial SWS recovery during an afternoon nap. *Sleep* **10**: 600–5.

Tilley, A., Brown, S., Donald, M., Ferguson, S., Piccone, J., Plasto, K. and Statham, D. (1991) Human sleep and memory processes. In *Sleep, Arousal and Performance,* edited by R. Broughton and R. Ogilvie. Boston: Birkhäuser.

Tyler, D.B. (1947) The effects of amphetamine sulfate and some barbiturates on the fatigue produced by prolonged wakefulness. *American Journal of Physiology* **150**: 253–62.

Tyler, D.B. (1955) Psychological changes during experimental sleep deprivation. *Diseases of the Nervous System* **16**: 293–9.

Warren, N. and Clark, B. (1937) Blocking in mental and motor tasks during a 65 hour vigil. *Journal of Experimental Psychology* **21**: 97–105.

Webb, W.B. (1985a) Experiments on extended performance: repetition, age, and limited sleep periods. *Behavior Research Methods, Instruments, and Computers* **17**: 27–36.

Webb, W.B. (1985b) A further analysis of age and sleep deprivation effects. *Psychophysiology* **22**: 156–61.

Webb, W.B. and Agnew, H.W. (1965) Sleep: effects of a restricted regime. *Science, New York* **150**: 1745–7.

Webb, W.B. and Agnew, H.W. (1973) Effects on performance of high and low energy expenditure during sleep deprivation. *Perceptual and Motor Skills* **37**: 511–4.

Webb, W.B. and Agnew, H.W. (1974) The effects of a chronic limitation on sleep length. *Psychophysiology* **11**: 265–74.

Webb, W.B. and Agnew, H.W. (1975) The effects of subsequent sleep of an acute restriction of sleep length. *Psychophysiology* **12**: 367–70.

Webb, W.B. and Levy, C.M. (1982) Age, sleep deprivation and performance. *Psychophysiology* **19**: 272–6.

Webb, W.B. and Levy, C.M. (1984) Effects of spaced and repeated total sleep deprivation. *Ergonomics* **27**: 45–58.

Weitzman, E.D., Nogeire, C., Perlow, M., Fukushima, D., Sassin, J., McGregor, P., Gallagher, T.F. and Hellman, L. (1974) Effects of a prolonged 3-hour sleep–wake cycle on sleep stages, plasma cortisol, growth hormone and body temperature in man. *Journal of Clinical Endocrinology and Metabolism* **38**: 1018–30.

Wilkinson, R.T. (1961) Interaction of lack of sleep with knowledge of results, repeated testing, and individual differences. *Journal of Experimental Psychology* **62**: 263–71.

Wilkinson, R.T. (1963) Interaction of noise with knowledge of results and sleep deprivation. *Journal of Experimental Psychology* **66**: 332–7.

Wilkinson, R.T. (1964) Effects of up to 60 hours sleep deprivation on different types of work. *Ergonomics* **7**: 175–86.

Wilkinson, R.T. (1965) Sleep deprivation. In *The Physiology of Human Survival,* edited by O.G. Edholm and A.L. Bacharach. New York and London: Academic Press.

Wilkinson, R.T., Fox, R.H., Goldsmith, R., Hampton, I.F.G. and Lewis, H.E. (1964) Psychological and physiological responses to raised body temperature. *Journal of Applied Physiology* **19**: 287–91.

Wilkinson, R.T., Edwards, R.S. and Haines, E. (1966) Performance following a night of reduced sleep. *Psychonomic Science* **5**: 471–2.

Williams, H.L. and Lubin, A. (1967) Speeded addition and sleep loss. *Journal of Experimental Psychology* **73**: 313–7.

Williams, H.L., Lubin, A. and Goodnow, J.J. (1959) Impaired performance with acute sleep loss. *Psychological Monograph 73.*

Williams, H.L., Hammack, J.T., Daly, R.L., Dement, W.C. and Lubin, A. (1964) Responses to auditory stimulation, sleep loss and the EEG stages of sleep. *Electroencephalography and Clinical Neurophysiology* **51**: 269–79.

Williams, H.L., Kearney, O.F. and Lubin, A. (1965) Signal uncertainty and sleep loss. *Journal of Experimental Psychology* **69**: 401–7.

Williams, H.L., Gieseking, C.F. and Lubin, A. (1966) Some effects of sleep loss on memory. *Perceptual and Motor Skills* **23**: 1287–93.

10

Vigilance

F. NACHREINER & K. HÄNECKE

INTRODUCTION

The vigilance phenomenon

Vigilance has become a major topic in (applied) psychological research since Mackworth published (1948, 1950) his results on the performance of operators in simulated radar watch-keeping tasks. Mackworth experimentally simulated a watch-keeping task in order to get insight into a phenomenon that had been observed by the British Admiralty when they found that the number of enemy contacts reported by sonar operators in World War II decreased with time on task. According to these reports, the cumulative distribution of reported contacts deviated considerably from any expected distribution in that about half of contacts were reported in the first half hour of the watch, whereas in the later parts of the vigil, decreasingly smaller numbers were detected (Figure 10.1).

Mackworth simulated this situation by asking his subjects to monitor a clock display whose arm required one hundred steps for one turn. Each of these steps was considered a non-critical event, requiring no action from the observer. At random intervals, however, and clearly detectable under 'alert' conditions, the arm would perform a double step, moving without stop to the next but one position. This was the critical signal that the subject was asked to detect and to respond to. Twelve such signals had to be detected per 30 minute period of the 2-hour watch, appearing at intervals from 45 seconds to 10 minutes.

Mackworth's experimental simulation of the watch-keeping performance under monotonous conditions with little requirement for active behaviour

HANDBOOK OF HUMAN PERFORMANCE
VOLUME 3 ISBN 0-12-650353-2

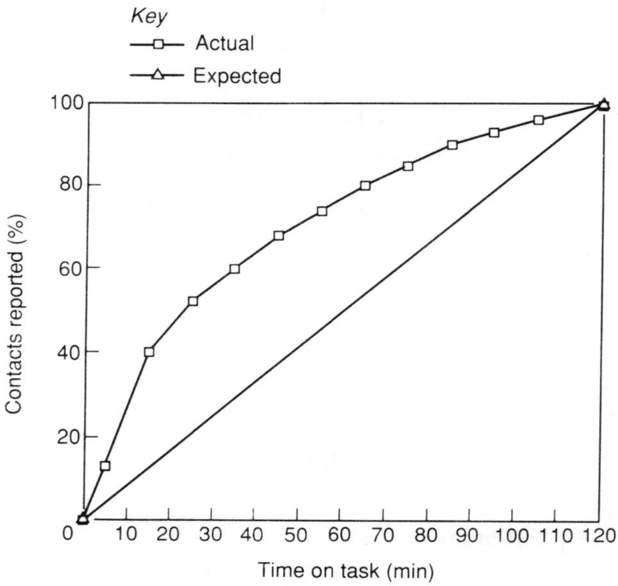

Figure 10.1 Cumulative proportion of contacts reported with time on task. (Based on Baker, 1959).

confirmed the results of the analysis of detections from real radar operations: performance under such conditions was *suboptimal* and *decreased with time on task*, especially within the first half hour of the vigil. Figure 10.2 shows a typical result from such an experiment. The operational relevance of these findings, first within military but soon also for industrial settings, was so evident that systematic research into the problems of watch-keeping or monitoring performance seemed mandatory. This, then, was the beginning of systematic experimental vigilance research.

The explanations for this phenomenon, which has been observed repeatedly in experimental research, are still unsatisfactory. Vigilance, as a hypothetical construct, is often conceived as a state of the nervous system between wakefulness and sleep leading to the performance described. The question, however, arises as to whether such a state can account for the performance and its dynamics in watch-keeping situations, which would justify the use of the term 'vigilance' for this state, or whether vigilance should be defined operationally through situational and operational conditions and requirements. It is a question to which we return later in the chapter.

Historical origins

Although Mackworth (1950) is usually credited as the originator of vigilance research, and this is certainly true for experimental vigilance research, the

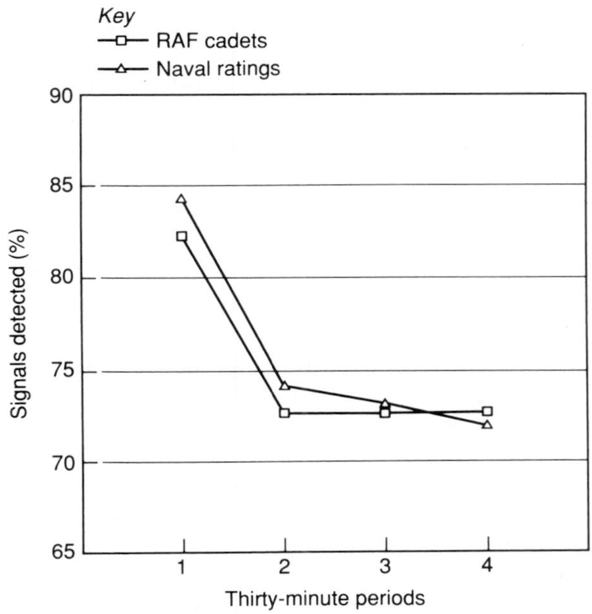

Figure 10.2 Hits as a function of time on task. (Based on results from Mackworth, 1950.)

phenomenon of suboptimal and decreasing performance at monotonous inspection tasks had been observed much earlier in industrial production (e.g. Wyatt and Langdon, 1932), and can be traced back to the research of the Industrial Fatigue Board on performance in the production and inspection of ammunition during World War I (Vernon, 1921).

Indeed, research on performance decrements with time on task under monotonous conditions, and research into monotony, fatigue and boredom, can, with certain limitations, be regarded as predecessors to vigilance research. Impaired performance with time on task and the effects of boredom derived from monotonous task and working conditions are common to both areas of study. Moreover, under certain job settings, all these effects may appear in a complex interaction.

Typical job settings

The job settings in question are, as can be seen from the origins of the problem, those which require prolonged monitoring of information displays in order to detect signals that require some action to be taken, for example in monitoring radar screens in air traffic control, or, more generally, in vehicle control, for example navigating a vessel by radar or flying an aircraft by instruments. This even applies to vehicle control without technical displays, where the only 'display' to be monitored for critical signals or events is the environment in which the vehicle is operating.

Monitoring is also a major requirement in industrial process and production control, with operators watching the process and its products for defects and critical states or preferably for signals or cues, which might indicate a future deviation from target values. This control may be by direct inspection of materials or remotely from a control room with displays and control actuators. Monitoring at some level is required in many occupational settings, for example in hospital intensive care units, where critical signals in physiological parameters of the patients have to be detected. Industrial inspection, though, perhaps provides the most obvious example of where the occurrence of faulty products has to be monitored against the background of fault-free products.

Within real-life job settings there is no clear-cut answer as to whether the conditions contain a vigilance problem. Rather, the problem seems to be one of the amount of monitoring required. Some jobs, like inspection, have a very clear vigilance component, while with others, vigilance seems to be a minor or borderline problem because neither the task nor the working conditions can be regarded as monotonous and a variety of (overt or mental) activities is required of the operator. An example would be controlling a process in an emergency situation, where nothing like a vigilance problem will be observed, although the operator is required to monitor displays for prolonged periods. Here the problem is one of overload, not one of sustaining attention under otherwise monotonous (underload) conditions.

In the future, monitoring will be a central requirement in many jobs, since increasing automation will allocate many decisions to the machine, leaving the monitoring (or in advanced systems, the monitoring of the monitoring system) to the operator (Nachreiner, 1988). This seems to be true not only in the traditional process industries, e.g. the chemical industry, but also in the manufacturing industries, where advanced technology is being applied in such areas as automobile assembly and vehicle control in advanced systems.

If this is true, then the vigilance problem will increase in importance and relevance for industrial settings, where reliable performance at high levels is requested from the operators in order to keep the whole system reliable and efficient. The problem, however, is to what extent the (experimental) vigilance research will remain relevant to these jobs. An answer to this question can only be given after a closer inspection of what the vigilance problem really is.

The vigilance problem

According to Mackworth the vigilance problem appears when operators have to detect:

- randomly or unpredictably occurring
- 'critical signals', which are easily detected under alerted conditions

- with low probability
- against a background of non-critical signals (or 'noise')
- over a prolonged period of time
- under monotonous conditions.

(For a more complete characterization of the typical vigilance task see McGrath, 1963.) Under such conditions performance is:

- suboptimal and
- decreases with time on task

in a characteristic way, where the number of signals correctly detected (hits) declines very early (within the first half hour of a vigil) and then tends to stabilize on that level for the rest of the vigil (with minor variations) (see Figure 10.2). This deterioration, which is typical for vigilance tasks, is called the *vigilance decrement*.

The vigilance problem can thus be characterized as consisting of suboptimal performance at a detection task with decreasing performance with time on task (Craig, 1984). The question, however, is whether suboptimal performance really is at the heart of the vigilance problem or whether this is only a matter of signal detectability or conspicuousness. McGrath (1963) has already raised this question: it should be simple to manipulate the overall level of performance by manipulating the detectability and physical characteristics of the critical and the non-critical signal. Since suboptimal performance is not specific to vigilance tasks, this does not seem to be a useful characteristic in the definition of the vigilance problem.

On the other hand, the variation in performance relative to the time on task, i.e. the vigilance decrement, is specific and thus central to vigilance performance. It is the time-locked dynamics of performance that has attracted the interest in the study of vigilance, and it should be kept in mind that it is a peculiar time function, not comparable with those of monotony or fatigue.

As our description of the problem suggests, vigilance can best be defined by the stimulus conditions and the performance function to which they are leading. This allows for a clear distinction from signal detection tasks, where the probability of critical signals is comparatively high, ideally approaching 0.5. Seen from the subject's point of view, this is quite a different task, leading to different time functions of performance.

In contrast to being able to specify the vigilance problem behaviourally, there are great difficulties in defining it conceptually. The question is, for example, how Mackworth's definition of vigilance as a state within the organism would help in understanding or explaining the problem. The same is true if vigilance is equated with or explained by attention, although this is a well known circumscription of the problem. It does help to distinguish problems of sustained attention (i.e. vigilance, Stroh, 1971) from those of selective attention (Jerison, 1977), although it does not explain why performance deteriorates in the manner specified.

The fact that concepts are so badly defined in this field may be a result of its practical origins. There was neither a theoretical basis nor an adequate conceptualization of its basic concepts in the beginning of vigilance research because the objective was to find solutions for practical problems, for example determining the optimal duration of a spell. It seems that much of this atheoretic approach still prevails in the field.

Another ill-defined area is the question of whether the decrement is attributable to changes in performance capacity, as would be suggested by a state interpretation; or in terms of a signal detection theory (SDT) interpretation, to changes in sensitivity, d' (Tanner and Swets, 1954); or whether motivational or strategic processes within the observer are responsible for the decrement, that is criterion (or β) shifts in terms of SDT (Craig, 1978; Craig and Davies, 1991). It may be, however, that both capacity and strategic processes are interactively involved, even though SDT tries to supply independent measures for both.

Related problems

Time-related deteriorations of performance are not specific to vigilance tasks but can also be found with fatigue, monotony or boredom. What is different, however, are the shapes of the decrement and recovery functions. Figure 10.3 gives some indication on the differences concerned.

In contrast with fatigue and monotony, the former of which takes a considerable time to manifest itself in performance and needs an adequate period of recuperation (the extent depending on the intensity and duration of the preceding workload) in order to recover rather slowly, while the latter also develops rather slowly but needs little time for recovery if the task is interrupted, vigilance performance is characterized by a quick deterioration of performance, right from the beginning, again with no time needed for recovery when the task is interrupted. The difference is thus to be found in the dynamics of the time-on-task-related performance and recovery functions, and it is again the time on task relation that distinguishes these forms of impairment from other impairing conditions that are not related to time on task, like time of day or sleep deprivation.

It should again be noted, that overload, resulting from high decision rates with equal or nearly equal probabilities of signals which are scarcely detectable, has more in common with fatigue than with vigilance. Discrimination should not be the problem. Signals should be easily detectable, at least in the beginning and under alerted conditions. The vigilance problem is not one of overload, but rather one of underload.

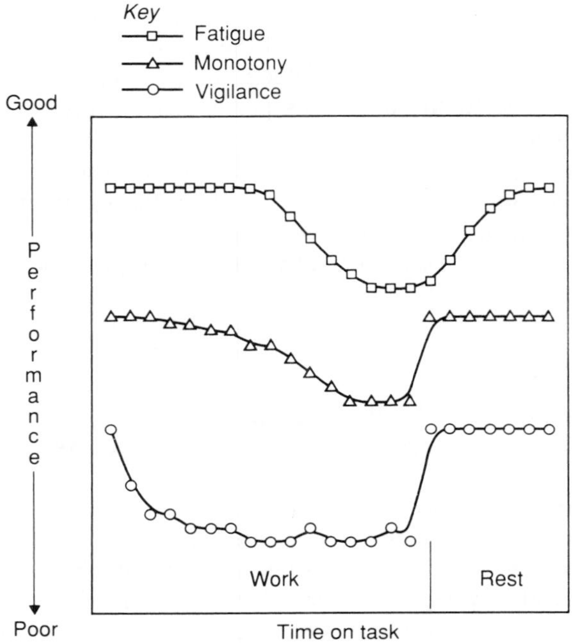

Figure 10.3 Typical performance and recovery functions for different forms of impairment.

CONDITIONS AFFECTING VIGILANCE PERFORMANCE

Task characteristics

Vigilance phenomena are clearly linked to certain kinds of task. However, these tasks still differ in a variety of characteristics which have to a great extent been considered as affecting the operator's performance and response behaviour.

SIGNAL AMBIGUITY

While Mackworth (1950) originally relates the vigilance phenomenon to 'faint' signals, 'difficult to see on the screen' (Mackworth, 1961, pp. 180, 185), further vigilance research provides evidence that suboptimal performance and the decrement also appear with clear signals, which can be easily detected under alerted conditions.

Variations in signal intensity or duration will, however, affect the overall level of performance, and hence the amount of the decrement will be affected only relatively. That is to say: with longer duration and greater intensity of the signals, the hit rate will increase and the decrement, in terms of d', will be less distinct (Baker, 1959). These effects, though, pertain mainly to signal detectability relative to the observer's perceptual sensitivity. It should be simple to manipulate the overall level of performance by manipulating the physical characteristics of the critical and the non-critical signals (McGrath, 1963), but there still remains the problem that the operator's suboptimal performance in vigilance does not only depend on low signal detectability or conspicuity, but can be due to inadequate decision processes and response strategies.

SENSORY MODALITY

Vigilance tasks mainly involve the visual and the auditory sense; other senses have seldom been investigated as they do not have great relevance for vigilance tasks in working life.

The level of performance and the extent of the vigilance decrement are similar for both visual and auditory modalities. Reported inter-task correlation in vigilance performance from recent studies (Davies and Parasuraman, 1981) proved to be relatively high when task factors are closely controlled. Even in combination with other task characteristics, like event rate, source complexity and type of discrimination, differential effects of sensory modality have not been revealed (Parasuraman and Davies, 1977; Parasuraman, 1979). This indicates that the vigilance phenomena are not of peripheral origin: rather they are due to central processes. Apart from the closer coupling of stimuli with the receptor in auditory tasks, differentiation by modality is not of great relevance, although internal (within-subjects) consistency between visual and auditory performance, especially with respect to the decrement, is low.

DISCRIMINATION REQUIREMENTS

Discrimination requirements of vigilance tasks can be distinguished according to basic performance abilities. Levine *et al.* (1973) consider *cognitive* abilities and *perceptual–sensory* abilities as the main domains relevant to monitoring and vigilance tasks. For the perceptual–sensory domain, which has been claimed to be of greater dominance in vigilance tasks, the primary abilities 'perceptual speed' and 'flexibility of closure' have been extracted. Perceptual speed refers to the ability to compare successively presented signals, involving high working memory load. Flexibility of closure refers to the ability to identify a previously defined pattern in a complex field of simultaneously presented stimuli, hence requiring only low, short term memory load. Levine *et al.* found that performance (in terms of hits) declines over time on task for both task types, but then shows an increase to the end of the task for flexibility of closure tasks, while performance in perceptual speed tasks remains low.

Parasuraman and Davies (1977) argued that a task specification with respect to discrimination requirements, in combination with high or low event rate, can be made responsible for some inconsistencies in vigilance research. A close examination of other studies as well as their own investigations (Parasuraman, 1979) suggested a differentiation of the possible sources of the vigilance decrement in terms of the discrimination requirements and event rates of the task. They postulated a decline in perceptual sensitivity (d'), when the task is of the perceptual speed type and the event rate is high, and a shift in the response criterion (β) at tasks with low event rate and/or of the flexibility of closure type.

EVENT RATE

In a vigilance task, at least two kinds of events are presented: critical signals, which ask for detection and response by the operator, and non-critical signals, which in most cases have not to be answered. With increasing event rate, defined as the sum of critical and non-critical signals, the overall detection rate will decrease (Nachreiner *et al.*, 1976). Jerison and Pickett (1964) found a detection rate of ninety per cent with five events per minute, and of only thirty per cent with thirty events per minute. Furthermore, with increasing event rate a steeper decrement can be demonstrated, due to the overload of the operator (Davies and Parasuraman, 1981). An interactive effect was found for event rate with type of task in terms of a decline in perceptual sensitivity over time on task for high event rate in perceptual speed tasks, whereas for low event rates and flexibility of closure tasks the vigilance decrement occurred in terms of a criterion shift (Parasuraman and Davies, 1977; Parasuraman, 1979; Craig and Davies, 1991).

SIGNAL PROBABILITY

Event rate may vary with or without a change in the critical signal rate, which may itself vary with or without changes in the event rate. Consequently, changes in signal probability may depend on variations in event rate or signal rate or both. By examining even rate and signal rate independently, Colquhoun (1961, 1969) found that signal probability affects the operator's response behaviour differently according to whether changes are due to variations in event rate or in signal rate.

Changes in signal probability, evoked by increasing or decreasing signal rate, have a greater impact on criterion (β) than on sensitivity (d'): the higher the signal probability, the less strict the criterion. This can be explained by the assumptions made by expectancy theory in vigilance research: according to known or experienced signal probabilities in the task, the operator establishes a subjective probability, namely specific expectancies, about the occurrence of critical signals and hence builds up and controls his response behaviour accordingly. As vigilance tasks are characterized by the irregular, and therefore unpredictable, occurrence of critical signals, recent studies are increasingly engaged in the question of within-task changes in operator's response behaviour (beyond the decrement!) due to within-task changes in signal probabilities (Vickers *et al.*, 1977; Vickers and Leary, 1983).

Personal characteristics

In addition to the characteristics of the vigilance task itself, the observer's personal characteristics have to be taken into consideration (Davies, 1985). The range of vigilance tasks span from quality control to process control: and different tasks require different abilities, knowledge and experience.

GENDER

The majority of studies about sex differences in vigilance tasks do not provide reliable differences between males and females in the performance of vigilance tasks (Davies and Parasuraman, 1981). In a study about the influence of sex as the main variable on monitoring performance Waag *et al.* (1973) found a difference between males and females in terms of the latter detecting fewer signals and producing more false alarms. But the difference was considered too small to indicate any practical relevance. However, for further investigations Waag *et al.* suggest matched groups to reduce the amount of unexplained variance in the data.

Usually the problem of gender itself is not of primary interest in vigilance investigations and occurs only sometimes as one variable in combination with others. Baker *et al.* (1984) produced evidence for an interactive effect of gender with difficulty of the task, time of day and noise; Green and Morgan (1985) reported interactive effects of gender, time of day, circadian type and task type. The problem with such kinds of higher interaction is to specify what they mean and whether they can be reliably reproduced.

AGE

Studies of vigilance performance of children have been conducted mainly to analyse the abilities of retarded children (e.g. Kirby *et al.*, 1979). They also investigate the relation between concentration, attention and motor activities in the classroom (Kupietz and Richardson, 1978; Azzarita, 1982) and attempt to find ways to predict 'school-readiness' (Simon, 1982). In general, it can be concluded that, even in children, the phenomenon of the vigilance decrement is always present. Gale and Lynn (1972) found that overall performance increases from the age of seven up to thirteen, but an interaction with gender shows that, at the ages of eight and nine years, girls' performance is superior to boys'.

Most studies considering effects of age in vigilance tasks deal with performance differences of younger and older adults. The event rate in a vigilance task has a stronger effect on the performance of older people than on that of younger; this could be attributed to the supposition that information processing in older adults is delayed. Some results show that, in general, older adults produce fewer hits and more false alarms than their younger counterparts. Furthermore, the vigilance decrement occurs earlier in the task for older than for younger adults. On the other hand, older people do adopt a stricter criterion and are less confident in their own responses (see Davies and Parasuraman 1981). These results are somewhat contradictory, which might be due to interactions with type of task, modality or other variables. Additionally, interactions of age with experience or personality, which can strengthen or even eliminate the age effect, have always to be taken into consideration.

EXPERIENCE

There is no doubt that the performance of well-trained operators differs from that of naive operators in a vigilance task. This is true for short-term practising as well as for long-term experience. A study by Bisseret (1981) reports that naive operators often discriminate better than experienced operators in terms of a higher value of d'. On the other hand, experienced operators show a laxer criterion in terms of a decreased β. As Bisseret's study concerns the jobs of air traffic controllers, the decrease in β is interpreted as an increase in caution. Experienced operators adopt a laxer criterion, when the costs for a miss are high but a false alarm is only a small nuisance. Conversely, the experienced operator is adopting a more conservative criterion when he has learned that missing a critical event does not mean a catastrophe, whereas the cost of a false alarm is high. While an increase in d' is unambiguously related to an increase in the level of performance, changes in the decision criterion can be attributed to different sources, for example to different pay-off matrices for consequences.

In conclusion, the task demands and the pay-off matrix determine the development of experience and general response strategies in vigilance tasks which will influence the response strategies of the operators. They thus provide evidence for the necessity of on-the-job training. Unfortunately, the question of whether training has more effects on knowledge and hence perceptual sensitivity or on motivation processes and hence criterion placement can still not be answered satisfactorily (Davies and Parasuraman, 1981).

PERSONALITY

The influence of the operator's personality on performance has often been investigated, mainly in terms of an introversion/extraversion distinction (Eysenck, 1957). In general, results claim that introverts perform better in prolonged and monotonous tasks than extraverts (Davies and Parasuraman, 1981). Introverts produce more hits and fewer false alarms, and show a smaller performance decrement over time on task relative to extraverts (Bakan, 1959). Extraverts, on the other hand, are less sensitive and adopt a laxer criterion; they seem to be less able to concentrate on a vigilance task than introverts. External conditions and situational factors are likely to affect the performance of extraverts, although they sometimes benefit from external stimuli, like secondary tasks (Bakan, 1959).

These results should be regarded only as indicating trends in operators' behaviour when they are divided into groups of extremely different personalities. There still remains a lack of consistency between studies and results, partly due to methodological problems, as for example in the operationalization of Eysenck's theoretical model when establishing introvert and extravert groups. Some studies separate subjects into extreme groups, sometimes with an intermediate group as a 'normal' control; others separate groups by certain, but often not identical, scores. All this, clearly, does not contribute towards consistency.

In addition, situational conditions might affect performance of the personality types differently. For example, Nachreiner and Eilers (1990) reported interactive effects of personality with time of day, indicating stronger differences over time-of-day for hits and sensitivity (d') in introverts. As a consequence, the time of testing should be taken into consideration because this might exaggerate or reduce differences between personality types. Additionally, the sensory modality and type of task seem to be of importance: while the differences in the overall performance level seem not to be affected, the decrement with extraverts increases when a task of the perceptual speed type with a high event rate is used.

Situational characteristics

Investigations of the influence of situational characteristics on vigilance performance revealed a variety of results, some of them contradictory.

NOISE

The effects of noise on vigilance performance are usually described on the basis of arousal theory by an inverted-U function, where the absence of noise as well as loud noise mean poorer performance, while moderate noise improves performance. Noise, though, is represented by many sounds including spoken language, music, white noise or intermittent noise, thus different parameters of noise, for example noise quality, sound pressure level and frequency distribution, have to be taken into account when describing the effects of noise on vigilance performance.

Poulton (1976, 1977) postulated that noise as a stressor increases arousal and, hence, the state of vigilance in man, which results in a beneficial effect on performance. He explained the undeniable detrimental effects of noise on vigilance performance by the influence of certain demands of the task itself: noise may mask auditory feedback which may be necessary in some tasks, or it may affect inner speech, which might have to assist short-term memory. Although regarded as a promising conception, it still raised counter-arguments (*cf.* Broadbent, 1976, 1978). Lysaght (1982) formulated a taxonomic approach to explain the effects of continuous noise on performance, where eight conditions were defined by two noise qualities (white versus varied), two noise levels (high versus low), and the processing demand of the task (high versus low). Results from various studies (see Hancock, 1984), examined by this approach, showed that varied noise at a low level has a beneficial effect on performance in simple tasks, while performance declined with high level white noise in complex tasks. No effect could be demonstrated in simple tasks with white noise, and only few investigations have been carried out for the remaining conditions. On the basis of evidence for interactive effects of noise with task difficulty, Smith in his *strategy choice theory* postulated that for tasks, which 'can be performed in several different ways, noise may lead to the adoption of certain strategies in preference to others' (1983, p. 799). Miles *et al.* (1984) examined the joint effects of noise and pre-test training, and found that noise impaired the development of the coping strategies which are important in complex tasks with high memory-load.

Studies of intermittent noise show that noise intensity and the on–off ratio are the main factors affecting performance, but they interact with the complexity of the task and the possible feedback-effect that intermittent noise may provide (Hancock, 1984). Poulton (1977) described intermittent noise, in contrast to continuous noise, as possibly distracting vigilance performance, but the results of only relatively few investigations on the effects of intermittent noise on vigilance performance are ambiguous. Carter and Beh (1989) reported a lower level of hits with intermittent noise, in contrast to a quiet condition, but found no decrement in either condition. On the other hand, reaction latencies decline over time on task in intermittent noise, but not in quiet conditions. This leads to the assumption of a speed–accuracy trade-off in vigilance performance when intermittent noise is present.

Some inconsistencies in the results can be explained by variations in methodology, such as the kind of noise presented or choice of performance measures. The same kind of noise may also have different effects on the mood of the operators, varying from enjoyment to annoyance, and this may affect performance in different ways.

CLIMATIC CONDITIONS

As climate is a combination of, amongst other things, air temperature, airflow, atmospheric humidity and radiant temperature, all these parameters have to be taken into consideration. Additionally, clothing and physical activity are relevant to the influence of climatic conditions on body temperature (Smith and Ottmann, 1987). The studies on the effects of different climatic conditions on performance revealed contradictory results: from improvement via no change to impairment (Hancock, 1984).

It is still controversial whether alterations in the climatic conditions of the environment can alter performance or whether effects only occur when changes in body temperature can be observed. Mackworth (1950) reported declining detection rates with rising environmental heat, while Wilkinson *et al.* (1964) found increasing detection rates when body temperature was raised. Differences in the methods of increasing subjects' body temperature and in the maximum temperature have caused some of these inconsistencies.

Colquhoun and Goldman (1972) observed that false alarm rates had not been reported in the earlier studies, so it was not clear whether the changes in hit rates were due to sensitivity changes or to criterion shifts. The results of their study showed no significant differences between heat conditions for hit rate and the decrement in hits, but a significant increase in the false alarm rate when body temperature was increased. So, according to Colquhoun and Goldman, effects on performance can be explained by a criterion shift from strict to risky response behaviour. Furthermore, they reported effects on performance only when body temperature had changed, and that these changes had to be considerable with highly trained subjects.

Extreme conditions of cold and heat have impaired vigilance performance (Davies and Parasuraman, 1981). This has been explained by the concept of arousal: with rising temperature, arousal will increase up to an optimal level and thereafter decrease. This, consequently, gives the well-known inverted-U relation between arousal and performance (Poulton, 1977).

However, results of studies dealing with the effects of climate show some interaction with other environmental and individual conditions, like type of task (Wilkinson *et al.*, 1964), noise or sleep deprivation (Smith and Ottmann, 1987), and observer's experience (Mackworth, 1950). This leads to the assumption that the effects of climatic conditions cannot simply be explained by the concept of arousal but rather by a multi-dimensional concept with tonic and phasic components (Pribram and McGuinness, 1975), where the tonic components refer to the general readiness to react, and the phasic components refer to reactions to task-specific stimuli. This model might be more appropriate for explaining performance in vigilance tasks where climatic conditions are extreme or changing, especially when it is taken into consideration that the recent research in vigilance is dealing with more differentiated methods of analysis.

TIME OF DAY

Time of day effects on performance are well-established but their direction seems to depend on the attention requirements and type of discrimination of the task. For simple tasks, without demands on working memory, performance increases over the waking day and generally covaries with body temperature fluctuations over a twenty-four hour period, reflecting changes in the diurnal rhythm of the general state of arousal (Davies and Parasuraman, 1981).

A decline in performance over the waking day can be observed for tasks with high demands on working memory, especially on short-term memory (Folkard and Monk, 1985). These results conform with the suggestion for a classification of vigilance tasks according to discrimination requirements in terms of perceptual speed and flexibility of closure by Parasuraman and Davies (1977; Parasuraman, 1979). These authors have consequently postulated different time of day effects for hit rate and perceptual sensitivity in these two task types. Indeed, in a study by Davies *et al.* (1984) the hypothesized results have been observed: the perceptual speed task, requiring successive discrimination with high load on short-term memory, showed a decline over the day, whereas the flexibility of closure task showed an increase in hits and perceptual sensitivity from morning to afternoon. However, a close replication of this study by Baer *et al.* (1986) failed to confirm these results, nor did subsequent studies by Eilers *et al.* (1988) and Eilers and Nachreiner (1990a), who analysed performance at both types of task around the clock provide any support for this hypothesis. Analysis of results from five recent studies, all using auditory perceptual speed tasks, showed that hits *as well as* false alarms increased from morning to evening (Craig *et al.*, 1981). Although the results did not reach significance in all cases, they indicate rather a criterion change from risky to lax instead of a change in perceptual sensitivity. Convincing evidence for the classification model of Parasuraman is, therefore, still lacking (Craig *et al.*, 1987).

The explanation of the observer's response behaviour should not be treated only in terms of the simple differentiation by the parameters' sensitivity and decision criterion. This argument is supported by the evidence of the speed–accuracy trade-off observed over the course of the day (Colquhoun, 1982). The results obtained by Craig and Condon (1985) revealed no change of the decision criterion (β) from morning to evening, but showed a speed–accuracy trade-off in terms of an increase in response latency and confidence and a decline in d'. The general tendency for subjects to react faster but less accurately as the day progresses has also been reported by Monk and Leng (1982).

An interaction between time of day and time on task has been observed by Eilers *et al.* (1988) and Eilers and Nachreiner (1990a). Subjects usually perform better at the beginning of night sessions than at the beginning of day sessions. However, night-time performance deteriorates rapidly during the night and reaches a very low level at the end of the task (Hänecke and Nachreiner, 1990); hence this decrement is more pronounced at night than in the day. It is interesting to note that time of day effects in vigilance performance are strongest in the later parts of the vigil. The absence of time-of-day-related differences in the first part of the vigil, however, might represent a time of day effect in compensation of expected impairments.

The increasing relevance of analysing and explaining changes in the operator's response behaviour over time of day in monitoring and supervisory tasks, which are often carried out in shift work under field conditions, has led to a trend to focus more on the relevance of changes in the observer's decision criterion and response strategy (Hänecke and Nachreiner, 1990; Queinnec and Terssac, 1987). Hänecke and Nachreiner (1991) reported that phases of attentiveness, in terms of two subsequent hits, do not differ from day to night, whereas phases of inattentiveness, in terms of a low probability of hits following a miss, do occur more frequently at night (see Figure 10.4). On the other hand, differences between day and night for the sequence false alarm – subsequent hit can be observed. This proves that not merely a (rather trivial) activity/inactivity difference is at stake, but also suggests differences

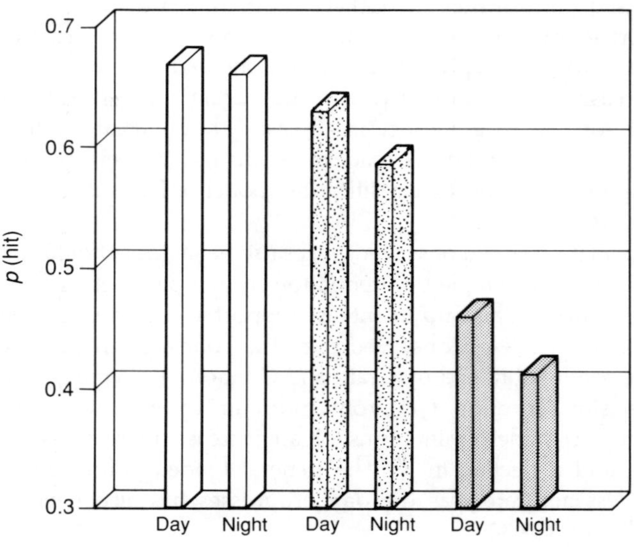

Figure 10.4 Probabilities of hits following different events at day and night-time. Preceeding event; ▭, hit; ▭, false alarm; ▭, miss. (From Hänecke and Nachreiner, 1991.)

in complex information processing and decision making at different times of the day.

These fine-grained and event-related analyses of vigilance data have revealed that circadian variations in vigilance performance are less affected by variations in attention *per se*, but rather by variations in the active control of attention by the operator.

Drugs

A severe problem in all jobs is the use and abuse of drugs. Drinking alcohol on the job is normally prohibited but nevertheless happens. Smoking and drinking coffee are common during working hours and are not usually prohibited. In vigilance, however, even small doses of alcohol and the intake of nicotine and caffeine might affect the operator's behaviour, not only in terms of performance decrements but also in terms of criterion alterations.

ALCOHOL

Effects of small doses of alcohol on vigilance performance have not been reliably demonstrated (Davies and Parasuraman, 1981). Some investigators report an increase in omission errors, which might be due to lapses of attention, while others find no effect. Methodological differences and deficiencies might be one of the causes for these inconclusive results. Different doses of alcohol and the respective actual temporal position in the absorption–elimination process (which changes with time on task) have to be taken into account. Grzech-Sukalo *et al.* (1988), controlling for these conditions, reported differential, time-dependent effects: a performance decrement in terms of d' together with an increase in the decision criterion in terms of β could be demonstrated early in the absorption–elimination process, and beginning at levels as low as 0.015 per cent blood alcohol content with some subjects. The higher the dose, the stronger the performance decrement early in the absorption– elimination process. Late in the absorption–elimination-process, however, no sensitivity decrement was registered for small and higher doses of alcohol, but the decision criterion was found to be rather lax. This might be interpreted as a compensation effect, but reducing the criterion must be regarded as precarious and thus unacceptable in some job settings.

Horne and Gibbons (1991) reported an interactive effect of time of day and the intake of alcohol where, in general, with a higher dose of alcohol the increase of reaction time as well as the decrease in hits was more marked at lunch-time as compared with the evening. Some subjects in this study, however, showed a speed–accuracy trade-off.

NICOTINE

Results on the effects of smoking on vigilance performance are again contradictory, showing detrimental, beneficial and null effects. In a review of all published studies on the effects of smoking on vigilance performance, Morris and Gale (1988) claim that poor methodology, poor theory and the absence of specific hypotheses in most studies are largely responsible for these inconsistencies.

Smokers, themselves, claim that smoking during a vigilance task maintains their attention, and indeed it appears that active smokers show less of a decrement when they are allowed to smoke during a vigilance task than when they are not allowed to. As smoking implies an additional motor activity, however, the vigilance situation itself is different for smokers and non-smokers. It cannot simply be concluded, then, that the nicotine itself is stimulating (Davies and Parasuraman, 1981) and might be used as a regulative mechanism in situations with a subjectively perceived performance decrement. The controls for other confounding variables seem to be neglected, for example consideration of the effects of deprivation of smoking, individual history in smoking, or smoking habits. Results on differences between smoking and non-smoking in vigilance performance are vague because only few studies introduce non-smokers as control group (Morris and Gale, 1988).

Passive smoking during a vigilance task detrimentally affected performance in terms of sensitivity and accuracy of non-smokers as well as smokers (Beh, 1989), but the effect appeared with non-smokers earlier and to a greater extent. Additionally, decision-time decreased for non-smokers while the decision criterion in terms of β was not affected. Reported feelings like anger and annoyance, which were greater in non-smokers than in smokers, might have influenced the operators' behaviour.

CAFFEINE

The effect of caffeine seems only to have been investigated to a limited extent (Davies and Parasuraman, 1981). It has been reported that caffeine reduces the vigilance decrement, but the results are combined with personality factors in terms of introversion and extraversion. Whereas introverts showed no decrement in either a non-caffeine or a caffeine condition, the provision of caffeine to extraverts prevented the decrement in comparison with the non-caffeine condition.

THEORETICAL AND METHODOLOGICAL PROBLEMS

Analysis of vigilance performance

One of the inherent general problems in the analysis of vigilance performance is the low probability of critical signals which leads to low response frequencies.

Based on such low response frequencies the reliability of the performance assessment itself must be rather low. To give an extreme example: hitting, just by chance, one signal out of two in a period of time yields a hit rate of $p = 0.5$; missing or hitting both signals leads to a hit rate of $p = 0$ or 1 respectively. But are these detection rates really different? The question is how reliable are such estimates? That is, how much is detection and performance measurement a function of chance, and how reliable are changes in performance with time on task based on such low probability events?

This problem has led some researchers to increase the number of critical signals to a level sufficient for purposes of analysis. This, however, changes the nature of the problem because the vigilance task is defined as one with a *low* probability of signals. Increasing the number of critical signals will result in problems of fatigue (overload) or monotony (underload). So this strategy does not solve the problem. Increasing the number of subjects, on the other hand, in order to get a more reliable performance estimate (for individual signals or periods of time) means that, with regard to the decrement function, the averaging takes place over different individual decrement functions and thus might not be a valid procedure. Since there is no possibility of hitting more than 100 per cent of the critical signals, performance increments (in general) cannot be observed, especially if the critical signal can be easily detected under alerted conditions (which is typical for real vigilance tasks), leading to high start levels for most subjects with the possibility of keeping performance at this level over time on task or to decline. There is, indeed, as can be shown by analyses of individual performance functions, a remarkable number of subjects who show no decrement over time on task, and there are also subjects who start at lower levels and improve their performance. The averaging of these different performance functions (with an naturally higher proportion of decreasing than increasing ones) should lead to the commonly reported decrement function; but the question remains as to what it really implies.

Another question is whether hits and correct rejections, or, on the other hand, false alarms and misses, do represent the same, or at least comparable, kinds of correct or erroneous decisions. It can be shown that the number and kinds of errors depend partly on the utility of the responses to the subject, thus representing not only attentiveness or performance *capacity* but also a *motivational* problem of response selection, or, in terms of signal detection analysis, criterion placement. The question can further be illustrated by looking at the meaning of correct rejections. Is such a response a correct answer because the subject, whether sure or according to the most suitable response under the given pay-off matrix, has decided that there was no critical signal present, or does it merely represent inattentiveness without any response, i.e. the subject did not make a decision at all, which is just the opposite of a correct response? Asking the subject to respond to each (critical and non-critical) signal does not solve the problem. Correct rejections and misses may represent both wrong decisions under high attentive conditions and inattentiveness with regard to the performance required. This questions both the validity of behavioural indicators (for example, for internal states) and the justification to treat different reactions under the same category, for example error or correct response, as in signal detection theory (SDT). Hänecke and Nachreiner (1990, 1991) have shown that this might not be justified because the underlying psychological processes leading to those outcomes are quite different. This, of course, apart from the statistical assumptions which can rarely be met under real vigilance conditions, would limit the applicability or utility of SDT-approaches in the analysis of vigilance performance and the associated interpretation of vigilance decrements as sensitivity or criterion shifts (Long and Waag, 1981).

Besides questions of what performance measures really stand for, another critical question is that of defining the time interval for integrating responses. Using half-hour intervals, as in the original experiments by Mackworth and many subsequent studies, might result in loosing track of the true dynamics of the vigilance decrement. Reducing the time interval in order to have more points to establish the decrement function more precisely inevitably leads to lower signal and response frequencies within such intervals, with the consequences described above. Lengthening the intervals in order to bring about more responses for a reliable performance assessment assumes rather stable performance within these intervals, an assumption that might not be warranted, as Mackworth's (1950) results already demonstrate. His analysis of signal-related detection probabilities shows that they vary considerably within intervals, especially within the first half-hour of the vigil (see also comparable results by Jerison, 1959). Using longer intervals thus might conceal systematic performance variations of shorter duration (Teichner, 1974) or serial dependencies.

Evidence that such serial dependencies exist has been provided by Peper *et al.* (1987) and Hänecke and Nachreiner (1990) using different methods of fine-grained analyses of performance. Besides the advantage of having a finer resolution of the decrement function (although with less reliable estimates of single points, which can be compensated, however, by smoothing adjacent points) such analyses can also provide some insight into phasic variations, ultradian rhythms or even strategic behaviour of active operators. The problem with such kinds of analysis, however, is that an enormous amount of data is required from each subject or for each experimental condition, in order to come to acceptable levels of reliability.

It has already been suggested that it is debatable whether the assumptions made in SDT analyses can be met with real vigilance tasks. Indeed, it seems a dubious policy to assume equality of variances for the probabilities of hits and false alarms when the probabilities of critical and non-critical signals are usually very different. Changing these probabilities in the direction of equal probabilities changes the characteristics from those of a vigilance task to those of an SDT task. Non-parametric parameters might look like a solution, but for β no satisfactory substitute has been found (McNicol, 1972; Craig, 1979). Furthermore, the different psychological backgrounds which may lead to hits and correct rejections and to false alarms and misses would again argue against treating them as of equal importance, as is done in the calculation of SDT parameters (Hänecke, in preparation). Their integration into d' and β and their graphical representation in a two-dimensional space as in receiver operating characteristics (ROC) analyses, suggests a questionable independence of hits and false alarms and their respective complements. This may be less suitable or even misleading for analysing what is really happening within the operator. It might, therefore, be more promising not to integrate the reactions into uni-dimensional parameters but rather to treat them separately.

Theoretical models

Although experimental vigilance research has a history of more than forty years, its theoretical foundations are rather weak. Many different theoretical approaches, for example inhibition theory, expectancy theory and activation theory, have been employed to account for the decline in performance with time on task and, although with less emphasis, the general suboptimal level of performance. None of these approaches, however, is able to account for *all* the results produced. Perhaps it would be rather unrealistic to expect to find a conclusive theory for a domain where it is not at all clear what has to be explained. It would thus be unrealistic to discuss all these approaches in detail, and introductions to these theories can already be found in Davies and Parasuraman (1981) and Craig (1985a).

Two main groups of theories can be identified: those concerned mainly with physiological processes like activation or arousal, and those that deal mainly with cognitive issues like expectancies or the filtering of incoming information. Whereas physiologically-oriented approaches, including inhibition theory, see the operator as a passive human being whose activation is controlled by external stimulus conditions, cognitive approaches put more emphasis on the active coping with the external situation by the operator.

Theories which consider vigilance as primarily depending on the degree of arousal or activation have difficulty explaining that although there is some association between performance and arousal (usually indicated by psychophysiological parameters), this association is by no means perfect. This is especially true with regard to phasic variations in performance which can be shown to be fairly independent of variations in arousal. It seems safe to assume that a certain level of arousal is necessary for acceptable task performance and that the typical experimental vigilance conditions will usually lead to deactivation, resulting in suboptimal performance. However, where more fine-grained analyses of the performance function over time on task are concerned, arousal models have little to offer to account for the observable variations in performance (Eilers and Nachreiner, 1990b; Eilers, in preparation).

Cognitive approaches to vigilance (e.g. Craig, 1988) place more emphasis upon the active nature of the observer in such tasks, by matching his responses to his subjective probabilities, by controlling his attempts to cope with the tasks demands, as he perceives them, or by changing his coping, decision and/or performance strategies (Craig, 1988; Hänecke in preparation). Such approaches have fewer problems explaining phasic fluctuations in performance. However, the problem of explaining these assumed changes in the operators' coping behaviour remains. It does not seem very promising to replace one overt performance description by another, less overt one. More specific experimental and analytical work is needed in order to show what is taking place in the operator, including the loss of activation and arousal.

Problems of external validity: laboratory versus real-life performance

Although vigilance research has an applied origin and a rather long tradition the question of whether vigilance problems occur in real life remains unanswered (Adams, 1987). The vigilance decrement in particular has been questioned and suspected to be an experimental artifact. Some authors (e.g. Kibler, 1965; Smith and Luccacini, 1969; Belt, 1971; Nachreiner, 1977) have seriously doubted that the typical vigilance decrement has ever been observed under real-life monitoring conditions. There is no doubt that performance is suboptimal, i.e. less than 100 per cent hits and more than 0 per cent false alarms. But this is, at least in part, a matter of signal characteristics or detectability. There is also no doubt that performance decrements with time on task do occur under field conditions (Craig, 1985b). But the question is whether they have the form typically found in vigilance experiments, i.e. a sharp drop right from the beginning and then levelling off, or whether performance functions over time are encountered which could be accounted for by concepts like overload, or fatigue or monotony.

There are some good reasons for being sceptical. Laboratory conditions and field conditions have little in common (Kibler, 1965; Nachreiner, 1977; Davies and Parasuraman, 1981). For example, differences can be demonstrated with regard to signal characteristics (for example, conspicuity, frequency or probability), task conditions (for example, uninterrupted time on task, task complexity, randomness versus serial dependency of critical events, which allows for strategy formation), environmental conditions (constant versus natural fluctuations), and motivational conditions (temporary versus occupational task orientation, goals associated with task performance). A very important difference between laboratory and field conditions is the outcome for the operator of successful or unsuccessful performance (in the laboratory – minimal monetary reward; in field conditions – from significant monetary rewards to potentially fatal events). If behaviour is controlled by the perception and interpretation of situational demands and the expected or perceived outcomes, these differences should be (and indeed have been) shown to be important in vigilance performance, both with regard to the general level and the dynamics or time function of performance (Smith and Luccacini, 1969; Belt, 1971; Nachreiner, 1977).

Declining performance at monitoring tasks under field conditions should be checked for decreasing probability of critical events with progressing time on task (possibly due to efficient prior performance), which as a reliable result of experimental investigations negatively influences detection probability. This has to be considered a possible explanation if easily detectable signals are removed first, leaving progressively fewer but progressively more difficult signals to be detected.

Another point is the distinction of two kinds of decrement (under laboratory conditions) made by Craig and Davies (1991). Independent of the validity of the results of the taxonomic analyses by Parasuraman and Davies (1977), on which this distinction between criterion and sensitivity shifts is based, and independent of whether such pure (either/or) kinds of decrement occur, this distinction may be interpreted as representing different kinds of workload leading to different kinds of effect. Whereas under high workload conditions (high event rates combined with memory requirements due to successive discrimination requirements) sensitivity shifts are said to be observed, low workload conditions (low event rates, giving opportunities for micro-breaks, and simultaneous discrimination requirements) are held to lead to criterion shifts. Thus the high workload condition may as well represent an overload condition, which can be managed only with additional effort, but only for a short period of time. The sensitivity decrement could thus be regarded too as resulting from an over-activation in the beginning of the vigil (Teichner, 1974). It is interesting to note that under high workload conditions imposed by signal ambiguity and irregular inter-signal intervals, sensitivity shifts can also be observed with low event rates at simultaneous discrimination tasks (Baer *et al.*, 1986; Eilers *et al.*, 1988; Eilers and Nachreiner, 1990a).

PRACTICAL IMPLICATIONS AND FUTURE PERSPECTIVES

The control of vigilance performance

Even if a direct generalization of experimental results to problems of monitoring or inspection performance under field conditions is questionable, some implications are relevant. In the first place, difficult tasks should be avoided. Conditions that are known to lead to performance decrements with time on task, at least in the laboratory and independent of the shape of that decrement function, should also be avoided under field conditions, especially if the risk associated with missing a signal or producing a false alarm is high. High event densities with low signal probabilities, high signal ambiguity, absence of reference standards, lack of feedback, prolonged time on task (especially at unfavourable working hours), monotonous stimulus conditions from both the task and the work environment, will all enhance problems of suboptimal and declining performance. Adequate task and equipment design, based on sound ergonomic principles, should be employed to avoid the risks associated with these conditions. If such conditions cannot be avoided, an adequate organization of task performance, such as design of work–rest cycles or provisions for job rotation, must be employed.

Future perspectives

One of the most urgent problems for future vigilance research is to determine whether, and if so where, when, and how vigilance problems occur under real-life conditions (Adams, 1987; Mackie, 1987). This is important for two reasons: in the first place, counter-measures might be suggested, based on existing evidence; and secondly, such results might guide the research paradigm in directions more relevant to practical applications (Wiener, 1987). Vigilance clearly has practical origins, but this orientation sometimes seems to have been lost in the interest of specific but, at least for practical purposes and the general problem, irrelevant subtleties.

What needs to be done is to simulate more precisely and with greater validity the *relevant* conditions in the laboratory, based on the above-mentioned analyses of present and probable future field conditions, instead of concentrating on conditions that should be avoided in the first place. Analyses of operator behaviour and performance under such conditions from a more complex, behavioural and cognitive point of view should help us to understand the real problems associated with monitoring, inspection, process or vehicle control, and to develop and suggest solutions for coping with them. Attention or vigilance would seem to play a major part in these considerations, but most probably the active control of attention by an active operator will be of even greater importance (Craig, 1988; Hänecke and Nachreiner, 1991; Hänecke, in preparation).

REFERENCES

Adams, J.A. (1987) Criticisms of vigilance research: a discussion. *Human Factors* **29**: 737–40.

Azzarita, F. (1982) The development of attention in the school-age children. *Acta Medica Auxologica* **14**: 199–205.

Baer, K., Eilers, K., Peper, J. and Nachreiner, F. (1986) Time of day effects in signal detection. In *Night and Shift Work: Long Term Effects and Their Prevention*, edited by M. Haider, M. Koller and R. Cervinka. Frankfurt: Lang, pp. 387–94.

Bakan, P. (1959) Extroversion–introversion and improvement in an auditory vigilance task. *British Journal of Psychology* **54**: 115–9.

Baker, C.H. (1959) Towards a theory of vigilance. *Canadian Journal of Psychology* **13**: 35–42.

Baker, M.A., Holding, D.H. and Loeb, M. (1984) Noise, sex and time of day effects in a mathematics task. *Ergonomics* **27**: 67–80.

Beh, H.C. (1989) The effect of passive smoking on vigilance performance. *Ergonomics* **32** 1227–36.

Belt, J.A. (1971) The applicability of vigilance laboratory research to a simulated industrial inspection task. PhD thesis, Texas Technical University.

Bisseret, A. (1981) Application of signal detection theory to decision making in supervisory control: the effect of the operator's experience. *Ergonomics* **24**: 81–94.

Broadbent, D.E. (1976) Noise and the details of experiments: a reply to Poulton. *Applied Ergonomics* **7**: 231–5.

Broadbent, D.E. (1978) The current state of noise research: reply to Poulton. *Psychological Bulletin* **85**: 1052–67.

Carter, N.L. and Beh, H.C. (1989) The effect of intermittent noise on cardiovascular functioning during vigilance task performance. *Psychophysiology* **26**: 548–59.

Colquhoun, W.P. (1961) The effect of unwanted signals on performance in a vigilance task. *Ergonomics* **4**: 41–52.

Colquhoun, W.P. (1969) Effects of raised ambient temperature and event rate on vigilance performance. *Aerospace Medicine* **40**: 413–7.

Colquhoun, W.P. (1982) Biological rhythms and performance. In *Biological Rhythms, Sleep, and Performance*, edited by W.B. Webb. Chichester: Wiley, pp. 59–86.

Colquhoun, W.P. and Goldman, R.F. (1972) Vigilance under induced hyperthermia. *Ergonomics* **15**: 621–32.

Craig, A. (1978) Is the vigilance decrement simply a response adjustment towards probability matching? *Human Factors* **20**: 441–6.

Craig, A. (1979) Nonparametric measures of sensory efficiency for sustained monitoring tasks. *Human Factors* **21**: 69–78.

Craig, A. (1984) Human engineering: the control of vigilance. In *Sustained Attention in Human Performance*, edited by J.S. Warm. New York: Wiley, pp. 247–91.

Craig, A. (1985a) Vigilance: theories and laboratory studies. In *Hours of Work: Temporal Factors in Work-Scheduling*, edited by S. Folkard and T.H. Monk. Chichester: Wiley, pp. 107–21.

Craig, A. (1985b) Field studies of human inspection: the application of vigilance research. In *Hours of Work: Temporal Factors in Work-Scheduling*, edited by S. Folkard and T.H. Monk. Chichester: Wiley, pp. 133–46.

Craig, A. (1988) Self-control over performance in situations that demand vigilance. In *Vigilance: Methods, Models, and Regulation*, edited by J.P. Leonard. Frankfurt: Lang, pp. 237–46.

Craig, A. and Condon, R. (1985) Speed–accuracy trade-off and time of day. *Acta Psychologica* **58**: 115–22.

Craig, A. and Davies, D.R. (1991) Vigilance: sustained visual monitoring and attention. In *Vision and Visual Dysfunction*, Vol. 15, *The Man–Machine Interface*, edited by J.A. Roufs. Basingstoke: Macmillan, pp. 83–98.

Craig, A., Wilkinson, R.T. and Colquhoun, W.P. (1981) Diurnal variation in vigilance efficiency. *Ergonomics* **24**: 641–51.

Craig, A., Davies, D.R. and Matthews, G. (1987) Diurnal variation, task characteristics, and vigilance performance. *Human Factors* **29**: 675–84.

Davies, D.R. (1985) Individual and group differences in sustained attention. In *Hours of Work: Temporal Factors in Work-Scheduling*, edited by S. Folkard and T.H. Monk. Chichester: Wiley, pp. 123–32.

Davies, D.R and Parasuraman, R. (1981) *The Psychology of Vigilance*. New York and London: Academic Press.

Davies, D.R., Parasuraman, R. and Toh, K.-Y. (1984) Time of day, memory load, and vigilance performance. In *Trends in Ergonomics. Human Factors I*, edited by A. Mital. Amsterdam: Elsevier/North-Holland, pp. 9–14.

Eilers, K. (in preparation) Reliabilität und Validität von Herzfrequenzvariabilitätsmaßen als Indikatoren psychischer Beanspruchung bei Daueraufmerksamkeitsbelastungen. Thesis, University of Oldenburg.

Eilers, K. and Nachreiner, F. (1990a) Time of day effects in vigilance performance at simultaneous and successive discrimination tasks. In *Shift-work: Health, Sleep and Performance*, edited by G. Costa, G. Cesana, K. Kogi and A. Wedderburn. Frankfurt: Lang, pp. 467–72.

Eilers, K. and Nachreiner, F. (1990b) Zur Reliabilität und Validität von Herzfrequenzvariabilitätsmaßen als Indikatoren psychischer Beanspruchung bei Daueraufmerksamkeitsbelastungen. In *Jahresdokumentation 1990 der Gesellschaft für Arbeitswissenschaft e.V., Bericht zum 36. Arbeitswissenschaftlichen Kongreß am 14.-16-3-1990 an der ETH Zürich*, edited by Gesellschaft für Arbeitswissenschaft. Cologne: Schmidt, pp. 36–7.

Eilers, K., Hänecke, K., Peper, J. and Nachreiner, F. (1988) Time of day effects in vigilance performance. In *Vigilance: Methods, Models, and Regulation*, edited by J.P. Leonard. Frankfurt: Lang, pp. 181–90.

Eysenck, H.J. (1957) *The Dynamics of Anxiety and Hysteria*. New York: Preager.

Folkard, S. and Monk, T.M. (1985) Circadian performance rhythms. In *Hours of Work. Temporal Factors in Work-Scheduling*, edited by S. Folkard and T.M. Monk. Chichester: Wiley, pp. 37–52.

Gale, A. and Lynn, R. (1972) A developmental study of attention. *British Journal of Educational Psychology* **42**: 260–6.

Green, G.K. and Morgan, B.B., Jr (1985) Task performances as functions of level of processing, morningness–eveningness, time of day, and gender. In *Trends in Ergonomics. Human Factors II*, edited by R.E Eberts and C.G. Eberts. Amsterdam: Elsevier/North-Holland, pp. 139–45.

Grzech-Sukalo, H., Hedden, I. and Nachreiner, F. (1988) Differentielle Effekte geringer Alkoholmengen auf Signalentdeckungsleistungen zu zwei Zeitpunkten im Eliminationsprozeß. *AtemAlkohol* **4**: 7–33.

Hänecke, K. (in preparation) Analyse des Antwortverhaltens bei Vigilanzaufgaben. Thesis, University of Oldenburg.

Hänecke, K. and Nachreiner, F. (1990) Strategy changes in monitoring behaviour at different times of the day. In *Shift-work: Health, Sleep and Performance*, edited by G. Costa, G. Cesana, K. Kogi and A. Wedderburn. Frankfurt: Lang, pp. 501–6.

Hänecke, K. and Nachreiner, F. (1991) Time of day effects in attentiveness and inattentiveness in vigilance performance. Poster at the Tenth International Symposium on Night and Shift Work, Sheffield.

Hancock, P.A. (1984) Environmental stressors. In *Sustained Attention in Human Performance*, edited by J.S. Warm. Chichester: Wiley, pp. 103–42.

Horne, J.A. and Gibbons, H. (1991) Effects on vigilance performance and sleepiness of alcohol given in the early afternoon ('post lunch') vs. early evening. *Ergonomics* **34**: 67–77.

Jerison, H.J. (1959) *Experiments on Vigilance. V: The Empirical Model for Human Vigilance*. Technical Report No. 58–526, US Air Force, Wright Air Development Center, Ohio.

Jerison, H.J. (1977) Vigilance: biology, psychology, theory, and practice. In *Vigilance: Theory, Operational Performance, and Physiological Correlates*, edited by R.R. Mackie. New York: Plenum, pp. 27–40.

Jerison, H.J. and Pickett, R.M. (1964) Vigilance: the importance of the elicited observing rate. *Science, New York* **143**: 970–1.

Kibler, A.W. (1965) The relevance of vigilance research to aerospace monitoring tasks. *Human Factors* **7**: 93–9.

Kirby, N.H., Nettelbeck, T. and Thomas, P. (1979) Vigilance performance of mildly mentally retarded children. *American Journal of Mental Deficiency* **84**: 184–7.

Kupietz, S.S. and Richardson, E. (1978) Children's vigilance performance in the classroom. *Journal of Child Psychology and Psychiatry* **19**: 145–54.

Levine, J.M., Romashko, T. and Fleishman, E.A. (1973) Evaluation of an abilities classification system for integrating and generalizing human performance research findings: an application to vigilance tasks. *Journal of Applied Psychology* **58**: 149–57.

Long, G.M. and Waag, W.L. (1981) Limitations on the practical applicability of d' and β measures. *Human Factors* **23**: 285–90.

Lysaght, R.J. (1982) The effects of noise on sustained attention and behavioral persistence. PhD thesis, University of Cincinnati.

Mackie, R.R. (1987) Vigilance research: Are we ready for countermeasures? *Human Factors* **29** 707–23.

Mackworth, N.H. (1948) The breakdown of vigilance during prolonged visual search. *Quarterly Journal of Experimental Psychology* **1**: 6–21.

Mackworth, N.H. (1950/1961) Researches of the measurement of human performance. *Medical Research Council Special Report No. 268.* London: HMSO. (Reprinted in Sinaiko, H.W. (ed.) (1961) *Selected Papers on Human Factors in the Design and Use of Control Systems.* New York: Dover, pp. 174–331.)

Mackworth, N.H. (1957) Some factors affecting vigilance. *Advancement of Science* **53**: 389–93.

McGrath, J.J. (1963) Some problems of definition and criteria in the study of vigilance performance. In *Vigilance: A Symposium,* edited by D.N. Buckner, and J.J. McGrath. New York: McGraw-Hill, pp. 227–37.

McNicol, D. (1972) *A Primer of Signal Detection Theory*. London: George Allen and Unwin.

Miles, C., Auburn, T.C. and Jones, D.M. (1984) Effects of loud noise and signal probability on visual vigilance. *Ergonomics* **27**: 855–62.

Monk, T.H. and Leng, V.C. (1982) Time of day effects in a simple repetitive tasks: some possible mechanisms. *Acta Psychologica* **51**: 207–21.

Morris, H. and Gale, A. (1988) Smoking and vigilance: a critical appraisal of research. In *Vigilance: Methods, Models, and Regulation,* edited by J.P. Leonard. Frankfurt: Lang, pp. 227–35.

Nachreiner, F. (1977) Experiments on the validity of vigilance experiments. In *Vigilance, Theory, Operational Performance, and Physiological Correlates,* edited by R.R. Mackie. New York: Plenum.

Nachreiner, F. (1988) Zur Belastung und Beanspruchung bei Überwachungs-, Kontroll- und Steuerungstätigkeiten. In *Aktuelle Probleme der Belastungs- und Beanspruchungsforschung.* Festschrift zum 60. Geburtstag von Joseph Rutenfranz, edited by F. Nachreiner. Frankfurt: Lang, pp. 111–30.

Nachreiner, F. and Eilers, K. (1990) Auswirkungen von Tageszeit und Belastungsdauer auf Vigilanzleistungen bei unterschiedlicher Aufgabenschwierigkeit. Final report to the German Research Foundation (DFG), contract no. NA 159/1–3, Oldenburg.

Nachreiner, F., Obliers, R. and Rutenfranz, J. (1976) Zur Frage einer Abhängigkeit der Entdeckungsleistung in Vigilanzversuchen von der Reizereignisrate. *Studia Psychologica* **18**: 26–39.

Parasuraman, R. (1979) Memory load and event rate control sensitivity decrements in sustained attention. *Science, New York:* **205**: 924–7.

Parasuraman, R. and Davies, D.R. (1977) A taxonomic analysis of vigilance perfrmance. In *Vigilance: Theory, Operational Performance, and Physiological Correlates,* edited by R.R. Mackie. New York: Plenum, pp. 559–74.

Peper, J., Eilers, K., Hänecke, K. and Nachreiner, F. (1987) Time of day effects in vigilance performance and its predictability. In *Contemporary Advances in Shiftwork Research*, edited by A. Oginsky, J. Pokorski and J. Rutenfranz. Krakow: Medical Academy, pp. 31–7.

Poulton, E.C. (1976) Continuous noise interferes with work by masking auditory feedback and inner speech. *Applied Ergonomics* **7**: 79–84.

Poulton, E.C. (1977) Arousing stresses increases vigilance. In *Vigilance: Theory, Operational Performance, and Physiological Correlates*, edited by R.R. Mackie. New York: Plenum, pp. 423–60.

Pribram, K.H. and McGuinness, D. (1975) Arousal, activation, and effort in the control of attention. *Psychological Review* **82**: 116–49.

Queinnec, Y. and Terssac, G. de (1987) Chronobiological approach of human errors in complex systems. In *New Technologies and Human Error*, edited by J. Rasmussen, K. Duncan and J. Leplat. Wiley, pp. 223–33.

Simon, M.J. (1982) Use of a vigilance task to determine school readiness of preschool children. *Perceptual and Motor Skills* **54**: 1020.

Smith, A.P. (1983) The effects of noise on strategies of human performance. In *The Proceedings of the Fourth International Congress on Noise as a Public Health Problem*, edited by G. Rossi. Milan: Centro Ricerche e Studi Amplifon, pp. 797–807.

Smith, A.P. and Ottmann, W. (1987) Einfluß von Umgebungsfaktoren auf die psychische Leistung. In *Arbeitspsychologie*, edited by U. Kleinbeck and J. Rutenfranz. Göttingen: Hogrefe, pp. 304–359.

Smith, R.L. and Luccacini, L.F. (1969) Vigilance research: its relevance to industrial problems. *Human Factors* **11**: 149–56.

Stroh, C.M. (1971) *Vigilance: The Problem of Sustained Attention*. Oxford: Pergamon.

Tanner, W.P. and Swets, J.A. (1954) A decision-making theory of visual detection. *Psychological Review* **61**: 401–9.

Teichner, W.H. (1974) The detection of a simple visual signal as a function of time on watch. *Human Factors* **16**: 339–53.

Vernon, H.M. (1921) *Industrial Fatigue and Efficiency*. London: Routledge.

Vickers, D. and Leary, J.N. (1983) Criterion control in signal detection. *Human Factors* **25**: 283–96.

Vickers, D., Leary, J. and Barnes, P. (1977) Adaptation to decreasing signal probability. In *Vigilance: Theory, Operational Performance, and Physiological Correlates*, edited by R.R. Mackie. New York: Plenum, pp. 679–703.

Waag, W.L., Halcomb, C.G. and Tyler, D.M. (1973) Sex differences in monitoring performance. *Journal of Applied Psychology* **58**: 272–4.

Wiener, E.L. (1987) Application of vigilance research: rare, medium, or well done? *Human Factors* **29**: 725–36.

Wilkinson, R.T., Fox, R.H., Goldsmith, R., Hampton, I.F.G. and Lewis, H.E. (1964) Psychological and physiological responses to raised body temperature. *Journal of Applied Psychology* **19**: 287–91.

Wyatt, S. and Langdon, J.N. (1932) Inspection processes in industry. Report no. 63, MRC, Industrial Health Research Board. London: HMSO.

11

Symptoms of Acute and Chronic Fatigue

A. CRAIG & R.E. COOPER

This chapter is about *fatigue*, the weariness that accrues from applying oneself to a task over a period of time. It is a readily understood blanket term that refers to the effects and after-effects of such diverse activities as digging a garden, spending a busy day at the office, driving a car on a long journey, or perhaps even staying awake to finish reading a book; it also applies to short-term activities such as concentrating for a few minutes on a rapid, speeded computer game as well as to long-term effects that can build up over weeks or months from the sustained pressures of work. Although fatigue is often seen as a consequence of maintaining an activity that is not entirely pleasant, it can equally be the result of doing something enjoyable – playing tennis or golf, for example; skiing or playing chess.

What will become apparent in this chapter is that our technical use of the term *fatigue* is just as ill-defined as the lay usage. It is applied to effects that develop over minutes – perhaps even seconds – or hours, and to effects that take weeks or months to develop. It is applied to an individual engaged on a specific task, and to a person working in a social milieu. The variety of situations, the time course of fatigue development and the outcomes, belie the notion of a single underlying set of processes leading to a single underlying state. Thus, while some attempt will be made to integrate the diversity of findings that relate to fatigue, one would search in vain for a single unifying account.

In this chapter, the authors skate across a wide expanse, ranging from a consideration of relatively brief, discrete tasks used in some laboratory research, to a discussion of the problems that derive from the demands of daily work situations. The broad coverage is incompatible with a detailed conceptual

HANDBOOK OF HUMAN PERFORMANCE
VOLUME 3 ISBN 0-12-650353-2

analysis. To compensate for our shortcomings, we refer the reader to the several collected works on fatigue. Among the most useful are: Bartley and Chute (1947), Ryan (1947), Floyd and Welford (1953), Ergonomics (special issues, 1971, 1978) and Hockey (1983).

Fatigue is a term used to cover a constellation of adverse, unwanted effects that can be traced to the continued exercise of an activity. The person may feel fatigued and disinclined to apply any more effort to the activity; performance may deteriorate or, if skilled, lose its smoothness of timing; and the body's physiological functioning or its chemistry may be affected. These three modes of effect, subjective, performance and organic are usually recognized as aspects of fatigue's symptoms, although it is probably true to say that most authorities (e.g. Holding, 1983) follow Bartley and Chute (1947) in giving greatest weight to the subjective mode, recognizing the condition by the reported feeling of fatigue and aversion towards applying further effort.

The three modes referred to in the previous paragraph are relevant to basic questions about fatigue: e.g. how can it be recognized in one's self or in others? or, when should an activity be discontinued if performance (and hence safety) or health is not to suffer? Some qualified answers are provided in the course of this chapter.

The chapter focuses on the effects of fatigue on performance. There are, as will be seen, two important aspects: the effects on continued performance at the task itself, and longer lasting effects or after-effects that carry over to subsequent performance at the same task or at another one. For example, the use of interpolated tasks to assess fatigue in field settings (e.g. Wiethoff and Hockey, 1989) depends on presumptions that after-effects exist, and that fatigue may generalize from one task to another, and hence is not task-specific (although it may be process-specific, as suggested by Zinchenko *et al.*, 1985). In lay terms, these issues translate into such considerations as: does a morning's weeding or digging in the garden interfere with the afternoon's game of golf; and do these activities influence the evening's chess match? One might also question whether any such carry-over effects are symmetric or not: is there a preferred order for spending four hours at a desk writing a chapter for a book and spending four hours out of doors walking, cycling and swimming?

These various issues about the appropriate indicators of fatigue, about the occurrence of immediate and after-effects, and about the specificity of fatigue effects are dealt with in the chapter, which, in addition, also looks at the problem of longer-term fatigue effects that build up over weeks and months, rather than over minutes or hours.

In assembling the material, it has proved convenient to adopt a sequence that approximates the chronological order of studies of fatigue. But this ordering is only approximate, and it would be false to conclude that the progression from simple to complex effects necessarily reflects the progression of ideas: some of the earliest work is among the most profound, while some current reports contain ideas that are naive in their simplicity.

In this chapter, the term fatigue is being used to refer to effects that stem from the continued exercise of an activity. This, it will be recognized, is a narrower view than the one that is commonly taken – people may feel just as tired, and be just as disinclined to work when they are sleepy, have eaten a large lunch or have ingested alcohol or a tranquillizing drug, as when they have worked for a long time. These various factors certainly do involve changes in the state of the person, and do modify the effects of time at work. For example, simple decrements in sustained performance are more likely after a large lunch (Smith and Miles, 1986), following alcohol ingestion (e.g. Rohrbaugh *et al.*, 1987) or when the people have not slept (Wilkinson, 1965) – although, as Horne *et al.* (1983) point out, sleep deprived subjects may retain undiminished enthusiasm and ability for interesting, complex tasks despite showing a loss of capacity on a simpler task requiring sustained attention. These and similar, related factors are covered in other chapters in this volume and in the two companion volumes in this series, and are addressed here in a superficial manner only.

The present chapter seeks, in particular, to avoid redundant overlap between its contents and those of the accompanying chapters in this volume on sleep deprivation (Tilley) and vigilance (Nachreiner and Hänecke), although some minimal coverage of the same ground is inevitable. For instance, a later section on what is termed 'continuous performance' necessarily involves some consideration of lack of sleep. Continuous performance certainly does look at the effects of prolonged work on that work itself, but it has become customary to regard continuous performance as referring to extended periods of several days over which the people, usually military personnel, have to operate without regular sleep at the usual times, and where the emphasis is frequently on disturbance of circadian rhythms, rather than on simple performance loss. Certain features of vigilance research are also relevant to the present chapter, since the maintenance of effective performance on most vigilance tasks often requires sustained attention over prolonged periods of time. Accordingly, this is dealt with in a later section.

To anticipate – early attempts to find simple decrements in mental activities paralleling those observed in muscular work were frustrated: simple decrements are seldom found. Attention then shifted to other changes in performance, notably to disturbances in timing, and to the frequently observed increase in its variability. The wartime focus on pilot fatigue moved attention still further, towards the analysis of complex skills and their breakdown. Subsequent research focused on selected aspects such as momentary lapses, forgetting of priorities, increased riskiness, lowered standards, reduced effort. Some effort too has gone towards identifying after-effects and indicators of these and, at the same time there has gradually emerged a view arguing that fatigue is non-specific, no different in essence from other stress responses, and, indeed, merely an aspect of a generalized stress syndrome. This view has stronger connections than previous ones with the physiological aftermath of fatiguing conditions and with longer-lasting effects on health and well-being.

It is best to regard these phases as complementary, the one building on what has gone before, rather than as competitive, with newer formulations superseding older ones; much data, collected seventy or more years ago, are as relevant now as they were then.

DIRECT PERFORMANCE INDICATORS

Simple response decrements

Early research on 'mental' fatigue was dominated by the analogy of muscular fatigue. It had been frequently shown that the strength of repeated muscular contractions against an opposing force declined over time as a function of the repetitions. Mosso (1890) demonstrated this by attaching a wire to a weight and to a finger, so that as the finger was flexed and extended, the weight would be raised and lowered. A linked pen-recording system produced a graph of the successive distances travelled by the weight, which typically reduced to zero within a few minutes. The distance clearly reflects the work done by the finger so that the resulting record is a work curve or ergogram.

By analogy, it was thought that, if a person is engaged on a task involving repetitive mental activity, the work done might be represented by the number of items completed per period of time. However, whereas muscular fatigue can invariably be demonstrated, evidence of a reduced output in mental work has been much less consistently forthcoming. Thorndike (1926), for example, concluded from a review of the then available evidence that there was little problem in maintaining efficiency for periods of up to two hours; that output on various mental tasks seldom fell below 90 per cent of the initial level.

Poffenberger (1928) reported output curves for five and a half hours of continuous work on four different tasks: digit addition, sentence completion, composition judgement and an intelligence test. For the first two hours, no curve shows a decrement; thereafter, additions decline, completion and composition are maintained, while intelligence test output improves. However, ratings of how the subjects felt, taken at twenty minute intervals, always declined steadily throughout, from 'extremely good' towards 'extremely tired', regardless of the task. (But Poffenberger did note that although there were wide individual differences in the uses of the rating scale, those who showed the greatest change in feeling, tended also to show the greatest loss of output, where this occurred.)

Muscio (1920) also reported a discrepancy between mean shifts in feelings and work output on an arithmetic task administered to college students at various times in the morning and afternoon. Usually, but not always, work output was lower at 5 p.m. than at 11 a.m.; feelings of weariness did not differ between morning and afternoon, but were consistently greater towards the end of the work periods in both morning and afternoon. A similar picture was emerging from industry – to which work decrements seemed particularly relevant. Whereas the output from heavy muscular work typically declined over the course of the usual day shift (Goldmark *et al.*, 1920), that from lighter work such as visual inspection might actually increase (Link, 1919). Other inconsistencies were also emerging. For example, although it was generally found that the hourly output was higher with reduced hours of work (Goldmark *et al.*, 1920; Vernon, 1921), there was little or no evidence that output was lower in the afternoon, the second half of a shift, than in the morning; and whereas there was usually a significant drop in the eighth hour of an eight-hour shift, the equivalent drop did not occur until the tenth hour of a ten-hour shift. It was recognized, however, that many factors including financial incentives in piece-rate work and accepted quotas for the day's output, influenced the production curve over the day.

In the absence of direct evidence that output varied inversely with the hours worked, Vernon (1921) examined the pattern of accidents in relation to time at work over a range of industries. In general, accidents tended to rise and fall with production rate, and differed little between morning and afternoon. Only in the case of excessively long twelve-hour shifts did he find a tendency for accidents to increase with time at work. In fact this was largely attributable to an increased risk of accidents among women employees, whose afternoon rate was 45 per cent greater than it had been in the morning; for a ten-hour shift, the accident rate among women was 17 per cent greater in the afternoon than in the morning. For men, the accident rate did not appreciably increase in the afternoon, and such increase as did occur (of the order of 7–8 per cent) did not differ between ten-hour and twelve-hour working days. The increased vulnerability of the women operators was also reflected in reported instances of feeling faint: these increased from being three times more likely than the men's rate on ten-hour shifts, to being nine times more likely on twelve-hour shifts.

In commenting on the effects of working hours on output, Wyatt *et al.* (1938), drawing on their experience of industrial fatigue, had suggested that for certain repetitive work, the output could be determined as much by boredom as by fatigue; that whereas output declined over time when the operator was fatigued, it could (especially in the case of self-paced work) increase when the worker was bored. They report an empirical association between ratings of boredom and the direction of the temporal drift in output.

The point to this is that the failure of these early studies to find a work decrement with gross measures of efficiency cast severe doubts on the simple mechanical metaphor of mental functioning and fatigue, and led to the development of more complex notions.

Among the early researchers, Muscio (1921–2) is noted for his often-quoted statement that we should abandon the fatigue concept. However, his own research offers one of the clearer examples of a simple fatigue effect.

As already mentioned, he had used an interpolated task technique to examine fatigue effects among college students. By comparing the hourly performance levels achieved on his interpolated arithmetic task by students pursuing their normal (and fairly demanding) course-work, and by students indulging in leisure activities such as walking, he demonstrated that rested students were consistently superior to those who were studying, and that this superiority increased towards the end of the morning and afternoon periods. He also showed that the difference, the fatigue effect, was superimposed on a diurnal rhythm whose peaks and troughs occurred at different times and with different amplitudes for different interpolated tasks, but which were coincident in time for rested and tired groups of students working on the same task.

The interpolated task technique represents an extension of the fatigue concept, from the specific to the general. With simple motor fatigue, as in the rapid finger-bending studies, there is no question of the fatigue being other than specific: a digit may be exhausted, but the subject can still walk or talk, or even write with his other hand. In Muscio's (1921) studies, however, the evidence was that the speed of doing arithmetic was influenced by the extent of the student's mental exertions in studying and attending lectures. An interesting early example was provided by Maggiora (1890), cited by Schneider (1939): using an ergograph, he electrically stimulated his finger so that the involuntary contractions raised a small weight; normally, fifty-three contractions occurred before exhaustion took place, but after a gruelling three and a half-hour exam, only twelve contractions were made before exhaustion. One should recall here that Mosso (1890) had previously shown that a muscle apparently exhausted following voluntary contractions was still capable of responding to electrical stimulation.

In a later study, Schwab (1953) used electrical stimulation to distinguish between voluntary and involuntary (i.e. actual effectors) neuromuscular fatigue, and demonstrated the influence of suggestibility and of financial incentives on the onset of voluntary fatigue. He showed, for example, that the maximum duration for which young men could suspend their weight, hanging by their hands from an elevated bar, could be increased by the offer of a substantial monetary reward. In keeping with his emphasis on the role of motivation in determining fatigue-like limits, he also introduced observational data showing that the physical capacity of commuters to sprint unsuccessfully for a train – measured by the distance run before they stopped – apparently increased with the cost of missing the train (though perhaps this example should be taken as showing a link between voluntary effort and cost of failure, rather than between fatigue and cost).

However, despite some successful demonstrations of fatigue-like effects, the prevailing view among the early researchers was that performance was remarkably resistant to fatigue. For example, Ryan and Warner (1936) tested six subjects for a total of 120 driving days on each of which they had

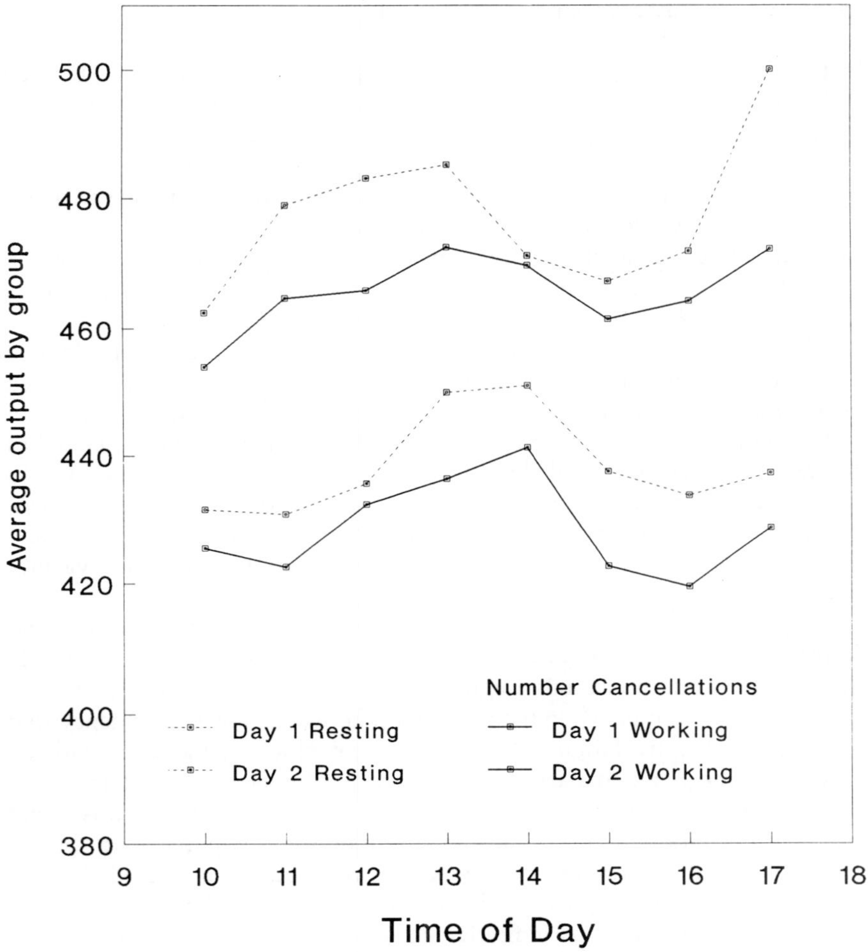

Figure 11.1 Average output on a number cancellation task by resting (broken line) and working (solid line) groups on successive days. The two upper curves were obtained on the second day. (Adapted from Muscio, 1920.)

completed an exhausting 300 mile drive, and on alternate control days when they had driven for an hour only. They found that although body-sway, eye–hand co-ordination, arithmetic, colour-naming and focused attention were all impaired by the driving, the extent of the impairment was slight. In other words, it may take a massive research effort and a very large difference between fatiguing and control conditions to obtain a reliable effect, when that effect is defined by a simple decrement in level.

Increased response variability and blocking

In the driving study just referred to, simple decrements were slight. Ryan and Warner (1936) also report, however, that several test scores were more variable following the long car drive. It had in fact long been recognized that increased variability was an aspect of the fatigue response. Weinland (1927), for example, had drawn attention to the characteristic increase in the variability of the stroke amplitude on the ergograph, and Woodworth and Wells (1911) had noted the variability in the timing of a sequence of colour-naming responses. This became an important focus in later research which gave a high profile to the work of Bills and his associates (Bills, 1931).

Bills (1931) focused on the occurrence of occasional pauses in a prolonged sequence of otherwise fast responses, such as in colour-naming. He referred to these as 'blocks' which, for measurement purposes, he defined as gaps of more than twice the normal response time. Their frequency, which tended to increase over time, averaged about three per minute on the rapid paced tasks he examined. Practice reduced the frequency and duration of the blocks, whereas fatigue increased them. Fast responders tended to incur fewer and briefer blocks. It was also observed that errors tended to occur in the vicinity of the blocks.

Fatigue increased the general irregularity of responding but produced no decrease in the overall response rate over the course of an hour's work – in fact, the overall response rate might well increase. Bills observed that most responses tended to bunch in the mid-period between blocks, a tendency that was exaggerated by fatigue. The incidence of blocking increases with an increase in the required pace of work, but the frequency and duration of blocks are lower with paced than with self-paced tasks – in fact it was found that when a task was paced at the mean of the self-paced rate, blocks disappeared. Bills interpreted these blocks as rest pauses, motivated shifts of attention away from the work in hand, and he regarded their increase over time on self-paced tasks as indicative of deterioration in voluntary control mechanisms. Although he did not specify a physiological basis for blocking, he clearly felt there was, indicating parallels between the fatigue effect of continuous work and anoxemia (he demonstrated that inhalation of pure oxygen may induce some recovery from 'mental fatigue' as indicated by reductions in blocking).

It may be mentioned here that in one of the most extensive studies of blocking, Warren and Clark (1936) observed that in sixty-five hours of continuous performance, the incidence of blocking gradually increased to reach a maximum at forty-eight hours, whereas the average response time remained almost constant throughout.

Bertelson and Joffe (1963) have provided a detailed analysis of blocking in a thirty-minute, four-choice reaction-time (RT) task. They found that the distribution of the final ten RTs differed in the long tail from the first ten

RTs obtained during the second minute; that short and median RTs did not change, only the longest ones. They observed that blocks, defined as RTs more than twice the mean RT, increased steeply in frequency over the first five minutes or so, and thereafter remained stable. They also noted that in the vicinity of blocks, RT increased sharply for four or five responses preceding the block, then declined again immediately after the block – rather like the undulations reported previously by Bills (1931). Errors were observed to rise and fall in parallel with reaction time, although as Bertelson and Joffe point out, the increase in RT in the couple of trials preceding a block is far greater than expected if it were just due to errors. They suggest that blocking permits accumulated fatigue to dissipate; that a block provides a rest pause which remains effective for about fifty responses or so. [More recently Rabbitt (1981) has suggested that blocking might reflect failures of self-regulation when the person is endeavouring to maintain performance within an appropriate speed–error trade-off band.]

Kogi and Saito (1973) have reported observed similar oscillations in performance on tracking tasks. They found that on a fifteen-minute continuous tracking task, there were steep error increases at intervals of about a minute. In compensatory tracking, they found that the critical flicker-fusion frequency (CFF), which is popularly regarded as an indicator of central nervous system effective state (see section below), was lower during a fifteen-second period prior to the error increase, than during steady state periods; and in pursuit

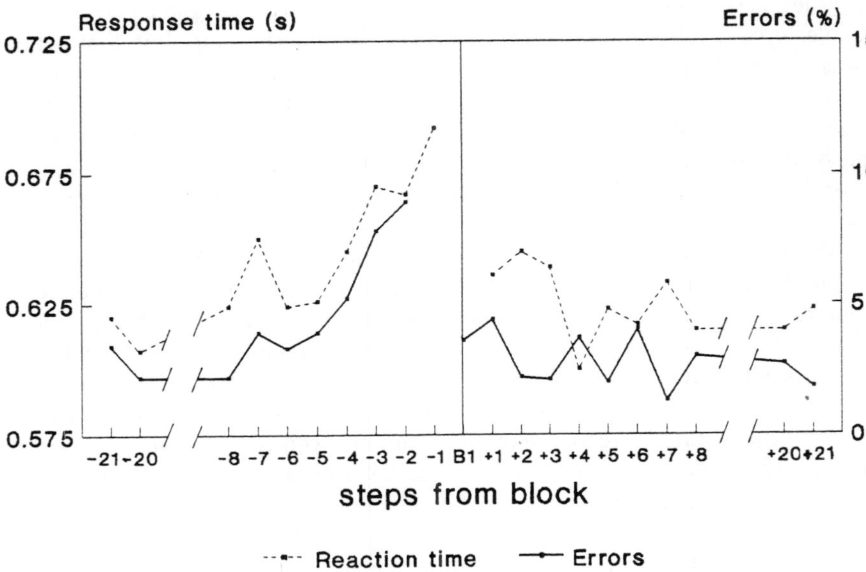

Figure 11.2 Blocks in prolonged serial responding: reaction times and errors in the vicinity of a block. (Redrawn from Bertelson and Joffe, 1963).

tracking they observed that saccades were less frequent during that fifteen-second period preceding the sharp error increase. In conjunction, they suggest that their results imply periodic loss of alertness whose symptoms include reduced orienting and an interruption of corrective efforts.

INDIRECT INDICATORS

Physiological measures

Some investigators argued that one could assess the fatiguing aspects of prolonged or excessive mental activity by measuring the expenditure of physical energy during mental processes. But such 'organic fatigue' as was measurable, seemed largely attributable to changes in muscular activity and tension during the performance of a task. For example, Benedict and Benedict (1933) report that the energy consumed in doing mental arithmetic was only some three to four per cent greater than the energy consumed at rest, that this small increment represented increased muscle tension and body movements, and that the consumption of energy by central nervous system activity was negligible. Goldstein (1934) demonstrated that three hours of work on a cancellation task, an intelligence test and a task involving overt physical activity all led to a similar pattern of increases in organic phosphorus, cholesterol and creatinine, and a decrease in blood sugar; but that when muscle activity on the mental tasks was minimized, metabolic levels did not differ from those of the resting state. Results like these were later to cause Bartley and Chute (1947) to conclude that the search for a direct energy basis for fatigue was futile. Van den Berg (1986) has recently voiced similar scepticism regarding efforts to date to identify the source of the brain's energy fuel.

With the development of recording techniques, muscle tension became a popular indicator, and Freeman (1931) demonstrated that the links between muscle tension and performance efficiency were congruent with his model that tension was under voluntary control and provided through its flow of proprioceptive impulses, the necessary non-specific bombardment to sustain cortical activity. According to Freeman, when this stimulation fell too low, cortical thresholds were not exceeded and the centres involved in mental activity were unresponsive; but beyond certain intensity levels, muscle tension could be too great, inhibiting the neural integration needed to perform a particular, precise task. Voluntary regulation of muscular activity, it was supposed, maintains it at or near an optimum level; habituation (from repetitive stimulation) may diminish this regulation, fatigue enhances it. Muscle tension was not taken to be an indicator of fatigue, *per se*, but rather of the effort applied in performing a task. This had, of course, been demonstrated previously by Ash (1914) who showed that as the finger in the ergograph became fatigued there were increasing signs of tension in more and more muscles whose involvement was quite irrelevant to the task of raising the weight. Also, as will be mentioned again in a subsequent section, Wilkinson (1962) found that the performance loss following a night without sleep was inversely related to the increased tension shown during task performance.

Critical flicker fusion (CFF)

The early period of research also saw the development of one of the most popular indicators of fatigue: the critical flicker-fusion rate (CFF). Snell (1933), for example, who was interested in the question of whether watching a cinema film had a fatiguing effect on the ocular mechanisms, demonstrated that prolonged exposure to visible flicker (of the sort produced by a film) reduced the critical frequency at which that flicker apparently fused into a steady signal. Subsequent studies have used the CFF as a general central nervous system (CNS) fatigue indicator, not merely as a specific, ocular fatigue indicator. Simonson and Enzer (1941), for example, showed that there was a decline in the later part of the day as compared to the morning, and that the decline could be eliminated by ingesting benzedrine. McFarland *et al.* (1942) demonstrated a modest effect of sleep deprivation, but found little evidence to support the notion that the CFF indexed general fatigue.

Perhaps more than others, the Japanese have placed reliance on the CFF as an indicator of cortical activation level. In this they pursue the position of Simonson and Enzer (1941) that the CFF reflects the handling capacity of the cortical visual information processing system, the capacity being presumed to depend on activation level. Kumashiro (1984), for example, has mapped out the decline in CFF in the course of a ninety-minute arithmetic task, and its subsequent recovery during a sixty-minute rest break, the recovery being only partial when the task was presented on a CRT display, but complete when a paper display was used (these changes were paralleled by shifts in EEG power towards the lower – delta, theta – end of the spectrum, and also by scores on the TAF, a specially devised fatigue test – see below). However a recent study by Iwasaki and Akiya (1991) casts some doubts on the general validity of these CFF interpretations. They presented a difficult arithmetic task (a version of the Kraepelin test) on a CRT display for a duration of thirty minutes, but used lenses so that the image was presented to one eye only. CFF declined to a significant extent for this loaded eye only; while the difference between loaded and unloaded eyes progressively increased over time. Eye-strain ratings also increased, but performance was maintained at a fairly constant level. The implication is that the CFF mainly reflects local, peripheral capacity rather than general cortical capacity.

Fatigue ratings

Mention of the Japanese work on the CFF reminds us that they, more than others, have worked on the development of a scale to measure the feeling of fatigue. The current version derives from factor-analytic procedures and seems a more sophisticated instrument than any of its predecessors, although much use had been made of fatigue ratings from the earliest period of research.

Japanese ergonomists have developed and validated a fatigue rating scale with three components: (1) general drowsiness and dullness; (2) difficulty concentrating and (3) projection onto specific physical disintegration (see e.g. Yoshitake, 1971, 1978). With this they have reliably distinguished between different types of jobs, both between industries (e.g. Kogi *et al.*, 1970) and within (e.g. Kishida, 1991); between part-time and full-time workers (the latter exhibiting more and stronger fatigue symptoms), and between lengths of working day among the part-timers (Kishida, 1991); and have shown that night work but not day work generally leads to increased symptoms of mental fatigue (difficulties concentrating) (Yoshitake, 1978). In addition, the self-ratings are related to observable signs recognized by others (Kashiwagi, 1971). Tanaka *et al.* (1989), in a recent review, confirm the ability of this rating scale to differentiate between the experiences of fatigue in different kinds of job, and show that between 1967/68, when the scale was first developed, and 1984, the changes in the obtained Japanese norms reflect the shift towards jobs that, although physically less demanding, increasingly produce feelings of mental fatigue. The scale has also been used in studies in the USA. Rosa *et al.* (1985), for example, used it in a study to examine the differential fatigue effects of working either six eight-hour days, or four twelve-hour days; they report a significant interaction with lack of concentration increasing across the last of the twelve-hour days, but not consistently otherwise. More recently, Washburn (1991) has found a consistent pattern of build up of fatigue during a shift, but no differences between eight- and twelve-hour shifts.

Conceptual notions about fatigue were also developing during the early era – or perhaps it would be better to say that notions were being expressed rather than developed since there is a familiarly modern ring about some of the earliest ideas. Thorndike (1900), for instance, in an early review of mental fatigue, pointed out that it involved not only an apparent inability to produce the right quantity of work, but also an inability to do the right *kind* of work. He suggested that fatigue involved a sense of mental repugnance to do the required work, and he stressed the importance of distinguishing between lack of ability and lack of desire to work. Thorndike also stated that an animal was likely to discontinue or decrease its mental work because continuing it annoyed it, rather than because some energy source (mental resources?) was running low. And he suggested that work without rest would become less satisfying because it: (1) loses its novelty (*cf.* Broadbent, 1958, on the activity and bias of an input filter), (2) produces ennui (*cf.* O'Hanlon, 1981, on the development of boredom), and (3) deprives the worker of the chance to do other things (sleep, leisure activities, socializing, etc.) – i.e. there is an opportunity cost to continuing the work.

Not too many years later, Ash (1914) indicated that one of the first symptoms of fatigue was a loss of control in co-ordinating activities which occurred before any signs of a loss of ability emerged. Ash also adopted a relatively modernist view in asserting that the state of one's energies and the ability to direct them to accomplishing a task are determined by a constellation of exogenous and endogenous factors including: environmental conditions, time of day, distraction, mental attitude towards the task, practice on the task and familiarity with its materials, and the state of health and nutrition of the person.

FATIGUE IN SKILLED WORK

Whereas most of the experimental work on fatigue in the era prior to World War II had focused on discrete, unitary tasks, it was to be research on the disintegration of complex skills that provided the major impact on thinking about fatigue in the period thereafter.

Wartime exigencies and the problems of maintaining both aircraft and pilots serviceable, had prompted research on 'pilot fatigue'. In England, this research was summarized and the results interpreted in the classic paper by Bartlett (1943), the report of his 1941 Royal Society Ferrier Lecture, 'Fatigue following highly skilled work'. For this, Bartlett made much use of the experimental work of George Drew, who has independently reported details of the study (Drew, 1940).

Drew investigated the behaviour of skilled pilots controlling a flight-simulator (the 'Cambridge cockpit') for periods of two hours or more. He reported that control of the aircraft (as indicated by side-slip and airspeed errors) deteriorated by as much as fifty per cent in the course of the flight scenario. The ability to perform the intellectual activities involved in correctly timing various required manoeuvres (as indicated by altitude and compass use) also deteriorated: errors in timing in fact decreased and then increased, as fatigue superseded practice, while actual errors just declined throughout. All of these scores showed a particularly pronounced deterioration between the final two periods (of about twenty minutes each), which was not present when the men were unaware that these were the final units. Standards of maintenance fell over time: at the start, when the men were fresh, two to three per cent fluctuation in bearing, airspeed, etc., was tolerated without correction; but progressively, this tolerance increased to five per cent, ten per cent and finally to twenty per cent before corrective action was taken.

A drift in standards also seemed evident in the manoeuvring error scores where it was found that there was a progressive rise in the rate of increase of large over small errors. It is noteworthy that the pilots seemed unaware of the drifting standards.

Some memory-lapse or inattention also appeared. After about an hour, an increasing proportion of pilots forgot to check the fuel and radiator gauges, and there was an increasing lapse in time between movements of the temperature needle, and reactions to it. At the end of the course, more than 80 out of 140 pilots forgot to lower the undercarriage – a lapse of some significance, one would have thought. The increases in manoeuvring control errors and in failures to check gauges are shown in Figure 3.

In addition to these general indications of a drop in skill effectiveness, Drew also noted that the task seemed to lose its integrity when the pilots were fatigued. This is reflected in their perceptions of what at first glance seems an unusual feature of the study. Balloons had been placed under the pilot's seat, and at various points in the scenario, these were inflated and deflated. At the beginning, when fresh, seventy-five per cent of the pilots perceived these as actual, realistic movements of the whole cockpit; in mid-flight, only thirty per cent perceived them in this way; and at the end, when fatigued, none of them saw them as integrated cockpit movements. As Drew points out, this is but one reflection of the way the task splits up into separate elements when the operator is fatigued.

Over time, the pilots became increasingly aware of physical discomfort, and grew more irritable. The balloons began to cause distraction; this was followed by an improvement in performance, followed by a slump again. With increasing fatigue, the distraction effect disappeared, the period of improvement grew shorter and the onset of the slump was hastened. The subjective impressions of the pilots became unreliable when they were fatigued: along with their increasing awareness of physical discomfort and their increasing irritability (especially towards their 'unresponsive' controls), the pilots made more and more unforced errors (doing completely the wrong thing, or interpreting something in quite the wrong way) and, often unaware of their drifting standards, actually thought they were performing better.

Davis (1948) also reports fatigue effects on the Cambridge cockpit. He adopted a rather different scoring procedure and examined behaviour over four twenty-minute periods. He failed to find a progressive deterioration over time: errors exceeding a criterion first increased and then decreased in a symmetric fashion. The duration of sideslip errors increased only during the final period, whereas for direction errors the duration increased throughout. Corrective aileron movements increased most in the first half. As Davis summarizes: in the second half, there were fewer errors overall, but those that did occur tended to be larger and to last longer. An important distinction that Davis makes is between the overactive pilots who make a lot of movement relative to the duration of their errors, and the inert ones, whose total error duration is high relative to the corrective movements they make.

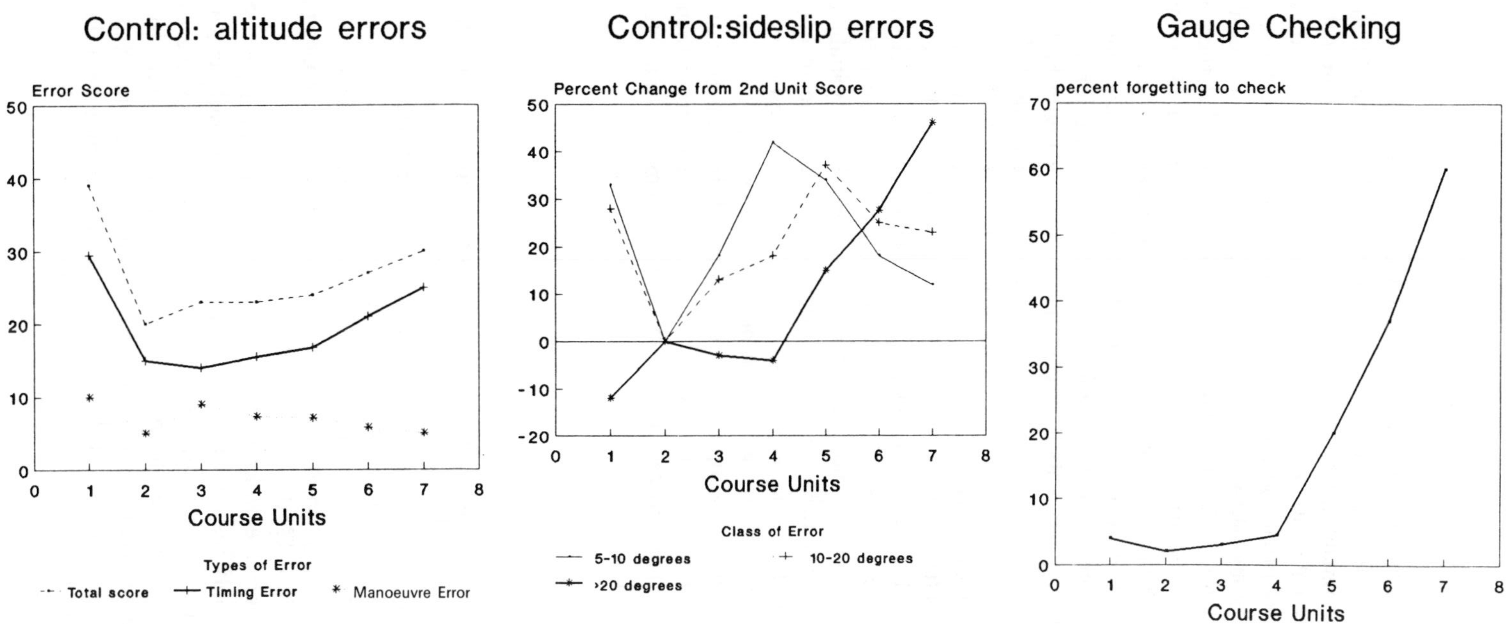

Figure 11.3 Pilot fatigue: the cumulative effect of successive course units on pilot errors in a simulated flight. (From Drew, 1940.)

From these simulation studies, from the work of Drew (1940) in particular, Bartlett (1943, 1953) formed his view of the criteria for identifying fatigue: (1) that there would appear increasing irregularity of the internal timing of the successive elements of performance that have to be repeated in carrying out the task; (2) that there would be a splitting up or disintegration of the field of display and lapses of memory, that the right actions might be done at the wrong time or even omitted altogether; and (3) that there would be a progressive reduction in the appropriate selectivity of behaviour, and a widening of the field from which selection was made, with a concurrent loss of direction and of increased attention to discomfort, hunger and so forth.

It should be noted that, contrary to what this description might lead us to expect, landing accidents in aircraft did not increase with flight time – at least for long flights up to ten hours. An analysis of accident data reported by Bradford Hill and Williams (1943) shows that more accidents occurred for flights of less than two hours or more than ten hours, but that between these times accident rates were unrelated to flight duration. Furthermore, Reid (1945) reports that navigator errors and variability actually decrease with time on non-operational sorties of four hours' duration. On operational sorties, however, this reduction did not occur; instead errors and variability waxed and waned with the risks encountered during the sortie, being high at high risk points. Reid pointedly attributes the performance disruption not so much to fatigue, as to anxiety – which can be regarded as a state of heightened – indeed, over – arousal coupled with emotional, distracting thoughts. Much recent work confirms that feelings of stress or anxiety rather than of plain fatigue are the common response to high work demands (e.g. Hockey and Wiethoff, 1990).

Vigilance

Perhaps rather surprisingly, in this atmosphere of work on the variability in performance caused by 'pilot fatigue', there emerged a task type that consistently and reliably yielded a simple decrement in performance. This was the *vigilance task* (see accompanying chapter by Nachreiner and Hanecke, this volume), designed to simulate military target surveillance. Much of the research on this topic was pioneered and directed by one of Bartlett's colleagues, N.H. Mackworth (1948, 1950).

Whereas cognitive tasks of the sort used by Poffenberger (1928) had proved remarkably resistant to a decrement with time-on-task, vigilance tasks as pioneered by Mackworth (1948) seemed especially sensitive to 'mental fatigue'. The vigilance task in generic form requires an observer to maintain a readiness to respond appropriately to specified rare events that occur at uncertain times. Detections of these events typically decline with the passage of time; detection response latency tends to increase; and there is usually a decline in emissions of false reports. Analyses of vigilance data using techniques derived from signal detection theory (Green and Swets, 1966) have revealed that the 'fatigue' effect, the vigilance decrement, is often due to a shift in the bias for reporting an event and, less frequently, to a demonstrable loss of capacity to distinguish the critical event from other, unwanted, events (Davies and Parasuraman, 1982). The noted criterion shift, a reduced inclination to respond, may be due to a change of state that involves a drop in arousal (Welford, 1968), but it may also result from an adaptive process as the observer comes to appreciate more accurately how infrequently the awaited event occurs (Vickers, 1979). There is less ambiguity about interpreting a loss of discriminability, which has been shown to be more likely when the event rate is high, and the event is rendered indistinct (Neuchterlein *et al.*, 1986); when repetitive, effortful processing is required (Fiske and Schneider, 1981); and when the discrimination involves memory for what constitutes the event. As with the less vulnerable tasks used by Poffenberger and others, prolonged vigilance is accompanied by feelings of fatigue (e.g. Koelega *et al.*, 1989). Mackworth, himself, suggested that the greater vulnerability of his vigilance tasks might be due to the reduced feedback the observers received about how well they were doing in the course of performing the task. In part, this may be so, but vigilance decrements in the form of increasingly slow reactions occur to even the most conspicuous of events – such as switching off a light (McCormack, 1967). It remains the case that, in general, tasks requiring sustained attention for the uncertain arrival of a rare event are especially vulnerable to any adverse state, including those induced by sleep deprivation, alcohol, drugs, noise (see e.g. Broadbent, 1971) – as well as to the fatiguing effects of time-on-task itself. Frankenhaeuser and her colleagues (e.g. Frankenhaeuser, 1986) have indicated that in terms of subjective ratings and catecholamine responses, a vigilance task can be just as demanding and stressful as a fast-paced, complex, choice RT task.

Task-dependent effects

Welford (1953) presented a perceptive analysis of the early research. He indicated that there were three fundamental task circumstances that resulted in three types of fatigue effect in performance:

1. On devised tasks that involve independent trials, and where accuracy is not dependent on speed of processing, fatigue may affect only one stage in the input–output chain, so that one observes a simple decrement in either speed or accuracy.
2. Disorganization of performance is only likely to be observed in skilled performance or on serial tasks, where actions are sequentially dependent. With skills, such as car driving, there is often a hierarchical organization

with each level steering the one below; with fatigue, there is often a focus on the smaller details rather than on the larger units, as though fatigue attacks the upper, executive level.

3. Finally, one finds a cumulative disruption of performance when actions form a sequential series and slowness affects accuracy. According to Welford, this arises because processing and responding take time, the central mechanisms that are continuously monitoring one's performance have to attend not only to the stimulus input but also to the kinaesthetic and other sensory feedback from responses; and since (according to Welford) the human is a limited, single-channel system, any delay at any point in the chain can be disruptive.

He suggests that if the task is self-paced, so that the operator can observe and respond in his/her own time, then fatigue will probably only produce a simple decrement; but if the performance is paced, then the more complex effects are likely to arise. These could occur if distraction or discomfort were to increase the total load being attended to. One response to overload might be to begin by reducing unnecessary activities, such as talking (*cf.* Haider, 1963; and L.C. Boer, personal communication, who uses reduced inclination to reply to questions as a sensitive indicator of workload in air traffic controllers).

Welford suggests we distinguish between increased load on the effector side, when actions may well remain smooth and rapid, but with increased error, and load on the receptor side which results in hasty decisions, too little evidence being accumulated or extracted from the input signal, and missed signals. In the latter case, because of the faulty processing of information, actions may become slow or jerky, or both, and the resulting changes in limb velocity may capture the attention and so further increase the receptor load. The process of breakdown under fatigue often occurs in a vicious circle. In tracking, for example, an increase in the time to detect a need for correction increases the error to be corrected and, if the time to correct is proportional to the size of the error, the process becomes cumulatively unstable leading to complete breakdown. On various tasks, whether paced or self-paced, slowing or inaccuracy may disturb expectancies about where and when future events are likely to occur, and the reduced expectancies may well lead to further slowing and inaccuracy. When events arrive in rapid succession, any slowing of the processing system may lead to increased demands on the short-term-memory stack, resulting in additional misses, inaccuracies and disturbed expectancies. Anxieties about one's own performance may increase the load, adding to the difficulties.

Welford also points out that the onset of fatigue may be delayed by changing the way a task is handled. People usually work within their capacities to their own standard of performance, trying to maintain but not exceed this standard. Although this sets limits to the overall performance that can be achieved, fatigue can accumulate some way before its influence is apparent. And in so far as fatigue can separately affect different parts of the system, fatigue in one part may be compensated for by operating closer to the margin in another – and until that spare capacity declines to a critical extent, performance may continue, undiminished. But if some additional load were now imposed, performance may break down in a way that would not occur with a fresh subject. It may even be that the attempt to compensate for some growing fatigue effect results in superior performance, as in Wilkinson's (1962) sleep deprived subjects who increased their concentration so as to maintain performance.

Finally it must be mentioned that the flexibility of the person allows the increased load to be handled by a reduction in the standards to be maintained. Attention was drawn to this in discussing the results of the Cambridge Cockpit Studies, and other have reported it more recently. Kantowitz *et al.* (1983), for example, report that pilots sometimes use this strategy when load becomes prohibitive: the reported load-stress declines along with performance (which is still within acceptable, external standards for safety), although the objective difficulty of a manoeuvre has increased.

AFTER EFFECTS

The work of Bartlett and his colleagues is often interpreted as implying that fatigue effects should be found in the work itself, especially in its internal organization rather than in one specific aspect of it. And it has been rightly argued that as soon as one introduces a subsequent test to examine for fatigue – on the reasonable assumption that fatigue persists beyond the task itself – the operator's state is already modified by the change in conditions. Notwithstanding this argument, a number of studies did successfully identify fatigue states *after* the completion of lengthy flights. For example, Welford *et al.* (1950) asked flight crew to perform tasks after they had completed a flight. One task required a number of resistance readings to be taken with a meter to map out a circuit. Many more readings were taken when the men encountered the task for the first time following a flight: they tended to forget one reading while they were taking another. The fatigue effects were most marked on the first occasion, and reduced on subsequent occasions as the men became familiar with the task; but those who first encountered the task when tired, remained disadvantaged compared to those whose first experience had been gained when fresh. Welford and his colleagues interpreted this as a transfer of the fatigue effects to subsequent sessions. They also noted that on a plotting task the men tended to perform better after a flight than when fresh – if the task was easy; the reverse occurred when a harder version of the plotting task was used: fatigued men were inferior to fresh ones.

Fraser (1955) also reports a series of studies in which he found after-effects of long flights. He used a prolonged (one-hour) task of the kind now referred to as a vigilance task, and measured the times taken to recognize an occasional discrepant item in a sequence of otherwise identical ones. He observed that for twenty-three out of thirty-six subjects, the timing variance increased between first and second halves of his test, with occasional reversals in subjects who, when fresh, had produced higher than average variance. In examining flight crew, he found that short sorties of one or two hours had no effect on test performances, but longer ones (e.g. those exceeding ten hours) reliably increased the variance overall, although in most cases (twenty-one out of thirty) this was coupled with a reduced variance in the second half hour (the magnitude of the reduction was equivalent to three times the increase that was found in the usual fresh condition). The increase in overall variance was especially marked after night flying, and Fraser noted that when four consecutive fifteen-hour night sorties were flown, the variance progressively increased from first to fourth sortie and was correlated with subjective feelings of fatigue. Later, Fraser noted that the variance tended to change over the course of the day, increasing for some who might be classed as 'morning' types, but decreasing for other 'evening' types. He also found that alcohol accelerated the appearance of the within-session fatigue effect.

Trading risk against effort

An interesting methodological and conceptual approach is found in the work of Holding and his colleagues. Holding focused on the long-held view (see Bartley and Chute, 1947) that the dominant symptom of fatigue is an aversion to apply further effort to the task. If fatigue is general, rather than specific, one might expect this aversion to effort to transfer to other tasks. In other words, it should be possible to assess the repugnance for effort using the interpolated task technique. The task, however, would have to be tailored to reveal the lack of willingness to expend effort. Holding's approach to this was to devise a problem-solving task in which the defined goal (solution) could be achieved in three different ways that required recognizably separate amounts of work (= effort); but where the effort required was balanced by the likelihood of success in achieving the goal. A key feature of the task is that the expected amount of work would be the same, regardless of whether one opted to start with a path high in effort and in probability of success, or low in effort and in probability of success. The interest of Holding and his colleagues lies in the original choice itself which indicates a willingness to expend effort, not in the successful achievement of the goal. Shingledecker and Holding (1974) reported on the use of a version of this choice of probability and effort (COPE) test for subjects who had performed 24–32 hours of continuous work on the multiple task performance battery (MTPB)

– an agglomeration of passive and active monitoring and cognitive processing tasks used by Alluisi and colleagues in their work for the US Army (Alluisi *et al.*, 1977). Shingledecker and Holding found that in a post-test evaluation, a fatigued group who had worked on the MTPB showed a lowered preference for high effort/probability choices. On mean choice scores, there was no overall difference between the fatigued group and a group of fresh controls. There was, however, an interaction between groups and their pre-test and post-test scores, with the scores of the fatigued groups declining (moving towards reduced effort) between pre- and post-test situations. This effect was only found on the first block of COPE trials (three blocks were given). Errors on COPE also increased for the fatigued group; this was especially evident when comparing the final pre-test block with the first post-test one. For controls, however, errors declined. In a subsequent study, it was observed that the mean choice scores on the last two post-test blocks of trials were significantly correlated with fatigue ratings: the higher the rating, the more likely a low effort/probability choice. Barth *et al.* (1976) reported that whereas the original circuit-testing COPE task was insensitive to physical fatigue a physical effort analogue was sensitive, regardless of whether the fatigue was induced in the arm or the leg; and as in the early study, COPE scores were correlated with ratings of fatigue. It seemed, therefore, that fatigue generalized to other tasks within a very broad category, mental or physical, but did not transfer between classes. Subsequently, Holding has been rather less successful with an arithmetic, paper and pencil version of the COPE task, although some results seemed promising. For example, Holding *et al.* (1983) reported that when subjects had to work at the Norinder arithmetic task during an interval between pre- and post-tests, the subsequent choice scores were lowered; and when the interval was filled with continuous loud (95 dBA) white noise there was an even greater reluctance to make an effortful choice. There was a suggestion that the effects of noise and work might be additive. A later report by Brand and Holding (1984), however, failed to find fatigue effects in a study involving repeated testing with three versions of the arithmetic COPE task.

TAF: function of maintaining concentration

Takakuwa (1962, 1977) has reported success with an interpolated fatigue test known as the TAF (target aiming function). This involves aiming a device like a rifle and maintaining the aim against a spring-loaded resistance for three consecutive periods of a minute. Both mean and variance of the aim are measured. Although Takakuwa has been at pains to point out the dangers of relying on single measures of fatigue, given the general lack of correlation among them, the TAF has proved differentially sensitive to the visual demands of CRT work, to frenetic mental activity of people involved in producing a live television programme, to the shifts and routes worked by bus-drivers, to the daily accumulation of fatigue in bankers during an especially busy week, and even to examination fatigue, over the period from the build-up to the exam to the aftermath of the exam, distinguishing the reduced symptoms of those facing the exam on meprobamate, from those not on drugs.

STRATEGY SHIFTS

We have seen that primary task performance is often insensitive to fatigue because performance is protected – albeit at some cost to the individual. Not only is the level of performance protected, but also the increased variability that is often seen as an indication of strain in the operator is frequently absent.

In addition, as was indicated in a previous section, interpolated tasks are often insensitive to fatigue. As Broadbent (1979) points out, their failure is attributed to (1) their usual brief duration, which enables even the very tired person to rouse him/herself for a few minutes' effort; and (2) their momentary arousing effect due to the usual difference between primary and interpolated tasks and the circumstances under which performance is extracted.

Recent attention has been directed at the possible changes in the way in which tasks are carried out, i.e. at strategy changes in information processing.

To take one simple initial example, Hockey (1986), speculated on the basis of earlier results reported by Hamilton *et al.* (1977), that a fatigued person would make less reliance on working memory than a fresh, alert person would. Just such a change in the pattern of behaviour has been shown by Schönpflug (1983) and his colleagues on a task that resembled business administration. On this task, information could be gathered and held in mind to aid in later decisions, or the earlier information could be referenced and consulted in the course of performing the task – but at the cost of time-out on the task. When operators were fatigued by having to work under time-pressure or in the presence of distracting noise, they placed less and less reliance on memory, and so either made increasing references to the information, thereby incurring time and effort costs, or they incurred the cost of errors by making risky decisions on the basis of incomplete (or incompletely remembered) information.

The study of fatigued aircrew, reported by Welford *et al.* (1950) quoted above, also indicates a working-memory deficit.

Changes in the way in which tasks are accomplished have also been reported by Hacker *et al.* (1978). They report a particularly interesting example in which subjects had to perform an arithmetic task for three hours. The task involved three levels of complexity and these were presented at random on the trials. Subjects were required to decide which complexity level was presented. For an experimental group, this decision could be aided or anticipated by a correct perceptual judgement prior to the arithmetic trial.

Not surprisingly, all subjects reported fatigue after about an hour on the task, and at that time no further improvements could be discerned in the records of those taking part (some even began to deteriorate). However, whereas the control group maintained their levels of judgements about the trial difficulty, the experimental group grew progressively less accurate, tending to regard each trial as a member of the 'easy' class, and these classification failures were found to be proportional to deterioration in other aspects of performance; interestingly there was no change in their perceptual ability (d') on the pre-trial anticipation judgement: merely a shift in the criterion for reporting each class of events, such that an increasing number were judged 'easy'. It seemed that as the subjects grew increasingly fatigued over time, the demands of the task produced a deterioration that was the combined result of a reduction in aspirations and a criterion shift.

Sperandio (1978) has reported adaptive changes by air traffic controllers in the strategies they use to cope as traffic density and workload increase. He notes in particular that working memory operates to delimit behaviour: with increasing load, less information about each aircraft is attended to, 'plans' are simplified and shortened in as economical a way as possible, according to a hierarchy of goals ranging from safety through speedy economical paths to ones favoured by pilots. As workload increases, there is progressively less focus on secondary goals. Sperandio suggests the controller monitors his own performance in relation to his own, internal standards as well as in relation to those that are externally imposed. At low loads he is operating comfortably within his standards and has no need to change anything; at average loads, he is still within the margin he sets, but has to choose the most economical method to remain there. When the workload increases to the point at which his own standards can no longer be met, the controller either changes his standards or the operating methods he uses to attain them. But when the load is so excessive that even external standards cannot be maintained, he is forced to refuse to work, to take a 'fatigue' break, or to ask for the sector load to be split between operators, e.g. one handling northbound flights, the other southbound ones, as is common on busy routes in the UK. Intriguingly, a recent study in the UK, by Farmer *et al.* (1991), suggests that the immediate impact of a particularly busy work-shift is to leave the controllers reporting *less* fatigue, rather than more: they are aroused rather than enervated by their high workload (CFF seems to reflect this, too).

FATIGUE AS STRESS

A very important contribution to thinking about fatigue was made by Cameron (1973). He argued that far from considering fatigue as separate from other stress effects, we should recognize that fatigue represents a generalized response to stress, extended over a period of time. It was the non-specificity of the fatigue response that he emphasized, thereby putting fatigue firmly into the domain of Selye's (1956) general adaptation syndrome, a view that is widely held today. While acknowledging the contribution of numerous early researchers, including those at Cambridge under Bartlett, who had highlighted the diagnostic value of disturbances of timing, and the adverse effect of fatigue in restricting the field of attention, Cameron argued that too little attention had been paid to the broader aspects of fatigue, including its links with sleep deprivation, and the role of anxiety – which emerges either directly, as part of the general stress response, or may be mediated by the awareness that one's performance is falling short of one's own standards. His conviction that the duration of the stress response, and its recovery time, were key indicators of severity, has prompted many research workers to attend to such aspects, including Frankenhaeuser's group at the Karolinska Institute in Sweden, and the various researchers who have examined the problem of 'burnout', which arises when fatigue from work is not dissipated during leisure, but continues to accumulate.

Neuroendocrine measures

Frankenhaeuser and her colleagues (Frankenhaeuser, 1980, 1986; Lundberg, 1980), continuing the tradition of Selye (1936, 1956), focus on the neuroendocrine response, and have argued cogently that fatigue is merely one aspect of the general stress response to the demands of the psycho-social environment. They focus on the responses of the adrenal hormones: (1) the catecholamines, adrenaline and noradrenaline, whose secretions are associated with activity of the sympathetic-adrenal-medullary system; and (2) the corticosteroid, cortisol, associated with the pituitary-adrenal-cortical system. They point out the complications of these since not only are the hormones secreted in response to stress, but also may themselves operate to activate the peripheral nervous system and so arouse the person, and they may function as cortical neurotransmitters.

According to Frankenhaeuser and her colleagues, the neuroendocrine response to the psychosocial environment reflects the emotional impact which is itself a result of the cognitive appraisal of the demands in relation to the individual's coping style.

Catecholamines reflect the general emotional experience of stress, whether the stressor is in the form of noise, shock, parachuting, radial acceleration, time pressure, workload or cognitive conflict (as on the Stroop task). These all represent disturbances from the optimal or preferred state, and in this respect, a vigilance task with its very low load is just as stressful as a fast-paced task involving cognitive overload (Lundberg, 1980). Generally, adrenaline is more sensitive than noradrenaline to mental stress; but the reverse seems to be true for physical stress, as induced for example by exercise or the cold pressor test.

By contrast with the general response of the catecholamines, corticosteroids are produced by conditions of novelty, strangeness, or unfamiliarity – in which uncertainty is paramount. In general, novel, unfamiliar situations produce feelings of uncertainty and anxiety – often associated with an anticipation of stress – which in turn trigger the secretion of cortisol. Cortisol levels are found to be particularly high in anxious or depressed patients, and in phobic reactions (e.g. arachnaphobics). However, environmental predictability and controllability – or at least the feeling of being in control – lead to suppressed corticosteroid production. Just such a reduction has been found by Hockey and Wiethoff (1990) in a recent study of naturally occurring variation in the daily workloads experienced by young hospital doctors: cortisol levels, which increased with rated workload, were significantly reduced on days when control of the workload was felt to be high.

Frankenhaeuser and her group consider that there are two main components of stress: firstly there is the effort expended in combating the stress, associated with active coping and the attempt to gain control of the situation, and with positive feelings of interest, engagement and determination; secondly there is the distress component, associated with the negative feelings of dissatisfaction, boredom, uncertainty and anxiety, and linked with a passive, helpless approach to confronting stressful situations.

They usefully distinguish between conditions depending on the conjunction of the presence or absence of effort and stress. Effort with distress is characterized by a significantly increased level of adrenaline and, to a lesser extent, of cortisol and is associated with the effects of repetitive, paced work, and with less than successful attempts to cope actively with daily pressures. On the other hand, when the effect is not accompanied by distress, cortisol production is reduced, although adrenaline still increases. This conjunction is associated with relatively happy, successful active coping, with involvement with the task and with the feeling of control. Distress without effort, however, results in a marked increase in cortisol production, accompanied by a more modest increase in adrenaline, the pattern associated with feelings of helplessness and of losing control, seen in depressed patients and those exhibiting 'learned helplessness'. These patterns and the moderating influence of perceived task control are illustrated in Figure 11.4.

In the laboratory, Lundberg (1980) has shown that a vigilance task, which is characterized by low control because of the uncertainty about when target events will arrive, produces heightened feelings of distress and effort, accompanied by increased production of adrenaline and cortisol. In contrast, a choice reaction time task, given the semblance of control by allowing subjects to choose the particular (fast) pace at which items were presented and to modify this if desired, yielded feelings of competence and of interest in the task, of increased effort but reduced distress, along with high levels

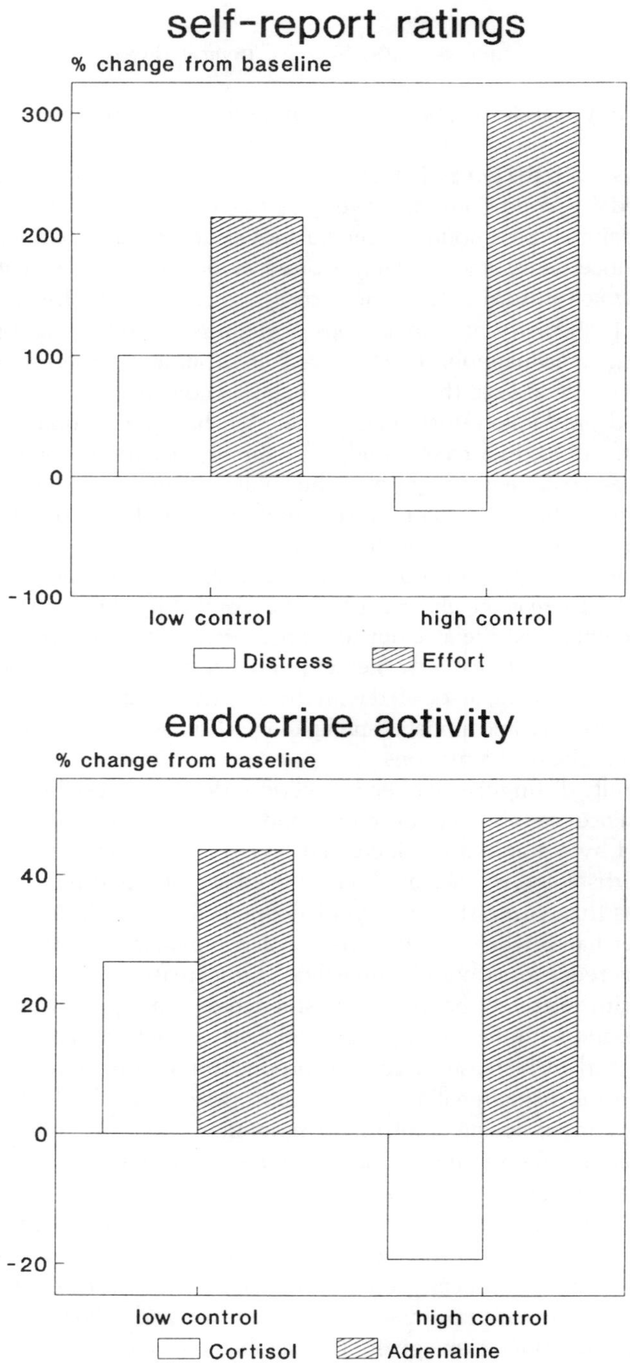

Figure 11.4 The moderating influence of perceived task control on the patterning of affective and biochemical responses to a demanding task. (Adapted from Frankenhaeuser, 1986.)

of adrenaline and noradrenaline but reduced cortisol secretion (below baseline). These same patterns have been observed with process controllers in a steel factory working on jobs classified as high or low in control (Johannson and Sanden, 1982).

An increase in task demands may be met either by increased effort to maintain performance at a standard level, or by maintaining the effort expended but allowing performance to drop. As noted above, Sperandio (1978) has observed both patterns in the behaviour of air traffic controllers. Frankenhaeuser reports that in the laboratory, increased demands on a Stroop-type task involving cognitive conflict were met by increased levels of adrenaline and feelings of distress, but without loss of performance. Again, when an arithmetic task had to be performed in noise, performance was maintained while secretions of adrenaline, noradrenaline and cortisol all increased, along with ratings of effort. However, when subjects were given prior exposure to noise, but to a level that was lower than that met in the experiment, they responded by letting performance levels drop while catecholamine secretion remained unchanged.

The effects reported by Frankenhaeuser and her colleagues are usually obtained from urine assays, less frequently from blood samples. They represent fairly immediate effects of the situational demands, although there is a short lag before secretions are detectable in urine.

However, Tsaneva (1972), among others, has reported that similar patterns of a more chronic nature are to be found in people who experience different stresses in the course of their everyday jobs. She observed increased levels of seventeen-ketosteroids in surgeons and air traffic controllers, and reported that in general the levels increased with the responsibility and mental loading of the job. She also noted that blood-glucose levels were particularly elevated in the air traffic controllers. Tsaneva has paid particular attention to diurnal variations in hormone secretion, and she notes that people whose jobs typically carry a higher mental load show a higher morning adrenaline surge – as the system adapts to the job requirements – the level of adrenaline being proportional to the complexity of the job. Interestingly, after the morning surge, adrenaline tends to decrease over the remainder of the day, whereas noradrenaline increases. Tsaneva suggests that adrenaline increases when adaptive reorganization is required to meet new demands, but that noradrenaline increases when the upper limits of normal physiological adaptation are exceeded. Compensated fatigue is characterized by an increased variability of the neuroendocrine measures due to the increased lability of the systems.

Frankenhaeuser acknowledges that there is only an indirect link between the short- and the long-term effects of stress, that in particular there is no direct evidence linking catecholamines with disease. There is, however, some suggestion that if raised levels are either maintained for too long a period of time or are repeated too frequently, this will lead to functional disturbances in various organs and organ systems making them more vulnerable. This view is linked with the notion that a quicker readjustment represents a more economical response mode, by a better balanced and more efficient system. In this sense, type A coronary prone individuals have less efficient systems than type B individuals, because when periods of work and inactivity alternate, type A persons seem to be inflexible and maintain the same arousal level (as indicated by catecholamine secretions and by heart rate), whereas type B people raise and lower their arousal appropriately.

In a sizeable group of subjects, the percentage of rapid readjusters was found to be higher immediately after a vacation – which was presumed to have improved the general state. Among women working overtime, the overload appears to spread into their leisure, and adrenaline, heart rate, fatigue and irritability all remain high in the evening. The effects of the work demands appear to be lagged, to accumulate progressively over days, and to decay slowly.

Frankenhaeuser's group have also observed that in an identified risk group of workers, namely, those on paced, assembly line work, catecholamine levels actually tend to increase over the shift, and along with feelings of irritability are proportional to the repetitiveness, physical (postural) constraint, and absence of any control over the pace of the line, whereas they may even show a slight decline during the shift in a comparison non-risk group of workers. Frankenhaeuser suggests the assembly line workers are drawing on their reserve capacities, and that this has a detrimental effect when prolonged: absenteeism, inability to relax, and various psychosomatic symptoms are high in this risk group.

However, epidemiological data reported by Karasek (1979) and by Theorell *et al.* (1981) indicate that high job demands have adverse health consequences only when combined with low decision latitude. It is apparent that repetitive, uncontrollable situations lead to slower unwinding, often with carry-over from one day to the next. As will be seen in a later section, this failure of complete recovery can lead to problems of 'burn-out'.

SLEEP DEPRIVATION AND CONTINUOUS PERFORMANCE

At some point in their lives, most people have spent at least one night without sleep and so are familiar with the effects: usually a feeling of fatigue, accompanied by a desire not to have to do anything that requires concentration, and, perhaps surprisingly, a feeling of mild euphoria; if asked to do something that does require concentration, there may well be an awareness of having to exert more effort than usual.

The accompanying chapter by Andrew Tilley, in the present volume, provides a detailed account of what is known about sleep deprivation effects. The present section will do no more than skim the surface of this evidence.

There are no apologies for any redundancy, however, because the question of how we feel when we lose our usual sleep ration, and how this interacts with a demand upon us to remain active, is intimately related to the issue of fatigue.

The importance of the distinction between paced and unpaced tasks, encountered in our discussion of blocking, and of the consequences of a slowing in processing speed, is again brought home dramatically in the Walter Reed studies on sleep deprivation which led them to propose their 'lapse' hypothesis regarding the effects (e.g. Williams *et al.*, 1959). According to this view, the primary impairment during sleep loss takes the form of lapses, or micro-sleeps. On a paced task, lapses would inevitably produce a performance decrement, because transient events coinciding with lapses would be missed and non-transient ones responded to only after a delay; on a self-paced task, such lapses merely slow down the process, they do not interfere with its accuracy – and even the slowing could be compensated for if necessary by bursts of speed at other moments. When a reaction time task is used, it is usually only the longest reaction times (RTs) that are affected by loss of sleep; shortest RTs are about as fast as ever. With a fast paced vigilance task requiring discriminations between signal and non-signal events, errors of omission and commission both increase under sleep loss, but it is the omission errors that are particularly vulnerable to the impaired state: as sleep loss builds up, their increased incidence takes place earlier and earlier in the task, and then rises in a near linear fashion over time. In addition, during sleep loss, omissions are considerably affected by the unpredictability of signal arrival times. Also, when workload is increased either by making the task more difficult (so that processing time is increased), or by increasing the time pressure (reducing the time allowed for responding), sleep loss causes increased errors of omission.

The elementary lapse hypothesis has its critics. Kjellberg (1977) suggests that sleep deprivation involves more than just lapses: it potentiates the de-arousing effect of certain situational variables; and more recently Broughton (1989) has suggested that sleep loss may produce a more continuous loss of alertness/arousal, involving smooth oscillations of state, rather than the step-like troughs associated with the lapse hypothesis.

Johnson (1982) has described the tasks most sensitive to sleep loss as those that are long, paced, complex, with high attention and vigilance requirements, with demands on a short-term memory chain and which do not provide information to the subject on how well he/she is performing. He also points out that controlled processes are more vulnerable than automatic ones to sleep loss – whether the level of processing is an inherent feature of the task or is due to the person's lack of proficiency. In addition to skill level, vulnerability to sleep loss is also affected by the person's level of motivation and by how interesting they find the task. This is clearly revealed in a study reported by Horne *et al.* (1983), in which subjects who were

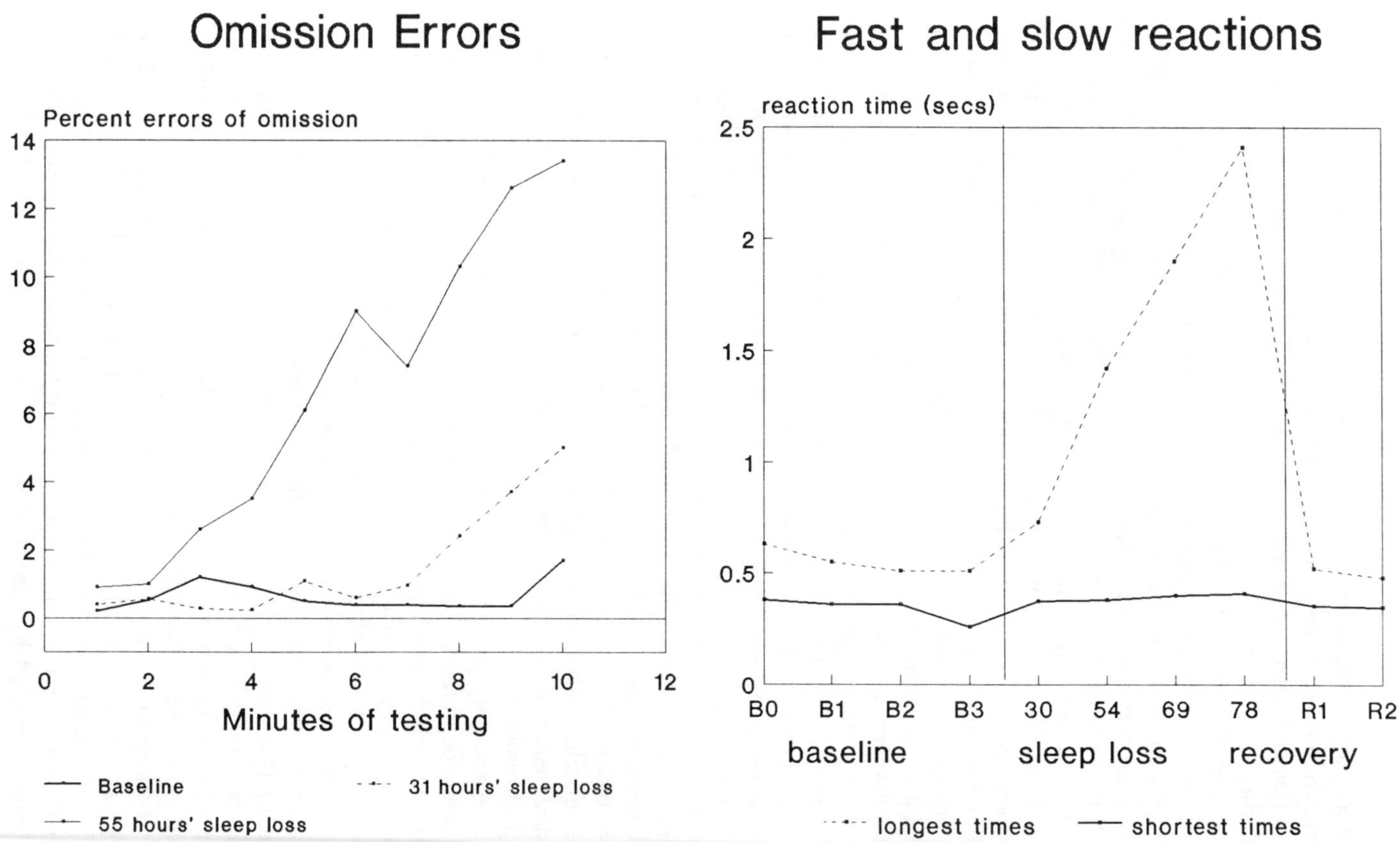

Figure 11.5 The influence of sleep loss on omissions on a fast paced task of sustained attention; and on the ten longest (broken line) and ten shortest (solid line) RTs on a reaction-time task. (Adapted from Williams *et al.*, 1959.)

fatigued by the sleep loss and who were growing progressively less effective at a vigilance task, were nevertheless enthusiastic to play a war game in between sessions on the vigilance task. These personal and task variables associated with vulnerability to sleep loss are so similar to the ones that produce sensitivity to fatigue that there can be little doubt that the two share much in common.

There is a general view that sleep deprivation is a stressor like any other. For example, Alluisi (1972) has stated that ten years' work with the MTPB had failed to indicate differential performance effects in the different functional areas from stresses such as (1) demanding work/rest schedules, (2) sleep loss, (3) operator loading, or (4) illness. He likened the situation to that in medicine where the somatic response to infection is very much a general response, without regard to the type of infection (bacterial, viral, parasitic). He thought it most likely that the behavioural effects of, or performance reactions to, stresses such as sleep loss are for the most part general effects, independent of the specific stress, except that when a specific function (channel, resource) is directly affected then the general behavioural reaction will show an overlaid effect based on the impairment of that function or channel.

In contrast to this commonly held view that all stresses produce the same syndrome (e.g. Alluisi, 1972; Selye, 1956), Froberg and his colleagues (e.g. Froberg *et al.*, 1972) have provided evidence that sleep deprivation is distinct from other stressors, in that it leaves the level and circadian rhythm in adrenaline and noradrenaline unperturbed; in addition, when a demanding task is given, the catecholamine response is as usual and is not accentuated by the sleep loss. In studies with soldiers deprived of sleep for three days, they found consistent evidence that subjective ratings of fatigue and stress increased from one day to the next, but did not find equivalent evidence of changes in adrenaline or noradrenaline or in performance at rifle shooting. They did find, however, that fatigue and performance (which were themselves negatively correlated) were significantly correlated with catecholamine levels: fatigue was negatively related to adrenaline, positively to noradrenaline; performance bore the opposite relations with the catecholamines. Further examination of the rhythmic fluctuations in their data led Froberg and his colleagues to conclude that the daily rhythms of adrenaline, fatigue and performance were related, and that this accounted fully for the correlations; but that the links with noradrenaline did not depend on the rhythms, and hence probably reflect a 'stress' factor – despite the absence of progressive trends in the noradrenaline levels with increasing sleep deprivation.

Not all studies, however, have found adrenaline to be independent of sleep need. Nishihara *et al.* (1985), for example, report that adrenaline – but not noradrenaline – was significantly, negatively, correlated with sleep efficiency in a group of young men who bed-rested for a week.

The general view, however, is that sympathoadrenal activity is little altered by sleep deprivation alone, but that changes may appear when the sleep loss is accompanied by demanding task activity (Horne, 1978, 1985). For example, in Froberg's studies, raised adrenocortical and adrenomedullary activities were found when the sleep loss was accompanied by simulated 'battle stress', but not when this was absent. Changes in corticosteroid or noradrenaline production may be related to distressing aspects of the experience rather than to the sleep loss itself; while attempts to inject compensatory effort in order to remain effective are likely to produce increased adrenaline output.

That sleep-deprived subjects may inject extra effort to compensate for their state-dependent impairment has been widely held. A compelling illustration is provided by Wilkinson (1962). He found that during performance at an adding task, the muscle tension in sleep-deprived subjects increased; that those whose tension increased most were the ones whose performance was least impaired; and that those whose tension increased least were the most impaired in terms of both speed and accuracy on the task. This finding, which brings to mind an earlier study by Freeman (1931), strongly suggests that the muscle tension reflects effort mobilized by the subjects to overcome their fatigue.

An interesting finding from a recent study of patients suffering from chronic sleep disturbance suggests that subjective reports of tiredness depend on decreased supranuclear or sympathetic activity; whereas if given the opportunity to sleep, the sleep latency depends on parasympathetic activity (Pressman and Fry, 1989).

Studies combining sleep deprivation with demands for sustained performance are grouped under the heading of 'continuous performance'.

Myles and Romet (1987), for example, conducted a study that simulated sustained combat engineering operations involving self-paced physical work. Their results suggest that, on its own, sleep deprivation for periods of forty-seven and sixty-nine hours has little effect, and they claim that physiological systems can tolerate up to sixty-five hours' sleep debt without ill-effect. They did find, however, that the intensity of the work and the rate of work both declined over time while fatigue ratings increased. Previously, referring to mental performance, Meddis (1982) had suggested that sleep deprivation mainly affects the ability to sustain performance, rather than causing a decline in any specific capacity; that it induces a disinclination towards activity, and, in particular, leads to a decrease in interest and motivation to initiate anything that does not lead to sleep.

Angus and Heslegrave (1985) suggested that performance under sleep deprivation appeared to be resource-limited, with reduced numbers of attempted trials, rather than data-limited, with declines in performance accuracy. In a recent study, reported by Mikulincer *et al.* (1989), subjects were required to perform a search and memory task at intervals throughout the course of a period of seventy-two hours' sleep loss. The authors found that both output and accuracy declined over time, but that subjective ratings of fatigue state were more closely related to output than to accuracy. Of particular significance, they found that rated motivation to initiate leisure activities declined more noticeably than motivation to perform an experimental trial. [We note that this contrasts with the enthusiastic war-gamers reported by Horne *et al.* (1983), referred to above.]

In a recent review of their work in the UK on continuous performance by soldiers, Allnutt *et al.* (1990) confirm the generally high level capability of these well-motivated teams to remain effective despite substantial sleep loss. They report that although members of platoons who received no sleep failed to last more than four days on a simulated combat exercise, half of those with only one-and-a-half hours' sleep in a twenty-four hour period survived for nine days, but with major degradation in their effectiveness, while ninety per cent of those with three hours' sleep per day lasted throughout with less deterioration. Interestingly, interpolated cognitive tasks failed to distinguish the platoons. In a partial follow-up study, it was found that after three and three-quarter days without sleep, a further three days with merely four-hours' sleep on each restored performance to eighty eight per cent of its control level. In one study, they examined sixty five hours' continuous performance at a ground control station (GCS) where crews alternated between five-hours operating the GCS and five hours working at a battery of laboratory tasks. Compared with baseline and recovery days, the period of sleep deprivation produced little evidence of any decline in operating the central GCS, although their was some blurring of the priorities of component tasks, higher priority tasks suffering more. On the laboratory tasks, however, where individual rather than team performance was being assessed, and where the soldiers were perhaps less dedicated to the job in hand, they found consistent evidence of deterioration due to sleep debt, and that the slower, less accurate performance was accompanied by an increase in fatigue, sleepiness and tension ratings, while hedonic tone declined. They also found that the salivary cortisol rhythm was disturbed but that total adrenocortical activity remained unaltered (*cf.* Froberg *et al.*, 1972).

PROLONGED FATIGUE FROM WORK

As was seen previously, Cameron (1973), among others, suggested that the term fatigue is synonymous with a generalized stress response over time; that it is a disease of adaptation to demands which tax or exceed an individual's resources.

The following sections examine prolonged fatigue at work from this perspective. Fatigue is firstly considered as a response to work demands, during which attempts are made to maintain or increase performance. It is then demonstrated that the effects of some demands persist beyond the demand itself and become known as after-effects. Despite the pleas of Cameron

(1973), research into the time course of after-effects has been somewhat neglected but an economic return to baseline physiological and emotional levels is acknowledged as vitally important if the consequences of longer-term/chronic effects are to be avoided (*cf.* Frankenhaeuser, 1980, 1986). Impaired recovery can lead to chronic fatigue; although in some cases, especially where the demands are of an intensely and persistently emotional nature, burnout may result. (Burnout includes a component related to chronic fatigue – emotional exhaustion – but also involves negative attitudinal changes.)

Stress from work

Given that we spend up to half our waking hours at work, it is unfortunate that so many people report feelings of stress and dissatisfaction associated with their work (Moos, 1988). 'For human beings, one of the most significant and persistent sources of stress is their job' (Hockey and Wiethoff, 1990, p. 231).

Fatigue is just one of the many symptoms that can result from work stressors. There is much consistency in the sources of work stress which are typically reported. For example, Cooper and Marshall (1976) identified five primary sources of stress at work:

1. Factors intrinsic to the job, such as work overload/underload, time pressures, shift work, physical working conditions and repetitive work.
2. Role-based stress; such as role ambiguity, role conflict and responsibility.
3. Relationships with subordinates, colleagues and superiors.
4. Career development factors; such as lack of job security, under/over-promotion, and thwarted ambition.
5. Organizational structure and climate; including office politics, communication, participation and organizational thrust.

There is, however, great individual variation in response to such stressors. That is, different job stressors may have different, specific consequences (see Gupta and Beehr, 1979).

In addition to the individual variation in the effects of occupational stressors, most studies do not easily accommodate the individual who feels under pressure but also derives satisfaction from that pressure. The person–environment (PE) interactional model of occupational stress was conceived in response to such criticism (e.g. French *et al.*, 1982). Stress is defined as a function of the discrepancy between the individual's resources and work demands. Thus, high job demands *per se* may not result in stress symptoms if they can be offset by, for example, a skilled performance.

PE fit forms the framework for many theories of organizational stress, such as Karasek's (1979) job demands–control model. Karasek (1979) found that high job demands need not automatically result in the experience of high strain; control (or job decision latitude, to use Karasek's terminology) is a major moderating factor. That is, only those jobs which were reported to have both high work demands and low opportunity for control were associated with stress symptoms.

Karasek's findings suggest that the individual can effectively manage his or her workload in controllable situations. In addition, we reiterate that individuals may exercise choice in resolving stressful situations. People may choose to maintain performance levels by increasing effort (which may be potentially costly in the long term), or they may decide to adopt a more passive strategy of allowing performance to deteriorate if necessary. In other words, the effects of work demands are more a function of how they are appraised (e.g. Lazarus and Folkman, 1984) and acted upon (Hockey and Wiethoff, 1990), than the demands themselves.

In preceding pages we have argued for the multi-level measurement of fatigue and work strain to include performance, physiological and psychological indicators. We agree with Hockey (1986) that it may be necessary practice in situations where performance goals are protected. The costs of an active coping strategy may only be detected in measures of endocrine activity, and/or subjective effort and fatigue. This methodology was applied in a study of junior house officers during their pre-registration year in a hospital, a study briefly referred to in preceding pages (Hockey and Wiethoff, 1990). Thirty-two junior doctors were examined over a five-month period, with an aim of investigating the moderating effects of coping styles on the work demands–strain relationship. Coping styles were identified by a specially designed checklist of fifteen stressful events and extreme coping groups (active versus passive) were selected. Not surprisingly, tension was experienced by both groups on high workload days. However, the active group showed an effect of workload on fatigue which was not demonstrated by the passive group. Fatigue is therefore viewed as the result of sustained mental effort in order to preserve performance, whereas tension appears to be concerned with how demands are appraised rather than with the individual's response to those demands.

After-effects

As we saw earlier, the notion of after-effects refers to the idea that prolonged/continuous exposure to a stressor may produce effects that appear after the stressor stimulation has ceased (Cohen, 1980). After-effects are the costs of adaptation to demands; part of Selye's (1956) 'diseases of adaptation'. Although individuals may adapt to extreme conditions, 'such adjustments often have indirect effects that are deleterious' (Dubos, 1968, p. 139). The after-effects of work have long been considered under the rubric of 'fatigue'.

Prolonged work or stress commonly gives rise to a general state, reflected in feelings of subjective tiredness or fatigue. This can be clearly seen in reports from a series of studies on city bus-drivers in the Netherlands (see Kompier, 1988). The drivers worked under very taxing conditions of double irregularity (shift schedules and starting times were irregular), in vehicles which displayed poor ergonomic design. Many of the men were leaving work on medical grounds, well before the age of fifty years. In addition to self-reported musculo-skeletal disorders and general health problems, sleep complaints were common. Feelings of fatigue both during and after work were reported. Work performance was maintained and accompanied by an increase in adrenaline secretion. Subjective workload measures suggested that this response was indicative of increased effort to meet task demands by maintaining adequate performance.

Broadbent (1979) noted the extent to which after-effects may affect the organization of complex performance. Some parts of a performance may be omitted, or performed out of sequence with the whole performance. Other parts may even be timed incorrectly. The extent to which such variations in performance may be tolerated will be a function of the personal and organization risk associated with the task. Van Dijk and Meijman (1986) called for special attention to be paid to the problem of fatigue with respect to safety procedures at work. Fatigue may limit an operator's field of perception and attention. His/her judgement may be impaired to the extent that risk-taking behaviour could result. Safety/protection devices may be discarded as slight bodily discomfort becomes significantly annoying under stress, and combined with a common rise in irritability, the fatigued operator may, in general, be less willing to conform to safety procedures.

As we have already intimated, fatigue after-effects are notoriously difficult to demonstrate with performance tasks alone. For example, in an oft quoted study, Chiles (1955) had subjects perform in an aircraft simulator for up to fifty-six hours without rest, except periodically performing a tracking task. As the experiment neared its conclusion, some subjects were so exhausted that it was necessary to carry them to the task, yet their subsequent performance was well within acceptable limits. In addition to the possibility of the fatigue indicator task acting as a novel/arousing stimulus, or as a compensatory activity, the theme of performance protection is prolific. Most people do not easily give up or disengage from a crisis or a salient task. They behave in a way that is necessary to maintain life, or to function properly, according to a personally salient goal structure (Kahneman, 1973). By a variety of mechanisms or strategies, the individual adjusts to the demands of a task, albeit accruing costs in the process.

Early empirical research on stress after-effects focused on the stressor effects on physical and psychological health. For example, many studies examined the cumulative effects of disease, malnutrition and toxic chemicals on normal bodily functioning (see Dubos, 1965). More recent work has examined post-stressor effects on social behaviour and performance (Glass and Singer, 1972). The post-stimulation effects of stressors on social and performance behaviour will be examined in turn, although more attention will be paid to the latter.

SOCIAL BEHAVIOUR

The effects of stressors on social behaviour can be summarized by a general decrease in sensitivity to others. Helping behaviour decreases (Cohen and Spacapan, 1978, experiment 2; Sherrod and Downs, 1974), and aggressive behaviour increases (Donnerstein and Wilson, 1976) after exposure to unpredictable, uncontrollable stress.

In a study of thirty-three air traffic controllers and twenty-seven wives, who completed surveys on three consecutive days, Repetti (1989) found that workload (objective and subjective) was related to the couples' descriptions of the air traffic controller's behaviour after work. On evenings when the spouse provided high emotional support, workload was associated with less expression of anger and increased social withdrawal. Repetti has suggested that social withdrawal may be a behavioural correlate of unwinding and that the spouse facilitates the stressed partner's return to baseline emotional and physiological levels.

A number of recent studies have investigated the association between daily stress events and affect (e.g. Bolger *et al.*, 1989a; Caspi *et al.*, 1987; Clark and Watson, 1988; DeLongis *et al.*, 1988; Watson, 1988; Stone, 1987). Although it has been suggested that the effects of daily stressors do not affect mood beyond the day of their occurrence (e.g. Rehm, 1978; Stone and Neale, 1984), Bolger *et al.* (1989) and DeLongis *et al.* (1988) demonstrated that mood is significantly improved on the day following a stressful event than on other 'stress-free' days. However, some people with low personal or social resources may not be amongst those who quickly recover from the effects of a stressor, particularly if it is a chronic event. Caspi *et al.* (1987) showed that the effects of stress persist beyond a single day for those individuals who are socially isolated or who endure chronically stressful demands.

PERFORMANCE

Performance was studied extensively in Glass and Singer's (1972) series of studies which aimed to investigate the cognitive aspects of stressor-mediated performance on tasks which were administered immediately after cessation of the stressor. Five studies were reported, in which post-stimulation effects of exposure to unpredictable, uncontrollable noise were examined. Immediately following noise exposure, subjects were administered one or more of three measures: the Feather (1961) tolerance for frustration task, a proofreading task, and the Stroop (1935) colour–word task. Post-stimulation deficits in performance occurred on all three of the tasks and was generally replicated across the five studies. The post-stimulation effect of lowered persistence in response to noise has been frequently replicated (e.g. Rotton *et al.*, 1978; Sherrod *et al.*, 1977; Wollwill *et al.*, 1976), and readers are referred to Cohen (1980) for a more detailed review. To summarize, the after-effects of noise on performance are consistent for variable continuous and steady-state continuous noise and somewhat mixed for intermittent exposure. This may be due to the greater exposure time during continuous stimulation. However, both findings provide considerable support for the reliability of the post-noise effect.

High work rate and duration (i.e. high taskload) acts as a stressor which shows post-stimulation effects. Cohen and Spacapan (1978, experiment 1) manipulated the taskload by having one group of subjects respond to one hundred lights per minute in a four-choice reaction time experiment, and another group respond to just fifty lights per minute. On completion of the tasks, those who had been subjected to the higher taskload had less tolerance for frustration than those who had responded to fifty lights per minute. Rotton *et al.* (1978) similarly showed reduced performance in a persistence test following high taskload.

Cohen (1980) lists various social and non-social stressors that produce after-effects and, in general, after-effects are most likely to occur when the stressor is clearly unpredictable/uncontrollable and when a sensitive indicator is used.

It may be argued that after-effects are merely the result of the experimenter mistreating or even offending his/her subjects, after which they do not feel inclined to co-operate further. However, after-effects have been shown to occur in studies which used a different experimenter for the subsequent task and also in some field studies where the experimenter and the stressor cannot be seen to be related.

Recovery

It can thus be seen that the stress reaction does not simply dissipate with termination of the stressor and that this may have implications for long-term individual health. After stressor termination the individual requires a recovery period, during which he/she can return to a normal/pre-stressor level of functioning. This is part of a normal, or non-pathological stress adaptation process, during which the individual may increase his/her activity in order to meet an episode of demands. This will be followed by a diminution of activity as the demands lessen, and a period of recovery (below baseline activity), during which the individual achieves a homeostatic balance of all physiological and psychological systems. Notably, however, a distinctly harmful, or pathological, stress reaction may be envisaged if the stressor is particularly ambiguous, exists over a long period of time, or is part of a constellation of stressors existing at once. In such a situation, the individual may persistently increase his/her activity in an attempt to meet ever increasing or durable demands. Energetic reserves may well be consumed during this time, but the important point is that the individual may maintain constant levels of increased activity without replenishing the body in a below-baseline recovery period. Under these conditions the individual does not return to normal physiological or emotional functioning as rapidly as from the non-pathological condition. Instead, the stress reaction continues and becomes potentially damaging. The economics of the stress response play an important role in determining the problem of chronic disturbance. It is in the individual's best interests to exhibit an 'economic' response and to deactivate/unwind quickly after stressor termination.

The after-effects of stressors have been well documented, but the time course of the effect has received little attention since post-stimulation tasks have usually been administered shortly after stressor termination (Cohen, 1980).

Attributes of the work situation may facilitate a rapid return to neuroendocrine and physiological baselines (e.g. control opportunity), whereas some conditions, such as repetitive and uncontrollable work, may slow down the unwinding process (Frankenhaeuser, 1981). The home/work interaction is also of importance in predicting unwinding from work. The physiological unwinding seen by Frankenhaeuser *et al.* (1987) in male managers following a stressful day, was not demonstrated for female managers. [This may be a result of the fact that males do not respond to their partner's demanding work day by increasing their efforts at home. In contrast, females tend to compensate for their partner's demanding day by lightening some of the tasks the men would normally undertake (Bolger *et al.*, 1989b).] Depue and Monroe (1986) suggest that stress may be more easily identified by the presence of variations in response over time, and by the time it takes the individual to recover from a stressor: stressed people show more variable responses and take longer to recover to physiological baseline levels than their lesser stressed counterparts. Similarly, Steptoe (1987) has argued that an individual's ability to deactivate after a stressful situation may be even more important for long-term health than the acute response itself. The need for research into unwinding during the recovery period is thus exemplified and underlines the view of Cameron (1973) that the time required for recovery provides the most promising method of assessing the severity of fatigue.

Chronic fatigue

As Cameron (1973) points out, fatigue is not likely to be considered a problem until normal rest and sleep do not lead to full recovery before the onset of the next set of demands. The importance of chronic fatigue effects was emphasized by Bartley and Chute (1947), who noted that chronic fatigue was prevalent in clinical practice. Chronic fatigue is fatigue which does not dissipate during the normal processes/period of rest and recuperation (Cameron, 1973). (We are suggesting that this pathological response is the inevitable result of prolonged demands and does not, as seems to be the case in 'chronic fatigue syndrome', imply any viral involvement.)

The protection of performance or active coping cannot be maintained indefinitely in the face of repeated or chronic demands, irrespective of the individual's 'sheer dogged fortitude' (Bartlett, 1953). A cumulative process is assumed ultimately to have serious negative consequences for the individual. For example, the city bus-drivers of The Netherlands (Kompier, 1988) showed progressive deterioration of health and well-being, with sleep complaints and subjective fatigue being early predictors of high absenteeism, disability and turnover.

The mechanism by which recovery from fatigue is retarded may comprise an emotional component of the previous demand. For example, whilst the individual is concerned with actually performing a task, anxiety may not interfere. However, Lovibond (1965) provides examples of anxiety which peaks after the demand, and Cameron (1973) suggested that this emotion may inhibit the recovery process and result in chronic fatigue.

Given that the response to chronic demands may be a significant mechanism in the aetiology of ill health, the duration of that response is a critical variable. Its importance becomes even greater for shift workers who may have little time in which to recover when working certain shift systems, and for working women whose partners do not relieve the dual load.

Burnout

Burnout is a special term which is used to describe a syndrome of negative consequences of relatively long-term occupational stress. The term was coined by Freudenberger in 1974 and broadly defined as a stress reaction caused by the relentless pursuit of success. Similarly, Cherniss (1980) described burnout as a disease of over-commitment. Other definitions (e.g. Maslach and Jackson, 1981) are narrower, relating burnout to interpersonal stress, inherent in the human service professions. Indeed, burnout is often exclusively applied to people who work in the caring professions. In addition to being strongly associated with health care professionals, however, burnout has been found in lawyers, prison warders, teachers and police (Maslach, 1976). Maslach and her associates have focused their definitions on behavioural and attitudinal changes: 'the loss of concern for people with whom one is working... characterized by an emotional exhaustion in which the professional no longer has any positive feelings, sympathy or respect for clients or patients. A very cynical and dehumanized perception of these people often develops, in which they are labelled in derogatory ways and treated accordingly' (Maslach and Pines, 1977, pp. 100, 101). Burnout can therefore be considered to be a change in motivation. What was once a calling becomes merely a job. Storlie (1979) took a somewhat dramatic view, defining burnout as a 'highly personal happening inside the nurse – the literal collapse of the human spirit' (p. 108).

It is hardly surprising that burnout has been seen to have a deleterious effect on work performance. Research (e.g. Freudenberger, 1974, 1975; Maslach, 1976, 1978a, 1978b, 1979; Maslach and Jackson, 1978, 1979; Jackson and Maslach, 1980; Maslach and Pines, 1977; Pines and Maslach, 1978, 1980) suggests that burnout can lead to a deterioration in the quality of care or service, as the professional care-worker experiences exhaustion and a lack of empathy for his/her clients. The process may even extend to the degree that the clients are seen as deserving of their present state. The professional who burns out is not able to cope with the emotional demands of the work (Maslach and Pines, 1977). Burnout is correlated with various self-report measures of personal distress (e.g. physical exhaustion, insomnia, increased use of drug/alcohol and marital/family problems) (Maslach and Jackson, 1981). These personal difficulties may eventually encroach upon the organization as low morale begins to be manifested in absenteeism and finally the act of quitting the job (Maslach and Pines, 1977). Burnout is therefore a serious issue for employee and organization alike.

Various researchers have categorized the concept and outlined stages in its development. Maslach outlines three stages (e.g. Maslach, 1976) in the gradual loss of caring:

1. Emotional exhaustion.
2. Cynicism and negative attitudes towards co-workers and patients.
3. Total disgust or terminal burnout.

It is generally regarded as important to recognize the symptoms of burnout in its early stages because the chances of recovery from the third stage are considered to be very slim. In contrast to this popular view, however, Edelwich and Brodsky (1980) and Numerof and Gillespie (1983) do not see burnout as a pathological event. Instead, burnout is regarded as a cyclical process of disillusionment. This perspective is more optimistic with respect to intervention and prognosis.

Golembiewski and Munzenrider (1981), Leiter and Maslach (1988) and Maslach and Jackson (1984b) agree and provide evidence to the fact that burnout profiles are related to profiles of work characteristics, rather than to demographic characteristics. Consonant with the view that burnout is a consequence of interpersonal demands, burnout *per se* has often been associated with the amount and type of such contact. For example, in a study of public contact workers, Maslach and Jackson (1984b) found that the number of clients and the emotional stressfulness of the contacts contributed to burnout. Furthermore, Burke *et al.* (1984) noted that burnout was correlated with low peer support. However, the three aspects of burnout (emotional exhaustion, depersonalization and feelings of low personal achievement) are each related to somewhat different sets of job conditions and behavioural reactions. To illustrate, Maslach and Jackson (1984a) discussed the differential effects of job conditions on burnout. Burnout in nurses was assessed by the Maslach Burnout Inventory (Maslach and Jackson, 1979, 1981) and it was found that lack of participation in organizational decision making was associated with feelings of depersonalization, but not with personal accomplishment or emotional exhaustion. Work pressure was related to emotional exhaustion and to low personal accomplishment, but not to depersonalization. Lack of feedback from clients was most strongly related to depersonalization, less related to low personal accomplishment and not related at all to emotional exhaustion. That is, burnout is not a unitary concept. The implication of this is that interventions may be targeted at decreasing the particular burnout aspect that is most problematic.

Despite the fact that burnout is a reaction to a stressful work situation, its effects commonly transcend the work setting. In other words, burnout becomes a post-stimulation effect, specifically relating to emotional, behavioural and social after-effects. In a study of police officers, Jackson and Maslach (1982) found that emotionally exhausted officers were described by their wives as returning home in an angry, upset, tense and anxious state. Emotional exhaustion in doctors was evinced by conscious efforts to withdraw socially (Maslach and Jackson, 1982). As is often the case, the family becomes the ultimate victim of the after-effects of work-related stress.

In sum, burnout may be seem as a stress reaction, characterized by attitudinal/motivational changes, which if left unrecognized or unresolved transcend the work setting and detract from the quality of non-work life. In turn, this impaired home life may subsequently serve to exacerbate the perceived working conditions and a chronic attitudinal disturbance may result.

Because burnout is considered to be a particular problem for individuals whose family or personal life and work are not clearly delineated (*cf.* the finding that fatigue after-effects are greater when indicator tests are very similar to the fatiguing task), most remedial measures involve either distancing or compensatory activities. Distancing may be either physical or psychological. Maslach (1978a) advocates the deliberate use of decompression routines, which are special activities performed outside work that allow individuals to relax and unwind. The use of social outlets and appropriate humour also provide elements by which the individual may compartmentalize his/her work and home life. Special leisure plans have even been designed to beat burnout (e.g. Dailey, 1985).

A lack of supportive relationships has consistently been shown to enhance vulnerability to burnout (Cronin-Stubbs, 1982; Cronin-Stubbs and Brophy, 1985; Hare *et al.*, 1988; Yasko, 1983), and the protective nature of adequate social support is a common theme in intervention studies.

CONCLUSIONS

While preparing this chapter, it has seemed that the story of fatigue has been very much a search for an effect whose existence is presumed, but whose appearance is elusive. For many, it is axiomatic that prolonged, demanding work is fatiguing; the problem has been to show it. It is the repeated failures to demonstrate the presence of fatigue, in the continued, firm conviction that it exists, that has prompted so much work on the problem; and it is this disparity that has led to the research effort on indirect ways of indicating fatigue. There seem parallels with Horne's (1985) comments on the presumed restorative powers of sleep.

Historically, it seems that the analytic endeavours of the early researchers looking for simple decrements, achieved a position where knowledge of the temporal structure of a task (including its sequential properties, and whether it was paced or not), helped to reduce the variance in predicting the typical outcome of any fatiguing effects. Much of this work, however, focused on the task itself, and paid relatively little heed to the active role of the individual performing the task. The more recent work which has focused on strategies, and on the variations in strategy that are dependent on the fatigue state of the operator, have helped further to reduce or explain the variance in fatigue effects. This variance has been reduced still further by the yet more recent work which looks at the part played by individual differences, most notably in coping style.

As Cameron (1973) recognized, fatigue involves the integration over time of the demands imposed by a task. We have always been able to measure the duration of a task, but it is doubtful if we were as reliably equipped to make a valid assessment of the imposed workload as we have become over the past decade. Research on workload and its measurement (e.g. Moray, 1979; O'Donnell and Eggemeier, 1986) has yielded subjective rating scales, secondary task techniques, and electro–physiological indicators that have the potential to provide convergent evidence on the task or work demands that are being experienced, and the effort expended in meeting them.

The notion that fatigue is measurable by its recovery seems a sound one, but whereas some advances can be claimed in looking at the more enduring effects, such as burnout or work stress, relatively little has been done on the shorter term, acute effects. This, it would seem, is more a question of focal interest than lack of techniques.

This sketch of the fatigue literature has shown that fatigue is intimately related to sleep deprivation. We have seen that in some tasks, the effects may show up in the form of a simple decrement in the speed of responding, while in other cases, the fatigue will be indicated by a decreased level of control. We have also seen that with more complex, skilled performance, the effect of fatigue is to disturb the essential timing, to impair memory for recently acquired information, and perhaps, to restrict attention increasingly with respect to sources of task-relevant information (although, paradoxically, we may become less resistant to distraction from task-irrelevant sources). There are also effects that seem to depend on the person who is performing the task, so that the observed effects depend on coping style, or personality type, as much as on the task demands themselves. We also recognize that many tasks contain as many solution paths as there are people attempting to solve them, and that therefore the effect of fatigue is to be inferred from changes in strategy, rather than from straightforward shifts in a simple parameter like speed or accuracy.

The general view that fatigue is non-specific, and so no different from any other stress-response is supported by numerous studies, but also refuted by the collation of data presented by Hockey (1986), although as has been seen, his analysis revealed little or no difference between fatigue arising from continued task performance and the fatigue associated with lack of sleep.

The reliable observation that sleep deprivation and time-on-task interact in determining the onset and extent of a performance decrement strongly suggests they share a common locus of effect. This broadly applies to total sleep deprivation. We are aware, however, that this view may be complicated by the possible differential effects of the quality of the sleep in partial sleep deprivation studies. The simplest view is that staying awake is itself fatiguing (see, for example, Folkard and Akerstedt, 1991); that working at a task is even more fatiguing, an influence that increases with the workload demands; and that sleep loss exacerbates or potentiates these effects. If performance is protected, we should seek indirect evidence of the costs, either during performance itself, or at its cessation; and if necessary pursue any after-effects (and recovery from them) that carry over after performance has ceased. Fatigue may be a state, but it is a state that is arrived at, and there remain many gaps in our knowledge about the dynamics of this process.

REFERENCES

Allnutt, M.F., Haslam, D.R., Rejman, M.H. and Green, S. (1990) Sustained performance and some effects on the design and operation of complex systems. *Philosophical Transforms of the Royal Society, Lond.* **B327**: 529–41.

Alluisi, E.A. (1972) Influence of work-rest scheduling and sleep loss on sustained performance. In *Aspects of Human Efficiency*, edited by W.P. Colquhoun. London: English Universities Press Ltd, pp. 199–215.

Alluisi, E.A., Coates, G.D. and Morgan, B.B. (1977) Effects of temporal stressors on vigilance and information processing. In *Vigilance, Theory, Operational Performance and Physiological Correlates*, edited by R.R. Mackie. New York: Plenum Press, pp. 361–421.

Angus, R.G. and Heslegrave, R.J. (1985) Effects of sleep loss on sustained cognitive performance during a command and control simulation. *Behavior Research Methods, Instruments & Computers* **17**(1): 55–67.

Ash, I.E. (1914) Fatigue and its effect upon control. *Arch. Psychology* **31**: 1–61.
Barth, J.L., Holding, D.H. and Stamford, B.A. (1976) Risk versus effort in the assessment of motor fatigue. *Journal of Motor Behavior* **8**: 189–194.
Bartlett, F.C. (1943) Fatigue following highly skilled work. *Proceedings of the Royal Society* (B) **131**: 147–257.
Bartlett, F.C. (1953) Psychological criteria of fatigue. In *Symposium on Fatigue*, edited by W.F Floyd and A.T. Welford. London: H.K. Lewis.
Bartley, S.H. and Chute, E. (1947) *Fatigue and Impairment in Man*. New York: McGraw-Hill.
Benedict, F.G. and Benedict, C.G. (1933) Mental effort in relation to gaseous exchange, heart rate and mechanics of respiration. Carnegie Institute of Washington **446**.
Bertelson, P. and Joffe, R. (1963) Blockings in prolonged serial responding. *Ergonomics* **6**: 109–16.
Bills, A.G. (1931) A new principle of mental fatigue. *Am. J. Psychol.* **43**: 230–45.
Bolger, N., DeLongis, A., Kessler, R.C. and Wethington, E. (1989a) The contagion of stress across multiple roles. *Journal of Marriage and the Family* **51**: 175–83.
Bolger, N., DeLongis, A., Kessler, R.C. and Schilling, E.A. (1989b) Effects of daily stress on negative mood. *Journal of Personality and Social Psychology* **57**: 808–18.
Bradford Hill, A. and Williams, G.O. (1943). *An Investigation of Landing Accidents in Relation to Fatigue*. Flying Personnel Research Committee Report 423, April 1943. Reprinted in E.J. Dearnaley and P.B. Warr (eds), 1979. *Aircrew Stress in Wartime Operations*. New York and London: Academic Press, pp. 89–108.
Brand, J.L. and Holding, D.H. (1984) Effects of different probability ratios on effortful choices. *Trends in Ergonomics/Human Factors* **I**: 131–6.
Broadbent, D.E. (1958) *Perception and Communication*. London: Pergamon.
Broadbent, D.E. (1971). *Decision and Stress*. New York: London: Academic Press.
Broadbent, D.E. (1979) Is a fatigue test now possible? *Ergonomics* **22**: 1277–90.
Broughton, R.J. (1989) Vigilance and Sleepiness: A Laboratory Analysis. In *Vigilance and Performance in Automatized Systems*, edited by A. Coblentz. London: Kluwer Academic Publishers, pp. 251–61.
Burke, R.J., Shearer, J. and Deszca, G. (1984) Burnout among men and women in police work: An examination of the Cherniss model. *Journal of Health and Human Resources Administration* **7**: 162–88.
Cameron, C. (1973) A theory of fatigue. *Ergonomics* **16**: 633–48.
Caspi, A., Bolger, N. and Eckenrode, J. (1987). Linking person and context in the daily stress process. *Journal of Personality and Social Psychology* **52**: 184–95.
Cherniss, C. (1980) *Staff Burnout: Job Stress in the Human Services*. Beverly Hills: Sage.
Chiles, W.D. (1955) *Experimental Studies of Prolonged Wakefulness* (W.A.D.C.) Tech. Report no. 55–395, Dayton, Ohio.
Clark, L.A. and Watson, D. (1988) Mood and the mundane: relations between daily life events and self-reported mood. *Journal of Personality and Social Psychology* **54**: 296–308.
Cohen, S. (1980) After-effects of stress on human performance and social behaviour: a review of research and theory. *Psychological Bulletin* **88**: 82–108.
Cohen, S. and Spacapan, S. (1978) The after-effects of stress: an attentional interpretation. *Environmental Psychology and Nonverbal Behavior* **3**: 43–57.
Cooper, C.L. and Marshall, J. (1976) Occupational source of stress: a review of the literature relating to coronary heart disease and mental ill health. *Journal of Occupational Psychology* **49**: 11–28.
Cronin-Stubbs, D. (1982) Professional burnout part two: a survey of enterostomal therapists. *Journal of Enterostomal Therapy* **9**: 14–6.
Cronin-Stubbs, D. and Brophy, E.B. (1985) Burnout: Can social support save the psychiatric nurse? *Journal of Psychosocial Nursing* **23**: 8–13.
Dailey, A.L. (1985) The burnout test. *American Journal of Nursing* **85**: 270–2.
Davies, D.R. and Parasuraman, R. (1982) *The Psychology of Vigilance*. New York and London: Academic Press.

Davis, D.R. (1948) *Pilot Error*. London: HMSO.

DeLongis, A., Folkman, S. and Lazarus, R.S. (1988) The impact of daily stress on health and mood: Psychological and social resources as mediators. *Journal of Personality and Social Psychology* **54**: 486–95.

Depue, R.A. and Monroe, S.M. (1986) Conceptualization and measurement of human disorder in life stress research: the problem of chronic life disturbance. *Psychological Bulletin* **99**: 36–51.

Donnerstein, E. and Wilson, D.W. (1976) Effects of noise and perceived control on ongoing and subsequent aggressive behaviour. *Journal of Personality and Social Psychology* **34**: 774–81.

Drew, G.C. (1940) *An Experimental Study of Mental Fatigue*. Flying Personnel Research Committee Report 227, December 1940. Reprinted in E.J. Dearnaley and P.B. Warr, 1979. *Aircrew Stress in Wartime Operations*. New York and London: Academic Press, pp. 135–77.

Dubos, R. (1965) *Man Adapting*. New Haven, Conn.: Yale University Press.

Dubos, R. (1968) Environmental determinants of human life. In *Biology and Behaviour: Environmental Influences*, edited by D.C. Glass. New York: Rockefeller University Press/Russel Sage Foundation.

Edelwich, J. and Brodsky, A. (1980) *Burnout: Stages of Disillusionment in the Helping Professions*. New York: Human Sciences Press.

Ergonomics (1971) Symposium on methodology of Fatigue Assessment (Kyoto, 1969). *Ergonomics* **14**: 1–186.

Ergonomics (1978) Symposium on Mental Work Load (Paris, 1976). *Ergonomics* **21**: 141–233

Farmer, E.W., Belyavin, A.J., Tattersall, A.J., Berry, A. and Hockey, G.R.J. (1991) *Stress in Air Traffic Control II: Effects of Increased Workload*. IAM report no 701. Royal Air Force Institute of Aviation Medicine.

Feather, N.T. (1961) The relationship of persistence at a task to expectation of success and achievement related motives. *Journal of Abnormal and Social Psychology* **63**: 552–61.

Fisk, A.D. and Schneider, W. (1981) Control and automatic processing during tasks requiring sustained attention: a new approach to vigilance. *Human Factors* **23**: 737–50.

Floyd, W.F. and Welford, A.T. (1953) *Fatigue*. London: H.K. Lewis & Co Ltd.

Folkard, S. and Akerstedt, T. (1992) A three process model of the regulation of alertness-sleepliness. In *Sleep, Arousal and Performance*, edited by R.J. Broughton and Robert D. Ogilvie. Boston: Birkhauser, pp. 11–26.

Frankenhaeuser, M. (1980) Psychoneuroendocrine approaches to the study of stressful person–environment transactions. In *Selye's Guide to Stress Research*, Vol. 1, edited by H. Selye. New York: Van Nostrand Reinhold.

Frankenhaeuser, M. (1981) Coping with stress at work. *International Journal of Health Services* **11**: 491–510.

Frankenhaeuser, M. (1986) A psychobiological framework for research on human stress and coping. In *Dynamics of Stress: Physiological, Psychological and Social Perspectives*, edited by H.H. Appley and R. Trumbull. New York: Plenum Press, pp. 101–16.

Frankenhaeuser, M. *et al.* (1987) *Stress On and Off the Job as related to Sex and Occupational Status in White Collar Workers*. Reports from the Department of Psychology, University of Stockholm, no. 666.

Fraser, D.C. (1955) Recent Experimental Work in the Study of Fatigue. *Reprinted from Occupational Psychology, October 1955.*

Freeman, G.L. (1931) Mental activity and the muscular processes. *Psychological Review* **38**: 428–49.

French, J.R.P., Jr, Caplan, R.D. and Harrison, R.V. (1982) *The Mechanisms of Job Stress and Strain*. London: Wiley.

Freudenberger, H.J. (1974) Staff burn-out. *Journal of Social Issues* **30**(1): 159–65.

Freudenberger, H.J. (1975) The staff burn-out syndrome in alternative institutions. *Psychotherapy: Theory, Research and Practice* **12**: 73–82.

Froberg, J., Karlsson, C.G., Levi, L. and Lidbert, L. (1972) Circadian variations in performance, psychological ratings, catecholamine excretion, and urine flow during prolonged sleep deprivation. In *Aspects of Human Efficiency*, edited by W.P. Colquhoun. London: The English Universities Press, pp. 247–60.

Glass, D.C. and Singer, J.E. (1972) *Urban Stress: Experiments on Noise and Social Stressors*. New York and London: Academic Press.

Goldmark, J., Hopkins, M.D., Florence, P.S. and Lee, F.S. (1920) *Studies in Industrial Physiology: Fatigue in Relation to Working Capacity: 1. Comparison of an Eight-hour Plant and a Ten-hour Plant*. US Public Health Service, Public Health Bulletin No. 106.

Goldstein, H. (1934) A biochemical study of the metabolism of mental work. *Arch. Psychology* **164**.

Golembiewski, R.T. and Munzenrider, R. (1981) Efficacy of 3 versions of one burnout measure: the MBI as total score, subscale scores, or phases? *Journal of Health and Human Resources Administration* **4**: 228–46.

Green, D.M. and Swets, J.A. (1966) *Signal Detection Theory and Psychophysics*. New York: Wiley.

Gupta, N. and Beehr, T.A. (1979) Job stress and employee behaviours. *Organizational Behaviour and Performance* **23**: 373–87.

Hacker, W., Plath, H.E., Richter, P. and Zimmer, K. (1978) Internal representation of task structure and mental load of work: approaches and methods of assessment. *Ergonomics* **21**: 187–94.

Haider, M. (1963) Experimentelle Untersuchungen uber Daueraufmerksamkeit und cerebrale Vigilanz bei einformigen Tatigkeiten. *Zeitschrift fur Experimentelle und Angewandte Psychologie* **1**: 1–18.

Hamilton, P., Hockey, B. and Rejman, M. (1977) The place of the concept of activation in human information processing theory: an integrative approach. In *Attention and Performance VI*, edited by S. Dornie. New York: Academic, pp. 463–486.

Hancock, P.A. and Warm, J.S. (1989) A dynamic model of stress and sustained attention. *Human Factors* **31**: 519–37.

Hare, J., Pratt, C.C. and Andrews, D. (1988) Predictors of burnout in professional and paraprofessional nurses working in hospitals and nursing homes. *International Journal of Nursing Studies* **25**: 105–15.

Hockey, G.R.J. (ed.) (1983) *Stress and Fatigue in Human Performance*. Chichester: Wiley.

Hockey, G.R.J. (1986) A state control theory of adaptation to stress and individual differences in stress management. In *Energetics and Human Information Processing*, edited by G.R.J. Hockey, A.W.K. Gaillard and M.G.H. Coles. Dordrecht: Martinus Nijhoff.

Hockey, G.R.J. and Wiethoff, M. (1990) Assessing patterns of adjustment to the demands of work. In *Psychobiology of Stress*, edited by A. Oliverio, S. Pugliso and A. Kejna. Dordrecht: Kluwer.

Hockey, G.R.J. (1991) The assessment of cognitive strain: a general framework for the study of performance under stress and high workload. Personal communication.

Holding, D.H. (1983) Fatigue. In *Stress and Fatigue in Human Performance*, edited by G.R.J. Hockey. Chichester: Wiley, pp. 145–67.

Holding, D.H., Loeb, M. and Baker, M.A. (1983) Effects and aftereffects of continuous noise and computation work on risk and effort choices. *Motivation and Emotion* **7**: 331–44.

Horne, J.A. (1978) A review of the biological effects of total sleep deprivation in man. *Biological Psychology* **7**: 55–102.

Horne, J.A. (1985) Sleep function, with particular reference to sleep deprivation. *Annals of Clinical Research* **17**: 199–208.

Horne, J.A., Anderson, N.R. and Wilkinson, R.T. (1983) Effects of sleep deprivation on signal detection measures of vigilance: implications for sleep function. *Sleep* **6**: 347–58.

Iwasaki, T. and Akiya, S. (1991) The significance of changes in CFF values during performance on a VDT-based visual task. In *Towards Human Work: Solutions to Problems in Occupational Health and Safety*, edited by M. Kumashiro and E.D. Megaw. London: Taylor and Francis, pp. 352–57.

Jackson, S.E. and Maslach, C. (1980) Job stress among helping professionals: the effects on

workers and their families. Presented at the Research Workshop on Current Issues in Occupational Stress: Theory, Research and Intervention, Downsview, Ontario, April.
Jackson, S.E. and Maslach, C. (1982) After-effects of job-related stress: families as victims. *Journal of Occupational Behaviour* **3**: 63–77.
Johansson, G. and Sanden, P.O. (1982) *Mental Load and Job Satisfaction of Control Room Operators*. Report No. 40, Dept. of Psychology, University of Stockholm.
Johnson, L.C. (1982) Sleep deprivation and performance. In *Biological Rhythms, Sleep and Performance*, edited by Wilse B. Webb. Chichester: Wiley, pp. 111–141.
Kahneman, D. (1973) *Attention and Effort*. Englewood Cliffs, NJ: Prentice Hall.
Kantowitz, B.H., Hart, S.G. and Bortolussi, M.R. (1983) Measuring pilot workload in a moving-base simulator: 1. Asynchronous secondary choice-reaction task. *Proceedings of the Human Factors Society* **27**: 319–322.
Karasek, R.A. (1979) Job demands, job decision latitude, and mental strain: implications for job redesign. *Administrative Science Quarterly* **24**: 285–308.
Kashiwagi, S. (1971) Psychological rating of human fatigue. *Ergonomics* **14**: 17–22.
Kishida, K. (1991) Workload of workers in supermarkets. In *Towards Human Work: Solutions to Problems in Occupational Health and Safety*, edited by M. Kumashiro and E.D. Megaw. London: Taylor and Francis, pp. 269–79.
Kjellberg, A. (1977) Sleep deprivation, arousal, and performance. In *Vigilance. Theory, Operational Performance, and Physiological Correlates*, edited by Robert R. Mackie. Plenum Press: London, pp. 529–535.
Koelega, H.S., Brinkman, J.A., Hendriks, L. and Verbaten, M.N. (1989) Processing demands, effort and individual differences in four different vigilance tasks. *Human Factors* **31**: 45–62.
Kogi, K. and Saito, Y. (1973) Rhythmic fluctuation of orientation to a continuous manual control task. *J. Human Ergol.* **2**: 169–84.
Kogi, K., Saito, Y. and Mitsuhashi, T. (1970) Validity of three components of subjective fatigue feelings. *J. Science of Labour* **46**(5).
Kompier, M.A.J. (1988) *Work and Health of City Bus Drivers*. Delft: Eburon.
Kumashiro, M. (1984) In *Ergonomics and Health in Modern Offices*, edited by E. Grandjean. London: Taylor & Francis.
Lazarus, R.S. and Folkman, S. (1984) *Stress, Appraisal and Coping*. New York: Springer.
Leiter, M.P. and Maslach, C. (1988) The impact of interpersonal environment on burnout and organizational commitment. *Journal of Organizational Behaviour* **9**: 297–308.
Link, H.C. (1919) A practical study in industrial fatigue. *Journal of Industrial Hygiene* **1**: 233–7.
Lovibond, S.H. (1965) Anxiety, Fear, Tension, and Stress Response. (Manuscript).
Lundberg, U. (1980) Catecholamine and cortisol excretion under psychologically different laboratory conditions. In *Catecholamines and Stress: Recent Advances*, edited by E. Usdin, R. Kventriansky and I.J. Kopin. New York: Elsevier/North-Holland, pp. 455–60.
Mackworth, N.H. (1948) The breakdown of vigilance during prolonged visual search. *Quarterly Journal of Experimental Psychology* **1**: 6–21.
Maggiora, A. (1890) Les lois de la fatigue etudiées dans les muscles de l'homme. II. *Archives of Italian Biology* **13**: 187–241.
Maslach, C. (1976) Burned-out. *Human Behaviour* **5**(9): 16–22.
Maslach, C. (1978c) Job burn-out: how people cope. *Public Welfare* **36**: 56–8.
Maslach, C. (1978b) The client role in staff burn-out. *Journal of Social Issues* **34**(4): 111–24.
Maslach, C. (1979) The burn-out syndrome and patient care. In *Stress and Survival: The Emotional Realities of Life-threatening Illness*, edited by C. Garfield. St Louis: Mosby.
Maslach, C. and Jackson, S.E. (1978) Lawyer burn-out. *Barrister* **5**(2): 52–4.
Maslach, C. and Jackson, S.E. (1979) Burned-out cops and their families. *Psychology Today*, **12**(58).
Maslach, C. and Jackson, S.E. (1981) Measurement of experienced burnout. *Journal of Occupational Behavior* **2**: 99–113.
Maslach, C. and Jackson, S.E. (1982) Burnout in the health professions: A social psychological

analysis. In *Social Psychology of Health and Illness*, edited by G. Sanders and J. Suls. Hillsdale, N.J.: Erlbaum.

Maslach, C. and Jackson, S.E. (1984a) Burnout in organizational settings. *Applied Social Psychology Annual* **5**: 133–53.

Maslach, C. and Jackson, S.E. (1984b) Patterns of burnout among a national sample of public contract workers. *Journal of Health and Human Resource Administration* **7**: 189–212.

Maslach, C. and Pines, A. (1977) The burnout syndrome in the day care center. *Child Care Quarterly* **6**: 100.

McCormack, P.D. (1967) A two-factor theory of vigilance in the light of recent studies. In *Attention and Performance*, Vol. I, edited by A.F. Sanders. Amsterdam: North-Holland, pp. 400–9.

McFarland, R.A., Holway, A.N. and Hurvich, L.M. (1942) *Studies of Visual Fatigue*. Harvard Graduate School of Business Administration Report.

Meddis, R. (1982) Cognitive dysfunction following loss of sleep. In *The Pathology and Psychology of Cognition*, edited by E. Burton. London: Methuen, pp. 225–252.

Mikulincer, M., Babkoff, H., Caspy, T. and Sing, H. (1989) The effects of 72 hours of sleep loss on psychological variables. *British Journal of Psychology* **80**: 145–162.

Moos, R.H. (1988) Psychosocial factors in the workplace. In *Handbook of Life Stress, Cognition and Health*, edited by S. Fisher and J. Reason. Chichester: Wiley.

Moray, N. (ed.) (1979) *Mental Workload. Its Theory and Measurement*. New York: Plenum Press.

Mosso, A. (1890) Les lois de la fatigue etudiées dans les muscles de l'homme. *Archives of Italian Biology* **13**: 123–86.

Muscio, B. (1920) Fluctuations in mental efficiency. *British Journal of Psychology* **10**: 327–44.

Muscio, B. (1921–2) Is a fatigue test possible? (A report to the Industrial Fatigue Research Board). *British Journal of Psychology* **12**: 31–46.

Myles, W.S. and Romet, T.T. (1987) Self-paced work in sleep deprived subjects. *Ergonomics* **30**: 1175–84.

Neuchterlein, K.H., Parasuraman, R. and Jiang, Q. (1983) Visual sustained attention: image degradation produces rapid sensitivity decrement over time. *Science, New York* **220**: 327–9.

Nishihara, K., Mori, K., Endo, S., Ohta, T. and Ohara, K. (1985) Relationship between sleep efficiency and urinary excretion of catecholamines in bed-rested humans. *Sleep* **8**(2): 110–117.

Numerof, R.E. and Gillespie, D.F. (1983) Developing a measure of burnout. Washington University.

O'Donnell, R.D. and Eggemeier, F.T. (1986) Workload assessment methodology. In *Handbook of Perception and Human Performance*, edited by K.R. Boff, L. Kaufman and J.P. Thomas, Vol. 2. New York: Wiley.

O'Hanlon, J.F. (1981) Boredom: practical consequences and a theory. *Acta Psychologica* **49**: 53–82.

Pines, A. and Maslach, C. (1978) Characteristics of staff burnout in mental health settings. *Hospital and Community Psychiatry* **29**: 233–7.

Pines, A. and Maslach, C. (1980) Combatting staff burnout in a day care center: A case study. *Child Care Quarterly* **9**: 5–16.

Poffenberger, A.T. (1928) The effects of continuous work upon output and feelings. *Journal of Applied Psychology* **12**: 459–67.

Pressman, M.R. and Fry, J.M. (1989) Relationship of autonomic nervous system activity to daytime sleepiness and prior sleep. *Sleep* **12**(3): 239–245.

Rabbitt, P.M.A. (1981) Sequential reactions. In *Human Skills*, edited by D.H. Holding. Chichester: Wiley, pp. 153–75.

Reid, M.D. (1945) *Fluctuations in Navigator Performance During Operational Sorties*. Flying Personnel Research Committee Report 615, April 1945. Reprinted in E.J. Dearnaley and P.B. Warr, 1979. *Aircrew Stress in Wartime Operations*. London: Academic Press, pp. 63–73.

Rehm, L.P. (1978) Mood, pleasant events, and unpleasant events: two pilot studies. *Journal of Consulting and Clinical Psychology* **46**: 854–59.

Repetti, R.L. (1989) Effects of daily workload on subsequent behaviour during marital interaction: the roles of social withdrawal and spouse support. *Journal of Personality and Social Psychology* **57**: 651–9.

Rohrbaugh, J.W., Stapleton, J.M., Parasuraman, R., Frowein, H.W., Eckardt, E. and Linolla, M. (1987) Alcohol intoxication in humans: effects on vigilance performance. *Alcohol and Alcoholism* (Supplement 1): 97–102.

Rosa, R.R., Wheeler, D.D., Warm, J.S. and Colligan, M.J. (1985) Extended workdays: effects on performance and ratings of fatigue and alertness. *Behavior Research Methods, Instruments & Computers* **17**(1) 6–15.

Rotton, J., Olszewski, D., Charleton, M. and Soler, E. (1978) Loud speech, conglomerate noise, and behavioural after-effects. *Journal of Applied Psychology* **63**: 360–5.

Ryan, T.A. (1947) *Work and Effort: the Psychology of Production*. New York: Ronald Press.

Ryan, A.H. and Warner, M. (1936) The effect of automobile driving on the reactions of the driver. *American Journal of Psychology* **48**: 403–21.

Schneider, E.C. (1939) *Physiology of Muscular Activity* (2nd edn). Philadelphia: W.B. Saunders.

Schönpflug, W. (1983) Coping efficiency and situational demands. In *Stress and Fatigue in Human Performance*, edited by G.R.J. Hockey. Chichester: Wiley, pp. 299–330.

Schwab, R.S. (1953) Motivation in measurements of fatigue. In *Symposium on Fatigue*, edited by W.F. Floyd and A.T. Welford. London: H.K. Lewis, pp. 143–9.

Selye, H. (1936) A syndrome produced by diverse nervous agents. *Nature, London* **138**: 32.

Selye, H. (1956) *The Stress of Life*. New York: McGraw-Hill.

Sherrod, D.R. and Downs, R. (1974) Environmental determinants of altruism: The effects of stimulus overload and perceived control on helping. *Journal of Experimental Social Psychology* **10**: 468–79.

Sherrod, D.R., Hage, J.N., Halpern, P.L. and Moore, B.S. (1977) Effects of personal causation and perceived control on responses to an aversive environment: the more control the better. *Journal of Experimental Social Psychology* **10**: 468–79.

Shingledecker, C.A. and Holding, D.H. (1974). Risk and effort measures of fatigue. *Journal of Motor Behaviour* **6**: 17–25.

Simonson, E. and Enzer, N. (1941) Measurement of fusion frequency of flicker as a test for fatigue of the central nervous system. *Journal of International Hygiene and Toxicology* **23**: 83–9.

Smith, A. and Miles, C. (1986) Acute effects of meals, noise and nightwork. *British Journal of Psychology* **77**: 377–87.

Snell, P.A. (1933) An introduction to the study of visual fatigue. *Journal of the Society of Motion Picture Engineers* **20**: 367–90.

Sperandio, J.C. (1978) The regulation of working methods as a function of work-load among air traffic controllers. *Ergonomics* **21**: 195–202.

Steptoe, A. (1987) The assessment of sympathetic nervous function in human stress research. *Journal of Psychosomatic Research* **31**(2): 141–52.

Stone, A.A. (1987) Event content in a daily survey is differentially associated with concurrent mood. *Journal of Personality and Social Psychology* **52**(1): 56–8.

Stone, A.A. and Neale, J.M. (1984) The effects of severe daily events on mood. *Journal of Personality and Social Psychology* **46**: 137–44.

Storlie, F. (1979) Burnout: the elaboration of a concept. *American Journal of Nursing* **79**: 108.

Stroop, J.R. (1935) Studies of interference in serial verbal reaction. *Journal of Experimental Psychology* **18**: 643–62.

Takakuwa, E. (1962) The function of concentration maintenance (TAF) as an evaluation of fatigue. *Ergonomics* **5**: 37–49.

Takakuwa, E. (1977) The function of maintaining concentration (TAF): an approach to the evaluation of mental stress. In *Vigilance: Theory, Operational Relevance and Physiological Correlates*, edited by R.R. Mackie. Chichester: Wiley, pp. 217–38.

Tanaka, J., Hiroaka, Y. and Okuda, H. (1989) A report of fatigue in Japanese workers based on subjective symptoms. *Journal of University of Occupational and Environmental Health* **11**

(Supplement): 622–630.

Theorell, T., Lind, E., Lundberg, U., Christensson, T. and Edhag, O. (1981) The individual and his work in relation to myocardial infarction. In *Society, Stress and Disease. Vol. IV: Working Life*, edited by L. Levi. New York and Toronto: Oxford University Press, pp. 191–200.

Thorndike, E. (1900) Mental fatigue. *Psychology Review* **7**: 466–82.

Thorndike, E.L. (1926) *Educational Psychology* Vol. III. *Mental Work and Fatigue, and Indvidual Differences and Their Causes*. New York: Teachers College, Columbia University.

Tsaneva, N. (1972) *Fatigue at Work*. Paper presented at the fourth Scandinavian Conference on Ergonomics, October 5–6, 1972. Helsinki.

Van den Berg, C.J. (1986) On the relation between energy transformations in the brain and mental activities. In *Energetics and Human Information Processing* edited by Hockey, G.R.J., Gaillard, A.W.K. and Coles, M.G.H. Dordrecht: Martinus Nijhoff, pp 131–135.

Van Dijk, F.J.H. and Meijman, T.F. (1986) Towards a dynamic model of exposure and susceptibility. *Heymans Bulletins Psychologische Instituten R.U. Groningen.*

Vernon, H.M. (1921) *Industrial Fatigue and Efficiency*. New York: E.P. Dutton & Co.

Vickers, D. (1979) *Decision Processes in Visual Perception*. London: Academic Press.

Warren, N. and Clark, B. (1936) Blocking in mental and motor tasks during a 65-hour vigil. *Psychological Bulletin* **33**: 814–15.

Washburn, M.S. (1991) Fatigue and critical thinking on eight and twelve-hour shifts. *Nursing Management* **22**: 80A-CC–80H-CC.

Watson, D. (1988) Intraindividual and interindividual analyses of positive and negative affect: Their relation to health complaints, perceived stress, and daily activities. *Journal of Personality and Social Psychology* **54**(6): 1020–30.

Weinland, J.D. (1927) Variability of performance in the curve of work. *Archives of Psychology* **87**.

Welford, A.T. (1953) The psychologist's problem in measuring fatigue. In *Symposium on Fatigue*, edited by W.F. Floyd and T. Welford. London: H.K. Lewis, pp. 183–91.

Welford, A.T. (1968) *Fundamentals of Skill*. London: Methuen and Co. Ltd.

Welford, A.T., Brown, R.A. and Gabb, J.E. (1950) Two experiments on fatigue as affecting skilled performance in civilian aircrew. *British Journal of Psychology* **40**: 195–211.

Wiethoff, M. and Hockey, G.R.J. (1989) Effort, fatigue and acute strain in a field study of natural variations in workload. Paper presented at the First European Congress of Psychology, Amsterdam, 2–7 July.

Wilkinson, R.T. (1962) Muscle tension during mental work under sleep deprivation. *Journal of Experimental Psychology* **64**: 565–71.

Wilkinson, R.T. (1965) Sleep deprivation. In *The Physiology of Human Survival*, edited by O.G. Edholm and A.L. Bacharach. New York and London: Academic Press, pp. 399–430.

Williams, H.I., Lubin, A. and Goodnow, J.J. (1959) Impaired performance with acute sleep loss. *Psychological Monographs* **73**: 14 (Whole No. 484).

Wollwill, J.F., Nasar, J.L., DeJoy, D.M. and Foruzani, H.H. (1976) Behavioural effects of a noisy environment: Task environment versus passive exposure. *Journal of Applied Psychology* **61**: 67–74.

Woodworth, R.S. and Wells, F.L. (1911) Association tests. *Psychological Monographs*, No. 57.

Wyatt, S., Langdon, J.N. and Stock, F.G.L. (1929) *Fatigue and Boredom in Repetitive Work*. Report No. 77, Industrial Health Research Board (Great Britain).

Yasko, J. (1983) The relationship between selected variables and the degree of burnout experienced by nurses prepared at the master's level functioning in the role of an oncology clinical nursing specialist. *Dissertation Abstracts International* **43**: 2165–B, (University Microfilms no. DA 8210643).

Yoshitake, H. (1971) Relations between the symptoms and the feeling of fatigue. *Ergonomics* **14**: 175–185.

Yoshitake, H. (1978) Three characteristic patterns of subjective fatigue symptoms. *Ergonomics* **21**: 231–3.

Zinchenko, V.P., Leonova, A.B. and Strelkov, Yu. K. (1985) *The Psychometrics of Fatigue*. London: Taylor & Francis.

Subject Index

Author Index